Fundamentals of Operating Systems

Fundamentals of Operating Systems

A. M. Lister
University of Queensland
Australia

Third Edition

Springer-Verlag New York Inc.

First edition 1975
Second edition 1979
Third edition 1984

Published by
Higher and Further Education Division
MACMILLAN PUBLISHERS LTD
London and Basingstoke

Sole distributors in the USA and Canada
Springer-Verlag New York Inc.
175 Fifth Avenue,
New York, NY 10010
USA.

Library of Congress Cataloguing in Publication Data
Lister, A. (Andrew), 1945–
    Fundamentals of operating systems.
    Bibliography: p.
    Includes index.
    1. Operating systems (Computers)   I. Title.
QA76.6.L57   1984   001.64′2   84–10685

Printed in the United States of America.

9 8 7 6 5 4 3 2 (Second printing, 1985)

ISBN 0-387-91251-7 Springer-Verlag New York

to my parents

Contents

Preface to the First Edition

An operating system is probably the most important part of the body of software which goes with any modern computer system. Its importance is reflected in the large amount of manpower usually invested in its construction, and in the mystique by which it is often surrounded. To the non-expert the design and construction of operating systems has often appeared an activity impenetrable to those who do not practise it. I hope this book will go some way toward dispelling the mystique, and encourage a greater general understanding of the principles on which operating systems are constructed.

The material in the book is based on a course of lectures I have given for the past few years to undergraduate students of computer science. The book is therefore a suitable introduction to operating systems for students who have a basic grounding in computer science, or for people who have worked with computers for some time. Ideally the reader should have a knowledge of programming and be familiar with general machine architecture, common data structures such as lists and trees, and the functions of system software such as compilers, loaders, and editors. It will also be helpful if he has had some experience of using a large operating system, seeing it, as it were, from the outside.

The first two chapters of the book define the functions of an operating system and describe some common operating system characteristics. Chapter 3 establishes the process as a basic concept in the discussion of the concurrent activities which go on inside an operating system, and describes how processes communicate with each other. The rest of the book then describes the construction of an operating system from the bottom up, starting at the interface with the machine hardware and ending at the interface with the user. By the end of the book the system which has been constructed is seen to possess the features demanded at the beginning.

Throughout the book I have tried to show how each stage in the construction of an operating system naturally follows on the previous ones, and have emphasised the logical structure of the system as a whole. I have done this for two reasons. The first is pedagogical: my experience indicates that students gain a better understanding of complex material if it is presented in a coherent manner. The second is frankly polemic: this is the way I believe operating systems should be built. Attention to structure and logical dependence are the best means we have of building operating systems which are easy to understand, easy to maintain, and relatively error free.

Finally, I would like to thank the many friends and colleagues who have helped in the writing of this book. In particular I would like to thank David Lyons, who has been a fertile source of ideas and comment; and David Howarth, who made valuable comments on an earlier draft. Thanks are also due to Colin Strutt, Morris Sloman, John Forecast, Ron Bushell and Bill Hart, who have made constructive suggestions for improving the text.

ANDREW LISTER

Preface to the Second Edition

Any book on computer science suffers from the fact that its subject matter is undergoing rapid change, both technological and conceptual. A book on operating systems is no exception: the hardware on which systems run is being revolutionised by the large scale integration of components, and ideas about what operating systems should do are being modified by changing user requirements and expectations. Although this book is about 'fundamentals', which can be expected to be less volatile than other topics, it would be foolish to ignore the developments which have occurred in the four years since publication.

Consequently I have amended the text in three main ways for this edition. First, there is an additional chapter on reliability, a topic whose importance has increased dramatically as reliance on computer systems has grown in many areas of life. Secondly, the references to real-life operating systems have been updated to include systems which have come into use since the first edition, and references to the literature have been similarly updated. Thirdly, I have altered the presentation of certain topics so as better to reflect current ideas, and have expanded the conclusion to indicate what developments can be expected in the future.

Other changes in the text have been motivated by feedback from readers of the first edition. Here I owe a great debt to my students, who have had the perception to point out errors, and the good sense to expose inadequate exposition. Any improvements in this respect are due largely to them, though any remaining inadequacies are, of course, my own.

A.L.

Preface to the Third Edition

Almost a decade after publication it is reassuring to know that the 'fundamentals' of the title remain essentially the same. However, as the systems of the early 1970s fade into distant memory I have found it necessary to update the text by reference to their successors. I have also taken the opportunity to introduce one or two new topics, and to improve the presentation of several others. In this latter respect I am indebted to Morris Sloman and Dirk Vermeir for their valuable suggestions, and, as ever, to my students.

A.L.

1 *Introduction*

In this chapter and the next we attempt to answer the questions

What is an operating system?
What does it do?
Why do we need one?

By answering these questions we hope to give the reader an idea of what we are trying to achieve when we discuss in later chapters how operating systems are constructed.

We start by examining the broad purpose of an operating system, and by classifying various types of operating system currently in existence.

Broadly speaking an operating system performs two main functions, as follows.

(1) Resource Sharing

An operating system must share the computer's resources among a number of simultaneous users. The aim is to increase the availability of the computer to its users, and at the same time to maximise the utilisation of such resources as the central processors, the memory, and the input/output devices. The importance of resource utilisation depends on the cost of the resources concerned – the continuing decline in hardware costs has led to decreasing emphasis on resource utilisation, to the extent that many microcomputers are dedicated to a single function and never shared at all. Large computers, however, are still expensive enough to warrant considerable effort in sharing their resources.

(2) Provision of a Virtual Machine

The second major operating system function is to transform a raw piece of hardware into a machine which is more easily used. This may be looked on as presenting the user with a *virtual machine* whose characteristics are different from, but more tractable than, those of the underlying physical machine. Some areas in which the virtual machine often differs from the underlying real machine are as follows.

(a)   Input/Output (I/O)

The I/O capabilities of the basic hardware may be extremely complex and require sophisticated programming in order to utilise them. An operating system will relieve the user of the burden of understanding this complexity, and will present to him a virtual machine with much simpler to use, though equally powerful, I/O capabilities.

(b)   Memory

Many operating systems present a virtual machine whose memory differs in size from that of the underlying real machine. For example, an operating system may use secondary memory (in the form of magnetic discs) to give the illusion of a larger main memory; alternatively, it may partition the main memory among users so that each user sees a virtual machine whose memory is smaller than that of the real machine.

(c)   Filing system

Most virtual machines include a *filing system* for the long-term storage of programs and data. The filing system is based on the disc or tape storage of the real machine, but the operating system allows the user to access the stored information by symbolic name rather than by its physical location on the storage medium.

(d)   Protection and error handling

Since most large computer systems are shared by a number of users it is essential that each user be protected against the effects of error or malice in others. Computers vary considerably in the degree of protection provided by the basic hardware, and the operating system must build on this to provide a virtual machine in which users cannot adversely affect each other.

(e)   Program interaction

A virtual machine may provide facilities for user programs to interact as they run, so that, for example, the output from one program is used as input to another.

(f)   Program control

A virtual machine provides the user with a means of manipulating programs and data within the computer system. The user is presented with a *command language* which allows him to convey what he wants the virtual machine to do — for example, the compilation and execution of a certain program, the amalgamation of two sets of data held in the filing system, and so on. The command language is at a much higher level, and is much easier to use, than the machine code instructions executable by the physical machine.

The precise nature of a virtual machine will depend on the application in which it is to be used. For example, the characteristics of a machine required for an airline seat reservation system will differ from those required for the control of scientific experiments. Clearly, the operating system design must be strongly influenced by the type of use for which the machine is intended. Unfortunately it is often the case with 'general purpose machines' that the type of use cannot easily be identified; a common criticism of many systems is that in attempting to be all things to all men they wind up being totally satisfactory to no-one. In the next section we shall examine various types of system and identify some of their characteristics.

1.1 TYPES OF OPERATING SYSTEM

(1) Single-user Systems

Single-user systems, as their name implies, provide a virtual machine for only one user at a time. They are appropriate for computers which are dedicated to a single function, or which are so inexpensive as to make sharing unworthwhile. Most microcomputer operating systems (for example, CP/M and MS-DOS, which run on many personal computers) are of the single-user type. Single-user systems generally provide a simple virtual machine which facilitates the running of a variety of software packages as well as allowing the user to develop and execute programs of his own. The major emphasis is on the provision of an easily used command language, a simple file system, and I/O facilities for terminal and disc.

(2) Process Control

The term process control generally implies the control by computer of an industrial process, such as the refining of oil or the manufacture of machine tools. It can be extended to include such things as environmental control in a space capsule or the monitoring of a patient's condition in a hospital. The common feature of all these applications is *feedback*; that is, the computer receives input from the controlled process, computes a response which will maintain its stability, and initiates the mechanism for giving it. If the input, for example, signifies a dangerous rise in temperature, then the response may well be to open a valve to increase the flow of coolant. Clearly there is a critical time in which the response must be given if the process is to remain in equilibrium, let alone safe! The main function of the operating system in process control is to provide maximum reliability with the minimum of operator intervention, and to 'fail safe' in the event of any hardware malfunctions.

(3) File Interrogation Systems

The distinguishing feature of these systems is a large set of data, or *data base*, which can be interrogated for information. The response to information requests must occur within a short time (typically less than a minute), and the data base must be capable of being modified as information is updated. Examples are management information systems, where the data base consists of information on company performance, and medical information systems, in which the data base is a set of patients' records. The user (company manager or doctor) expects to be able to access information without any knowledge of how the data base is organised, either in terms of software structure or hardware storage devices. Hence the operating system must make interrogation facilities available without involving the user in details of implementation.

(4) Transaction Processing

Transaction processing systems are characterised by a data base which is frequently being modified, perhaps several times a second. Typical applications are in airline seat-reservations and banking. In the former the data base contains information on seat availability, and is modified each time a seat is booked; in the latter it consists of details of accounts, which are updated for every credit and debit. The major constraint in transaction processing is the necessity of keeping the data base up to date; clearly the system is useless if transactions are made on incorrect data. Further problems arise in dealing with simultaneous transactions on the same piece of data (for example two travel agents trying to book the same seat). The individual user should of course be unaware of these problems, and the operating system must resolve them so that he has the impression of being the sole user of the system.

(5) General Purpose Systems

General purpose operating systems are employed on computers characterised by a large number of users performing a wide range of tasks. Such systems are designed to handle a continuous flow of work in the form of jobs to be run on the computer. Each job performs a specific task for a particular user (for example, analysis of survey data, solution of differential equations, calculation of monthly payroll) and typically consists of running one or more programs. In a simple case, say that of survey analysis, the job may be no more than the running of an already compiled program with a particular set of data. More complicated jobs may involve modifying a program by use of an editor, compiling it, and finally running it. Because of the variety of jobs which may be submitted, the system must be able to support a large number of utilities such as compilers for various languages, assemblers, editors, debugging packages, word processors, and a file system for long-term storage of information. It must also be able to handle the wide variety of peripherals which may be required (for example, card reader and punch, terminal, line printer, magnetic tapes and discs, graph plotter). The provision and control of these facilities, together with the organisation of the flow of work, are the broad functions of a general purpose operating system.

General purpose systems can be classified into two groups: (1) *batch*, and (2) *multi-access*. The chief characteristic of a batch system is that once a job enters the computer the user has no further contact with it until it has been completed. A typical job is punched on cards or stored on magnetic tape and is passed to an operator for submission to the machine. When the job is complete the operator dispatches the output back to the user. In most cases the job is submitted to the computer through input and output devices within the computer room itself; however some batch systems, called *remote job entry* (RJE) systems allow submission of jobs through I/O devices which may be at some distance from the central installation and connected to it by a data transmission line. An RJE system may support several outlying I/O stations, and must of course return output to the station at which a job was submitted. In neither a straightforward batch system nor an RJE system is there any opportunity for a user to interact with his job while it is running.

In a multi-access system, on the other hand, a user may submit a job by typing on a terminal and may use the terminal to monitor and control the job as it runs. He may for example correct the syntax errors reported by a compiler, or supply data which is dependent on the results so far received. The operating system shares the computing resources among the different jobs so that it appears to each user that he has the entire machine to himself.

Many operating systems combine both the batch and multi-access modes of operation. Because of the advantages of interaction the multi-access mode tends to be used for activities such as program development and document preparation, while batch mode is used only for routine non-interactive tasks such as payroll and stock inventory.

Many of the systems described above may be implemented on either a single computer, or on a number of connected computers. In the latter case the separate computers may share the workload equally between them, or each computer may be dedicated to servicing only one particular aspect of it. For example, one computer may be devoted to handling all I/O from remote stations, while another performs all work requiring intensive numeric processing. The computers may be located in the same room, possibly sharing memory and backing store, or they may be located at some distance from each other and communicate by means of data transmission lines. In such *distributed systems* the operating system must coordinate the activities of each computer, and ensure that the appropriate information flows between them as required.

1.2 THE 'PAPER' OPERATING SYSTEM

The majority of this book will be devoted to general purpose systems. However, several of the problems discussed also arise in other systems, and we shall indicate the relevance of our discussion to other systems wherever appropriate.

In order to study the way in which a general purpose system is constructed we shall build a 'paper' operating system; that is, we shall develop a hypothetical system on paper, in the hope that this will illustrate the principles involved. It will be our aim to develop this system in a logical manner, in that each stage of development will follow naturally from the previous one. The final structure will in some ways resemble an onion, in which each layer provides a set of functions which are dependent only on the layers within it. The direction of construction will be from the inside outwards, or 'bottom up', so that starting from a nucleus we shall add layers for memory management, I/O handling, file access, and so on.

It must be admitted that only a few real-life operating systems actually exhibit the neatly layered structure suggested; notable examples are T.H.E. (Dijkstra, 1968), RC-4000 (Hansen, 1970), UNIX (Ritchie and Thompson, 1974), and, in the commercial world, VME for the ICL 2900 series (Keedy, 1976; Huxtable and Pinkerton, 1977). Indeed it can fairly be said that many existing systems display very little logical structure at all. This sad fact may be attributed to three factors: first, most current systems were designed at a time when the principles of operating system construction were far less clear than they are now; second, the common technique of using large numbers of people to write complex software seldom results in a 'clean' product; and third, the previously mentioned desire for a system to be all things to all men often leads to the *ad hoc* attachment of new features long after the initial design stage. It is also the case that constraints imposed by peculiarities of hardware may often cause a well structured design to become blurred in implementation. However, we can reasonably hope that these constraints will become fewer as hardware design is modified to meet the needs of operating system construction.

As the development of our paper operating system proceeds we shall compare it with existing systems, and relate the techniques we use to those employed elsewhere. In this way we shall keep our operating system firmly rooted in current practice, while using it as a vehicle for conveying the principles of operating system construction.

2 Functions and Characteristics of an Operating System

In this chapter we discuss in more detail the functions which we expect an operating system to fulfil, and isolate some of the characteristics it must exhibit in order to do so.

2.1 OPERATING SYSTEM FUNCTIONS

We take as our starting point the raw machine — the basic computer hardware consisting of central processor, memory, and various peripherals. (We defer until later consideration of computers with more than one central processor.) In the absence of any software aids, the operation of loading and running a user program must be performed entirely under human control. Assuming batch operation, the operator must perform a tedious sequence of tasks something like this

(1) place the source program cards in the card reader (or other input device)
(2) initiate a program to read in the cards
(3) initiate a compiler to compile the source program
(4) place the data cards, if any, in the card reader
(5) initiate execution of the compiled program
(6) remove results from the line printer

The speed of the machine is obviously dependent on the rate at which the operator can press buttons and feed peripherals, and the system is therefore very much operator-limited.

An obvious first improvement is to make the machine carry out automatically, without operator intervention, the sequence of steps necessary to read-in, compile, load and execute programs. The operator's role is thus reduced to loading cards at one end of the machine and tearing off paper at the other, and throughput is consequently increased. Of course one rarely gets something for nothing, and the price paid for increased speed is the dedication of part of the machine to a program which can perform the necessary job sequencing operations. Since all jobs do not require the same sequencing operations (some jobs, for example, may not need compilation) the control program must be able to infer from one or more control cards precisely what operations are to be performed in any particular case. In other words the control program must be capable of interpreting a *job control language*. Furthermore, the errors which will inevitably occur in some jobs cannot be allowed to affect jobs later in the sequence, and so the control program must be responsible for handling errors in some rational fashion. A control program with these features is in fact an embryonic operating system.

A system of this type is clearly limited by the speed at which it can perform I/O, and the next stage in improving efficiency is to reduce the I/O dependency. Historically, this was first achieved by the technique of *off-lining*, whereby all output and input was performed to and from magnetic tape. The task of converting card (or paper tape) input to magnetic tape, and magnetic tape output to line printer or punch, was relegated to a satellite computer of less power and cost. The transfer of magnetic tapes between satellite and main computer was by hand. Off-lining systems, notably the IBM Fortran Monitor System, ran successfully from the late 1950s into the mid 1960s.

Off-lining reduced I/O dependency by ensuring that all I/O was performed on magnetic tape, which was at the time the fastest cheaply available medium. The price paid was the addition to the embryonic operating system of a set of routines for coding and packing on magnetic tape data eventually destined for some other peripheral (and conversely for input). It should also be noted that because magnetic tape is essentially a serial medium there was no notion of scheduling jobs to run in any order other than that in which they were presented.

In order to eliminate I/O dependency rather than merely reduce it, techniques must be employed whereby I/O can be overlapped with processing. This is possible with the aid of two hardware devices -- the *channel* and the *interrupt*. A channel is a device which controls one or more peripherals, performing data transfers between the peripherals and memory quite independently of the central processor. An interrupt is a signal which transfers control of the central processor to a fixed location, while at the same time storing the previous value of the program counter. Thus the program being executed at the time of the interrupt is temporarily abandoned but can be resumed later (that is, it is *interrupted*). An interrupt from a channel acts as a signal to indicate that a data transfer has been completed. Hence it is possible for the central processor to initiate a peripheral transfer, to continue processing while the channel controls the transfer, and to receive notification by means of an interrupt when the transfer is complete. (The reader who wishes to learn more about channels and interrupt hardware is referred to any text on computer architecture, such as Foster, 1970, or Stone, 1975.)

It now becomes possible to read-in jobs on to some suitable storage medium, usually disc, and to execute them one by one at the same time as other jobs are being read-in. The additions to our rapidly growing operating system are a routine to handle the interrupts and a routine to decide which of the several jobs on disc to run next. This latter function, that of *scheduling*, derives from the use as input medium of disc, which is a random access device, rather than magnetic tape, which is serial. A system working in this way is known as a *single stream batch monitor*. (Single stream means only one job is executed at a time.) Such systems were predominant in the mid 1960s.

The main disadvantage of a single stream system is the dedication of the entire machine to the execution of a single job, no matter how large or small. This disadvantage can be overcome by *multiprogramming* — the running of several programs in the same machine at the same time. The idea is that several programs are held simultaneously in memory, and the central processor divides its time between them according to the resources (such as channels or peripherals) that each one needs at any instant. In this way it is possible, by having a suitable mix of jobs in the machine at any time, to achieve optimal utilisation of resources. This includes central processor utilisation, as whenever a job is waiting for an I/O transfer to be completed the processor can switch to some other job currently in the machine. The additional load on the operating system is the control of resources and the protection of one job from the activities of another. An operating system of this type is called a *multi-stream batch monitor*, and versions abounded on all large computers of the early 1970s (for example GEORGE 3 on the ICL 1900 series, and OS/360 on the IBM 360 and 370 series). The development of these systems owed much to the pioneering work done in the early 1960s on the Atlas computer at Manchester University.

At this stage of our progression from the raw machine we have quite a sophisticated system which is making good use of the hardware available. Its main disadvantage from the user's point of view is the lack of any interaction with his job as it passes through the computer. Interaction is valuable in many situations, particularly during the development and debugging of a program. For example, debugging becomes easier if the programmer is immediately able to test modifications and see their effect, making further modifications as necessary. Similarly, many problem-solving programs require 'steering' by the user, that is, the user directs the further action of the program after examining the results so far. In order for interaction to be feasible, the multi-stream batch system must be modified to accept input from users typing at remote terminals; in other words it must become a multi-access system as described in the previous chapter. In the early 1970s most manufacturers produced multi-access operating systems for their larger computers; examples were MINIMOP (ICL 1900), TSS/360 (IBM 360 and 370), and TOPS-10 (DEC System-10). In the mid 1970s the batch and multi-access modes of operation were combined in such systems as MVS (IBM 370), MCP (Burroughs 6700 and 7700), and VME (ICL 2900).

The foregoing discussion has led us to an operating system which must perform at least the following functions

(1)   Job sequencing
(2)   Job control language interpretation
(3)   Error handling
(4)   I/O handling
(5)   Interrupt handling
(6)   Scheduling
(7)   Resource control
(8)   Protection
(9)   Multi-access

Additionally, the operating system should be easy to run from the operator's point of view, and easy to control from the installation manager's point of view. We can therefore add the further functions

(10) Provision of good interface to the operator
(11) Accounting of computing resources

It will be clear from this that operating systems are decidely non-trivial animals, and it is not surprising that an enormous amount of effort has been spent in writing them. As a step towards a coherent structure for an operating system we can abstract from the above list of functions certain characteristics which the system must exhibit. These, together with the attendant problems in displaying them, are listed in the following section.

2.2 OPERATING SYSTEM CHARACTERISTICS

(1) Concurrency

Concurrency is the existence of several simultaneous, or parallel, activities. Examples are the overlapping of I/O operations with computation, and the coexistence in memory of several user programs. Concurrency raises problems of switching from one activity to another, of protecting one activity against the effects of another, and synchronising activities which are mutually dependent.

(2) Sharing

Concurrent activities may be required to share resources or information. The motivation for this is fourfold.

(a)   Cost: it is extravagant to provide sufficient resources for all users separately.
(b)   Building on the work of others: it is useful to be able to use other people's programs or routines.
(c)   Sharing data: it may be necessary to use the same data base for several different programs, possibly working for several different users.
(d)   Removing redundancy: it is economical to share a single copy of a program (for example a compiler) between several users, rather than provide a separate copy for each user.

Problems associated with sharing are resource allocation, simultaneous access to data, simultaneous execution of programs, and protection against corruption.

(3) Long-term Storage

The need for sharing programs and data implies the need for long-term storage of information. Long-term storage also allows a user the convenience of keeping his programs or data in the computer rather than on some external medium (for example, cards). The problems arising are those of providing easy access, protection against interference (malicious or otherwise), and protection against system failure.

(4) Nondeterminacy

An operating system must be *determinate* in the sense that the same program run today or tomorrow with the same data should produce the same results. On the other hand it is *indeterminate* in that it must respond to events which will occur in an unpredictable order. These events are such things as resource requests, run-time errors in programs, and interrupts from peripheral devices. Because of the enormous number of contingencies which can arise it is clearly unreasonable to expect to write the operating system to cater for them all individually. Instead the system must be written so as to handle *any* sequence of events.

It is worth pointing out that none of these characteristics is peculiar to general purpose systems alone. Long-term storage, for example, is clearly required in file interrogation systems, and concurrency is a prime feature of transaction processing systems.

To conclude this chapter we mention briefly a few features which it is desirable for a general purpose operating system to display.

2.3 DESIRABLE FEATURES

(1) Efficiency

The need for efficiency has already been alluded to. Unfortunately, it is difficult to light on one single criterion by which the efficiency of an operating system can be judged: various possible criteria are listed below.

(a)   mean time between jobs
(b)   unused central processor time
(c)   turn-round time for batch jobs
(d)   response time (in multi-access systems)
(e)   resource utilisation
(f)   throughput (jobs per hour)

Not all these criteria can be satisfied simultaneously; we shall have more to say in later chapters about design decisions which effectively give more weight to some than to others.

(2) Reliability

Ideally an operating system should be completely error-free, and be able to handle all contingencies. In practice this is never the case, but we shall see in chapter 10 how considerable progress can be made towards this goal.

(3) Maintainability

It should be possible to maintain an operating system — enhancing it or correcting errors — without employing an army of systems programmers. This implies that the system should be modular in construction, with clearly defined interfaces between the modules, and that it should be well documented.

(4) Small Size

Space used to hold the operating system, whether in memory or on backing store, is wasted as far as productive computing is concerned. Furthermore, a large system is liable to be more prone to error, and take longer to write, than a small one.

To summarise what has been done in this chapter: we have discussed the general functions we expect an operating system to fulfil; we have isolated some crucial operating system characteristics; and we have enumerated some desirable system features. In the next chapter we shall examine some basic tools which will help us construct the system we require.

3 Concurrent Processes

Before we can start a detailed study of operating systems, we need to introduce some basic concepts and develop a few tools. This will be the purpose of the present chapter.

3.1 PROGRAMS, PROCESSES AND PROCESSORS

We start by considering an operating system as a set of activities, each providing one of the functions, such as scheduling or I/O handling, described in chapter 2. Each activity consists of the execution of one or more programs, and will be invoked whenever the corresponding function is to be provided. We use the word *process* to describe an activity of this kind. (Other names in the literature are *task* and *computation*.) A process may thus be thought of as a sequence of actions, performed by executing a sequence of instructions (a program), whose net result is the provision of some system function. We can extend the concept to include the provision of user functions as well as system functions, so that the execution of a user program is also called a process.

A process may involve the execution of more than one program; conversely, a single program or routine may be involved in more than one process. For example, a routine for adding an item to a list might be used by any process engaged in queue manipulation. Hence the knowledge that a particular program is currently being executed does not tell us much about what activity is being pursued or what function is being implemented. It is largely for this reason that the concept of a process is more useful than that of a program when talking about operating systems.

A process is able to proceed by virtue of an agent which executes the associated program. This agent is known as a *processor*. We say that a processor *runs* a process, or that a process *runs on* a processor. A processor is something which executes instructions; depending on the nature of the instructions the processor may be implemented in hardware alone, or in a combination of both hardware and software. For example, a central processing unit (CPU) is a processor for executing machine language instructions, while a CPU together with a BASIC interpreter can form a processor for executing BASIC instructions. The transformation, discussed in chapter 1, of a raw computer into a virtual machine may in fact be regarded as the combination of the computer hardware and the

13

operating system to provide a processor capable of running user processes (that is, a processor capable of executing user instructions).

The program or programs associated with a process need not be implemented as software. The action of a channel, for example, in performing a data transfer, may be looked on as a process in which the associated program is wired into the channel hardware. Viewed in this way the channel, or indeed any peripheral device, is a processor which is capable of executing only a single process.

The concepts of process and processor can readily be used to interpret both concurrency and nondeterminacy, which were two of the operating system characteristics outlined in the last chapter.

Concurrency can be regarded as the activation of several processes (that is, the execution of several programs) at the same time. Provided there are as many processors as processes this presents no logical difficulty. If, as is more usual, there are fewer processors than processes then apparent concurrency can be obtained by switching processors from one process to another. If the switching is done at suitably small intervals of time then the system will give the illusion of concurrency when viewed on a longer time scale. Apparent concurrency is in effect achieved by interleaving processes on a single processor.

It may be helpful at this point to draw an analogy with the activities of a secretary in a general office. Each of the jobs a secretary has to perform, such as typing letters, filing invoices, or taking dictation, can be likened to a process in an operating system. The processor is the secretary herself, and the sequence of instructions which defines each job is analogous to a program. If the office is busy then the secretary may have to break off one job to do another, and in this situation she would probably complain of 'doing several jobs at the same time'. Of course she is only doing one job at once, but the frequent switching from one activity to another gives an overall impression of concurrency. We may pursue the analogy further by observing that before the secretary can change to another activity she must make sufficient note of what she is currently doing in order to pick up the thread again later. Similarly, a processor in a computing system must record information about the process it is currently running before it can switch to some other process. The precise nature of the information to be stored will be discussed in the next chapter; for the moment we remark only that it must be sufficient to enable the process to be resumed at some later time.

Carrying the analogy still further, we can introduce additional secretaries (processors) into the office. True concurrency can now exist between the various secretaries performing different tasks, though apparent concurrency may still persist as each secretary switches from one task to another and back again. Only when the number of secretaries is equal to the number of jobs to be done can all the jobs be performed in a truly concurrent manner. The analogue of the processor, such as an I/O device, which can perform only a single process, is the junior secretary who is capable only of making the tea.

Bearing in mind the foregoing discussion, we define *concurrent processing* (or *parallel processing*) to mean that if a snapshot is taken of the system as a whole then several processes may be found somewhere between their starting points and their end points. This definition clearly includes both true and apparent concurrency.

Nondeterminacy is the second operating system characteristic which can easily be described in terms of processes. If we regard processes as sequences of actions which can be interrupted between steps, then nondeterminacy is reflected in the unpredictable order in which the interruptions may occur, and hence the unpredictable order in which the sequences proceed. Reverting to our secretarial analogy, we can liken the unpredictable events which occur in an operating system to telephones ringing in an office. It cannot be known in advance when a particular telephone will ring, how long it will take to deal with the call, or what effect the call will have on the various jobs being done in the office. We can observe, however, that the secretary who answers the telephone must note what she is currently doing so that she can return to it later. Similarly, the interruption of a process must be accompanied by the recording of information which will subsequently enable the process to be resumed. The information recorded is the same as that required when processors switch among processes in order to achieve concurrency. Indeed, interruption of a process can be regarded as a switch, caused by some unpredictable event, of a processor away from the process.

We can summarise what has been said so far as follows. A process is a sequence of actions, and is therefore dynamic, whereas a program is a sequence of instructions, and is therefore static. A processor is an agent for running a process. Nondeterminacy and concurrency can be described in terms of interrupting processes between actions and of switching processors among processes. In order to effect interruption and switching sufficient information about a process must be stored in order that it may later be resumed.

3.2 COMMUNICATION BETWEEN PROCESSES

The processes within a computing system do not of course act in isolation. On the one hand they must co-operate to achieve the desired objective of running user jobs; on the other hand they are in competition for the use of limited resources such as processors, memory, or files. The two elements of co-operation and competition imply the need for some form of communication between processes. The areas in which communication is essential may be categorised as follows.

(1) Mutual Exclusion

System resources may be classified as *shareable*, meaning that they may be used by several processes concurrently (in the sense defined in the previous section), or *non-shareable*, meaning that their use is restricted to one process at a time. The non-shareability of a resource derives from one of two reasons.

(a)   The physical nature of the resource makes it impracticable for it to be shared. A typical example is a paper tape reader, where it is impracticable to switch tapes between successive characters.

(b)   The resource is such that if it were used by several processes concurrently the actions of one process could interfere with those of another. A particularly common example is a memory location which contains a variable accessible to more than one process: if one process tests the variable while another modifies it then the result will be unpredictable and usually disastrous. For instance, suppose that in an airline booking system the availability of a particular seat is represented by the contents of a certain location in memory. Then if the location were accessible to more than one process at a time it would be possible for two travel agents to reserve the seat simultaneously by following the unfortunate sequence of actions below.

Agent A sees the seat is free
and consults his client

.   Agent B sees the seat is free
.   and consults his client
.
.   .
.   .
Agent A reserves the seat   .
.
Agent B reserves the seat

Non-shareable resources therefore include most peripherals, writeable files, and data areas which are subject to modification; shareable resources include CPUs, read-only files, and areas of memory which contain pure procedures or data protected against modification.

The mutual exclusion problem is that of ensuring that non-shareable resources are accessed by only one process at a time.

(2) Synchronisation

Generally speaking the speed of one process relative to another is unpredictable, since it depends on the frequency of interruption of each process and on how often and for how long each process is granted a processor. We say that processes run *asynchronously* with respect to each other. However, to achieve successful co-operation there are certain points at which processes must synchronise their activities. These are points beyond which a process cannot proceed until another process has completed some activity. For example, a process which schedules user jobs cannot proceed until an input process has read at least one job into the machine. Similarly, a computational process producing output may not be able to proceed until its previous output has been printed. It is the operating system's responsibility to provide mechanisms by which synchronisation can be effected.

(3) Deadlock

When several processes compete for resources it is possible for a situation to arise in which no process can continue because the resources each one requires are held by another. This situation is called *deadlock*, or *deadly embrace*. It is analogous to the traffic jam which occurs when two opposing streams of traffic, in trying to turn across each other's path, become completely immobilised because each stream occupies the road space needed by the other. The avoidance of deadlock, or the limitation of its effects, is clearly one of the functions of the operating system.

3.3 SEMAPHORES

The most important single contribution towards inter-process communication was the introduction (Dijkstra, 1965) of the concept of *semaphores* and the primitive operations *wait* and *signal* which act on them. (*Wait* and *signal* are often referred to by Dijkstra's original names P and V which are the initial letters of the corresponding Dutch words. We shall, however, adopt the more recent and descriptive terminology.)

A semaphore is a non-negative integer which, apart from initialisation of its value, can be acted upon only by the operations *wait* and *signal*. These operations act only on semaphores, and their effect is defined as follows.

signal(s)

The effect is to increase the value of the semaphore s by one, the increase being regarded as an indivisible operation. Indivisibility implies that *signal(s)* is not equivalent to the assignment statement '$s: = s + 1$'. For suppose that two processes A and B both wish to perform the operation '*signal* (s)' when the value of s is, say, 3. Then the value of s when both operations are complete will be 5. Suppose on the other hand that in similar circumstances both processes wish to execute '$s: = s + 1$'. Then A could evaluate the expression $s + 1$, finding it equal to 4; before A can assign the result to s, B also evaluates $s + 1$ with the same result. Each process then assigns the value 4 to s, and one of the desired increments is lost.

wait(s)

The effect is to decrease the value of the semaphore s by 1 as soon as the result would be non-negative. Again the operation is indivisible. The *wait* operation implies a potential delay, for when it acts on a semaphore whose value is 0, the process executing the operation can proceed only when some other process has increased the value of the semaphore to 1 by a *signal* operation. The indivisibility of the operation means that if several processes are delayed then only one of them can successfully complete the operation when the semaphore becomes positive. No assumption is made about which process this is.

The effects of the wait and signal operations may be summarised as

$$wait(s) \quad : \quad \textbf{when } s > 0 \textbf{ do } \text{decrement } s$$
$$signal(s) \quad : \quad \text{increment } s$$

where s is any semaphore.

It can be seen from these definitions that every *signal* operation on a semaphore increases its value by 1 and every successful (that is, completed) *wait* operation decreases its value by 1. Hence the value of a semaphore is related to the number of *wait* and *signal* operations on it by the relation

$$val\ (sem) = C\ (sem) + ns\ (sem) - nw\ (sem) \tag{3.1}$$

where

$val\ (sem)$	is the value of semaphore *sem*
$C\ (sem)$	is its initial value
$ns\ (sem)$	is the number of *signal* operations on it
$nw\ (sem)$	is the number of successful *wait* operations on it

But, by definition

$$val\ (sem) \geqslant 0$$

Hence we derive the important relation

$$nw\ (sem) \leqslant ns\ (sem) + C\ (sem) \tag{3.2}$$

in which equality holds if and only if $val\ (sem) = 0$.

The relation 3.2 is invariant under *wait* and *signal* operations; that is, it is true however many operations are performed.

The implementation of semaphores and of the *wait* and *signal* operations will be discussed in the next chapter. For the present we shall take their implementability for granted, and use them to solve the problems listed earlier.

(1) Mutual Exclusion

Non-shareable resources, whether peripherals, files, or data in memory, can be protected from simultaneous access by several processes by preventing the processes from concurrently executing the pieces of program through which access is made. These pieces of program are called *critical sections*, and mutual exclusion in the use of resources can be regarded as mutual exclusion in the execution of critical sections. For example, processes may be mutually excluded from accessing a table of data if all the routines which read or update the table are written as critical sections such that only one may be executed at once.

Exclusion can be achieved by the simple expedient of enclosing each critical section by *wait* and *signal* operations on a single semaphore whose initial value is 1. Thus each critical section is programmed as

> *wait (mutex)*;
>> critical section
>
> *signal (mutex)*;

where *mutex* is the name of a semaphore.

The reader will see by inspection that if the initial value of *mutex* is 1 then mutual exclusion is indeed assured, since at most one process can execute *wait (mutex)* before another executes *signal (mutex)*. More formally, application of relation 3.2 gives

$$nw \ (mutex) \leqslant ns \ (mutex) + 1$$

which implies that at most one process can be inside its critical section at any time.

Furthermore, a process is never unnecessarily prevented from entering its critical section; entry is prevented only if some other process is already inside its own critical section. We can see this by observing that a process is denied entry only if the value of *mutex* is 0. In this case relation 3.2 indicates that

$$nw \ (mutex) = ns \ (mutex) + 1$$

In other words the number of successful *wait* operations on *mutex* exceeds the number of signal operations by 1, which implies that some process is within its critical section.

Our conclusion is that each time a process wishes to access a shared variable or a shared resource then it must effect the access via a critical section which is protected by a semaphore as above.

As an example suppose that an operating system contains two processes *A* and *B* which respectively add items to and remove items from a queue. In order that the queue pointers do not become confused it may be necessary to restrict access to the queue to only one process at a time. Thus the addition and removal of items would be coded as critical sections as below.

Program for Process A	*Program for Process B*
.	.
.	.
.	.
wait (mutex);	*wait (mutex)*;
add item to queue	remove item from queue
signal (mutex);	*signal (mutex)*;
.	.
.	.
.	.

At this point the suspicious reader may wonder whether the mutual exclusion problem could have been solved without the additional formalism of semaphores and their associated operations. On the face of it this suspicion might appear well founded, for it seems possible to derive a solution by protecting each critical section by a single simple variable (called *gate*, say). When *gate* is set to *open* (represented by the value 1, say), entry to the critical section is allowed; when it is set to *closed* (represented by 0), entry is not allowed. Thus a critical section would be coded as

> **while** *gate* = *closed* **do** null operation;
>
> *gate* := *closed*;
>
>> critical section
>
> *gate* := *open*;

Thus each process entering the critical section tests that *gate* is *open* (and loops until it is); it then sets *gate* to *closed*, preventing other processes entering the section. On exit, the process resets *gate* to *open*, freeing the section for execution by another process.

Unfortunately this simple solution will not work. The reason lies in the separation of the test for an open gate in line 1 from the closing of the gate in line 2. As a consequence of this separation two processes executing in parallel may each find an open gate at line 1 before either has the chance to close it at line 2. The result is that both processes enter the critical section together.

Semaphores avoid a similar difficulty by the insistence that the *wait* and *signal* operations are indivisible; there is no possibility of two processes acting on the same semaphore at the same time. The implementation of semaphores, to be discussed in chapter 4, must of course ensure that this is so.

(2) Synchronisation

The simplest form of synchronisation is that a process *A* should not proceed beyond a point L1 until some other process *B* has reached L2. Examples of this situation arise whenever *A* requires information at point L1 which is provided by *B* when it reaches L2. The synchronisation can be programmed as follows

Program for Process A	*Program for Process B*
.	.
.	.
.	.
L1 : *wait* (*proceed*);	L2 : *signal* (*proceed*);
.	.
.	.
.	.

where *proceed* is a semaphore with initial value 0.

It is clear from the above programs that *A* cannot proceed beyond L1 until *B* has executed the signal operation at L2. (Of course if *B* executes the signal operation before *A* reaches L1 then *A* is not delayed at all.) Again we can use relation 3.2 to demonstrate this more formally; we have

$$nw \ (proceed) \leqslant ns \ (proceed)$$

which implies that *A* cannot pass L1 before *B* passes L2.

The above example is asymmetric in that the progress of *A* is regulated by that of *B* but not vice versa. The case in which two processes each regulate the progress of the other is exemplified by the classic problem of the producer and consumer. Since this problem is typical of many which arise in inter-process communication we shall describe it in some detail.

A set of 'producer' processes and a set of 'consumer' processes communicate by means of a buffer into which the producers deposit items and from which the consumers extract them. The producers continually repeat the cycle 'produce item – deposit item in buffer', and the consumers repeat a similar cycle 'extract item from buffer – consume item'. A typical producer might be a computational process placing lines of ouput in a buffer, while the corresponding consumer might be the process which prints each line. The buffer is of limited capacity, being large enough to hold *N* items of equal size. The synchronisation required is twofold: firstly, the producers cannot put items into the buffer if it is already full, and secondly, the consumers cannot extract items if the buffer is empty. In other words, if the number of items deposited is *d*, and the number of items extracted is *e*, we must ensure that

$$0 \leqslant d - e \leqslant N \tag{3.3}$$

Furthermore, the buffer must be protected from simultaneous access by several processes, lest the actions of one (for example in updating pointers) disturb the actions of another. Hence both the deposition and extraction of items must be coded as critical sections.

We postulate the following solution to the problem

Program for producers	*Program for consumers*
repeat indefinitely	**repeat** indefinitely
begin	**begin**
produce item;	*wait(item available)*;
wait(space available);	*wait(buffer*
wait(buffer	*manipulation)*;
manipulation);	extract item from buffer;
deposit item in buffer;	*signal(buffer*
signal(buffer	*manipulation)*;
manipulation);	*signal(space available)*;
signal(item available)	consume item
end	**end**

Synchronisation is achieved through the semaphores *space available* and *item available* whose initial values are N and 0 respectively. Mutual exclusion of processes from accessing the buffer is effected by the semaphore *buffer manipulation* with initial value 1.

We must now show that this solution satisfies relation 3.3. If we apply the invariance relation 3.2. to the two synchronisation semaphores we obtain

$$nw\ (space\ available) \leqslant ns\ (space\ available) + N \qquad\qquad (3.4)$$

and

$$nw\ (item\ available) \leqslant ns\ (item\ available) \qquad\qquad (3.5)$$

But we observe from the order of operations in the program for the producers that

$$ns\ (item\ available) \leqslant d \leqslant nw\ (space\ available) \qquad\qquad (3.6)$$

and from the order of operations in the program for the consumers that

$$ns\ (space\ available) \leqslant e \leqslant nw\ (item\ available) \qquad\qquad (3.7)$$

Hence, from relation 3.6

$$d \leqslant nw\ (space\ available)$$
$$\leqslant ns\ (space\ available) + N \qquad\text{by 3.4}$$
$$\leqslant e + N \qquad\qquad\qquad\text{by 3.7}$$

Similarly, from relation 3.7

$$e \leqslant nw\ (item\ available)$$
$$\leqslant ns\ (item\ available) \qquad\text{by 3.5}$$
$$\leqslant d \qquad\qquad\qquad\text{by 3.6}$$

Combination of these two results gives

$$e \leqslant d \leqslant e + N$$

which shows that relation 3.3 is satisfied as required.

The solution to the producer–consumer problem can be used as a guide in any situation where one process passes information to another. In particular, processes which drive input peripherals act as producers for those processes which consume the input, and processes which drive output peripherals act as consumers for those processes which produce the output.

(3) Deadlock

As pointed out earlier, deadlock can occur whenever a set of processes compete for resources. As such it is a problem that we will leave for full discussion until chapter 8.

In this section we remark that deadlock may also occur because processes are waiting for each other to complete certain actions. As an example, consider two processes *A* and *B* which operate on semaphores *X* and *Y* as below.

process A	*process B*
.	.
.	.
.	.
wait(*X*);	*wait*(*Y*);
.	.
.	.
wait (Y);	*wait*(*X*);
.	.
.	.
.	.

If the initial values of *X* and *Y* are 1 then each process can complete its first *wait* operation, reducing the semaphore values to 0. Clearly, neither process can then proceed beyond its next *wait* operation, and deadlock prevails.

The situation is in fact analogous to that in which deadlock arises from competing resource requests. If a semaphore is regarded as a resource, and *wait* and *signal* operations regarded as claiming and releasing it, then deadlock has ensued because both *A* and *B* hold the resource required by the other. The 'shareability' of a semaphore is determined by its initial value: if the value is n (>1) the semaphore can be shared by n processes; if it is 1 (as above) then the semaphore is unshareable.

A similar but more complex case of deadlock can be derived from the producer–consumer problem by reversing the order of the *wait* operations performed by the consumers. If the buffer is empty it is possible for a consumer to gain access to the buffer by executing '*wait* (*buffer manipulation*)' and then to be suspended on '*wait* (*item available*)'. The only way in which the consumer can be freed is for a producer to deposit an item in the buffer and execute '*signal* (*item available*)'. However, no producer can gain access to the buffer since it is held by the blocked consumer. Hence deadlock results. Again the situation is analogous to that resulting from competing resource requests. In this case the resources are the buffer, held by the consumer, and a new item, held by a producer.

The lesson to be learned from these examples is that deadlock can occur as a result of an incorrectly ordered sequence of *wait* operations even when no explicit resource requests are being made. It may be salutary to realise that the deadlock threat inherent in the wrong solution to the producer–consumer problem would not be detected by the validation carried out in the last section.

Both the deadlock-free and deadlock-prone solutions satisfy relation 3.3, and thus appear equally correct by that criterion. Criteria for recognising deadlock in respect of resource allocation will be discussed in chapter 8; the recognition of deadlock (or lack of it) in a sequence of *wait* operations can be performed by an analysis similar to the following.

Consider the solution to the producer–consumer problem given in section (2) above. We shall show that it is in fact deadlock-free. Firstly we observe that the inner sections of the programs for the producers and consumers are simply critical sections protected by the semaphore *buffer manipulation*, and therefore in themselves possess no deadlock potential. Hence deadlock can prevail only if

(a)   no producer can pass *wait* (*space available*) and no consumer is in a position to execute *signal* (*space available*) (that is, no consumer is extracting);

and

(b)   no consumer can pass *wait* (*item available*) and no producer is in a position to execute *signal* (*item available*) (that is, no producer is depositing).

Condition (a), with relation 3.2, implies

$$nw \ (space \ available) = ns \ (space \ available) + N$$

and

$$nw \ (item \ available) = ns \ (space \ available)$$

Condition (b), with relation 3.2, implies

$$nw \ (item \ available) = ns \ (item \ available)$$

and

$$nw \ (space \ available) = ns \ (item \ available)$$

Putting these relations together we get

$$nw \ (space \ available) = nw \ (space \ available) + N$$

which is a contradiction (since $N > 0$).

A similar analysis for the case in which the order of *wait* operations in the consumer program is reversed is not possible, since the inner section of the program for the consumers is no longer a simple critical section (it now contains a *wait* operation). A more complex analysis (for example, Habermann, 1972; Lister, 1974) is needed to show that deadlock can in fact occur.

3.4 MONITORS

In the previous section we saw how semaphores can be used to effect synchronisation and communication between processes. The undisciplined use of semaphores is, however, rather prone to error — a programmer can easily place *wait* and *signal* operations in the wrong places, or even omit them altogether. For example, if a programmer fails to realise that a particular data structure is to be shared by several processes he will omit to enclose in *wait* and *signal* operations the critical sections of program which access it. The data structure will then be unprotected from simultaneous manipulation by several processes, and inconsistencies in its contents will probably ensue.

To avoid such problems there have been a number of proposals for programming language constructs which oblige the programmer to declare shared data and resources explicitly, and which enforce mutual exclusion of access to such shared objects. One of the most influential and widely adopted constructs is the *monitor* (Hoare, 1974), which we describe briefly below, and in more detail in the Appendix.

A monitor consists of

(1) the data comprising a shared object
(2) a set of procedures which can be called to access the object
(3) a piece of program which initialises the object (this program is executed only once, when the object is created)

For example, a buffer (such as that described in the previous section) for passing data items between producer processes and consumer processes might be represented by a monitor consisting of

(1) the buffer space and pointers (for example, an array, and indices into it)
(2) two procedures *deposit* and *extract* which can be called by processes to place an item in the buffer or remove an item from it
(3) a piece of program which initialises the buffer pointers to the start of the buffer

The compiler for a language incorporating monitors must ensure that access to a shared object can be made only by calling a procedure of the corresponding monitor (this can be achieved fairly easily through the scope mechanism of most block structured languages). The compiler must also ensure that the procedures of each monitor are implemented as mutually exclusive critical sections. The compiler may well do this by generating *wait* and *signal* operations on appropriate semaphores in the compiled program. Thus, in the buffer example, the compiler guarantees that access to the buffer is restricted to the *deposit* and *extract* procedures, and that these procedures are mutually exclusive.

It should be apparent that monitors eliminate a potentially fertile source of error by transferring the responsibility for mutual exclusion from the programmer to the compiler. Responsibility for other forms of synchronisation remains, however, with the programmer, who must use semaphores (or something equivalent) to effect it. For example, the representation of a buffer as a monitor (as above) ensures through the mutual exclusion of *deposit* and *extract* that items cannot be simultaneously inserted and removed. It does not, however, prevent processes depositing items in a full buffer or removing them from an empty one. Such disasters must be prevented by placing appropriate synchronisation operations inside the *deposit* and *extract* procedures. The details are given in the Appendix.

The monitor construct has been implemented in a number of programming languages, such as Concurrent Pascal (Hansen, 1975), Pascal-plus (Welsh and Bustard, 1979), and Mesa (Lampson and Redell, 1980). For the operating system implementor it has the advantage of restricting all operations on a shared object to a set of well-defined procedures, and of ensuring that these operations are mutually exclusive. Synchronisation for purposes other than mutual exclusion remains the responsibility of the programmer.

3.5 SUMMARY

In this chapter we have introduced the notion of a process, as opposed to a program, and have shown that it is a useful concept in the study of operating system characteristics. In particular we have seen that both concurrency and nondeterminacy can be described in terms of switching processors between processes. We have also introduced semaphores and the operations on them as a mechanism for inter-process communication, and have demonstrated that they are a sufficient tool for solving problems of mutual exclusion and synchronisation. Finally we have seen that it is possible in some cases to use certain relations about the values of semaphores to demonstrate that processes exhibit the properties we expect.

In the next chapter we shall use these tools to start the construction of our paper operating system.

4 *The System Nucleus*

In the last chapter we developed the concepts and tools needed to build the paper operating system outlined in chapter 1. As mentioned there, the paper operating system will resemble an onion in which each layer provides a set of functions dependent only on the layers within it. At the centre of the onion are the facilities provided by the hardware of the machine itself. The onion layers can be regarded as implementing successive virtual machines, so that the onion as a whole implements the virtual machine required by the user.

The major interface between the basic machine hardware and the operating system is provided by the system *nucleus*, which is the innermost layer of the onion. The purpose of the nucleus is to provide an environment in which processes can exist; this implies handling interrupts, switching processors between processes, and implementing mechanisms for inter-process communication. Before describing these functions in detail we shall look at the essential hardware required to support the operating system we are trying to build.

4.1 ESSENTIAL HARDWARE FACILITIES

(1) Interrupt Mechanism

It was mentioned in chapter 2 that in order for I/O activities to be overlapped with central processing it must be possible to interrupt the running process when a peripheral transfer is complete. We therefore demand that our computer should provide an interrupt mechanism which at least saves the value of the program counter for the interrupted process and transfers control to a fixed location in memory. This location will be used as the start of a piece of program known as an *interrupt routine*, or *interrupt handler,* whose purpose is to determine the source of the interrupt and respond to it in an appropriate manner. We will describe the interrupt handler in section 4.4, and will discuss the various forms it can take according to the precise nature of the interrupt mechanism available.

(For the sake of completeness we mention that some computers, for example, the CDC CYBER 170 range, operate without an explicit interrupt mechanism. In such a computer one or more processors must be dedicated to monitoring the status of the I/O devices to detect when transfers are complete. In the case of the CYBER this function is performed by a number of so-called 'peripheral processors', while the CPU is relieved of all I/O handling. A restricted form of interrupt still exists, however, since the peripheral processors can force the CPU to jump to a different location.)

(2) Memory Protection

When several processes are running concurrently it is necessary to protect the memory used by one process from unauthorised access by another. The protection mechanisms which must be built into the memory addressing hardware are described in detail in the next chapter; for the present we take their existence for granted.

(3) Privileged Instruction Set

In order that concurrent processes cannot interfere with each other, part of the instruction set of the computer must be reserved for use by the operating system only. These privileged instructions perform such functions as

(a)   enabling and disabling interrupts
(b)   switching a processor between processes
(c)   accessing registers used by the memory protection hardware
(d)   performing input or output
(e)   halting a central processor

To distinguish between times when privileged instructions are or are not allowed, most computers operate in one of two modes, usually known as *supervisor mode* and *user mode*. Privileged instructions can be used only in supervisor mode. The switch from user to supervisor mode is made automatically in any of the following circumstances.

(a)   A user process calls on the operating system to execute some function requiring the use of a privileged instruction. Such a call is termed an *extracode*, or *supervisor call*.
(b)   An interrupt occurs.
(c)   An error condition occurs in a user process. The condition can be treated as an 'internal interrupt', and handled in the first instance by an interrupt routine.
(d)   An attempt is made to execute a privileged instruction while in user mode. The attempt can be regarded as a particular kind of error, and handled as in (c) above.

The switch from supervisor mode back to user mode is effected by an instruction which is itself privileged.

It should perhaps be mentioned that the scheme above, which involves two levels of privilege, is extended on some computers (for example, the ICL 2900, CYBER 180, and Honeywell 645) to incorporate several levels. We shall defer discussion of such multilevel machines until chapter 9.

(4) Real-time Clock

A hardware clock which interrupts at fixed intervals of real-time (that is, time as measured in the outside world rather than time required for computation by any particular process) is essential for the implementation of scheduling policies and for the accounting of resources consumed by the various users.

We shall assume from this point on that the machine on which we are building our paper operating system has the hardware facilities outlined above. More precisely, since we allow the possibility of including several central processors in a single configuration, we shall assume that each processor has facilities (1) to (3) and that there is a single real-time clock which can interrupt each processor. In addition we shall restrict ourselves to *tightly coupled* configurations in which the processors are identical and share a common memory. This excludes consideration of computer networks, in which the processors have separate memories and communicate by some form of data transmission, and of systems in which dissimilar processors are organised so as to share a workload in a way best suited to their particular characteristics. The former topic merits a book on its own; the latter is still a fertile field for research in which no clear trends have yet emerged.

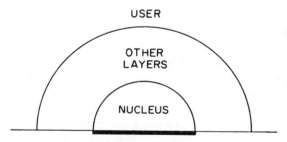

Figure 4.1 Structure of the paper operating system

4.2 OUTLINE OF THE NUCLEUS

The relationship between the nucleus and the rest of the operating system is illustrated in figure 4.1. The horizontal line at the base of the diagram represents the computer hardware; the thickened portion of this line is the privileged instruction set, whose use we restrict to the nucleus. (Exceptions to this rule are some privileged instructions concerned with memory protection and I/O, discussed in later chapters.)

The nucleus consists of three pieces of program

(1)   the *first-level interrupt handler*, which performs the initial handling of all interrupts;

(2)   the *dispatcher*, which switches the central processors between processes;

(3)   two procedures (routines) which implement the inter-process communication primitives *wait* and *signal* described in chapter 3. These procedures are called via extracodes in the processes concerned.

Because the nucleus is built directly on the basic hardware we can expect it to be the most heavily machine-dependent part of an operating system. Indeed it is probably the only part of the operating system which need be written substantially in assembly language: with a few small exceptions, mainly related to I/O, the other layers can be most conveniently coded in a high-level language. Suitable systems programming languages, to which the reader may care to refer, are BCPL (Richards, 1969), BLISS (Wulf *et al.*, 1971) and C (Kernighan and Ritchie, 1978). Other languages, like Concurrent Pascal (Hansen, 1975) and Modula (Wirth, 1977 and 1983), are intended specifically for writing operating systems, though they impose certain constraints on the system designer. The restriction of assembly language to one small (probably no more than 400 instructions) part of the operating system, made possible by the system's hierarchical structure, can contribute greatly towards realising the goal of an error-free, comprehensible, and maintainable product.

4.3 REPRESENTATION OF PROCESSES

The programs within the nucleus are responsible for maintaining the environment in which processes exist. Consequently they are required to operate on some data structure which is the physical representation of all processes within the system. The nature of this data structure is the concern of the current section.

Each process can be represented by a *process descriptor* (sometimes known as a *control block* or *state vector*) which is an area of memory containing all relevant information about the process. The composition of this information will become apparent as we progress; for the present we include in it some identification of the process (the *process name*) and an indication of the process's *status*. A process can have one of three principal statuses: it may be *running*, which means that it is executing on a processor; it may be *runnable*, meaning that it could run if a processor were allocated to it; or it may be *unrunnable*, meaning that it could not use a processor even if one were allocated. The most common reason for a process being unrunnable is that it is waiting for the completion of a peripheral transfer. The status of a process is an essential piece of information for the dispatcher when it comes to allocate a central processor.

We shall refer to a process which is running on a central processor as the *current process* for that processor; the number of current processes within the system at any time is of course less than or equal to the number of processors available.

A further part of the process descriptor can be used to store all information about the process which needs to be saved when it loses control of a processor. This information, required for subsequent resumption of the process, includes the values of all machine registers, such as program counter, accumulators, and index registers, which could be changed by another process. It also includes the values of any registers used in addressing the memory owned by the process (see chapter 5). We call the whole of this information the *volatile environment* of the process (other names in the literature are *context block* and *process state*). More formally, the volatile environment of a process can be defined as that subset of the modifiable shared facilities of the system which are accessible to the process.

The process descriptor of each process is linked into a *process structure*, which acts as a description of all processes within the system. For the present we shall adopt an elementary form of process structure, in which the process descriptors are linked into a simple list. The process structure is the first data structure we have introduced into our operating system; since it will be by no means the last, we also introduce a *central table* whose purpose is to serve as a means of access to all system structures. The central table will contain a pointer to each data structure, and may also be used to hold any other global information, such as the date, time of day, and system version number, which might from time to time be required. The central table and process structure are illustrated in figure 4.2.

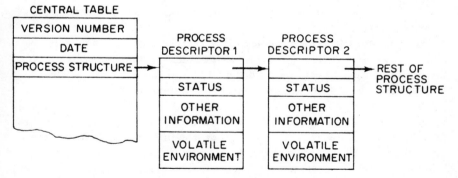

Figure 4.2 Central table and process structure

4.4 THE FIRST-LEVEL INTERRUPT HANDLER

The first-level interrupt handler (FLIH) is the part of the operating system which is responsible for responding to signals both from the outside world (interrupts) and from within the computing system itself (error traps and extracodes). We shall refer collectively to both types of signal as interrupts and use the adjectives 'external' and 'internal' to distinguish between them where necessary. The function of the FLIH is twofold

(1)   to determine the source of the interrupt
(2)   to initiate service of the interrupt

We have already stated in section 4.1 that the computer's interrupt mechanism is responsible for saving at least the value of the program counter for the interrupted process. It must also be ensured that other registers required by the FLIH which may be being used by the interrupted process are appropriately saved. If this is not done by the interrupt mechanism it must be performed as the first operation of the FLIH itself. Because the FLIH is a relatively simple program operating in a dedicated area of memory the set of registers involved will not be large, perhaps only a single accumulator. It will certainly be considerably smaller than the volatile environment of the interrupted process, which need not be saved in its entirety since the process may be resumed once the interrupt has been serviced.

An alternative strategy to saving register values, adopted for example on the Zilog Z80, the IBM Series 1, and some of the PDP-11 range, is to provide an extra set of registers for use in supervisor mode only. The FLIH can use these registers and leave those of the interrupted process intact.

Determination of the source of the interrupt can be performed more or less easily depending on the hardware provided. In the case of the most primitive hardware, in which all interrupts transfer control to the same location, identification must be achieved by a sequence of tests on the status flags of all possible sources. This sequence, often called a *skip chain*, is illustrated in figure 4.3. It is clearly advantageous to code the skip chain so that the most frequent sources of interrupts occur near its head.

On some computers (for example the PDP-11) the skip chain is rendered unnecessary by the inclusion of hardware which distinguishes between interrupt sources by transferring control to a different location for each source. This reduces the time to identify an interrupt at the cost of the extra interrupt locations required. A compromise arrangement employed on several computers, including the IBM 370 series, is to provide a small number of interrupt locations each of which is shared by a group of devices. The first stage of interrupt identification is then achieved by hardware, and a short skip chain starting at each location is sufficient to complete it. The distinction between external interrupts, error traps, and extracodes is often made in this way. The interrupt mechanism, as on the IBM 370, may give further aids to identification by planting information about the interrupt in some fixed memory location.

Interrupts to a central processor are normally inhibited when it switches from user to supervisor mode. This ensures that the values of registers saved on entry to the FLIH cannot be overwritten by a subsequent interrupt occurring before the FLIH is left. An interrupt which occurs while the interrupt mechanism is disabled is held pending until the mechanism is re-enabled on resumption of user mode. This arrangement becomes inoperable in situations where some peripheral devices require response far more quickly than others if, for example, data is not to be lost. In these cases it is convenient to introduce the notion of *priority* among the various interrupt sources, and to allow an interrupt routine to be itself interrupted by a request for service from a device of a higher priority. Some computers (for example the IBM 370) allow this to be done by selectively disabling interrupts within the FLIH; when the FLIH is servicing an interrupt it disables all those of equal or lower priority. Care must of course be taken to store the program registers of the interrupted process in different locations according to the priority level of the interrupt received. Alternatively, the interrupt hardware may itself distinguish between various priority levels, transferring control to and saving registers at different locations for each level. An interrupt at one level automatically inhibits others at the same or lower levels. The DEC System-10, PDP-11, and M6800 are examples of processors with this kind of priority interrupt mechanism, each having eight priority levels.

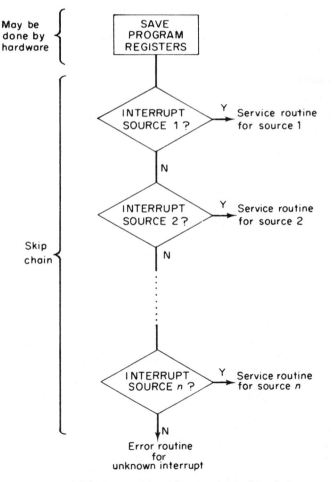

Figure 4.3 Interrupt identification by a skip chain

The second function of the FLIH is to initiate service of an interrupt by calling an interrupt service routine appropriate to the type of interrupt involved. We shall give details in chapter 6 of service routines for I/O devices, and in chapter 11 of handling error traps. At this stage we remark only that because the interrupt routines run in supervisor mode with interrupts wholly or partially inhibited it is desirable to keep them as short as possible. In general each routine will perform some minimal action, for example transferring a character from an input device into a buffer, and hand over responsibility for further action, such as reacting to the character received, to a process which runs in normal user mode.

It is important to note that the occurrence of an interrupt, either external or internal, will often alter the status of some process. For instance, a process which has requested a peripheral transfer and which is unrunnable while the transfer is in progress will be made runnable again by the interrupt which occurs at its completion. Again, certain extracodes, such as a *wait* operation on a zero-valued semaphore or a request for I/O, will result in the current process being unable to continue. In all cases the change of status is effected by the interrupt routine changing the status entry in the process descriptor of the process concerned.

A consequence of the status change is that the process which was running on the processor concerned before the interrupt occurred may not be the most suitable to run afterwards. It may be the case, for example, that the interrupt makes runnable a process which in some sense has a higher priority than the currently running one. The question of when to switch a central processor between processes, and which process to favour, is considered in the next section.

4.5 THE DISPATCHER

It is the function of the dispatcher (sometimes known as the *low-level scheduler*) to allocate the central processors among the various processes in the system. The dispatcher is entered whenever a current process cannot continue, or whenever there are grounds to suppose that a processor might be better employed elsewhere. These occasions may be detailed as follows

(1) after an external interrupt which changes the status of some process;
(2) after an extracode which results in the current process being temporarily unable to continue;
(3) after an error trap which causes suspension of the current process while the error is dealt with.

These occasions are all special cases of interrupts; that is, they are all interrupts which alter the status of some process. For the sake of simplicity we do not distinguish them from those interrupts, such as a *wait* operation on a positive-valued semaphore, which have no effect on the status of any process; we say, in effect, that the dispatcher is ultimately entered after *all* interrupts. The overhead in entering the dispatcher on occasions when no process status has changed is

more than offset by the advantages gained from a uniform treatment of all
interrupts.

The operation of the dispatcher is quite simple.

(1)   Is the current process on this processor still the most suitable to run? If so
       then return control to it at the point indicated by the program counter
       stored by the interrupt hardware. If not, then ...
(2)   Save the volatile environment of the current process in its process
       descriptor.
(3)   Retrieve the volatile environment of the most suitable process from its
       process descriptor.
(4)   Transfer control to it at the location indicated by the restored program
       counter.

To determine the most suitable process to run it is sufficient to order all
runnable processes by some priority. The assignment of priorities to processes
is not a function of the dispatcher but of the high-level scheduler to be described
in chapter 8. For the present we remark that priorities are calculated according
to such factors as the amount of resources required, the length of time since the
process last ran, and the relative importance of the originating user. As far as the
dispatcher is concerned the process priorities are given *a priori*.

In our paper operating system we link the process descriptors of all runnable
processes into a queue ordered by decreasing priority, so that the most eligible
process is at its head. We call this queue the *processor queue*, illustrated in
figure 4.4. Thus the role of the dispatcher is to run the first process on the
processor queue which is not already running on some other processor. This may
or may not be the same process as was running before the dispatcher was invoked.

We note in passing that the introduction of the processor queue means that
the action taken by an interrupt routine to make a process runnable is now twofold. Firstly it must alter the status entry in the process descriptor and secondly
it must link the process descriptor into the processor queue at the position
indicated by its priority. We shall see in the next section that this operation can
conveniently be done by executing a *signal* operation on a semaphore on which
the process concerned has executed *wait*.

It is of course possible that at a particular moment the processor queue
contains fewer processes than there are processors, perhaps because several
processes are waiting for input or output. This situation, which is probably the
result of a poor high-level scheduling decision, implies that there is no work for
some central processors to do. Rather than allowing a processor to loop within
the dispatcher it is convenient to introduce an extra process, called the *null
process*, which has the lowest priority and is always runnable. The null process
may be nothing more than an idle loop, or it may perform some useful function
such as executing processor test programs. It has been known for the null process

to be used for such esoteric purposes as solving chess endgame problems or
calculating the decimal expansion of π. Its position at the end of the processor
queue is shown in figure 4.4.

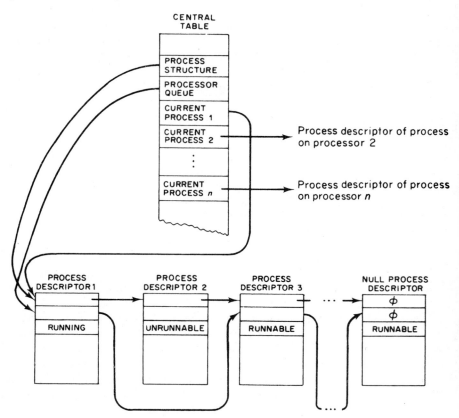

Figure 4.4 Process structure and processor queue

The operation of the dispatcher can now be summarised as follows.

(1)   Is the current process on this processor still the first non-running process
       on the processor queue? If so then resume it. If not then ...
(2)   Save the volatile environment of the current process.
(3)   Restore the volatile environment of the first non-running process in the
       processor queue.
(4)   Resume running this process.

Before leaving the dispatcher we should point out that we have chosen a very
simple structure for the runnable processes. Many operating systems divide the
runnable processes into several classes, distinguished by such criteria as resources

required, the maximum waiting time to be tolerated, or the amount of processor time to be allowed before pre-emption. The DEC System-10 monitor for example has three processor queues, one each for processes which are allowed 2 seconds, 0.25 seconds, and 0.02 seconds respectively before pre-emption. Each queue is serviced on a first come, first served basis, with the shorter pre-emption time queues having the higher priority. A process is originally placed in the 0.02 second queue; if it runs for the whole of its allowed quantum it is relegated to the 0.25 second queue, and similarly, if it runs for the whole of its increased quantum it is relegated to the 2 second queue. The effect is to ensure that processes associated with on-line terminals, which typically have low processor requirements, receive a rapid service, whereas processor bound jobs receive longer but less frequent attention. We shall say more about this when we discuss scheduling in chapter 8.

We conclude this section by summarising the relationship between the FLIH and the dispatcher in the diagram below.

Interrupt mechanism	Save program counter
	Save other registers (optional)
	Enter FLIH
↓	
FLIH	Save program registers (if not done above)
	Identify interrupt (aided by hardware)
	Enter some service routine
↓	
Service routine	Service interrupt, possibly altering status
	of some process
↓	
Dispatcher	Processor switch necessary? If not, resume
	interrupted process
	Save volatile environment of current process
	Restore volatile environment of first
	eligible process in processor queue
	Transfer control to new process

4.6 IMPLEMENTATION OF *wait* AND *signal*

The final part of the nucleus is the implementation of some form of inter-process communication mechanism. As indicated in chapter 3 we shall use the operations *wait* and *signal* as our communication primitives, a choice which is based on the widespread understanding and ease of implementation of semaphores. Other communication mechanisms can be found in the literature (Andrews and Schneider, 1983). Some of these, like monitors (see section 3.4), may themselves be implemented in terms of semaphores.

Wait and *signal* are included in the nucleus because

(1)   they must be available to all processes, and hence must be implemented at a low level;

(2)   the *wait* operation may result in a process being blocked, causing an entry
       to the dispatcher to reallocate the processor. Hence the *wait* operation
       must have access to the dispatcher;
(3)   a convenient way for an interrupt routine to awaken (make runnable) a
       process is to execute *signal* on a semaphore on which the process has
       executed *wait*. Hence *signal* must be accessible to the interrupt routines.

The operations we have to implement (see chapter 3) are

    wait(s)   :   **when** $s > 0$ **do** decrement s
    signal(s)   :   increment s

where s is any semaphore. We develop our implementation as follows.

(1) Blocking and Unblocking

The *wait* operation implies that processes are blocked when a semaphore has value
0 and freed when a *signal* operation increases the value to 1. The natural way to
implement this is to associate with each semaphore a *semaphore queue*. When a
process performs an 'unsuccessful' *wait* operation (that is, it operates on a zero-
value semaphore) it is added to the semaphore queue and made unrunnable.
Conversely, when a *signal* operation is performed on a semaphore some process
can be taken off the semaphore queue (unless empty) and made runnable again.
The semaphore must therefore be implemented with two components: an integer
and a queue pointer (which may be null).
    At this point our implementation is as follows

    wait(s)   :   **if** $s \neq 0$ **then** $s := s - 1$
                       else add process to semaphore queue and make
                       unrunnable;
    signal(s)   :   **if** queue empty **then** $s := s + 1$
                       else remove some process from semaphore queue and
                       make runnable;

    Note that the semaphore need not be incremented within *signal* if a process is
to be freed, since the freed process would immediately have to decrement the
semaphore again in completing its *wait* operation.

(2) Queueing and Dequeueing

We have said nothing yet about which process is lucky enough to be removed from
the semaphore queue after a *signal* operation. Nor have we stated whether a
process which is added to the queue on an unsuccessful *wait* operation should be
added at the head, tail, or somewhere in the middle. In other words we have not
yet specified the queue organisation.

For most semaphores a simple first in, first out queue is adequate, since it ensures that all blocked processes are eventually freed. In some cases it may be preferable to order the queue on some other basis, perhaps by a priority similar to that used in the processor queue. This latter organisation ensures that processes with high processor priority do not languish for long periods of time on a semaphore queue. The important point is that different semaphores may require different queue organisations, so that an extra component must be included in the semaphore implementation to indicate which queue organisation applies. This component may simply be a coded description of the queue organisation, or in more complex cases it may be a pointer to a small piece of program which will perform the queueing and dequeueing operations. The structure of a semaphore in our implementation is shown in figure 4.5.

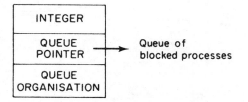

Figure 4.5 Structure of a semaphore

(3) Processor Allocation

Both *wait* and *signal* may alter the status of a process, the former by making it unrunnable and the latter by doing the opposite. An exit must therefore be made to the dispatcher for a decision on which process to run next. In cases where no process status has changed (that is, a *wait* on a positive valued semaphore or a *signal* on a semaphore with an empty queue) the dispatcher will resume the current process since it will still be the first non-running process in the processor queue. It is arguable that in this case the return from *wait* or *signal* should be directly to the current process rather than via the dispatcher; the resulting gain in efficiency would be at the expense of a slight extra complexity in the code for *wait* and *signal*. In this discussion we shall opt for simplicity over efficiency, while recognising that the opposite viewpoint may be equally valid.

(4) Indivisibility

As pointed out in chapter 3 both *wait* and *signal* must be indivisable operations in the sense that only one process can be allowed to execute them at any time. Hence they must both be implemented as procedures which begin with some kind of *lock* operation and end with an *unlock* operation. On a single processor configuration the lock operation can most easily be implemented by disabling the interrupt mechanism. This ensures that a process cannot lose control of the central processor while executing *wait* and *signal* since there is no way in which it can be interrupted. The unlock operation is performed by simply re-enabling the interrupts. On a machine with several central processors this procedure is inadequate since it is possible for two processes simultaneously to enter *wait* or *signal* by running on separate processors. In this case we need some other mechanism, such as a 'test and set' instruction. This is an instruction which tests and modifies the content of a memory location in a single operation. During execution of the instruction attempts by other processes to access the location are inhibited.

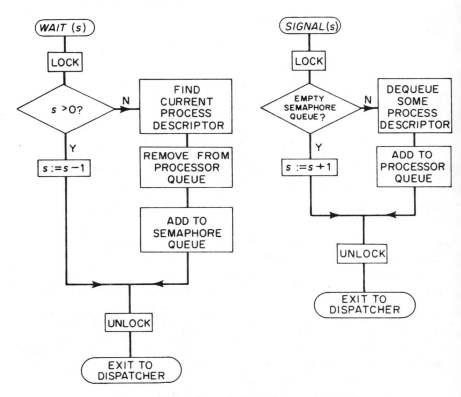

Figure 4.6 Implementation of wait and signal

The idea is that a particular location is used as a flag (similar to the variable *gate* in section 3.3) which indicates whether entry to the *wait* and *signal* procedures is allowed. If the flag is non-zero (say) entry is permitted, otherwise it is not. The lock operation consists of executing a test and set instruction on the flag, which determines its value and at the same time sets it to zero. If the value of the flag is non-zero then the process proceeds, otherwise it loops on the test and set instruction until the process currently inside the *wait* or *signal* procedure unlocks the flag by setting it to some non-zero value. Note that difficulties similar to those which arose in respect of the variable *gate* in section

3.3 are avoided by implementing the entire test and set instruction as a single indivisible operation. This lock/unlock mechanism is adopted on many computers, such as the IBM 370 series.

An alternative to test and set, adopted on the Burroughs 6000 series and the Plessey 250, is an instruction to interchange the contents of two memory locations. The lock operation starts by interchanging the values of a flag and a location which has previously been set to zero. The value of this second location is then examined to see whether entry is permitted, while any other process trying to gain entry will find the zero left by the interchange. A process which finds after the interchange that the flag was zero simply repeats the lock operation until the flag is made non-zero by some other process executing an unlock operation.

It should be noted that both these mechanisms imply some form of *busy waiting*. That is, a process which cannot pass the lock operation ties up its processor in a tight loop repeatedly trying the operation until the flag becomes unset. So long as the *wait* and *signal* procedures are simple the length of time involved in busy waiting should be quite short.

It is worth emphasising that the lock and unlock operations cannot be used as a substitute for *wait* and *signal*. The busy waiting or interrupt inhibition used to implement the lock operation would not be acceptable over the time scale for which processes can be delayed by a *wait* operation. The table below shows the conceptually different levels at which the two kinds of operation exist.

	Wait and *Signal*	Lock and Unlock
Purpose	General process synchronisation	Mutual exclusion of processes from *wait* and *signal* procedures
Implementation level	Software	Hardware
Delaying mechanism	Queueing	Busy waiting/interrupt inhibition
Typical delay time	Several seconds	Several microseconds

The result of the foregoing discussion is that we can implement *wait* and *signal* as two related procedures as shown in figure 4.6. The procedures will be called by extracodes which are part of the instruction repertoire of all processes.

We have now completed the system nucleus, which consists of the first-level interrupt handler, the dispatcher and the procedures for *wait* and *signal*, all running in supervisor mode.

5 *Memory Management*

Memory management is the next layer of our 'onion'. We put it next to the nucleus because unless a process possesses some memory there is very little it can do. It certainly cannot execute, since there is no room for the associated program, nor can it perform input or output without space for buffers.

In this chapter we shall first of all discuss the objectives of memory management and introduce the concept of virtual memory. We shall describe ways in which virtual memory can be implemented, and then discuss various policies for regulating the implementation. Finally, we shall see how memory management can be included in our paper operating system.

5.1 OBJECTIVES

The objectives of memory management are fivefold.

(1) Relocation

In a multiprogrammed computer the available memory will generally be shared at any given time between a number of processes, and it is not possible for the individual programmer to know in advance what other programs will be resident in memory when his own program is run. This means that he does not know at the time he writes the program precisely whereabouts in memory it will be located, and hence he cannot write the program in terms of absolute memory addresses. If the memory allocated to his program remained fixed during its entire run, then it would of course be possible to transform symbolic or relative addresses into absolute addresses at the time the program was loaded, but in fact this is seldom the case. As processes run to completion the space they use become free for other processes, and it may be necessary to move processes around in memory in order to make the best use of the space available. In particular, it may be desirable to move processes so that small non-contiguous areas of free memory become compacted into a larger, more useful, single area. Thus the region of memory allocated to a process may change during the process's lifetime, and the system must be responsible for transforming the addresses used by the programmer into the actual addresses in which the process is physically located.

(2) Protection

When several processes are sharing memory it is of course essential for their integrity that none of them is permitted to alter the contents of memory locations which are currently allocated to the others. Compile time checks on program addresses are an inadequate protection since most languages allow the dynamic calculation of addresses at run time, for example by computing array subscripts or pointers into data structures. Hence all memory references generated by a process must be checked at run time to ensure that they refer only to the memory space allocated to that process. (Strictly speaking, only write accesses need be checked, but if privacy of information is required then read accesses must also be checked.)

(3) Sharing

Despite the need for protection, there are occasions when several processes should be allowed access to the same portion of memory. For example, if a number of processes are executing the same program it is advantageous to allow each process to access the same copy of the program, rather than have its own separate copy. Similarly, processes may sometimes need to share a data structure and thus have common access to the area of memory holding it. The memory management system must therefore allow controlled access to shared areas of memory without compromising essential protection.

(4) Logical Organisation

The traditional computer has a one-dimensional, or linear address space in that addresses are numbered sequentially from zero to the upper limit of memory. While this organisation closely mirrors the hardware of the machine it does not really reflect the ways in which programs are usually written. Most programs are structured in some way – into modules or procedures – and refer to distinct areas of modifiable or unmodifiable data. For example, a compiler may be written with separate modules for lexical analysis, syntax analysis, and code generation, and among its data areas may be a table of reserved words (unmodifiable) and a symbol table (modified as new identifiers are encountered during compilation). If the logical divisions into program and data are reflected in a corresponding *segmentation* of address space then several advantages accrue. Firstly, it is possible for segments to be coded independently and for all references from one segment to another to be filled in by the system at run time; secondly, it is possible with little extra overhead to give different degrees of protection (for example, read only, execute only) to different segments; and thirdly, it is possible to introduce mechanisms by which segments can be shared among processes.

(5) Physical Organisation

Historically, the general desire for large amounts of storage space and the high cost of fast memory have led to the almost universal adoption of two-level storage systems. The compromise between speed and cost is typically achieved by supplementing a relatively small amount (up to a few million bytes) of direct access main memory by a much larger amount (perhaps several hundred million bytes) of secondary memory, or backing store. Main memory uses semiconductor technology, and has an access time of the order of 100 nanoseconds; backing store is usually based on magnetic discs, with an access time of up to 100 milliseconds.

Since in typical systems only information in main memory can be accessed directly, the organisation of the flow of information between main and secondary memories is obviously of prime importance. It is of course possible to rest the onus of organisation on the individual programmer, making him responsible for moving sections of program or data to or from main memory as required. Indeed, in the early days of computing this is what was done, and the technique of *overlay programming* — writing sections of program which overlaid themselves in memory — became an art in itself. However, there are two sound reasons which militate against such an approach. The first is that the programmer does not want to expend a great deal of effort in writing complicated overlays: he is too interested in solving his own problems to waste energy on side issues. Clever compilers can help by automatically generating overlay code at appropriate points in the program, but in many cases the compiler does not have sufficient information to know when the overlays will be required. The second reason is that because of dynamic relocation the programmer does not know at the time of writing how much space will be available or whereabouts in memory that space will be. Overlay programming thus becomes impracticable.

It is clear from these arguments that the task of moving information between the two levels of memory should be a system responsibility. How this responsibility can be carried out is discussed later in this chapter.

5.2 VIRTUAL MEMORY

The objectives listed above can be achieved by the conceptually simple (and pleasingly elegant) device of using an address translation mechanism, or *address map*, to transform the addresses used by the programmer into the corresponding physical memory locations actually allocated to the program. The maintenance of the address map is a system function, and possible implementations are discussed in the next section. The crucial point at this stage is the distinction between *program addresses* — addresses used by the programmer — and the physical *memory locations* into which they are mapped. The range of program addresses is known as the *address space* (or *name space*); the range of memory locations in the computer is the *memory space*. If the address space is denoted by N, and the memory space by M, then the address map can be denoted by

$$f \; : \; N \rightarrow M$$

On current computers the memory space is linear -- that is, the memory locations are numbered sequentially from zero − and its size is equal to the amount of main memory included in the configuration. We shall see that the address space, however, need not be linear, and depending on the particular implementation of the address map its size may be smaller than, equal to, or greater than that of the memory space.

An alternative way of looking at the address map is to regard it as a means of allowing the programmer to use a range of program addresses which may be quite different from the range of memory locations available. Thus the program- mer 'sees', and programs for, a *virtual memory* whose characteristics differ from those of the real memory. The address map is designed so as to produce a virtual memory convenient for the programmer, and so as to achieve some or all of the objectives listed in the previous section. The provision of virtual memory is a good example of the transformation (discussed in chapter 1) of the basic computer into a more convenient virtual machine.

In the next section we shall describe various virtual memories and the address maps which provide them.

5.3 IMPLEMENTATION OF VIRTUAL MEMORY

(1) Base and Limit Registers

The first two objectives listed in section 5.1, namely relocation and protection, can be achieved by a fairly simple address map as follows.

When a process is loaded into memory the address of the lowest location used is placed in a *base register* (or *datum register*), and all program addresses are interpreted as being relative to this *base address*. The address map thus consists simply of adding the program address to the base address to produce the cor- responding memory location; that is

$$f(a) = B + a$$

where a is the program address, and B is the base address of the process.

Relocation is accomplished by simply moving the process and resetting the base address to the appropriate value. Protection of memory space among processes can be achieved by including a second register − the *limit register* − which contains the address of the highest location which a particular process is permitted to access. The address map (see figure 5.1) performed by the memory addressing hardware then proceeds according to the following scheme

(a) if $a < 0$ then memory violation
(b) $a' := B + a$
(c) if $a' > limit$ then memory violation
(d) a' is required location

It is worth noting that the address space mapped by this scheme is linear, and its size, being the difference between the base and limit registers, is necessarily less than or equal to the size of the memory space. Thus objectives (3) and (4) of section 5.1 are not achieved.

In order that the address mapping operation shall not be prohibitively time consuming the base and limit registers must be implemented in fast hardware. The cost of the registers can be reduced, and the mapping speeded up, by removing the lower order bits, implying that the size of the address space must be a multiple of 2^n (where n is the number of bits removed).

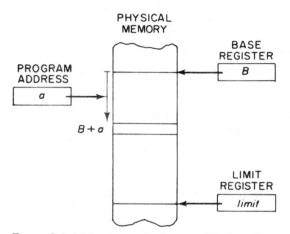

Figure 5.1 Address map for base and limit registers

A slight variation on the base–limit scheme is to use the limit register to hold the *length* of the memory space rather than its upper limit. In this case the address map is

(a)   if $a < 0$ or $a > length$ then memory violation
(b) $a' := B + a$
(c) a' is required location

The advantage is that the limit check does not depend on the result of the additition, so both the checks and the addition can be performed in parallel. (The addition is aborted if a memory violation occurs.)

It is impracticable, for economic reasons, to provide a pair of base and limit registers for each process which may be present in memory. Instead, a single pair of registers is provided for each processor, and is loaded with the base and limit addresses of the currently active process. These values form part of the volatile environment of the process and are stored when the process is suspended.

The sharing of re-entrant programs can be effected by providing two pairs of registers rather than one. One pair is used to demarcate the memory space occupied by the re-entrant code, and the values in them are common to all processes using the code; the other pair is used to demarcate the data areas associated with the code, and hold different values for each process concerned. The older DEC System-10 is an example of a machine employing this technique.

(2) Paging

In the base–limit scheme described above, the size of the address space is necessarily less than or equal to that of the memory space. If we wish to give the programmer a virtual memory which is larger than the available physical memory, thus relieving him of the burden of writing overlays, then we must devise an address map which apparently abolishes the distinction between main and secondary memory. The concept of the *one-level store*, in which secondary memory is made to appear as an extension of main memory, was first introduced on the Atlas computer at Manchester University around 1960, and has since had a profound influence on computer design.

The one-level store can be realised by the technique of *paging*, whereby the virtual address space is divided into *pages* of equal size (on Atlas 512 words), and the main memory is similarly divided into *page frames* of the same size. The page frames are shared between the processes currently in the system, so that at any time a given process will have a few pages resident in main memory (its *active* pages) and the rest resident in secondary memory (its *inactive* pages). The paging mechanism has two functions

(a)   to perform the address mapping operation; that is, to determine which page a program address refers to, and find which page frame, if any, the page currently occupies;

(b)   to transfer pages from secondary memory to main memory when required, and to transfer them back to secondary memory when they are no longer being used.

We describe these functions in turn.

In order to determine which page a program address refers to, the high order bits of the address are interpreted as a page number and the low order bits as the word number within the page. Thus if the page size is 2^n then the bottom n bits of the address represent the word number, and the remaining bits the page number. The total number of bits in the address is sufficient to address the entire virtual memory. For example, on Atlas the program address was 20 bits long, giving a virtual memory of 2^{20} words; the page size was 512 words (2^9), and so the bottom 9 bits represented the word number and the top 11 bits represented the page number. The total number of pages in the virtual memory was therefore 2^{11} (as opposed to 32 page frames in the original physical memory).

It is worth emphasising that the division of the address into word and page number is a function of the hardware and is transparent to the programmer; as far as he is concerned he is programming in a large sequential address space.

The address map from page and word number to physical memory location is made by means of a *page table*, the pth entry of which contains the location p' of the page frame containing page number p. (The possibility that the pth page is not in main memory will be dealt with in a moment.) The word number, w, is added to p' to obtain the required location (see figure 5.2).

The address map is therefore

$$f(a) = f(p,w) = p' + w$$

where program address a, page number p, and word number w are related to the page size Z by

$$p = \text{integral part of } (a/Z)$$
$$w = \text{remainder of } (a/Z)$$

Since the number of pages frames (amount of real memory) allocated to a process will usually be less than the number of pages it actually uses, it is quite possible that a program address will refer to a page which is not currently held in main memory. In this case the corresponding entry in the page table will be empty, and a 'page fault' interrupt is given if an attempt is made to access it. The interrupt causes the paging mechanism to initiate the transfer of the missing page from secondary to main memory and update the page table accordingly. The current process is made unrunnable until the transfer is complete. The location of the page in secondary memory can be held in a separate table or in the page table itself. In the latter case a 'presence bit' in each page table entry is needed to indicate whether or not the page is present in main memory and whether the address field is to be interpreted as a page frame address or a backing store location.

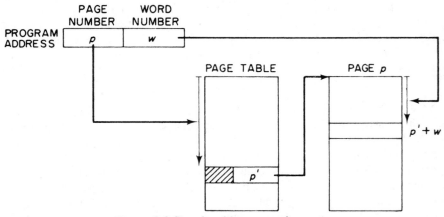

Figure 5.2 Simple address map for paging

If no empty page frame exists at the time the page fault occurs then some other page must be moved into secondary memory in order to make room for the incoming page. The choice of which page to swap out in this way is the result of a *page turning algorithm*; we discuss various algorithms in later sections. For the present we remark that information required by the page turning algorithm can be held in a few bits added to each page table entry (the shaded section of figure 5.2). This information might be

(a)   how many times the page has been referenced
(b)   the time the page was last referenced
(c)   whether the page has been written to

It should perhaps be made clear that the entire address mapping operation is performed by hardware except when a page has to be brought in from secondary memory. In this case the application of the page turning algorithm and the updating of the page table are performed by software.

The foregoing discussion gives a general outline of how paging works; in practice several modifications must be made to obtain a viable implementation. In particular, in the system as described the time required for each memory reference is effectively doubled by the necessity of first accessing the page table. A way of overcoming this would be to keep the page table in a set of fast registers rather than in ordinary memory. However, the size of the page table is proportional to the size of the address space and hence the number of registers required would be too large to be economically feasible. The solution to the problem is to adopt a quite different technique for accessing active pages. This technique involves the addition to the machine of an *associative store*, which consists of a small set of *page address registers* (PARs), each of which contains the page number of an active page. The PARs have the property that they can be searched *simultaneously* for the page number occurring in a particular program address. For example, in figure 5.3 the program address 3243 is split up into page number 3 and word number 243. (For convenience the page size is assumed to be 1000.) The page number is then simultaneously compared with the contents of all the PARs, and is found to correspond to that of PAR 5. This indicates that page number 3 currently occupies page frame 5 and so the required memory location is 5243.

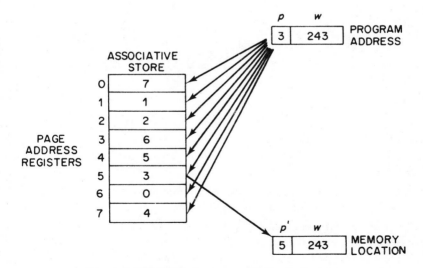

Figure 5.3 Mapping by means of associative store

The use of an associative store reduces the overhead of the address map by an order of magnitude from that incurred by a page table held in main memory.

In order that all active pages should be referenced by a PAR one needs as many PARs as there are page frames in memory. This is possible in systems with small memories (for example, Atlas), but on larger systems, it is not economically feasible to provide all the PARs required. (One might, however, expect that economic arguments will change as technology develops.) In such cases a compromise can be reached by holding a complete page table in memory for each process, and by using a small associative store to reference a few pages of the most recently active processes. In this case the page frame referred to by each PAR is no longer implicit in the PAR's position within the associative store, but must be included as an extra field in the PAR itself. The memory addressing hardware then performs the address mapping operation shown in figure 5.4. As before, software intervention is required only for page replacement.

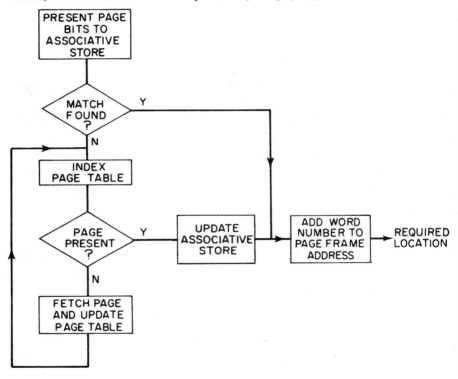

*Figure 5.4 Address mapping operation for paging with
a small associative store*

One problem not illustrated by figure 5.4 is that of distinguishing in the associative store between pages belonging to the current process and pages belonging to other processes. One solution is to extend the PARs to include process identification as well as page number. Each address presented to the associative store must then include the process identification as well as the page bits. An alternative solution is to extend the PARs by a single bit which is set to one in entries belonging to the current process and to zero elsewhere. This solution necessarily implies having a separate associative store for each processor in the configuration. (This is probably advisable in any case in order that the memory addressing logic does not form a bottleneck between processors and memory.)

It is clearly desirable that the associative store contains the page numbers of those pages which are most likely to be referenced. Unfortunately there is no general algorithm for ensuring that this is so (compare section 5.4 on the traffic of pages between main and secondary memories); in practice the associative store is usually filled cyclically with the addresses of the most recently referenced pages. This rather crude algorithm is in fact quite effective; depending on memory size a store of only 8 or 16 registers can be expected to give an average hit rate of better than 99 per cent.

As a final observation on the mechanics of paging it is worth pointing out the large amount of main memory which can be occupied by the page tables themselves. For example, on the paged version of the DEC System-10 the address space consists of 512 pages of 512 words each; this implies a page table of 256 words (entries are packed two to a word) for each process in memory. In fact the page table is placed in a page of its own, the other half of which is used to hold the process descriptor.

The size of page tables can be reduced to the number of pages actually used, rather than the number in the address space, by accessing them by hashing rather than by indexing. The idea is that instead of containing an entry for every page in the address space the page table refers only to those pages which have been used. Each time a new page is brought into main memory the page number and corresponding page frame address are entered in the table at a point determined by a suitable hash function. The same hash function can then be used to locate the page during the address mapping operation. The penalty paid for the reduction in size of the page table is an increase in memory access time for some references. The increase is due to two factors: first there is the time required to compute the hash function itself, and second, in the case that the hashed entries in the page table collide, it may be necessary to access the table more than once before the required page is located. Despite this the scheme can be made viable by using an associative store, which can reduce the number of occasions on which the page table is referenced to about one per cent of the total, and by performing the hashing operation by hardware.

(3) Segmentation

The third objective of section 5.1, namely the organisation of address space to reflect logical divisions in program and data, can be achieved by using the technique of *segmentation*. The idea is that the address space is divided into *segments*, each segment corresponding to a procedure, program module, or collection of data. This can be done in a simple way by adding several pairs of base and limit registers to each processor so that the address space can be demarcated into several areas. For example, the Modular One computer has three pairs of registers, and the three segments are used respectively for program, data private to a process, and data shared between processes. The disadvantages of this simple

mechanism are that the number of segments is for economic reasons necessarily
small, and that there needs to be a convention as to which segments are used for
what purpose.

A more flexible arrangement of virtual memory is to allow the programmer to
use a large number of segments according to his wishes, and to reference the
segments by names assigned by himself. The address space thus becomes two-
dimensional, since individual program addresses are identified by giving both a
segment name and an address within the segment. (In fact for convenience of
implementation the operating system replaces the segment name by a unique
segment number when the segment is first referenced.) A generalised program
address therefore consists of a pair (s,a), where s is the segment number and a is
the address within the segment.

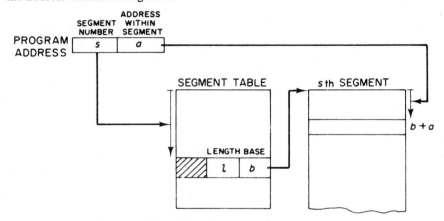

Figure 5.5 Simple address map for segmentation

The address map can be implemented by means of a *segment table* for each
process, the sth entry of which contains the base location and length of the sth
segment of the process. The segment table entries are sometimes referred to as
segment descriptors. In simplified form the mapping operation is (see figure 5.5)

(a)   Extract program address (s,a)
(b)   Use s to index segment table
(c)   If $a < 0$ or $a > l$ then memory violation
(d) $(b + a)$ is the required memory location

Protection against memory violation is provided by comparing the word
address with the segment length l. Additional protection may be given by incorporating into each segment descriptor a number of *protection bits* (shown shaded
in figure 5.5), which specify the modes in which the corresponding segment can
be accessed.

Note that a segment may readily be shared by a number of processes. All
that is needed is a descriptor for the segment concerned in the segment table
of each process. The protection bits in each descriptor may be different, so that,
for example, one process may have read only access to a shared segment while

another process is able to write into it. Thus segmentation allows flexible sharing
of programs and data among processes.

It is worth emphasising that despite the apparent similarity between figures
5.2 and 5.5 the address maps for paging and for segmentation are quite different
in the following respects.

(a)   The purpose of segmentation is the logical division of address space; the
       purpose of paging is the physical division of memory to implement a one-
       level store.
(b)   Pages are of a fixed size determined by the machine architecture; segments
       can be of any size determined by the user (up to a limit fixed by the way
       in which the program address is partitioned into segment and word numbers).
(c)   The division of program address into page and word numbers is a function
       of the hardware, and overflow of the word number automatically incre-
       ments the page number; the division into segment and word numbers is a
       logical one, and there is no overflow from word number to segment number.
       (If the word number overflows then a memory violation is generated.)

In practice the address mapping operation is not as simple as the foregoing
description suggests. The major complication is that for large programs it may
not be possible to hold all segments in main memory, particularly since the
memory will be shared between several processes. This is effectively a situation
in which the virtual memory is larger than the physical memory, and it can be
treated either by employing paging or by swapping entire segments in and out of
memory as required.

When paging is employed each segment generally consists of several pages and
has its own page table. Provided that some of the segment's pages are in memory,
the segment table entry points to the segment's page table; otherwise it is empty.
The address mapping operation performed by the addressing hardware is as
follows.

(a)   Extract program address (s,a)
(b)   Use s to index segment table
(c)   If sth entry is empty then create a new (empty) page table, otherwise extract
       address of page table
(d)   Split word address a into page number p and word number w
(e)   Use p to index page table
(f)   If pth entry is empty then fetch page from backing store, otherwise extract
       page frame address p'
(g)   Add p' to word number w to obtain required location

Steps (a) to (c) represent the mapping due to segmentation; steps (d) to (g)
(which correspond to figure 5.2) represent the mapping due to paging the
segments.

The extra memory references required to access the segment and page tables
can be avoided by the use of an associative store in a way similar to that described
earlier for paging alone. In this case each entry in the associative store contains
both the segment and page numbers of the most recently accessed pages. The
segment and page bits of each program address are presented to the associative

store (figure 5.6) and if a match is found the word number is added to the corresponding page frame address to obtain the required memory location. Only when no match is found is the full operation described above invoked.

If paging is not employed then segment table entries are as shown in figure 5.5. A missing segment fault causes the whole of the required segment to be brought into main memory; some other segment may have to be relegated to backing store to create sufficient space. Policies for allocating memory among segments will be described in the next section.

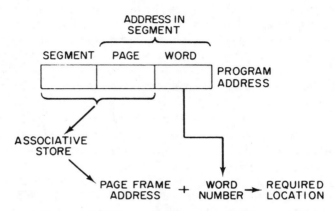

Figure 5.6 Address mapping operation for paged segments using associative store

The advantages of using paging to implement a segmented address space are twofold. Firstly, the entire segment need not be present in main memory — only those pages currently in use need be accommodated; secondly, it is not necessary that the pages occupy contiguous areas of memory — they can be dispersed throughout memory wherever a suitable page frame is found. Against paging must be set the complexity of the address map and the overhead of the page tables. Examples of systems which have paged segments are the Honeywell 645, ICL 2900 and large IBM 370s; those which have unpaged segments are the large Burroughs machines (for example, B6700) and the PDP-11/45.

5.4 MEMORY ALLOCATION POLICIES

The discussions in the last section were concerned exclusively with the *mechanisms* of memory management rather than with the *policies* governing them. In this section we shall concentrate on the policies which enable the mechanisms to be put to good use.

Policies for managing memory fall into three broad categories.

(1)   *Replacement policies*, which determine what information is to be removed from main memory, that is, create unallocated regions of memory.

(2)   *Fetch policies*, which determine when information is to be loaded into main memory, for example on demand or in advance.
(3)   *Placement policies*, which determine where information is to be placed in main memory, that is choose a subset of some unallocated region.

We shall see that policies of type (2) are very much the same for both paged and non-paged systems. Policies of types (1) and (3), however, differ between paged and non-paged systems: the differences arise from the fixed size of pages as opposed to the variable sizes of the blocks of information which have to be handled in non-paged systems.

(1) Placement Policies for Non-paged Systems

In this subsection we are considering the transfer of information into main memory in the cases where the virtual address space is either segmented or implemented by base–limit pairs. In either case we shall denote the blocks of information which are being transferred by the word 'segment', with the understanding that if a single base–limit system is being used then a segment will be the entire address space of a process.

The situation is that from time to time segments are inserted into or deleted from the main memory. (The insertions and deletions occur on invocations of the fetch and replacement policies respectively.) If the system is in equilibrium, (that is, over a period of time the space freed by deletion is equal to that filled by insertion) then the memory has the chequer-board appearance of figure 5.7.

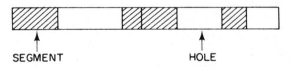

SEGMENT   HOLE

Figure 5.7 Segmented memory

It is clear that the placement policy must maintain a list of the locations and sizes of all unallocated 'holes'; we shall call this the *hole list*. Its task is to decide which hole to use, and to update the hole list after each insertion. If the segment to be placed is smaller than the hole to be used, then the segment is placed at the 'left-hand' or 'bottom end' of the hole. This tactic minimises the amount by which the hole is fragmented. If, on the other hand, the segment is larger than any available hole then the placement policy has the additional task of moving around the segments already in memory to create a hole large enough for its purpose.

Numerous placement algorithms are described in the literature, for example Knuth, (1968); we shall give four principal ones here. In each case the sizes of the holes are denoted by $x_1, x_2, ..., x_n$.

(a) Best Fit

The holes are listed in order of increasing size, that is $x_1 \leqslant x_2 \leqslant ... \leqslant x_n$. If s is the size of the segment to be placed, then find the smallest i such that $s \leqslant x_i$.

(b) Worst Fit

The holes are listed in order of decreasing size, that is $x_1 \geqslant x_2 \geqslant ... \geqslant x_n$. Place the segment in the first hole, and link the hole formed by the remaining space back into the appropriate position in the list.

(c) First Fit

The holes are listed in order of increasing base address. Find the smallest i such that $s \leqslant x_i$. The use of the algorithm leads, after a time, to an accumulation of small holes near the head of the list. To avoid excessive search time for large segments the start position can be advanced cyclically by one element after each search.

(d) Buddy

For this algorithm segment sizes must be powers of 2, that is $s = 2^i$ for some i less than a maximum k. A separate list is maintained for holes of each size $2^1, 2^2, ...,$ 2^k. A hole may be removed from the $(i + 1)$-list by splitting it in half, thereby creating a pair of 'buddies' of size 2^i on the i-list. Conversely a pair of buddies may be removed from the i-list, coalesced, and put on the $(i + 1)$-list. The algorithm for finding a hole of size 2^i is recursive

```
procedure get hole (i);
begin  if i = k + 1 then failure;
        if i-list empty then
        begin get hole (i + 1);
              split hole into buddies;
              put buddies on i-list
        end;
        take first hole in i-list
end
```

To the more suspicious reader it may appear strange that algorithms (a) and (b) are both viable since they adopt directly opposing strategies regarding the ordering of the hole list. Algorithm (a) is perhaps the more intuitively appealing since it appears to minimise the wastage in each hole it selects (that is, it selects the smallest hole that will do the job). Algorithm (b), however, works on the philosophy that making an allocation from a large hole is likely to leave a hole large enough to be useful in future, whereas making an allocation from a small hole will leave an even smaller hole which will probably be quite useless.

A problem common to all the placement policies described is *fragmentation* — the splitting up of free memory into holes so small that new segments cannot be fitted in. When this occurs some *compaction* of memory is necessary; that is, all segments must be moved downwards so that a single large hole appears at the top of memory. Compaction is most easily achieved if the holes are listed in address order, as in the first-fit algorithm. An alternative approach is to compact memory every time a segment is removed, thus avoiding fragmentation altogether; the overhead of frequent compaction is offset by not having to search a hole list whenever a segment is to be placed.

(2) Placement Policies for Paged Systems

Placement policies for paged systems are far simpler than for non-paged systems; to place k pages we simply use a replacement policy to free k page frames. Fragmentation, in the sense described for non-paged systems, cannot occur, since all pages and page frames are of equal size. However, a paged system can suffer from a different form of fragmentation, *internal fragmentation*, which arises because the space required by a process is not usually an exact multiple of the page size. Consequently a part of the last page frame allocated is generally wasted: the average wastage can be expected to be half the page size. If the address space consists of several paged segments, the degree of internal fragmentation is multiplied by the number of segments currently held in main memory.

(3) Replacement Policies for Paged Systems

The job of a replacement policy is to decide which blocks of information to relegate to secondary memory when space has to be found in main memory for new blocks. In this subsection we consider the case where the blocks of information are pages; we shall see later that the same policies can be applied, with appropriate modifications, in the non-paged situation.

Ideally one wants to replace the page which is not going to be referenced for the longest time in the future. Unfortunately, knowledge of the future is hard to come by: the best one can do is infer from past behaviour what future behaviour is likely to be. The accuracy of the inference depends on the predictability of program behaviour, which we shall discuss further in the section on fetch policies.

Three common replacement algorithms are

(a) Least Recently Used (LRU)

'Replace the page which has least recently been used.' The assumption is that future behaviour will closely follow recent behaviour. The overhead is that of recording the sequence of access to all pages.

(b) Least Frequently Used (LFU)

'Replace the page which has been used least frequently during some immediately preceding time interval.' The justification is similar to (a), and the overhead is that of keeping a 'use count' for each page. One drawback is that a recently loaded page will in general have a low use count and may be replaced inadvisedly. A way to avoid this is to inhibit the replacement of pages loaded within the last time interval.

(c) First-in First-out

'Replace the page which has been resident longest.' This is a simpler algorithm, whose overhead is only that of recording the loading sequence of pages. It ignores the possibility that the oldest page may be the most heavily referenced.

Simulation studies (Colin, 1971) have shown a difference in performance of the three algorithms (in terms of the number of transfers required during the running of a number of jobs) which varies according to the type of jobs being run, but which is rarely more than fifteen per cent. Algorithm (c) gives a generally poorer performance than the other two.

Finally, it is worth noting that pages which have not been written to need not be transferred back to secondary memory provided a copy already exists there. A record of whether a particular page has been written to can be kept in a single bit in the corresponding page table entry.

(4) Replacement Policies for Non-paged Systems

In this subsection we consider policies for the situation where the blocks of information to be replaced are segments in the broad sense defined in (1) above.

The major objective is the same as for paged systems — that is, to replace the segment which is least likely to be referenced in the immediate future. One might therefore expect the same policies to be applicable, and this is indeed the case, but with one major qualification. The qualification arises from the fact that not all segments occupy equal amounts of memory, so consideration of which segment to relegate to secondary memory is influenced by the size of the segment to be placed. If a small segment is to be brought into main memory then only a small segment need be replaced; on the other hand, the placement of a large segment requires the replacement of another large segment (or several smaller ones).

Possibly the simplest algorithm is to replace the single segment (if one exists) which, together with any adjacent holes, will free enough space for the incoming segment. If there are several such segments, then one of the policies discussed earlier, such as LRU, can be used to discriminate between them. If no single segment is large enough to create sufficient space, then several segments have to be replaced: a possible choice is the smallest set of contiguous segments which will free the space required.

The danger with such an algorithm is that the segment (or segments) replaced, being selected mainly on criteria of size, may be referenced again shortly afterwards. The danger can be reduced by selecting segments purely on an LRU (say) basis, but since the selected segments are not likely to be contiguous some compaction of memory will be required. The reader will readily appreciate that the relative emphasis given to segment size, expectation of future reference, and compaction, can produce a variety of complex algorithms which are difficult to assess except in practice. We shall not pursue the subject further here, but refer the interested reader to more detailed studies such as Knuth (1968) and Denning (1970).

(5) Fetch Policies

Fetch policies determine when to move a block of information from secondary to main memory. The arguments for choosing a policy are roughly the same whether the blocks are pages or segments (in the broad sense we have been using). Fetch policies are divided into two broad classes: *demand* and *anticipatory*. Demand policies fetch blocks when they are needed; anticipatory policies fetch them in advance.

Demand policies are clearly the easier to implement — a missing block (segment or page) fault generates a fetch request, and the placement and/or replacement policies allocate memory for the new block. In non-paged systems (for example Burroughs machines) the transfer of blocks is usually on demand, as it is on some paged machines (for example Atlas).

Anticipatory policies rely on predictions of future program behaviour in order to be fully effective. Prediction can be based on two things

(a)   the nature of construction of programs
(b)   inference from a process's past behaviour

Consider (a) for a moment.

Many programs exhibit behaviour known as *operating in context*; that is, in any small time interval a program tends to operate within a particular logical module, drawing its instructions from a single procedure and its data from a single data area. Thus program references tend to be grouped into small localities of address space. The locality of reference is strengthened by the frequent occurrence of looping; the tighter the loop, the smaller the spread of references. The observation of this behaviour leads to the postulation (Denning, 1970) of the so called *principle of locality*: 'program references tend to be grouped into small localities of address space, and these localities tend to change only intermittently'

The validity of the principle of locality will vary from program to program; it will, for example, be more valid for programs making sequential array accesses than for programs accessing complex data structures. The principle is used by Denning in the context of paged memory to formulate the *working set* model of program behaviour which we briefly describe in the next section.

5.5 THE WORKING SET MODEL

The working set model of program behaviour (Denning, 1968) is an attempt to establish a framework for understanding the performance of paging systems in a multiprogramming environment. The policies for memory management which we discussed in the last section are based on a study of how processes behave in isolation; they do not take into account any effects which may arise from having several processes in the machine at once. The competition for memory space between processes can in fact lead to behaviour which would not occur if each process ran separately.

As an illustration of what can happen, consider a single processor system with a paged memory in which the degree of multiprogramming (that is, the number of processes present in memory) is steadily increased. As the degree of multiprogramming rises one might expect that the processor utilisation would also rise, since the dispatcher would always have a greater chance of finding a process to run. Indeed observation confirms that this is generally the case, so long as the degree of multiprogramming is kept below a certain level which is dependent on the size of memory available. However, if the degree of multiprogramming exceeds this level then it is found (see figure 5.8) that there is a marked increase in the paging traffic between main and secondary memories accompanied by a sudden decrease in processor utilisation. The explanation for this is that the high degree of multiprogramming makes it impossible for every process to keep sufficient pages in memory to avoid generating a large number of page faults. This means that the backing store channel can become saturated, that most processes are blocked awaiting a page transfer, and that the processor is under-utilised. This state of affairs is referred to by the descriptive term *thrashing*.

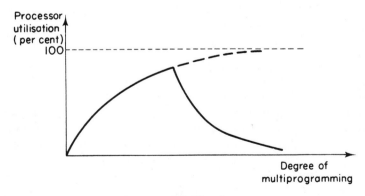

Figure 5.8 Thrashing

The lesson to be learned from this illustration is that each process requires a certain minimum number of pages, called its *working set*, to be held in main memory before it can effectively use the central processor. If less than this number are present then the process is continually interrupted by page faults which contribute towards thrashing. For thrashing to be avoided the degree of multiprogramming must be no greater than the level at which the working sets of all processes can be held in main memory.

The question now arises of how to determine which pages constitute the working set of a process. The answer is to inspect the process's recent history and to appeal to the principle of locality mentioned in the last section. More formally, the working set of a process at time t is defined to be

$$w(t,h) = \{\text{page } i \mid \text{page } i \in N \text{ and page } i \text{ appears in the last } h \text{ references}\}$$

In other words the working set is the set of pages which have recently been referred to, 'recentness' being one of the parameters (h) of the set. From the principle of locality one would expect the working set to change membership slowly in time. Denning has shown that the expected size $w(h)$ of the working set varies with h as shown in figure 5.9.

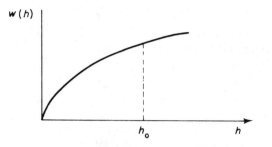

Figure 5.9 Expected size of the working set

As h is increased (that is, the further into the past one looks), the fewer extra pages one expects to find in the working set. This enables one to establish a reasonably small value for h (for example h_0) in the knowledge that a larger value of h would not significantly increase the working set size.

As far as fetch and replacement policies are concerned the value of the working set lies in the following rule

'Run a process only if its entire working set is in main memory, and never remove a page which is part of the working set of some process.'

Although the working sets of some processes may be rather arbitrarily defined, and although the principle of locality does not apply to some programs, application of the above rule can make a significant contribution towards the prevention of thrashing. The working set model is widely used, though the definition of working set varies somewhat from one operating system to another.

It is important to realise that the rule given above is more than a pure memory management policy since it implies a correlation between memory allocation and processor allocation. So far in this chapter we have treated memory management as an issue distinct from the management of other resources. In practice management of a single resource cannot always be divorced from consideration of other resources, but we shall defer a full treatment of resource allocation until chapter 8.

5.6 IMPLEMENTATION IN THE PAPER SYSTEM

It may appear to the reader that the memory management policies discussed in this chapter have a rather *ad hoc* air, and that the choice of algorithm in a particular case is somewhat arbitrary. To a certain extent this is true; many of the policies are founded on common sense and experience, backed up in some cases by analytical or statistical justification. A powerful aid in the choice of algorithm is simulation; ideally each option should be tested with a simulation of the job mix expected. Some studies are reported by Knuth (1968), and an extensive bibliography is given by Denning (1970).

In order to implement in our paper operating system the mechanisms of section 5.3 we add to the volatile environment of each process

> (1)   a copy of the contents of the base and limit registers
>
> or (2)   a pointer to its segment table
>
> or (3)   a pointer to its page table

depending on the architecture of our machine.

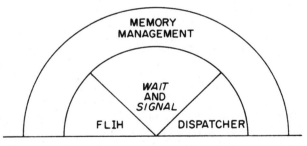

Figure 5.10 Current state of the paper operating system

If we have a non-paged machine then we introduce the hole list as a further data structure pointed to from the central table. The memory management layer of our system consists of code to implement the policies discussed in section 5.4.

Our system has now reached the stage shown in figure 5.10.

6 *Input and Output*

At this stage in the development of our paper operating system we have established
an environment in which processes can exist and in which memory can be
allocated to hold the associated programs and data. We now turn our attention
to the means by which processes communicate with the outside world; that is,
to mechanisms for the input and output of information.

Traditionally I/O is regarded as one of the more sordid areas of operating
system design in that it is a field in which generalisation is difficult and *ad hoc*
methods abound. The reason for this is the wide variety of peripheral devices
employed; a particular configuration may include devices which differ greatly in
their characteristics and mode of operation. Specifically, devices may differ on
one or more of the following counts.

(1) Speed

There may be a difference of several orders of magnitude between the data
transfer rates of various devices. A magnetic disc, for instance, may be able to
transfer 10^6 characters per second, compared with a terminal keyboard speed of
only a few characters per second (depending on the typist!).

(2) Unit of Transfer

Data may be transferred in units of characters, words, bytes, blocks or records,
according to the peripheral used.

(3) Data Representation

An item of data may be encoded in different ways on different I/O media. Even
on a single medium such as magnetic tape several different codes may be employed.

(4) Permissible Operations

Devices differ in the kind of operation they can perform. One example is the
obvious distinction between input and output; another is the ability to rewind
magnetic tape but not line printer paper.

(5) Error Conditions

Failure to complete a data transfer may have such various causes as a parity error, a card wreck, or a checksum error, depending on the peripheral being used.

Clearly the diversity exemplified above is difficult to handle in a uniform manner. However we shall attempt in this chapter to construct a framework for an I/O system in which device-dependent characteristics are isolated as far as possible and in which some degree of uniformity is achieved. We start by considering some design objectives and their implications.

6.1 DESIGN OBJECTIVES AND IMPLICATIONS

(1) Character Code Independence

It is obviously undesirable that in order to write his programs a user should require detailed knowledge of the character codes used by various peripherals. The I/O system must take responsibility for recognising different character codes and for presenting data to user programs in a standard form.

(2) Device Independence

There are two aspects to device independence. First, a program should be independent of the particular device of a given type which it happens to be allocated. For example, it should not matter on which magnetic tape deck a particular tape is mounted, or which line printer is used for a program's output. Device independence of this kind ensures that a program does not fail simply because a particular device is broken or allocated elsewhere. It gives the operating system the freedom to allocate a device of the appropriate type according to overall availability at the time.

Second and more demanding, it is desirable that programs should as far as possible be independent of the device type used for their I/O. Clearly device independence of this nature cannot be carried as far as sending output to a card reader; what we have in mind is that only minimal changes to a job should be required for it to receive its data from disc rather than magnetic tape.

(3) Efficiency

Since I/O operations often form a bottleneck in a computing system it is desirable to perform them as efficiently as possible.

(4) Uniform Treatment of Devices

In the interests of simplicity and freedom from error it is desirable to handle all devices in a uniform manner. For reasons already mentioned this may be difficult in practice.

Some implications of these objectives are immediately apparent. First, character code independence implies the existence of a uniform internal representation of all characters. This representation is called the *internal character code*, and translation mechanisms must be associated with each peripheral to perform the appropriate conversions on input and output. For peripherals which may handle a variety of character codes a separate translation mechanism must be supplied for each code supported. Translation is performed immediately on input and immediately before output, so that only those processes intimately connected with peripheral handling need be aware of anything but the standard internal code. The translation mechanism will generally be a table, or in some cases a short piece of program.

Next, device independence implies that programs should operate not on actual devices but on virtual devices, variously called *streams* (Atlas), *files* (MULTICS), or *data sets* (IBM). The streams are used within a program without any reference to physical devices; the programmer merely directs output and input to or from particular streams. The association of streams with real devices is usually made by the operating system on the basis of information supplied by the user in the job description. We shall discuss job descriptions in detail in chapter 11; for our present purpose it is sufficient to say that the job description is a collection of user-supplied information, usually presented at the head of the job, which helps the operating system decide when and how to run it. A typical job description statement for the binding of a stream to a peripheral device is

OUTPUT 1 = LPT

meaning that output stream 1 is to be a line printer. Independence of a particular line printer is guaranteed by the operating system's freedom to associate the stream with any available printer; independence of device type is achieved by a trivial change to the job description (for example, magnetic tape output might be obtained by changing LPT to MT).

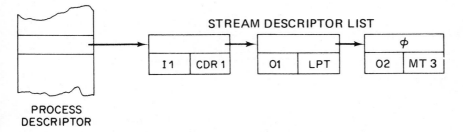

PROCESS
DESCRIPTOR

Figure 6.1 Device and stream information for a process

The equivalence of streams and device types for a particular process can be recorded in a list of *stream descriptors* pointed to from its process descriptor (see figure 6.1); the allocation of a particular device of a given type is made when the process first uses the corresponding stream. We say that at this point the process *opens* the stream; the stream is *closed*, indicating that it is no longer to be used, either explicitly by the process or implicitly when the process terminates. For the process shown in figure 6.1, card reader 1 has been allocated as input stream 1, tape drive 3 has been allocated as output stream 2, and output stream 1, which has not yet been opened, is to be a line printer.

A third implication of our design objectives is that the I/O system should be constructed in such a way that device characteristics are clearly associated with the devices themselves rather than with the routines which handle them (the *device handlers*). In this way it is possible for device handlers to show great similarities, and for their differences of operation to derive solely from parametric information obtained from the characteristics of the particular device concerned. The necessary isolation of device characteristics can be achieved by encoding them in a *device descriptor* associated with each device, and by using the descriptor as a source of information for the device handler. The characteristic information about a device which may be stored in its descriptor is

(1)   the device identification
(2)   the instructions which operate the device
(3)   pointers to character translation tables
(4)   the current status: whether the device is busy, free, or broken
(5)   the current user process: a pointer to the process descriptor of the process, if any, which is currently using the device

All device descriptors can be linked together in a *device structure* which is pointed to from the central table.

6.2 THE I/O PROCEDURES

In the last section we made significant progress towards the uniform treatment of devices by isolating all device dependent characteristics in the device descriptors. We are now in a position to consider how the operating system handles a request for I/O from a user process.

A typical request from a process will be a call to the operating system of the general form

DOIO (*stream, mode, amount, destination, semaphore*)

where

DOIO	is the name of a system *I/O procedure*
stream	is the number of the stream on which I/O is to take place
mode	indicates what operation, such as data transfers or rewind, is required; it may also indicate, if relevant, what character code is to be used
amount	is the amount of data to be transferred, if any
destination	(or source) is the location into which (or from which) the

transfer, if any is to occur
semaphore   is the address of a semaphore *request serviced* which is to be
signalled when the I/O operation is complete

The I/O procedure DOIO is re-entrant, so that it may be used by several
processes at once. Its function is to map the stream number to the appropriate
physical device, to check the consistency of the parameters supplied to it, and to
initiate service of the request.

The first of these operations is straightforward. The device which corresponds
to the specified stream is determined from the information placed in the stream
descriptor list of the calling process at the time the stream was opened (see
figure 6.1). Once the device is identified the parameters of the I/O request can
be checked for consistency against the information held in the device descriptor,
and if an error is detected an exit can be made to the caller. One particular
check which may be performed is that the device is capable of operating in the
desired mode, another is that the size and destination of the data transfer
correspond to the mode of operation. In the case of devices which can transfer
only single characters the specified quantity of data to be transferred must
be 1 and the destination either a register or memory location; for devices which
transfer blocks of data directly to memory the specified quantity must be equal
to the block size (fixed or variable according to the device) and the destination
the memory location at which the transfer is to start.

When the checks have been completed the I/O procedure assembles the parameters of the request into an *I/O request block* (IORB) which it adds to a queue
of similar blocks which represent other requests for use of the same device. These
other requests may come from the same process, or, in the case of a shared
device such as a disc, from other processes. The *device request queue* is attached
to the descriptor of the device concerned (see figure 6.2), and is serviced by a
separate process called a *device handler* which we shall describe in the next
section. The I/O procedure notifies the device handler that it has placed a request
on the queue by signalling a semaphore *request pending* associated with the
device and which is contained in the device descriptor. Similarly, once the I/O
operation is complete the device handler notifies the user process by means of
the semaphore *request serviced* whose address was a parameter of the I/O procedure and was passed to the device handler as an element of the IORB. This
semaphore can be initialised either by the user process or by the I/O procedure
when the IORB is created.

The complete I/O routine is

```
procedure DOIO (stream, mode, amount, destination, semaphore);
begin  lookup device in process descriptor;
       check parameters against device characteristics;
       if error then error exit;
       assemble IORB;
       add IORB to device request queue;
       signal (request pending)
end;
```

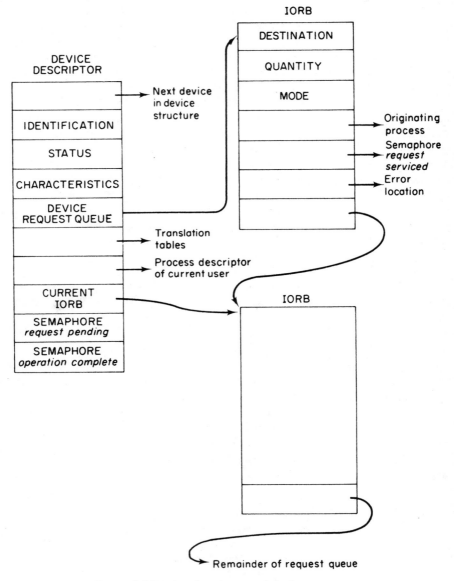

Figure 6.2 Device descriptor and device request queue

6.3 THE DEVICE HANDLERS

As mentioned in the last section a device handler is a process which is responsible for servicing the requests on a device request queue and for notifying the originating process when the service has been completed. There is a separate handler for each device, but since all handlers operate in a similar way they can make use of shareable programs. Any differences in behaviour between handlers are derived from the characteristics stored in the descriptors of the particular devices.

A device handler operates in a continuous cycle during which it removes an IORB from the request queue, initiates the corresponding I/O operation, waits for the operation to be completed, and notifies the originating process. The complete cycle for an input operation is

> **repeat** indefinitely
> **begin**   *wait* (*request pending*);
>   pick an IORB from request queue;
>   extract details of request;
>   initiate I/O operation;
>   *wait* (*operation complete*);
>   **if** error **then** plant error information;
>   translate character(s) if necessary;
>   transfer data to destination;
>   *signal* (*request serviced*);
>   delete IORB
> **end**;

The following notes, which should be read with reference to figure 6.2, may clarify the details.

(1) The semaphore *request pending*, contained in the device descriptor, is signalled by the I/O procedure each time it places an IORB on the request queue for this device. If the queue is empty the semaphore is zero and the device handler is suspended.

(2) The device handler may pick an IORB from the queue according to any desired priority algorithm. A first come, first served algorithm is usually adequate, but the handler could be influenced by priority information placed in the IORB by the I/O procedure. In the case of a disc the device handler may service requests in an order which minimises head movements.

(3) The instructions to initiate the I/O operation can be extracted from the device characteristics held in the device descriptor.

(4) The semaphore *operation complete* is signalled by the interrupt routine after an interrupt is generated for this device. The outline program of the interrupt routine, which is entered from the first-level interrupt handler, is

> locate device descriptor;
> *signal* (*operation complete*);

The semaphore *operation complete* is held in the device descriptor. Note that the interrupt routine is very short; all housekeeping is performed by the device handler, which operates in user mode as a normal process.

(5)   The error check is made by interrogating the device status when the operation is complete. If there has been an error, such as parity or card wreck, or even end of file, information about it is deposited in an *error location* whose address is included by the I/O procedure in the IORB.

(6)   Character translation is made according to the mode specified in the IORB and the tables pointed to from the device descriptor.

(7)   The cycle shown above is for an input operation. In the case of an output operation the extraction of data from its source and any character translation occurs before the operation rather than after.

(8)   The address of the semaphore *request serviced* is passed to the device handler as a component of the IORB. It is supplied by the process requesting I/O as a parameter of the I/O procedure.

The synchronisation and flow of control between the process requesting I/O, the I/O procedure, and the appropriate device handler and interrupt routine are summarised in figure 6.3. Solid arrows represent transfers of control; broken arrows represent synchronisation by means of semaphores. It is important to note that in the scheme illustrated the requesting process proceeds asynchronously with the device handler so that it may perform other computations or make other I/O requests while the original request is being serviced. The requesting process need be held up only on occasions when the I/O operation is incomplete when it executes *wait (request serviced)*.

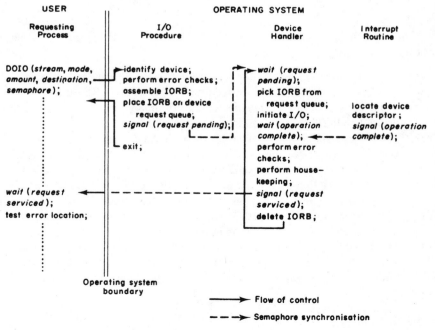

Figure 6.3 Sketch of the I/O system

The disadvantage of this arrangement is that the requesting process must take responsibility for synchronising its activities with those of the device handler. It must not, for example, attempt to use input data which has not yet been provided. This means that the author of the process must be aware that I/O operations are not instantaneous and must be capable of achieving the desired synchronisation by appropriate use of the semaphore *request serviced*.

An alternative arrangement is to place the responsibility for synchronisation within the I/O procedure, which is part of the operating system. This can be done by making the semaphore *request serviced* local to the I/O procedure (that is, its address need no longer be supplied by the requesting process) and by inserting the operations

wait (*request serviced*);

test error location;

in the I/O procedure immediately before its exit. The delay implicit in an I/O operation is now hidden within the operating system; as far as the requesting process is concerned the operation is instantaneous in the sense that when the next instruction after the request is obeyed the operation can be assumed complete. To put it another way, the requesting process is executing on a virtual machine in which I/O operations are achieved by a single instantaneous instruction.

The two possible arrangements discussed above may be summarised as follows. In the first the user has the freedom to continue in parallel with the I/O operation but has the responsibility of detecting its completion; in the second the responsibility is taken away from him but he also loses the freedom.

6.4 BUFFERING

The description of the I/O procedure and the device handlers given above assumes that all data transfers are unbuffered. That is, each I/O request from a process causes a physical transfer to occur on the appropriate peripheral. If the process is performing repeated transfers on the same stream it will repeatedly be suspended (on *wait* (*request serviced*)) while the transfers take place. In order to avoid heavy overheads in process switching it is sometimes convenient to perform I/O transfers in advance of requests being made, thus ensuring that data is available when required. This technique is known as *buffering*.

Input transfers are made by the operating system into an area of memory called an input buffer; the user process takes its data from the buffer and is forced to wait only when the buffer becomes empty. When this occurs the operating system refills the buffer and the process continues. Similarly, ouput transfers from a process are directed to an output buffer, and the operating system empties the entire buffer when it is full. The process has to wait only if it tries to output an item before the system has emptied the buffer.

The technique can be refined by the use of two buffers rather than one: so called *double buffering*. A process now transfers data to (or from) one buffer while the operating system empties (or fills) the other. This ensures that the process will wait only if both buffers are filled (or exhausted) before the operating

system has taken action. This will happen only when the process performs a
rapid burst of I/O, and in this case the problem can often be solved by the
addition of yet more buffers (*multiple buffering*). Of course no amount of
buffering can help those cases in which a process demands I/O at a rate which is
consistently higher than that at which the I/O devices can work. The usefulness
of buffering is restricted to smoothing out peaks in I/O demand in situations
where the *average* demand is no greater than the I/O devices can service. In
general, the higher the peaks the greater is the number of buffers required to
achieve the smoothing.

   Whether or not a stream is to be buffered may be declared by an appropriate
statement in the job description; in the buffered case the user may specify how
many buffers are to be used or allow the system to supply a default value,
usually two. The operating system allocates space for buffers when the stream is
opened, and records the buffer address in the stream descriptor.

   A slightly different I/O procedure is needed to allow for buffered operation.
The new procedure handles an input request by extracting the next item from
the appropriate buffer and passing it directly to the calling process. Only when
a buffer becomes empty does the procedure generate an IORB and signal to the
device handler to supply more input. When the stream is opened the I/O procedure
generates enough IORBs to fill all the buffers. The device handler operates as
before, initiating a data transfer into the buffer whose location is indicated in the
IORB. Similar remarks apply, *mutatis mutandis*, to output requests. In both
cases the I/O procedure and the device handler together form a variation of the
producer-consumer pair described in chapter 3.

   The I/O procedure for buffered operations can be called from a user process
by a statement of the general form

DOBUFFIO (*stream, mode, destination*)

where *stream*, *mode*, and *destination* are as described for procedure DOIO in
section 6.2. The amount of information transferred will be a single item. Note
that since any delays arising from full or empty buffers are hidden in the I/O
procedure there is no need to pass a semaphore address as one of the parameters.
The type of buffering, if any, the addresses of the buffers, and the semaphores
to be used by the I/O procedures are all accessible from the stream descriptor list
of the calling process (see figure 6.4b). The first element of this information can
be used to determine which I/O procedure to call to effect a transfer.

6.5 FILE DEVICES

In the foregoing discussion we have implicitly assumed that the name of a
peripheral device is sufficient information to determine the external source or
destination of a given transfer. This is true of peripherals which operate sequentially, so that there is no ambiguity about what area of the external medium a
data transfer is directed to or from. A keyboard reader, for example, can read

only the next character typed, while a line printer can print only on the current line. In some cases it may be possible to advance the medium by a certain amount (to a new page, say), but there is no question of being able to direct a transfer to any part of the medium at will. Other devices, such as disc drives and drums, which operate in a random access mode, provide the facility of selecting a particular area of the medium (disc or drum) on which to effect the transfer. In these cases it is not sufficient to name the device involved; it is also necessary to specify what data area on the medium is to be used.

Each data area which can exist on such media is called a *file*, and usually has an arbitrary size which is defined when it is created or updated. A device which supports files is called a *file device*. We shall say more in the next chapter about the organisation of files; for the moment we shall assume that each file has a unique name which can be used by the operating system to determine the location of the file on the appropriate medium. A directory of file names and the corresponding locations is kept by the operating system for this purpose.

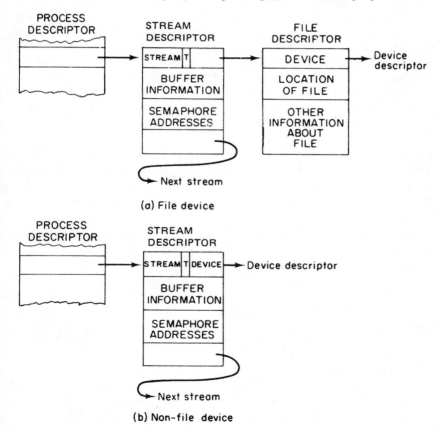

Figure 6.4 Stream information for file and non-file devices (T = device type)

When a data stream is to be directed to or from a file device the stream is associated in the job description with the name of a particular file rather than with the name of the device. A typical job description statement might be

INPUT 1 = 'TESTDATA'

indicating that data on stream 1 is to come from the file named TESTDATA. When the stream is opened the operating system looks up the file name in the directory, to find the particular device and location where the file is stored. This procedure, known as *opening* the file, includes various checks which will be detailed in the next chapter; because it can be a lengthy operation it is not desirable to repeat it for each data transfer. Consequently each time a file is opened a *file descriptor* is created to hold the information which will be required for forthcoming transfers. This information includes the address of the device descriptor of the device on which the file is stored, the location of the file on that device, whether the file is to be written to or read from, and details of the file's internal organisation. A pointer to the file descriptor is placed in the appropriate stream descriptor of the process opening the file, as illustrated in figure 6.4a. The reader will see from a comparison of figures 6.4a and 6.4b that the file descriptor adds extra information to the association of streams with physical devices. The I/O procedures, which perform the association for each data transfer, can readily be modified to take this information into account when assembling an IORB.

6.6 SPOOLING

The preceding sections have made an implicit distinction between shareable devices, such as disc drives, which can handle successive requests from different processes, and unshareable devices, such as line printers, which can necessarily be allocated to only one process at a time. The unshareable devices are those which operate in such a way that their allocation to several processes at once would lead to an inextricable intermingling of I/O transactions. As pointed out in section 6.1, the allocation of an unshareable device is made when a process opens a stream associated with it; the device is released only when the stream is closed or the process terminates. Processes which wish to use a device when it is already allocated must wait for it to be released. This implies that during periods of high demand several processes may be held up waiting for the use of scarce devices, while during other periods these same devices may be lying unused. In order to spread the load and reduce the possibility of bottlenecks some other strategy may be needed.

The solution adopted by many systems is to *spool* all I/O for heavily used devices. This means that instead of performing a transfer directly on the device associated with a stream the I/O procedures execute the transfer on some intermediate medium, usually disc. The responsibility of moving data between the disc and the required device is vested in a separate process, called a *spooler*, which is associated with that device. As an example, consider a system in which all line printer output is spooled. Each process which opens a line printer stream is allocated an anonymous file on disc, and all output on the stream is directed to this file by the I/O procedure. The file is in effect acting as a virtual line printer. When the stream is closed the file is added to a queue of similar files created by other processes, all of which are waiting to be printed. The function of the line printer spooler is to take files from the queue and send them to the printer. It is assumed, of course, that over a period of time the speed of the printer is adequate to handle all the output files generated. A skeletal structure for the spooler is

```
repeat indefinitely
begin   wait (something to spool);
        pick file from queue;
        open file;
        repeat until end of file
        begin DOIO (parameters for disc read);
              wait (disc request serviced);
              DOIO (parameters for line printer output);
              wait (printer request serviced)
        end
end;
```

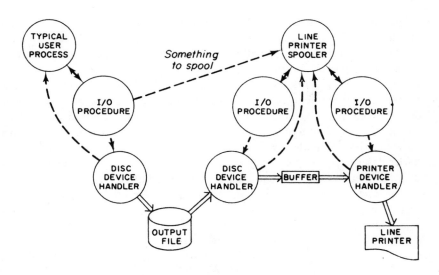

Procedure call and exit

Process communication via semaphore

Data transfer

Figure 6.5 Output spooling

The reader may note the following points.

(1)   The structure will in practice be modified to allow for buffering the data between disc and printer.
(2)   The semaphore *something to spool* is signalled by any process which closes a line printer stream (that is, completes an output file).
(3)   The output queue need not be processed on a first come, first served basis; the spooler may for example favour short files over long ones.

The relationships between the spooler, the device handlers, and the processes producing the output are summarised in figure 6.5. A similar diagram, based on an analogous discussion to the above, could be drawn for an input spooler.

In summary we can say that spooling evens out the pressure of demand on heavily used peripherals. As we shall see in chapter 8 it also reduces the possibility of deadlock arising from injudicious peripheral allocation. A further advantage is that it is relatively easy to produce several copies of the same output without rerunning the job. On the debit side are the large amounts of disc space needed to hold the input and output queues, and the heavy traffic on the disc channel. Finally, spooling is of course not feasible in a real-time environment since I/O transactions are required immediately.

6.7 CONCLUSION

In the preceding sections we have outlined an I/O system which satisfies the objectives of character code independence, device independence, and the uniform treatment of devices. These qualities have been gained at the expense of efficiency the I/O procedures and device handlers we presented will, because of their generalised nature, work more slowly than specialised pieces of code tailor-made for particular I/O operations or devices. However, the framework we have laid down is conceptually sound, and may be used as a basis for optimisation. The greatest gains would in practice come from replacing the code of the I/O procedures and device handlers, which is driven by information in I/O requests and device descriptors, by pieces of device and operation specific program. This would of course blur the uniform approach we have established.

The current stage of development of the paper operating system is shown in figure 6.6.

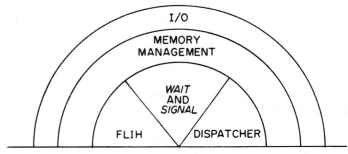

Figure 6.6 Current state of the paper operating system

7 *The Filing System*

7.1 OBJECTIVES

It was mentioned in chapter 2 that the facility for long-term storage is a desirable characteristic of an operating system. The motivation for long-term storage varies according to the nature of the system, but generally derives from consideration of one or both of the following benefits.

(1) On-line Storage

For certain applications concerned with information retrieval (such as management information systems) it is necessary to store large quantities of data in such a way that they are always accessible. Even in a general purpose system where a large on-line data base may not be essential, it is a great convenience to the user to be able to store programs or data within the computing system itself rather than on some external medium such as punched cards. In multi-access systems in particular it is impracticable to expect the user to manage without on-line storage, since the only I/O device at his disposal is the terminal on which he types. Few users would tolerate a system in which all their programs and data had to be typed in afresh at the start of every session on the terminal. Even in batch systems on-line storage of information can increase throughput by reducing dependency on slow peripherals.

(2) Sharing of Information

In some systems it is desirable that users should be able to share information. For example, the users of a general purpose system may wish to use each other's programs or data, and in a transaction processing system many separate processes may use the same data base. In most general purpose systems it is desirable for the installation to provide a set of *library* programs, such as editors, compilers, or scientific subroutines, which are commonly available to its users. If information is to be shared in this way then it must be stored on-line over long periods of time.

For reasons of economy long-term storage is effected on secondary media such as discs, drums and magnetic tapes, and it is the purpose of the *filing system* to provide the means of organising and accessing the data in a way convenient to the user. The way this is done will naturally depend on the kind of data and the uses to which it is to be put; the filing system for a transaction processing system can be expected to be quite different from that for a process control system. In this chapter we shall keep to the spirit of the book in confining ourselves to general purpose systems, in which the filing systems are generally disc based; the reader who is interested in other areas is referred to the extensive literature elsewhere (for example IFIP, 1969; Judd, 1973; Martin, 1977).

The user of a general purpose system arranges his data in *files* of arbitrary size. Each file is thus a collection of data which is regarded as an entity by the user; it may be a program, a set of procedures, or the results of an experiment. The file is the logical unit which is stored and manipulated by the filing system. The medium on which files are stored is usually divided into *blocks* of fixed length (typically 512 to 2048 bytes), and the filing system must allocate the appropriate number of blocks to each file. In order to be useful the filing system must

(1)   Allow creation and deletion of files.
(2)   Allow access to files for reading or writing.
(3)   Perform automatic management of secondary memory space. It should be of no concern to the user whereabouts his files are located in secondary memory.
(4)   Allow reference to files by symbolic name. Since the user does not know, nor wish to know, the physical location of his files, he should be required only to quote their names in order to refer to them.
(5)   Protect files against system failure. Users will be reluctant to commit themselves to the system unless convinced of its integrity.
(6)   Allow the sharing of files between co-operating users but protect files against access by unauthorised users.

In the following sections we examine how the above objectives can be achieved.

7.2 FILE DIRECTORIES

The basic problem in accessing a file is to map a symbolic file name to a physical location in secondary memory. The mapping is achieved by means of a *file directory*, or *catalogue*, which is basically a table containing information about the locations of named files. Since the directory is the mechanism through which the file is accessed it is natural to include in it some means of protection against unauthorised access. We shall discuss this further in the next section; for the present we observe that an immediate measure of security can be afforded by dividing the directory into two levels as shown in figure 7.1. At the upper level a *master file directory* (MFD) contains for each user in the system a pointer to a *user file directory* (UFD) for that user; at the lower level each UFD contains the names and locations of a single user's files. Since a UFD can be accessed only via the MFD the privacy of a user's files can be assured by a simple identity check at the MFD level. Moreover, it is possible for different users to use the same name for a file without confusion, since the *full name* of a file can be regarded as the concatenation of the user name (or number) with the *individual name* of the file. For example, the individual name of the file shown in figure 7.1 is PROG, and its full name is FRED.PROG. Another file with the same individual name, but belonging to a user BILL, would have full name BILL.PROG. In practice it is not always necessary to specify the full name of a file, since the filing system can use the identity of the person requesting access as the default value for the first component. Only when a user requests access to another user's file does he need to quote the name in full.

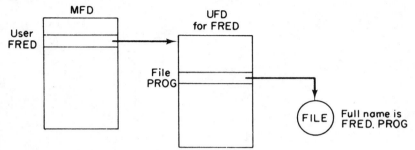

Figure 7.1 Two-level directory structure

The information in each UFD entry generally consists of

(1)   The file name.
(2)   The physical location of the file in secondary memory. The form of this entry will depend on the way in which the file is stored (see section 7.4).
(3)   The file type (character, binary, relocatable, etc.). This information is kept largely for user convenience, and also for the convenience of systems programs, such as loaders or editors, which may be used to operate on the file. As far as the filing system itself is concerned each file is simply a string of bits.
(4)   Access control information (for example read only; see section 7.3).
(5)   Administrative information (for example time of last update). This information is used to provide data for the system activities of preserving duplicate copies as insurance against hardware failure (see section 7.5).

Many systems (for example the DEC System-10) adopt the two-level directory structure described above. Others, such as UNIX, extend the concept to a multi-level structure, in which directory entries may be pointers to either files or other directories (see figure 7.2). A multi-level structure is useful in situations where the stored information has a tree-like classification, or where the users are grouped in hierarchies such as individuals within project teams within departments. In the latter case a hierarchical protection mechanism can be applied by making increasingly stringent checks as one progresses further down the tree. As in the two-level system, conflicting file names can be resolved by regarding the full name of the file as the concatenation of its individual name with the names of the directories on its access path.

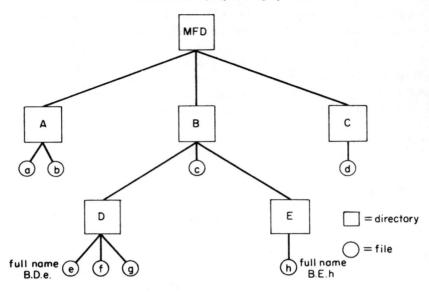

Figure 7.2 Multi-level directory structure

The disadvantage of a multi-level system lies in the length of the path to any particular file and the number of disc accesses which must be made to follow the path through the various directories. This can be alleviated to some extent by making use of the tendency of successive file accesses to be directed to files in the same directory. Once a route is established through the tree structure to a particular directory then this directory can be designated the *current directory* and subsequent file references need quote only the individual file name. A change of current directory is made by quoting the file name in full. This technique is used in UNIX and in MULTICS (Daley and Neumann, 1965).

7.3 SHARING AND SECURITY

The problem of the security of files arises directly from the desire to share them. In a non-sharing environment, where the only person allowed to access a file is the owner himself, security can be achieved by making an identity check in the MFD. When files are to be shared, however, the owner requires a means of specifying which users are to be allowed access to his files, and which are not. Moreover it is convenient for the owner to be able to specify *what kind* of access is to be permitted; he may wish some of his friends to be able to update his files, others only to read them, and others merely to load them for execution. We may summarise this by saying that the owner must be able to specify what *access privileges* other users may have.

A particularly simple way of doing this is to associate with each file a set of access privileges applicable to various classes of user. The user classes might be

(1)   the owner
(2)   partners
(3)   others

and typical access privileges are

(1)   no access (N)
(2)   execute only (E)
(3)   read only (R)
(4)   append only (A)
(5)   update (U)
(6)   change protection (P)
(7)   delete (D)

Each access privilege generally implies the ones above it. A typical *file protection key* assigned by the owner when creating the file, would be DAR, meaning that the owner can do anything, partners can append, and anyone else can only read. The file protection key resides in the owner's UFD as part of the entry for that particular file. Note that in some cases it may be sensible for the owner to grant himself only a low access privilege in order to protect himself from his own mistakes. Despite this the filing system must always allow the owner the change protection privilege, since otherwise he would have no way of altering or deleting his own file.

An implication of this method is that the owner must list in his UFD those users who are designated partners, and this list must be checked for all accesses other than by the owner himself. In some systems it is possible to avoid this by defining partnerships implicitly: the identification by which the user is known to the system may be structured so that its first component indicates partnership and its second component the individual user identity. For example, on the DEC System-10 the user identification consists of the pair (*project number, user number*), and all users with the same project number are deemed to be partners as far as file access is concerned. This technique is clearly inadequate when different but overlapping partnerships are required for different files.

The user class method of protection was initially developed in the mid-1960s for the Atlas 2, which had seven different access privileges and four classes of user (partnerships were defined explicitly by the user); it is now employed in several systems, such as the DEC System-10, which has eight access privileges and three classes of user (partnerships are defined implicitly).

A more general technique, which overcomes the hierarchical limitations of user classes, is for the owner to list in his UFD all users to whom he has accorded access privileges, together with a specification of what the privileges are. If a single list is associated with the entire UFD then the privileges accorded are necessarily the same for all files; alternatively, separate lists may be associated with each UFD entry, so that different privileges may be given to different sets of users for different files. In the latter case a great deal of space may be taken up by the lists, and unless the increased flexibility is essential this method should probably not be used.

A variation of this technique, used in MULTICS (Daley and Neumann, 1965), is for the owner to allow other users to create links in their UFDs to entries within his own UFD. Figure 7.3 shows a user Fred who has a link to a file entry in another user Jim's UFD. The link allows Fred to access the corresponding file belonging to Jim. Jim's UFD will contain a list of all users whom he allows to make such links. The great disadvantage of this method is that when a file is deleted all links to it must also be deleted, which means that the system must have a way of finding where all the links are. Alternatively, as in UNIX, a count can be kept of the number of links, and the file deleted only when the count is zero.

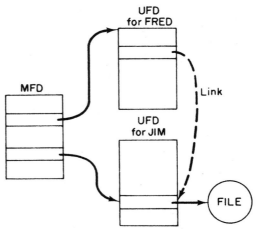

Figure 7.3 Links between UFDs

Summarising, the techniques described above offer various solutions to the problem of sharing and security. In general the more flexible the method adopted the greater is the space overhead in the UFDs and the longer the time to perform an access.

7.4 SECONDARY MEMORY ORGANISATION

As mentioned in section 7.1 file storage space is generally allocated in fixed size blocks, and since file sizes are variable, some kind of dynamic storage technique is required for both files and free space. There are several ways of organising the blocks within a file, three of which we describe below.

(1) Block Linkage

One word in each block of the file is used as a pointer to the next block (see figure 7.4). The UFD entry for the file points to the first block in the chain. The space overhead involved is one word per block for each file.

A disadvantage of this method of chaining is the large number of disc accesses which are needed to find the end of the file. This can be particularly inconvenient if the file is to be deleted and the space occupied returned to a free list; the alterations to pointers which are required to return the space rely on a knowledge of the position of the end of the file. For this reason the UFD entry is often extended to point to the last block in the file as well as to the first.

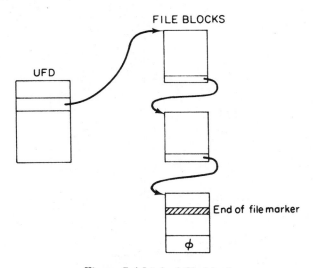

Figure 7.4 Linked file blocks

The reader will note that access to the file is necessarily sequential since all blocks can be reached only by passing down the chain. This method of chaining is therefore best suited to situations in which the files are processed sequentially. In these cases the overhead in accessing the file is only that of reading the successive blocks.

(2) File Map

For this method of file linkage the state of the disc is recorded in a *file map* in which each disc block is represented by a single word. The UFD entry for a file points to the location in the file map which represents the first block in the file. This location in turn points to the location in the map which represents the next block in the file, and so on (see figure 7.5). The last block in the file is represented by a null pointer. Thus the file shown in figure 7.5 occupies blocks 3, 6, 4 and 8 of the disc. The space overhead of the method is one word for every disc block.

As with the block linkage method access to the file is necessarily sequential. As an aid to extending and deleting a file the UFD entry may contain a pointer to the location in the file map which represents the file's last block.

Since the file map is generally too large to be held in main memory it must be stored on disc as a file itself and brought into memory a block at a time as required. This means that to read a file of N blocks may require an extra N disc accesses to read the appropriate parts of the file map. The overhead will be less than this only if some of the locations representing successive blocks of the file happen to lie in the same block of the file map. For this reason it is clearly advantageous to keep the space occupied by each file as near contiguous as possible, rather than allowing the file to be spread over the entire disc.

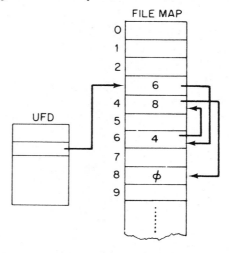

Figure 7.5 File map

(3) Index Blocks

The linkage pointers for each file are stored in a separate *index block* on disc. If the file is large then several index blocks may be needed, each one chained to the next (see figure 7.6). The UFD entry for the file points to the first index block in the chain. Since the last index block for a file is unlikely to be fully used the average space overhead is slightly more than one word per block for each file. The overhead for small files is proportionately greater than for large ones.

The great advantage of index blocks is that the file need not be accessed sequentially; any block may be accessed at random simply by specifying the name of the file and an offset in the index block. This method of file storage therefore lends itself to situations in which files possess an internal structure and in which the individual components are to be accessed separately.

The time overhead in accessing the file is small: the first access requires the index block to be read, but subsequent accesses carry no overhead unless different index blocks are needed. However, the addition or deletion of blocks in the middle of the file implies a rearrangement of pointers in the index blocks. This can be a lengthy operation and means that this method of storage is unsuitable for files which change frequently.

We remark in passing that in each of the above methods the end of each file can be denoted by a special marker at the appropriate place in the last block. This can be done for any type of file for which a unique marker can be defined which cannot be interpreted as data. For example, the end of file marker for character files could be a bit pattern which does not represent any known characters. However, no such marker can be defined for binary files since all bit patterns form valid data. In this case it is necessary to record the length of a file (in words or bytes) as an extra component of its UFD entry. (This is probably a good idea in any case, since it can give an extra check against corruption of a file.)

As a final observation on file block linkage we remark that a system may allow several forms of linkage, particularly where some files are likely to be accessed sequentially and others non-sequentially. The type of linkage required may be specified by the user when a file is created, with a suitable default being supplied by the system.

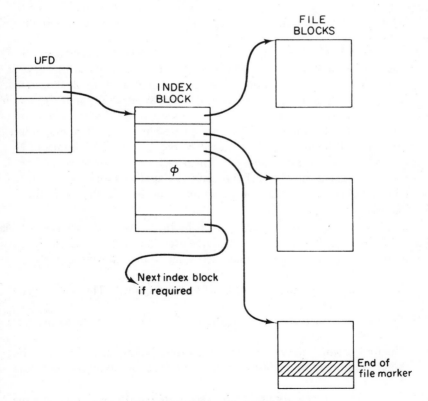

Figure 7.6 Use of index blocks

An equally important aspect of secondary memory organisation is the management of free space. One method is to regard free blocks as constituting a file in their own right, and to link them by one of the techniques described above. If the index block technique is used then all operations on a free chain (that is, allocating and returning free blocks) must take place at its tail since operations at the head would involve the rearrangement of a large number of pointers. If the block linkage or file map technique is used the operations may take place at either end of the chain. The index block technique has the further disadvantage that when N blocks are allocated or returned then N pointers must be deleted from or inserted in the last index block. By contrast only two pointers need changing when the other two techniques are used, no matter how many blocks are allocated or returned. (For example, when blocks are returned to the end of the free chain the two pointers which need changing are one from the last block of the old chain to the first block of the addition, and one from the system directory to the end of the new chain.)

A different method of recording free space is to use a *bit map*, which is an area of memory in which each bit represents a disc block. If a block is free the corresponding bit is set to zero; if the block is being used the bit is set to one. In order to find N free blocks it is necessary only to search the bit map for the first N zero bits, and then perform a simple calculation to obtain the corresponding block addresses.

In some situations the bit map may be too large to be held conveniently in main memory. In these cases the map can be stored in secondary memory, with only a section of it in main memory. This section can be used for all allocations, and when it is full (that is, all bits are one) it can be swapped for another section. The return of free space involves retrieving that section of the map corresponding to the returned blocks, and setting the appropriate bits to zero. This may result in heavy traffic of the disc map, but this can be reduced by keeping a list of all returned blocks and using it to update the map each time a new section of it comes into main memory. This technique must be applied with care, so that in the event of a disc crash the state of the bit map remains consistent with the space allocated.

The choice of block size is generally made by the hardware designer (a notable exception being the IBM 370 series, where the user may make a separate choice for each file). The choice is made according to the following criteria.

(1)   The waste of space due to some blocks not being filled. This will increase as the block size increases.

(2)   The waste of space due to chain pointers. The smaller the blocks the more pointers are required.

(3)   The unit in which the storage device transfers data to main memory. The block size should be a multiple of this unit so as to fully utilise each data transfer.

(4)   The amount of memory needed for each read or write operation on a file. Depending on the method of disc organisation, space may have to be found

in memory for the current index block or the current file map block, as well as for the block being read or written.

Typical block sizes are 512 to 2048 bytes.

Space allocation strategies can range from the straightforward (use the first block on the free block chain or the first block in the bit map) to the sophisticated (use the block which will minimise the amount of disc head movement when reading the file). The overhead of seek time in reading a file whose blocks are scattered all over the disc can in fact be quite large and can lead to saturation of the disc channel. It can be reduced by the strategy outlined above, or by periodically going through the file structure concatenating files as much as possible. This latter technique can be built into the back-up procedures described in the next section.

7.5 FILE SYSTEM INTEGRITY

Since the content of files may represent many months' work or may consist of irreplaceable data it is essential that a filing system provides adequate mechanisms for back-up and recovery in the not unlikely event of hardware or software failure. This means that the system must maintain duplicate copies of all files so that they can be restored after any unfortunate occurrence.

There are two principal ways of making copies of files, the first and simpler of which is known as the *periodic* (or *massive*) *dump*. At fixed intervals of time the contents of the entire file store are dumped onto some medium, usually magnetic tape, and in the event of failure all files can be recreated in the state they were in when the last dump was taken. Single files which are inadvertently deleted may be retrieved at the expense of scanning the entire dump tape. The disadvantages of the periodic dump are

(1) The file system may have to be placed out of use during the period of the dump. The alternative is not to dump any files which are open for writing.
(2) The dump usually takes a long time (20 minutes to 2 hours, depending on the size of the system and the speed of the tape decks). This means that the dump cannot be performed very often, and so a retrieved file may well be out of date.

The second and more sophisticated technique is the *incremental dump* (Fraser, 1969). With this technique a dump is made only of that information which has been changed since the previous dump was taken. This means that only files which have been created or altered, and directory entries which have been modified, will be dumped on each occasion. The amount of such information will be small, and so the dump can be made at frequent intervals. In order to determine which files are to be dumped a flag in the directory entry of each file is set whenever the file is altered, and cleared when it is dumped. So that the dumping process does not have to examine all directory entries, a global flag in each UFD can be used to indicate whether any individual flags within the UFD are set. Since the dumping process will skip all files whose flags are not set, which includes all files which are currently being updated, it can run in parallel with normal work. It is even possible, as in MULTICS, for the dumper to be a low priority process which is always present in the machine and which continually searches directories looking for updated information.

The disadvantages of the incremental dump lie in the large quantities of data which are generated and in the complexity of the recovery procedure. After a failure information must be reconstructed from the sequence of events recorded on the dump tapes. The tapes are mounted in inverse chronological order, and the filing system is restored back to the time that the last periodic dump was taken. (Periodic dumps will be made at rare intervals, typically once a week.) During this procedure the reloading process picks out from the dump tapes only those files it has not already restored, so that recent files are not superseded by earlier versions. Finally the last periodic dump tape is used to complete the recovery operation. This method of procedure is superior to starting with the periodic dump tape and working forwards, since no redundant information is restored.

It is worth noting that whatever method of dumping is used the recovery of the system affords a good opportunity to compact files into contiguous blocks. This reduces file access overheads at the expense of slightly lengthening the recovery procedure.

7.6 OPENING AND CLOSING FILES

We remarked in the last chapter that when an I/O stream is associated with a file the operating system must look up the device and location where the file is stored. This procedure is known as *opening* the file; the inverse procedure of *closing* the file is performed either explicitly when all I/O to the file has been completed or implicitly when the process using the file terminates.

To implement these operations we require within the operating system two procedures of the form

$$open \ (filename, mode) \qquad\qquad close \ (filename)$$

where *filename* is the name of the file to be opened or closed, and *mode* is the type of access required (for example read, write, or create). The operations performed by *open* are

(1)　Look up the directory entry for the file.
(2)　Check that the requesting process was instigated by a user with the requisite privileges for access in the specified mode.
(3)　Perform checks to ensure that if the file is already open for reading (possibly by another process) it cannot now be opened for writing, and

that if it is already open for writing it cannot now be opened at all. These checks will be described in a moment.

(4) Ascertain the device and location where the file is stored. If the file is to be newly created then the location is specified by the space allocation routine.

(5) Create a *file descriptor* which contains all information about the file relevant to forthcoming data transfers. The file descriptor, as mentioned in section 6.5, is used by I/O procedures as a source of information for constructing I/O requests, thus avoiding the necessity of going through the open procedure for each data transfer involving the file.

The information required in the file descriptor includes

(1) the file name
(2) the address of the device descriptor of the device on which the file is stored
(3) the location of the first block in the file
(4) the location of the next block to be read or written (assuming that access is sequential)
(5) the mode of access

The file descriptor is pointed to from the appropriate stream descriptor of the process which has opened the file, as shown in figure 6.4a.

The read/write interlocks referred to in part (3) of the description of *open* may be implemented by including two extra items in the directory entry of each file. The first is a 'write bit' which is set whenever the file is opened for writing: the second is a 'use count' of the number of processes which currently have the file open for reading. A process may open a file for reading only if the write bit is zero, and may open it for writing only if the write bit and the use count are both zero. Unfortunately there is a problem with this technique in that several processes might simultaneously wish to open or close the same file, thus making simultaneous changes to the directory entry. This can be overcome by writing the *open* and *close* procedures as critical sections, each enclosed by the same mutual exclusion semaphore, but this has the serious disadvantage that if a process is interrupted while opening or closing a file then these operations are unavailable to all other processes.

An alternative technique is to form a list of the file descriptors of all files which are open on each particular device. This list can be pointed to from the device descriptor of the device concerned. When a file is to be opened the *open* procedure inspects the list to see whether any file descriptors already exist for the file, and if so what mode of access they indicate. The procedure refuses to open the file unless the read/write constraints are satisfied. A mutual exclusion semaphore can be used to protect the list from simultaneous access by processes which wish to open or close the same file at the same time. The disadvantage of this technique lies in the time required to inspect the list, which in a large multiaccess system might easily contain 100 descriptors. This time is particularly critical since the list can be inspected by only one process at a time, and if the process is interrupted then the list becomes inaccessible to other processes.

A partial solution to these problems is to divide each file descriptor into two separate structures: a *central file descriptor* for each open file and a *local file descriptor* for each process using a file. A local file descriptor is created each time a process opens a file, and all the local file descriptors for a particular file point to the single central file descriptor for that file. The central file descriptors are linked to the appropriate device descriptor (see figure 7.7). A central file descriptor contains information which is the same for any process using the file, namely

(1)   the file name
(2)   the address of the device descriptor of the device on which the file is stored
(3)   the location of the first block in the file
(4)   the use count for the file
(5)   the write bit for the file

A local file descriptor contains information which is particular to the process using the file, namely

(1)   the location of the next block to be read or written
(2)   the mode of access

plus a pointer to the central file descriptor for the file. The introduction of central file descriptors eliminates the storage of duplicate information in separate descriptors and reduces the length of the descriptor list for each device. It also reduces the amount of work the *open* and *close* procedures have to do in searching the descriptor list. More significantly, it allows mutual exclusion to be applied to each descriptor separately rather than to the list as a whole, and thus it avoids the bottleneck dangers mentioned earlier. The mutual exclusion semaphore can be held in the central file descriptor for each file.

A variation of this technique (Courtois *et al.*, 1971) is to replace the write bit in the central file descriptor by another semaphore *w*. The *open* and *close* procedures are then written to include the following pieces of code.

Open	*Close*
if *mode* = read **then**	**if** *mode* = read **then**
begin *wait* (*mutex*);	**begin** *wait* (*mutex*);
usecount: = *usecount* + 1;	*usecount:* = *usecount* − 1;
if *usecount* = 1 **then** *wait* (*w*);	**if** *usecount* = 0 **then** *signal* (*w*);
signal (*mutex*)	*signal* (*mutex*)
end	**end**
else *wait* (*w*)	**else** *signal* (*w*)

In this variation those access requests which are refused are implicitly queued on the semaphore *w*, while in the original version the system designer retains the freedom to queue requests or not, according to the application.

The operation of the *close* procedure is relatively simple. It consists of deleting the local file descriptor and decrementing the use count in the central file descriptor. If the use count is zero the central file descriptor is also deleted and the directory updated where necessary (if, for example, the file has just been created).

Deletion of a file may be treated as a call of *open* with an appropriate *mode* parameter. However this has the disadvantage that if the file is already open, as will often be the case with library files, the delete request will be refused. This

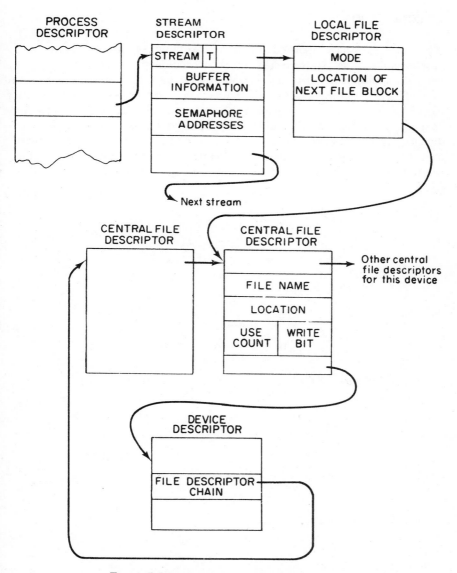

Figure 7.7 Local and central file descriptors

makes the replacement of library files somewhat awkward. A way round this problem is to include in each central file descriptor a 'delete pending bit' which is set whenever a delete request is made on an open file. The *close* procedure checks this bit: if it is set and the use count falls to zero the file can be deleted. Deletion is hastened if *open* refuses access to a file whose delete pending bit is set.

7.7 CONCLUSION

In this chapter we have discussed various aspects of filing systems for general purpose applications. The next step in the construction of our paper operating system is the adoption of a particular system based on the techniques we have described. This will give us another layer of our 'onion', consisting of code for implementing particular security and integrity mechanisms, for administering free space, and for opening and closing files. The additional permanent data structures are the file directories and whatever structure is used to record space allocation. Temporary data structures which exist only while a file is open are the local and central file descriptors. The current state of the system is shown in figure 7.8.

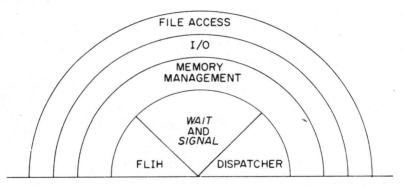

Figure 7.8 Current state of the paper operating system

8 *Resource Allocation and Scheduling*

Up to this point in the development of our paper operating system we have assumed that all processes have the resources they need. It is now time to consider how processes acquire their resources, and how a limited set of resources can be effectively shared among several processes. Our discussion of resource allocation will also include scheduling since the two functions are closely related: decisions on process priority can be dependent on where resources are committed, and the introduction of new processes into the system is clearly influenced by the amount of spare resource capacity. In fact scheduling, being concerned with the allocation of central processors, can be regarded as a subtopic of resource allocation as a whole.

8.1 GENERAL OBSERVATIONS

In an environment in which resources were unlimited a 'grab it when you need it' method of acquisition would be perfectly acceptable. Unfortunately it is rarely feasible to provide resources to satisfy the concurrent demands of all processes in the system, and so techniques must be devised to share a limited set of resources among a number of competing processes. The objectives of these techniques are to

(1) mutually exclude processes from unshareable resources
(2) prevent deadlock (see section 3.2) arising in respect of resource requests
(3) ensure a high level of resource utilisation
(4) allow all processes an opportunity of acquiring the resources they need within a 'reasonable' time

   The reader will see that these objectives are not necessarily mutually consistent. In particular, the user satisfaction implied by objective (4) can generally be gained only by compromising objective (3). This is because the higher the level of resource utilisation the longer will be the average wait before a resource request can be granted. The trade-off between user satisfaction and resource utilisation is one of the criteria by which resource allocation and scheduling policies can be evaluated. In a real-time system with a guaranteed response time one would expect the trade-off to be in favour of the user; in a batch system it might be in favour of high utilisation. This can create a difficult managerial problem in a system which attempts to provide both batch and multi-access service.

It is useful to discuss resource allocation under two headings: the *mechanisms* and the *policies*. By *mechanisms* we mean the nuts and bolts aspect of how allocation is made. This includes such things as data structures for describing the state of resources, techniques for ensuring the exclusive use of unshareable resources, and means for queueing resource requests which cannot be granted immediately. The *policies* govern the ways in which the mechanisms are applied. They are concerned with the wisdom of granting requests even when the appropriate resources are available. This involves the questions of deadlock and system balance: an unwise allocation may lead to a situation in which some processes cannot proceed or in which the system is overloaded with respect to one particular class of resource. It is at this latter point that resource allocation becomes linked with scheduling, since the likelihood of overload can be reduced by judicious scheduling decisions on process priority and on the introduction of new processes into the system. We shall discuss both mechanisms and policies in the following sections.

8.2 ALLOCATION MECHANISMS

From the observations above it should be apparent that any element of a computing system which is in limited supply and which has to be shared can be regarded as a resource. In fact resources generally fall into one of the categories mentioned below. We shall review the allocation mechanisms for each category, giving consideration to what part of the system makes the allocation, the data structures used to describe the resources, and the means by which processes are queued while awaiting allocation.

(1) Central Processors

We have already discussed in chapter 4 how a central processor is allocated by the dispatcher to the first non-running process in the processor queue. The data describing a central processor can be held in a processor descriptor which is similar to the device descriptor used for data relating to a peripheral (see chapter 6). The processor descriptor might typically contain

(a)   the processor identification
(b)   the current status — whether in user or supervisor mode
(c)   a pointer to the process descriptor of the current process

The processor descriptors can be contained within the central table, or be pointed to from it.

In a configuration in which processors are dissimilar the processor descriptors can be extended to hold an indication of the individual processor characteristics (whether it has floating point hardware for example). In this case each processor might be best suited to running a particular kind of process, and so might have its own processor queue pointed to from its descriptor. The processor queues are then analogous to the device request queues for peripherals. The assignment of processes to different processor queues is a subject still largely unexplored, and we shall not deal further with it here.

(2) Memory

In chapter 5 we saw how memory can be allocated by the memory management layer of the operating system in both the paged and non-paged cases. The data structures describing the state of memory are the page tables, segment tables, or free block lists, depending on the machine architecture involved. A process waiting for the transfer of a new page or segment from secondary memory is made unrunnable, with the status bits in its process descriptor indicating the reason. Page and segment requests are queued as I/O request blocks by the memory management system, and serviced by the device handler for the appropriate secondary memory device.

(3) Peripherals

We described in chapter 6 how in systems with stream based I/O an unshareable peripheral is allocated to a process when the corresponding stream is opened. In systems which do not use streams a peripheral may be allocated after a direct request to the operating system. In both cases the allocation mechanism is the same. The data structure describing a peripheral is its device descriptor, and processes awaiting allocation of a peripheral can be queued on a semaphore which is included in the descriptor. Mutual exclusion in the use of the peripheral is ensured by initialising the semaphore value to 1.

(4) Backing Store

Backing store which is used in the implementation of virtual memory is allocated by the memory management system, and that used as file space is allocated by the filing system. Some operating systems, notably MULTICS, make no distinction between files and segments, so that the file store becomes part of the virtual memory and the filing system is responsible for all allocations. The data structure used for allocation is some kind of free block list or bit map as described in section 7.4.

Requests for file space are refused only when an individual user has exceeded his quota, or when all backing store is full. In neither case is it sensible to queue requests; the former situation can be resolved only by the user's own action, and the latter situation cannot be guaranteed to change within any small space of time.

(5) Files

An individual file may be regarded as a resource in the sense that several processes may wish to share it. As long as all processes operate in a 'read only' mode the resource is shareable; if one process wishes to write to the file then the resource is unshareable.

Allocation of a file to a process is made by the filing system when the file is opened, and write interlocks are achieved by the methods described in section 7.6. The data structures describing files are of course the file directories.

Batch systems do not usually queue file requests since simultaneous (non-read) requests are usually indicative of user error. However, in transaction processing or process control it may well be sensible to establish access queues within the filing system. These queues may be associated with semaphores as discussed in section 7.6.

It is apparent from the above review that allocation mechanisms are implemented at various levels of the operating system, each mechanism being found at the level appropriate to the resource being allocated. We shall see, however, that the policies for using the mechanisms must be global to the entire system.

8.3 DEADLOCK

The first resource allocation policies we consider are concerned with the problem of deadlock, which was described in section 3.2.

If resources are allocated to processes solely on the basis of their availability then deadlock may easily occur. In its simplest form deadlock will happen in the following circumstances: process *A* is granted resource *X* and then requests resource *Y*; process *B* is granted resource *Y* and then requests resource *X*. If both resources are unshareable and neither process will release the resource it holds then deadlock ensues. In general the necessary and sufficient conditions for deadlock (Coffman *et al.*, 1971) are

(1) the resources involved are unshareable
(2) processes hold the resources they have already been allocated while waiting for new ones
(3) resources cannot be pre-empted while being used
(4) a circular chain of processes exists such that each process holds resources which are currently being requested by the next process in the chain

The problem of deadlock may be solved by adopting one of the following strategies

(1) prevent deadlock by ensuring at all times that at least one of the four conditions above does not hold
(2) detect deadlock when it occurs and then try to recover
(3) avoid deadlock by suitable anticipatory action

We consider each of these strategies in turn.

(1) Deadlock Prevention

To prevent deadlock at least one of the four necessary conditions above must be denied.

Condition (1) is difficult to deny since some resources (for example a card reader or a writeable file) are by nature unshareable. However, the use of spooling (see section 6.6) can remove the deadlock potential of unshareable peripherals.

Condition (2) can be denied by stipulating that processes request all their resources at once and that they cannot proceed until all the requests are granted. This has the disadvantage that resources which are used only for a short time are nevertheless allocated and therefore inaccessible for long periods. It is, however, easy to implement, and may prove more economical in the long run than some more complex algorithm.

Condition (3) is easily denied by imposing the rule that if a process is refused a resource request then it must release all resources it currently holds, and if necessary request them again together with the additional resources. Unfortunately this Draconian strategy can be rather inconvenient in practice, since pre-empting a line printer (say) would result in the interleaving of the output from several jobs. Furthermore, even if a resource is conveniently pre-emptible, the overhead of storing and restoring its state at the time of pre-emption can be quite high. In the case of a central processor, however, the overhead is relatively small (namely storing the volatile environment of the current process), and the processor can always be regarded as pre-emptible.

Denial of condition (4) can be effected by imposing an order on resource types so that if a process has been allocated resources of type k then it may request only resources of types which follow k in the order. This ensures that the circular wait condition can never arise. The disadvantage is the constraint imposed on the natural order of resource requests, though this can be mitigated by placing commonly used resources early in the order.

An interesting example of these three ways of preventing deadlock occurs in OS/360 (Havender, 1968). In this system jobs are divided into 'job steps', and there is a job step initiator which is responsible for getting the resources necessary for each job step. The concurrent initiation of several job steps for different jobs is achieved by having several copies of the job step initiator. Deadlock between the copies is prevented by ensuring that each initiator always acquires resources in the order files, memory, peripherals. Deadlock between different job steps wishing to access the same files is prevented by making the initiator acquire files for a whole job at once. It should be noted that in this case pre-emption would not be appropriate, since a job would not want its files to be tampered with by alien job steps while it was itself between job steps. Neither can any reasonable order be placed on file requests. Deadlock over peripheral allocation is prevented by forcing jobs to release resources (except files) between job steps and to re-request them for the next step if required.

(2) Deadlock Detection and Recovery

If the prevention policies detailed above are considered too restrictive then an alternative approach may be acceptable. This allows the possibility of deadlock but relies on detecting it when it occurs and on being able to stage a recovery. The value of this approach depends on the frequency with which deadlock occurs and on the kind of recovery it is possible to make.

Detection algorithms work by detecting the circular wait expressed by condition (4) above. The state of the system at any time can be represented by a *state graph* in which the nodes are resources and an arc between nodes *A* and *B* implies that there exists a process which holds resource *A* and is requesting resource *B* (see figure 8.1).

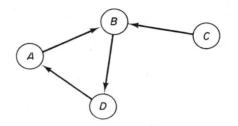

*Figure 8.1 Example state graph (resources A, B and D
are involved in deadlock)*

The circular wait condition is represented as a closed loop in the state graph (for example *A*, *B*, *D* in figure 8.1). The detection algorithm maintains a representation of the state graph in some convenient form and inspects it at intervals for the existence of closed loops. The inspection may occur after each allocation or, since the overhead of doing this is probably too high, at fixed intervals of time.

Detection of deadlock is useful only if an acceptable attempt at recovery can be made. The definition of 'acceptable' can be stretched according to circumstance to include any of the following techniques, which are listed in order of increasing sophistication.

(a)   Abort all deadlocked processes. This is roughly equivalent to the Post Office burning the occasional sack of mail whenever it gets overloaded, but is the method adopted in most general purpose systems.

(b)   Restart the deadlocked processes from some intermediate checkpoint, if one exists. If naïvely applied this method may lead straight back to the original deadlock, but the nondeterminacy of the system will usually ensure that this does not happen.

(c)   Successively abort deadlocked processes until deadlock no longer exists. The order of abortion can be such as to minimise the cost of losing the investment of resources already used. This approach implies that after each abortion the detection algorithm must be reinvoked to see whether deadlock still exists.

(d)   Successively pre-empt resources from deadlocked processes until deadlock
no longer exists. As in (c) the order of pre-emption can be such as to
minimise some cost function. Reinvocation of the detection algorithm is
required after each pre-emption. A process which has a resource pre-empted
from it must make a subsequent request for the resource to be reallocated
to it.

It is worth remarking before we leave the subject that detection of deadlock
is often left to the computer operators rather than performed by the system
itself. An observant operator will eventually notice that certain processes appear
to be stuck, and on further investigation he will realise that deadlock has occurred.
The customary recovery action is to abort and restart (if possible) the deadlocked
processes.

(3) Deadlock Avoidance

By deadlock avoidance we mean the use of an algorithm which will anticipate
that deadlock is likely to occur and which will therefore refuse a resource request
which would otherwise have been granted. This is a notion distinct from prevention, which ensures *a priori* that deadlock cannot occur by denying one of the
necessary conditions.

A tempting line of approach to devising an avoidance algorithm is as follows.
Before granting a resource request, tentatively change the state graph to what it
would be if the request were granted, and then apply a deadlock detection
algorithm. If the detection algorithm gives the all clear then grant the request;
otherwise refuse the request and restore the state graph to its original form.
Unfortunately this technique will not always work since it relies on the premise
that if an allocation is going to result in deadlock then it will do so immediately.
That this premise is false can be shown by study of figure 8.2 (due to Dijkstra),
which illustrates a two-process, two-resource system.

The joint progress of processes P_1 and P_2 is represented by plotting a trajectory, shown in the diagram as the heavy arrowed line. The horizontal portions of
the trajectory represent periods when P_1 is running, the vertical portions
represent the periods when P_2 is running, and the sloping portions represent
periods when both P_1 and P_2 are running simultaneously. (In a single processor
configuration only horizontal and vertical portions can exist.) The trajectory is
constrained from entering the shaded region on the diagram since this is an
interval during which at least one of the resources R_1 and R_2 is required by both
processes. The important point is that if the trajectory enters the region D then
eventual deadlock is inevitable, since in that case there is no way that the
trajectory can avoid meeting the shaded area (the trajectory can move only
upwards and to the right, in the directions of positive progress). However, deadlock does not exist in region D itself, and so entering D would provoke no
objection from any deadlock detection algorithm. Thus the use of a detection
algorithm would not avoid deadlock in this case. To put it another way, a
detection algorithm can see only one step ahead, whereas deadlock may be

inevitable several steps ahead.

It is apparent from the above discussion that a successful avoidance algorithm must possess some prior knowledge of the possible pattern of future events so that it can spot potential deadlocks before they arise. The type of prior knowledge assumed is the feature which distinguishes one algorithm from another. We discuss below the *banker's algorithm*, which is probably the best known.

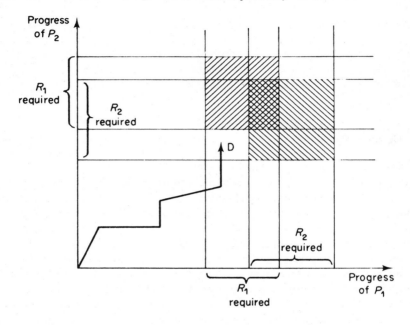

| | interval during which R_1 is required by both processes |
| | interval during which R_2 is required by both processes |

Figure 8.2 Illustration of deadlock

The prior knowledge demanded by the banker's algorithm is the maximum quantity of each resource which a process will require during its lifetime. We call this quantity the *claim* of a process on a resource. In batch systems this demand is quite reasonable, since job descriptions can be used to specify maximum resource requirements in advance. The algorithm allows a resource request only if

(a)   the request plus the current usage is less than the claim

and (b)   after doing so there exists a sequence in which all processes can run to completion even if they all demand their full claims.

Thus before making an allocation the algorithm checks that enough resources will be left to enable such a sequence to be constructed. It has been shown (Habermann, 1969) that the work involved in making the check is proportional to the square of the number of processes in the system.

As an example of how the algorithm works, consider again figure 8.2. The claims of P_1 and P_2 are each R_1 and R_2. Before entry into region D, R_1 is allocated to P_1 and R_2 is free. Thus there are sufficient resources left to run both P_1 and P_2 to completion even if both processes demand their full claims. The appropriate sequence in this case is P_1 followed by P_2. Inside region D, R_1 is allocated to P_1 and R_2 to P_2. Thus if both processes demand their claims there is no sequence (neither P_1 before P_2 nor vice versa) in which they can run to completion. The banker's algorithm therefore refuses entry into region D by denying the request for R_2 by P_2. P_2 will be suspended, and only P_1 will be able to run. The trajectory will therefore follow a horizontal course along the lower edge of the shaded area until P_1 releases R_2. At this point the original request by P_2 for R_2 can be granted since there are now sufficient resources available to complete both processes.

It should be noted that the banker's algorithm always allows for the worst possible case (that in which all processes demand their full claims). It may therefore sometimes refuse a request because deadlock *might* ensue, whereas if the request had been granted no deadlock would in fact have occurred. For example, in figure 8.2 entry into region D is forbidden because of the possibility that P_1 might exercise its claim on R_2 and P_2 might exercise its claim on R_1. If in fact either process chooses not to exercise its claim at an awkward moment then region D would be quite safe (since the shaded areas would not occupy the positions shown), and the refusal of P_2's request for R_2 would have been unnecessarily restrictive. The tendency of the banker's algorithm towards over-cautiousness, together with the overheads of applying it, are the main drawbacks to its use.

We conclude our discussion of deadlock by considering the level in the operating system at which policies to deal with it should be implemented.

If a prevention strategy is used then all parts of the system which allocate resources operate under one or more of the constraints described earlier. The constraints can be implemented as part of the resource allocation mechanisms at the appropriate levels.

If detection is used then no alteration to the allocation mechanisms is required. The detection algorithm, which must have access to all allocation data structures, can be implemented at a high level, possibly within the scheduler itself. (The scheduler is described in later sections.)

In the case of deadlock avoidance all resource requests must be vetted by the avoidance algorithm. We shall see in the next section that all resource requests can be made via the scheduler, which thus becomes the natural place in which to implement the algorithm.

8.4 THE SCHEDULER

The term scheduling is generally understood to cover the questions of when to introduce new processes into the system and the order in which processes should run. As mentioned earlier these subjects are intimately related to resource allocation. In fact decisions on scheduling and decisions on resource allocation are so closely linked that it is often sensible to place responsibility for both in the hands of a single system process. We shall call this process the *scheduler*. The duties of the scheduler are described below.

(1) Introduction of New Processes

In a batch system jobs awaiting execution are stored in a *job pool* which is held in secondary memory. (How they get there will be discussed in chapter 11.) The scheduler starts execution of a job by initiating an appropriate process such as compilation. The choice of which job to start next depends on the resources each job requires (as stated in its job description) and on the current pattern of resource allocation in the system. In order to achieve high throughput the scheduler should initiate a new process as soon as resource capacity warrants it.

In a multi-access system processes are created when users log-in to the system. Each new user increases the demand on resources, and access can be refused when the number of logged-in users is such as to increase response time to the limit of acceptability.

(2) Assignment of Process Priorities

The order in which processes are run is determined either by the order of the processor queue or by the order in which the dispatcher selects processes from the queue. We suggested in chapter 4 that to minimise dispatching overheads the dispatcher should always pick the first eligible process in the queue; this implies that the order of the queue will be the determining factor. The scheduler is responsible for assigning priorities to processes so that when they become runnable they are linked into the appropriate place in the queue. Algorithms for determining suitable priorities will be discussed in the next section.

(3) Implementation of Resource Allocation Policies

The policies implied here are those concerned with deadlock avoidance and with system balance; that is, with ensuring that no type of resource is either over- or under-committed. Criteria for evaluating balance will be discussed in the next section.

Since the behaviour of the system is largely determined by the activities of the scheduler it is important that the scheduler should have a high priority relative to other processes. If the scheduler has top priority the dispatcher will pick it whenever it is runnable in preference to all other processes. This ensures that the system reacts quickly to changes in circumstance, particularly to changes in demand. The occasions on which the scheduler might be activated are

(1) a resource is requested
(2) a resource is released
(3) a process terminates
(4) a new job arrives in the job pool (or a new user attempts to log-in)

It is instructive to note the analogy between interrupts and the scheduling events above. Both occur at unpredictable intervals, and both may cause the system to modify its behaviour. In the case of scheduling events the modifications are at a high level, affecting such global parameters as process priorities and the number of processes in the system; modifications due to interrupts are at a low level, affecting the runnability of processes and the allocation of the central processors. Interrupts may be expected to occur every few milliseconds, whereas scheduling events will probably occur only every second or so.

When the scheduler has finished its work it suspends itself by executing a *wait* operation on a semaphore; this semaphore is signalled whenever a scheduling event occurs. However, in an operating system which neither prevents nor avoids deadlock it is possible that no scheduling event does in fact occur. In this situation it is vital that the scheduler is reawakened in order to detect that deadlock prevails; this can be done by signalling the semaphore on certain clock interrupts, say every ten seconds.

The request and release of resources (the first two scheduling events above) can be implemented by providing two operating system procedures

request resource (*resource*, *result*)   *release resource* (*resource*)

These procedures place the necessary information about the resource concerned and the identity of the calling process in a data area accessible to the scheduler, and then signal the scheduler semaphore. The scheduler will respond according to criteria to be discussed in the next section. The second parameter of *request resource* is used to convey the result of the request, and may also give an indication of the reason for any refusal. Note that a request which is at first refused may be queued by the scheduler until the resource becomes available. In this case the request will eventually be granted and the *result* parameter of *request resource* will indicate this. The queueing operation and the associated delay are transparent to the requesting process.

A disadvantage of combining the scheduling and resource allocation functions in a single process is the overhead of process switching incurred whenever a resource is requested or released. If this overhead is thought to outweigh the gains that can be obtained from system balance and high resource utilisation then the two functions may be separated. In this case the routines *request resource* and *release resource* perform the resource allocation functions without invoking the scheduler.

8.5 SCHEDULING ALGORITHMS

The general objective of a scheduling algorithm is to arrange the pattern of work performed by the computing system so as to maximise some measure of user satisfaction. This measure may differ from system to system: in a batch environment it may be total throughput or the average turnround time for a certain class of job; in a multi-access system it may be the average response time offered to users, or the response time offered to certain kinds of interaction. The scheduling algorithm used will naturally depend on the goal desired.

We start by considering algorithms which are based on the assumption that central processors are the resources of prime importance. We have already implied at the start of this chapter that in many cases this assumption is false and that other resources may also be of importance. However, by studying processor-bound systems we may gain insight into the more complex cases to be discussed later.

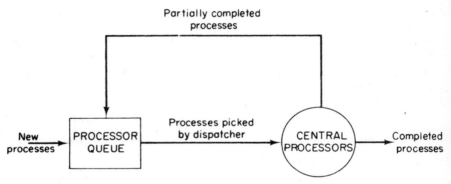

Figure 8.3 Scheduling model of a processor-bound system

A general model of a processor-bound system is illustrated in figure 8.3. New processes arrive on the processor queue and are serviced by a number of processors (We are assuming that the processors are identical.) After receiving a certain amount of service a process may be completed, in which case it leaves the system; otherwise it is returned to the queue to await further service at a later time. The model represents processes only in the runnable and running states; the omission of the blocked state of chapter 4 reflects the fact that in a processor-bound system the only significant delays which can occur are due to waiting in the processor que A particular scheduling algorithm is characterised by the order of processes in the queue and the conditions under which processes are fed back into it. We consider several popular algorithms below.

(1) Shortest Job First

As the name implies the queue is ordered according to the running time required by each process. The algorithm is suitable only for batch systems, where an estimate of the running time can be acquired from the job description. Its aim is to minimise the turnround time of short jobs, and it is therefore best used in an environment in which short jobs form the bulk of the load. In its simplest form the algorithm allows all processes to run to completion, but a modification can be made by which a new process may pre-empt a processor if it has a running time less than that required to finish the current process. This version, known as *pre-emptive shortest job first*, is even more favourable to short jobs. Another modification, which ensures that long jobs are not delayed indefinitely, is gradually to increase the priority of a process according to the length of time it has been in the queue.

(2) Round Robin

This algorithm was developed as a means of giving rapid response to short service requests when running times are not known in advance. Each process in the system receives a fixed quantum of service before being returned to the end of the queue. The queue is therefore circular, and ordered by length of time since the last service. Processes which require lengthy service will cycle round the queue several times before being completed, while processes whose service time is less than the quantum will terminate on the first cycle. The round robin algorithm was used in the early time-sharing system CTSS (Corbató *et al.*, 1962) and has subsequently been implemented with several variations in many other systems. Most variations have the aim of reducing the tendency of the system to collapse under heavy loading. Analysis and experience both show that if the load becomes too heavy for a given quantum size then performance is suddenly degraded. One way of overcoming this is to increase the quantum size as the number of processes rises. This increases the probability that a process will terminate within the quantum, and so reduces the overhead of process switching.

(3) Two-level Queue

This is another variation of the round robin algorithm which attempts to overcome sudden load degradation. Processes which are not completed within a fixed number of quanta are syphoned off into a 'background' queue which is serviced only if there are no other processes in the system. The background queue may itself be treated on a round robin basis with a larger quantum, or it may be simply first come, first served. The two-level system is often used in mixed batch and multi-access environments, where the longer batch processes tend to sink into the background and are serviced only when no terminal initiated processes are present. The algorithm can of course be generalised to a *multi-level system* if this is considered appropriate. An example of this occurs in the DEC System-10 Monitor, where there are three round robin queues with quanta set at 0.02 seconds, 0.25 seconds, and 2 seconds respectively. (These values may in fact be changed if desired.)

The optimal values of the parameters of the round robin algorithm and its descendants, such as quantum size and when to move processes to a background queue, are difficult to determine analytically (but see Coffman and Denning, 1973, for some attempts). Approximations may be found by simulation, and adjusted after experience of real life running conditions.

The algorithms above form the basis of most popular scheduling policies. Other algorithms and variations can be found in the excellent survey by Coffman and Kleinrock (1968). One particular variation of note is to allow the inclusion of externally specified priorities. The effect is that processes with high external priority receive a better service than would be the case with the pure form of an algorithm. This enables users with tight deadlines or VIP status to obtain better response from the system, though they may be charged more for the privilege.

Systems in which central processors are not the sole resources of importance can be described by the model shown in figure 8.4. This model differs from that of figure 8.3 by the inclusion of the blocked state, in which processes wait for resource requests or I/O transfers. The addition of this state greatly increases the complexity of the model. Firstly, the state is characterised not by a single queue but by a multiplicity of queues associated with the various semaphores which cause blocking to occur. Secondly, processes move from the blocked to the runnable state after events such as the signalling of a semaphore which occur at unpredictable intervals. The movement of processes between queues can be studied for different scheduling strategies either by formal analysis or by simulation (Coffman and Denning, 1973; Svobodova, 1976), though the complexity of the model makes both techniques difficult to apply.

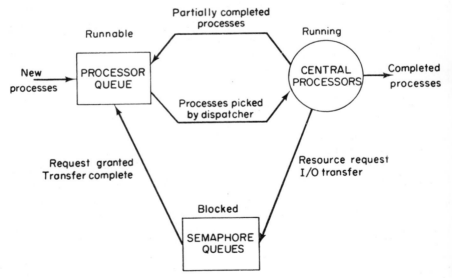

Figure 8.4 General scheduling model

The reader will see from figure 8.4 that one of the aims of a scheduling algorithm could be to minimise the number of transitions from the running to the blocked state. Since the transitions due to I/O transfers are outside its control it follows that the algorithm should minimise the number of resource requests which are refused. This implies that processes should be introduced into the system only if their likely resource demands can be satisfied by the resources currently available. This policy is more easily implemented in batch syst'ms, where maximum resource demands can be specified in advance, than in n.ulti-access systems, where demands are virtually unpredictable. An example of batch implementation was the Atlas operating system, in which jobs were divided into three classes: short jobs, requiring little processor time and no esoteric peripherals; magnetic tape jobs, whose name is self-explanatory; and long jobs, comprising the rest. The scheduler attempted to maintain at least one job of each class in the system at any given time.

It is worth noting that policies such as this will not necessarily result in high resource utilisation. The reason is that a process is unlikely to use throughout its life all the resources of which it has given notice. The resources claimed, and allowed for by the scheduler, may therefore lie idle for considerable periods. If higher utilisation is required the scheduler must make policy decisions on resource allocation not only when introducing a new process but also when each resource request or release occurs. The criteria for making such decisions and for assigning process priorities are generally empirical; we discuss a few of them below.

(1) Processes which possess a large number of resources may be given high priority in an attempt to speed their completion and regain the resources for deployment elsewhere. The danger of pursuing this strategy is that large jobs might monopolise the machine or that users may generate dummy resource requests in order to gain favourable treatment. This latter danger can be avoided in a batch system by ensuring that jobs with small resource requirements are selected for running in preference to others.

(2) Processes which possess a large number of resources could have further requests granted whenever possible. The justification is similar to that above, and again there is a danger that large jobs might monopolise the system.

(3) Memory allocation in paged machines can be performed according to the working set principle described in chapter 5.

(4) Operating system processes should have priorities which reflect the urgency of the functions they perform. The scale will range from the scheduler itself at the top to such processes as the incremental file dumper at the bottom. Most system processes will have higher priorities than user processes.

(5) As a special case of (4) peripheral device handlers should have high priority. In general the faster the device the higher should be the priority of the associated handler. This ensures that peripherals are kept busy as much as possible, thereby reducing the potential of I/O bottlenecks. If spooling is used then the spoolers should also have high priority.

(6) Unless deadlock prevention measures are in force all resource requests should be subjected to a deadlock avoidance algorithm.

(7) The overhead in making scheduling decisions should not be out of proportion to the ensuing gains.

The considerations above may be used to modify one of the processor scheduling algorithms described earlier. The result will be an algorithm in which process priorities are continually being updated according to the pattern of resource demand and the state of the system. The performance of such an algorithm is difficult to gauge except by observation; it can often be substantially improved by quite minor alterations to its parameters. An interesting example of such an improvement arose in the DEC System-10 Monitor. In an early version of the scheduling algorithm processes which re-entered the runnable state after being blocked while awaiting terminal I/O were placed on the end of the first level processor queue. This procedure was subsequently changed so as to place these processes on the front of the first level queue. The improvement of response to multi-access users was dramatic.

We may summarise this section by saying that the number of possible scheduling algorithms is very large, but that at present we have no means of selecting an optimal algorithm for a specific case other than by experiment. Analysis and simulation can be of some help, but their value is restricted by the complexity of most systems.

8.6 PROCESS HIERARCHIES

We saw in section 8.4 that the scheduler is responsible for initiating new processes. Thus in a sense the scheduler is the parent of all processes introduced into the system. Moreover, it is responsible for the welfare of its offspring in that it governs policies of resource allocation and influences the order in which processes are selected by the dispatcher. This parental role need not be restricted to the scheduler; it can be extended to other processes by allowing them the capability to

(1)   create subprocesses
(2)   allocate to their subprocesses a subset of their own resources (the resources being returned when the subprocess terminates)
(3)   determine the relative priority of their subprocesses

The effect is to enable the creation of a hierarchy of processes with the scheduler at the head. Thus the natural form of the process structure is no longer the simple list of chapter 4, but a tree as shown in figure 8.5. The tree is partially threaded by the processor queue, which links all the nodes (processes) which are currently runnable.

The advantages of a hierarchical organisation are twofold. First, it allows a process which performs several independent tasks to create a subsidiary process for each task so that the tasks may be executed in parallel. Of course nothing is gained on a machine with a single central processor since only apparent concurrency can be achieved, but when several processors are available real gains may result.

Second, it allows several versions of the operating system, each oriented towards a different application, to run independently and in parallel. The different versions, or subsystems, will each be based on the facilities provided by the system nucleus (see chapter 4,) but may use different algorithms for the implementation of the higher system functions which appear in the outer layers. Thus each subsystem is a particular version of our 'onion', though all subsystems have the same core. The various subsystems each implement a virtual machine which is suitable for a particular class of users, and all the virtual machines coexist in the same physical configuration.

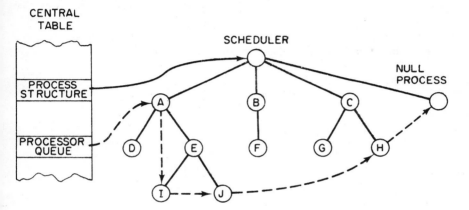

Figure 8.5 A process hierarchy

As an example consider figure 8.6, which illustrates a situation in which two different subsystems are responsible for batch and on-line work respectively. The performance of the two subsystems is governed by the resources and relative priorities allocated by the scheduler; within these constraints each subsystem can control its subordinate processes according to any appropriate algorithms. Within the batch subsystem, for example, all I/O may be spooled and user processes ordered on a shortest first principle; within the on-line subsystem I/O may be unspooled and processes ordered in a round robin. One can imagine an extension of the hierarchy in which, for instance, the batch subsystem is divided into further subsystems which handle different classes of job.

One advantage of the subsystem arrangement is the coexistence of different virtual machines. Another is the ability to develop new versions of an operating system while the old version runs in parallel. Against this must be set the loss of global control over resource allocation which results from the way in which resources are passed up and down the process structure. Resources which have been allocated to a subsystem or to an inferior process, and which are not being used, cannot be transferred elsewhere in the system unless they are first returned to a common ancestor. Since processes are free to allocate subsets of their resources as they wish there is no guarantee that the overall pattern of resource utilisation will in any way be optimal.

The assignment of priorities by a process to its offspring can also create problems. Unless some restrictions are imposed it is possible for a process to gain an unfair scheduling advantage by delegating its task to a subprocess to which it assigns a very high priority. One form of restriction which will overcome this problem is to insist that all priorities are assigned relative to that of the parent process, and that the range over which relative priorities may vary successively decreases at each level down the hierarchy. For example, suppose that in figure 8.5 the range of relative priorities at the top level is 0-99, and at the second level is 0-9, and so on. Then if the priority of process B is 20 no subprocess of B may have a priority outside the range 20±9. This implies that if the priority of process A is greater than 29 then B cannot gain any advantage over A by splitting itself up into subprocesses. If the priority of A is greater than 39 then all subprocesses of A will be guaranteed preference over subprocesses of B.

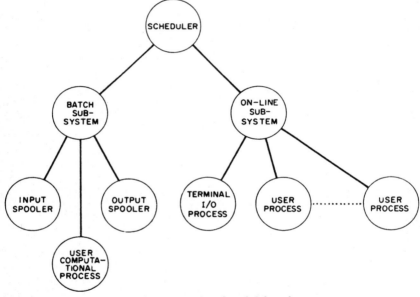

Figure 8.6 Example of multiple subsystems

In the situation shown in figure 8.6 the relative priorities assigned by the scheduler to the batch and on-line subsystems effectively determine the response of the system to the two classes of job. A large difference in priority between the subsystems will ensure that one class of user always gains preference over the other; a small difference will result in competition for the central processor(s) on more equal terms. The relative priority of processes within each subsystem is, as mentioned earlier, a matter for the subsystem concerned.

One of the earliest operating systems displaying a hierarchical process structure was that on the RC-4000 computer (Hansen, 1970). The nucleus of this system was referred to as the Monitor, and the head of the hierarchy, which corresponded to our scheduler, was called the Basic Operating·System. Up to 23 processes (the restriction was for reasons of space) could exist in the structure, and resources were passed from parents to offspring as described above. One difference between the RC-4000 system and the one we have outlined is that parents could not assign priorities to their children; all processes had equal priority except in so far as they were selected by the dispatcher on a round robin basis.

A limited hierarchy is also implemented by the IBM VM/370 operating system (VM stands for Virtual Machine). The structure is restricted to three levels: at the root is the VM/370 system itself, at the next level may occur any of a number of other standard IBM operating systems (acting as subsystems), and at the lowest level are the user tasks. The standard operating systems which run at the second level provide various virtual machines on the same configuration. The dispatcher works according to a two-level round robin discipline which can be modified by assigning relative priorities to each subsystem.

The implementation of a hierarchical process structure requires the provision of the system procedures

create process (*name, relative priority*)   *delete process* (*name*)
start process (*name*)   *stop process* (*name*)

The function of *create process* is to set up a process descriptor for the new process and link it into the process structure. *Start process* adds the process descriptor to the processor queue, that is, it marks the process as eligible to run. *Stop process* and *delete process* perform the inverse functions, and allow a parent to control its children. Children may of course terminate of their own accord, in which case the use of *stop process* is unnecessary. All four procedures manipulate process descriptors or the processor queue, and should therefore be implemented within the system nucleus. The procedures *request resource* and *release resource* described in section 8.4 are amended so as to invoke the parent process rather than the scheduler. The parent process is thus made responsible for allocation to its off-spring.

8.7 CONTROL AND ACCOUNTING

The previous sections have been concerned with the allocation of resources on a time scale which is comparable with job running times. We now turn our attention to longer term aspects of resource allocation, that is to such questions as charging for resource usage, estimating and influencing the pattern of demand, and ensuring that all users receive an appropriate proportion of the computing facilities available. These matters are usually described by the term *resource control*. Strictly speaking, resource control is the concern of the computer manager rather than the operating system designer, but unless the designer provides the appropriate tools the manager is impotent. In particular the designer must provide tools for measurement, since without measurement no control is possible.

The aims of resource control depend on the installation concerned. Broadly speaking installations are of two types; *service* and *in-house*. The purpose of a service installation, such as exists in a bureau, is to provide computing facilities for a number of paying users. No restrictions, other than the ability to pay, are placed upon users; indeed it is in the interests of management to sell as many facilities to as many users as possible. Resource control is thus reduced to *accounting*, that is, to recording the amount of each chargeable resource used and billing each user accordingly.

An in-house installation on the other hand is owned by a single company, university, or other institution, and provides facilities only to members of that institution. Because of constraints imposed on his budget the manager has the problem of dealing with a demand for service which nearly always exceeds the installation's capacity. Unlike a bureau no profit is gained from providing service, and so the option of increasing capacity to meet demand is not usually open. Thus the manager must ration the resources available according to the relative needs or importance of the various users. Resource control in this case provides a tool for discrimination between users. It must fulfil the dual function of accounting for resources and ensuring that no user exceeds his ration.

It should be clear that the control mechanisms required for service installations are a subset of those required for in-house installations. We shall therefore concentrate on the latter.

(1) Restriction of Access

Access to facilities which entail heavy resource usage can be denied to certain classes of user such as junior programmers or students. Again, users working in multi-access mode might be restricted to editing and small scale testing, while batch users are allowed free range of all facilities.

(2) Rationing

A rationing policy may be either long or short term, or a combination of both. Short term rationing applies a limit to the amount of resource, such as processor time or memory space, which can be used by a single job. In long term rationing a budget is given to each user indicating the amount of resources which he can use in a given period, for example, a week or a month. Attempts by a user to exceed his ration result in job abortion or refusal of access to the system.

Both methods of control can be implemented by maintaining an accounting file which contains the following information for each accredited user of the system.

(1)   The user identification. This is an 'account number' quoted by the user when he logs in or at the head of a job description. It serves to identify the user to the system.

(2)   A password known only to the user and to the system. This is presented by the user as proof of his identity. (Passwords are not normally required in batch systems, since their secrecy is difficult to maintain when punched on cards or similar medium.)

(3)   A 'permission vector' in which each bit represents the permission to use a certain facility. Permission is granted only if the appropriate bit is set.

(4)   The resource limits for a single job.

(5)   The budget for the current accounting period.

(6)   The resources still outstanding in the budget for the current period.

The details of how control is applied vary from system to system. In batch-oriented systems the outstanding resource balance is debited at the end of each job, and jobs are accepted by the scheduler only if the balance is positive. An alternative is to accept a job only if its stated resource requirements are less than the current balance; this prevents a user exceeding his ration by running a large job when his balance is almost zero. In a multi-access system the balance may be debited at regular intervals during a terminal session and the user forcibly logged off (after an appropriate warning) if the balance reaches zero.

Rationing may be applied to each resource separately or, more commonly, the usage of each resource may be compounded through some specified charging formula into some kind of global resource consumption units. In this case the relative weights given to each resource in the charging formula are chosen so as to reflect the resource's importance or scarcity value. An example of such a charging formula, taken from the Essex University DEC System-10 is

$$\text{number of units used} = (133.0P + 6.0C + 13.3K + 5.5W)$$

where

$$P = \text{central processor time in seconds}$$
$$C = \text{terminal connect time in seconds}$$
$$K = \text{memory occupancy, that is the integral over processor time of the number of 1024 word memory blocks used}$$
$$W = \text{number of disc transfers}$$

It is worth noting that the parameters in a charging formula can be altered in order to influence the way in which users work. For example, a dramatic increase in the charge for terminal connect time would encourage users to make greater use of batch facilities, while an increase in the memory occupancy charge might be an incentive to writing small jobs.

Another important feature of a rationing policy is that the total allocated amount of each resource should be related to the amount of the resource which the system can supply in the given time period. The amount allocated and the amount in supply need not be equal, since there is a good chance that most users will not consume their entire allocation; the degree of safe over-allocation can be gauged by experience. In the case of global charging formulae the allocation and supply are more difficult to match, for if all users decided to use their allocation in the form of the same resource then the system could not cope. In practice the existence of a large user population makes this eventuality unlikely.

More sophisticated rationing policies (for example, Hartley, 1970) may employ different charging rates at different times of the day. This encourages use of the machine at unpopular times and gives a more even distribution of the work load. Similarly, charges may vary according to the external priority a user has requested for his work.

The system designer's responsibility is to provide the tools for implementing policies such as just described. These tools include

(1)   routines for administering the accounting file
(2)   mechanisms for measuring resource usage
(3)   mechanisms for refusing facilities to users who have overdrawn their budgets

The measurement of resource usage is a function which is distributed throughout the system at the points where resources are allocated. It can be greatly facilitated by the provision of suitable hardware, such as a counter in the disc controller to record the number of transfers. A real-time clock is of course essential to accurate measurement. Measurements on an individual process can be stored as part of the process descriptor, and statistics on total system usage can be gathered in a central file. The latter figures can be regarded as an indicator of system performance and used as a basis of comparison and enhancement.

Consideration should perhaps also be given to the question of whether operating system overheads should be charged to the user. On the one hand it can be argued that the operating system is acting on behalf of the user, and that the user should therefore be charged. This would have the beneficial side effect of encouraging users to write programs in such a way as to minimise system overhead, by avoiding redundant file accesses for example. On the other hand the overheads will vary according to the current load, and it might be considered unfair to charge a user more simply because the machine is busy or because his job interacts unfavourably with some other job which happens to be present at the same time. It could also be argued that the ordinary user should not be expected to acquire the detailed knowledge of the operating system that would be needed for him to modify his work to reduce overheads. A possible compromise is to charge the user for all system activities, such as I/O handling, performed specifically on his behalf, but not to charge for activities such as process switching which are outside his control. However, even this leaves some areas subject to dispute; paging traffic for example is dependent both on the user, who can increase the locality of his memory references, and on the current pressure of demand for memory. Ultimately decisions in this field are necessarily arbitrary, and must be left to the individual designer.

8.8 SUMMARY

In this chapter we have seen how policies for resource allocation and scheduling can be implemented in a single process which we called the scheduler. We have described how the functions of the scheduler can be extended to other processes, thus establishing a hierarchical process structure. The nucleus of our paper operating system has been enlarged by the inclusion of procedures for creating and deleting processes. The mechanisms for allocating resources and for measuring resource usage are distributed thoughout the system at the levels appropriate to the resources concerned. The current state of our system is as shown in figure 8.7.

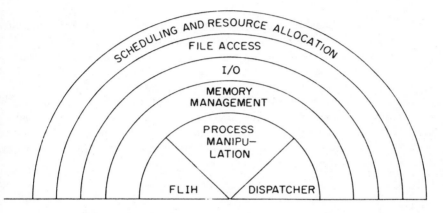

Figure 8.7 Current state of the paper operating system

The additional data structures are

(1)   a record of available resources
(2)   for each process a list of resources allocated to it, pointed to from the process descriptor
(3)   if deadlock detection is employed then a representation of the state graph
(4)   if deadlock avoidance is employed then a record of resource claims and allocations
(5)   a possible elaboration of the processor queue to include several levels
(6)   a possible modification of the process structure which turns it into a tree
(7)   an accounting file

9 *Protection*

We have already alluded several times to the fact that processes within a computing system must be protected from each other's activities. We have introduced mechanisms at various points in our paper operating system which ensure that the memory, files, and resources belonging to a process cannot be accessed by another process except in a controlled manner. The mechanisms have been **distributed** throughout the system in such places as the memory addressing hardware, file directories, and resource allocation procedures, and have functioned more or less independently of each other. In this chapter we take a closer look at the subject of protection as a whole and indicate how it is possible to implement protection mechanisms on a unified system-wide basis.

9.1 MOTIVATION

The motivation for protection mechanisms in a multi-user computing system may be summarised as follows.

(1) Protection from Faults

When several processes, possibly working for different users, are executing on the same machine it is clearly desirable that faults in any one of them should not be allowed to affect the running of the others. Few users would tolerate a system in which every process had to be guaranteed fault-free before they could be confident that their own work would be run without interference. Mechanisms must therefore be devised to erect 'fire walls' between the different processes in the system. Protection from faults applies not only to user processes but also to the operating system itself. If the operating system can be corrupted by faults in a user process then it is unlikely to perform well (or at all) for very long.

Protection is desirable even in the case of a single user with a private machine. In this situation protection can be an aid to debugging by limiting the propagation of errors and localising the original source. Even when programs are fully debugged protection can minimise the damage caused by hardware malfunction or operator error. These considerations apply even more forcefully in multi-user systems.

(2) Protection from Malice

At a time when computers are increasingly being used for storing and processing data bases, many of which contain confidential information, it is essential that the security of data can be guaranteed. The guarantee may be required for commercial reasons, as in the case of an installation which provides a service to users with divergent interests, or it may be required for reasons of privacy. For example, employees of government agencies such as the Health Service or the Inland Revenue must be prevented from accessing confidential personal records without authorisation. The safeguards required for data apply equally to programs. For example, a company which has invested a great deal of money in developing a program which it intends to sell or hire will not be happy if its customers or competitors are able to copy the program and install it elsewhere. Similarly, the Inland Revenue would be dismayed to find that one of its employees had modified a program so that he had paid no tax for the past five years.

An operating system itself is a collection of programs and data which must be protected from malice. It is not difficult to imagine a user modifying an unprotected system so that his jobs are always scheduled first, or so that he is never charged for the resources he uses.

If protection were simply a matter of isolating all processes from each other then adequate mechanisms could readily be devised. Unfortunately processes may well have legitimate grounds for wishing to share resources, access common data, or execute the same programs. A worthwhile protection system must therefore allow legitimate sharing while preventing unauthorised interference. It is the coexistence in a computing system of elements of both co-operation and competition which makes protection a problem.

9.2 DEVELOPMENT OF PROTECTION MECHANISMS

Protection in the elementary sense of totally excluding unauthorised users from the system can be achieved by requiring that a user presents some proof of his identity when he logs-in or submits a job. The user generally does this by quoting his account number, which is used in charging for the resources used, and a password known only to himself and the operating system. The account number and the password are checked against the system accounting file, as described in section 8.7. Provided the accounting file is inaccessible to users, and provided that each user keeps his password secret, then entry to the system can be made by authorised users only. Unfortunately this latter proviso is difficult to enforce in practice since users have a habit of disclosing their passwords, either inadvertently or through a misplaced sense of generosity. In batch systems in particular it is difficult to keep passwords secret since they have to be punched on cards or similar medium, and consequently many batch systems do not demand passwords at all. Even in multi-access systems where the users observe strict secrecy it has been proved that a determined intruder, through a process of inspired trial and error, can eventually discover a valid password and penetrate the system. We shall not discuss this topic any further here, but shall concentrate for the rest of this chapter on the protection measures that can be applied once users have gained some form of access (legitimate or otherwise) to the system.

A rudimentary form of protection can be achieved by including in the hardware of the host machine a *mode switch* and a pair of *base and limit registers*. The mode switch governs the ability to execute privileged instructions as described in section 4.1, and the base and limit registers demarcate the area of memory accessible to a process when in user mode (see section 5.3). Information which is resident in main memory is protected by the base and limit registers, whose values can be altered only when the processor is in supervisor mode; information on backing store is protected by virtue of the fact that I/O instructions are privileged and thus all data transfers can occur only via the operating system. Validation of the transfers can be achieved by using information held in the file directories when the files are opened and closed, as described in chapter 7.

This form of protection is found in most computers of the mid 1960s (for example the ICL 1900 series). It is unsatisfactory in that it is an 'all or nothing' solution to the protection problem: a process either has no privileges (executing in user mode) or all privileges (executing in supervisor mode). Thus, for example, processes executing any system procedures have the same absolute privileges, irrespective of whether they need them. Furthermore, sharing of data or programs between processes is possible only by making their memory spaces overlap, in which case the processes are completely unprotected from each other.

A more flexible protection scheme can be implemented if the host machine is equipped with segmentation hardware (see section 5.3). In this case the address space of each process is divided into logical segments, and each segment can be given a particular degree of protection (such as execute only or read only) by incorporating a protection indicator into its descriptor. The situation is illustrated in figure 5.5. The memory addressing hardware checks all accesses to the segment to ensure that the protection specified in the descriptor is not violated.

Since each process references its segments through its own set of segment descriptors (held in its segment table) it is possible for two processes to reference the same physical segment through descriptors which have different protection indicators. This allows segments to be shared between processes with different access rights. Figure 9.1 shows an example in which a process A reads information which is deposited in a buffer by process B. The buffer appears as a segment in the address spaces of both A and B; its descriptor in process A specifies read only access while its descriptor in process B allows write access. Both descriptors point to the same location in memory.

Although this scheme is an improvement on the previous one it still does not provide us with adequate protection. The reason is that the access rights which a process has for a segment remain unchanged throughout the process's lifetime. This means that whatever program or procedure the process is executing it maintains constant privileges over all its segments. (An exception to this is when the process enters supervisor mode, when it assumes absolute privileges over all segments.) A preferable arrangement, not provided for by the scheme above, is that a process should at all times possess only those privileges which it needs for the activity it is currently engaged in. This philosophy of 'minimum necessary privilege' is essential to the aim of limiting the effects of erroneous or malicious processes.

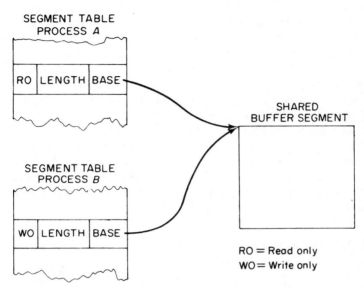

Figure 9.1 Segment sharing with different access privileges

As an example consider again processes *A* and *B* of figure 9.1. If use of the buffer is extended to include two-way communication between the processes then both *A* and *B* require write access to it. This means that each process has the ability to write to the buffer even at those times when it is supposed to be reading, and thus the information in the buffer cannot be guaranteed against malfunction in either process. What is required is that the access privileges of *A* and *B* for the buffer should be dependent on whether they are currently engaged in sending or receiving information. Thus when either process is executing a procedure for sending information it should have write access to the buffer, but when it is executing a procedure for receiving information the access should be read only.

As a result of this discussion we introduce the idea of a *domain* of protection (other terms are *sphere*, *context* and *regime*) in which a process executes. Each domain defines a set of privileges or *capabilities* which can be exercised by a process executing in it. A change of capabilities can be achieved only by a transition from one domain to another; we naturally insist that such transitions are strictly controlled.

Primitive examples of domains are the supervisor and user modes of execution mentioned earlier. When a process executes in supervisor mode its capabilities include the right to execute privileged instructions and to reference the whole memory; when it is in user mode its capabilities are restricted to the use of non-privileged instructions and to accessing only its own memory space. For reasons discussed earlier this two-domain system is inadequate for our purposes: what we have in mind is a more complex arrangement in which a number of domains define a large variety of capabilities and in which a process runs in the domain which contains just those capabilities which allow it to transact its legitimate business. We shall examine in the following sections how such an arrangement can be implemented.

It is worth noting at this point that capabilities for all objects which require protection can be expressed in terms of capabilities for memory segments. Access to a system data structure can, for example, be expressed in terms of access to the segment containing it while permission to operate a peripheral device depends on access to the segment containing the device descriptor. (Some computers, such as the PDP-11 and many microprocessors, incorporate device addresses within the overall address space; in these computers access to devices can be controlled in exactly the same way as access to memory.) This observation leads to a significant simplification of protection schemes since it allows all protection to be performed by means of segment capabilities, which in turn can be implemented as part of the memory addressing mechanisms. This approach is followed in the schemes described below.

9.3 A HIERARCHICAL PROTECTION SYSTEM

In this section we describe the protection scheme implemented in MULTICS (Graham, 1968; Schroeder and Saltzer, 1972). MULTICS was one of the earliest systems to treat protection in a generalised way and has inspired several similar systems such as VME on the ICL 2900 and NOS/VE on the CYBER 180. Our description is somewhat simplified, but will serve to illustrate the ideas behind a hierarchically organised protection scheme.

Domains in MULTICS are called *rings*, and are ordered so that each ring contains a subset of the capabilities of the one inside it. Conceptually the arrangement can be viewed as shown in figure 9.2, where the progression from the outermost (high numbered) rings to the innermost (low numbered) rings bestows successively greater privileges. The reader will see that this is a refinement of the supervisor/user mode system of protection, which can in fact be considered as a two-ring system.

A ring in MULTICS is a collection of segments, and for the moment we shall consider that each segment is assigned to one and only one ring. Procedures which require a large number of privileges reside in segments in inner rings, while procedures needing less privileges, or which cannot be trusted to be error-free, are contained in segments in outer rings.

In order to identify the ring to which a segment belongs its segment descriptor is extended to include a field holding the ring number. The program counter is similarly extended to identify the ring in which the current process is executing (that is, the ring number of the segment from which it is executing instructions). The protection indicator in the segment descriptor includes flags which denote whether the segment can be written, read, or executed (see figure 9.3). A process executing in ring i has no access whatever to segments in ring j, where $j < i$; its access to segments in ring k, where $k \geq i$, is governed by the access indicators of the segments concerned. In other words access to inner rings is prohibited, while access to outer rings is subject to the access indicators. An attempt by a process to cross a ring boundary by calling a procedure in a different ring results in the generation of an error trap. The trap causes entry to a special trap handler which performs certain checks on the transfer of control. These checks will be described in a moment.

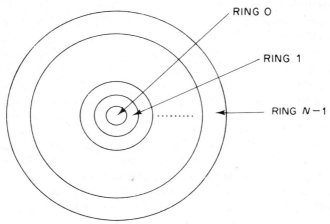

Figure 9.2 Rings of protection

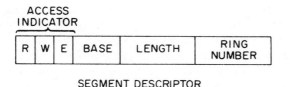

SEGMENT DESCRIPTOR

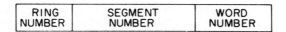

PROGRAM COUNTER

Figure 9.3 MULTICS segment descriptor and program counter

The mechanism described above is adequate for the provision of hierarchical protection. However, the fact that a segment is assigned to only one ring leads to inefficiencies arising from the large number of procedure calls across ring boundaries. A more flexible arrangement, adopted in MULTICS, is to allocate each segment to a set of consecutive rings known as its *access bracket*. The ring field of the segment descriptor then contains two integers $n1$ and $n2$ which specify the lowest and highest rings of the access bracket. A call by a process executing in ring i to a procedure in a segment with access bracket $(n1,n2)$ does not now cause a trap so long as $n1 \leqslant i \leqslant n2$, and in this case control remains in ring i.

If $i > n2$ or $i < n1$ a trap is generated, and the corresponding trap handler must decide whether the call is to be allowed. (The trap handler may be a procedure in ring 0 or, as in MULTICS, it may be largely integrated into the memory addressing hardware.) The case $i < n1$ represents an outward call, that is, a transfer of control to a ring with lesser privileges, and can therefore always be allowed. However, the parameters of the call may refer to segments which are inaccessible to the called procedure because of its inferior status. In this case the parameters must be copied into a data area accessible to the called procedure.

A call in the reverse direction $(i > n2)$ is more difficult to handle. Since the call represents a transfer of control to a ring with higher privileges care must be taken that the caller cannot in any way cause the called procedure to malfunction. A first step in this direction is to allow calls only from rings which are not too far distant from the access bracket of the called procedure. An integer $n3$ $(n3 > n2)$ held in each segment descriptor is used to define the limit of the segment's *call bracket*; a call from ring i, where $i > n3$, is not permitted. Further, each segment possesses a list (which may be empty) of the entry points, or *gates*, at which it may be called. The trap handler checks that all inward procedure calls are directed to one of these gates, and generates an error if not. The trap handler also records on a stack the return point and ring number corresponding to the call. Returns across rings are validated against the top of the stack to ensure that a procedure cannot be tricked into returning to a ring lower than that prevailing before the call. The parameters of an inward call also require validation in case they refer to segments which should be protected against the caller.

The disadvantage of hierarchical protection systems such as the one outlined above is that if an object must be accessible in domain A which is not accessible in domain B then A must be higher up the hierarchy than B. This implies that everything accessible in B must necessarily be accessible in A. This can be regarded as falling a long way short of the goal of giving a process the minimum necessary privileges at all times. However, the various layers of protection do to some extent mirror the layers of construction of an operating system, and therefore form a naturally attractive way of reinforcing operating system structure. The designers of the MULTICS system claim that the hierarchical structure does not in practice impose embarrassing constraints, and that satisfactory protection can be provided. In the next section we shall examine an alternative which does not depend on a hierarchical organisation.

9.4 GENERAL SYSTEMS

In the hierarchical protection scheme described above the capabilities which can be exercised by a process are implicit in the number of the ring in which it is executing. Furthermore, transfers of control from one ring to another imply either an extension or a reduction of the capabilities currently available. In a non-hierarchical system, on the other hand, transfers in control between domains are accompanied by quite arbitrary changes in a process's capabilities. The set of capabilities belonging to a process in a particular domain is known as its *capability list*: a change of domain implies a change of capability list. In a hierarchical system the new capability list is always either an extension or subset of the old, while in a non-hierarchical system there is no obvious relationship.

An abstract model for a general protection system (Graham and Denning, 1972) is an *access matrix* (figure 9.4) which denotes the capabilities of various *subjects* for all system *objects* which need protection. A subject is a pair (*process, domain*), so each row in the matrix represents the capability list of a particular process executing in a particular domain. When a process changes domain it becomes a different subject and its capability list is represented by a different row of the access matrix. In general subjects require protection from each other, and so subjects are also regarded as objects.

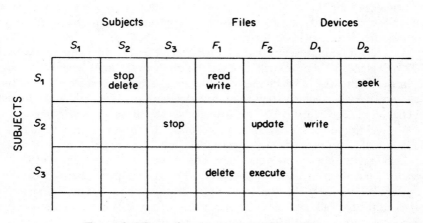

Figure 9.4 Part of an access control matrix

Associated with each object is a *controller* which is entered whenever the object is accessed. Depending on the type of object concerned the controller could be implemented in hardware or software: typical examples might be

Type of object	Controller
file	filing system
segment	memory addressing hardware
peripheral	device handler

The controller is responsible for ensuring that a subject possesses the appropriate capability for the type of access requested. A particular protection scheme is characterised by the choice of subjects and objects, by the capabilities denoted by the elements of the access matrix, and by the way in which capabilities can be modified or transferred.

The model includes all the elements of a general protection system, but an efficient implementation for a wide range of object types is difficult to envisage. However, if, as suggested in section 9.2, the range of objects is restricted to memory segments and if a process may change domain only when entering a new segment then implementation can be achieved in terms of the memory addressing hardware. Two approaches to such implementation are described below.

The first approach (Evans and Leclerc, 1967) is to regard a capability, which takes the form (*access indicator, segment base, segment length*), as equivalent to a segment descriptor, and to identify the capability list of a process with its segment table. A change of domain by a process implies a change of segment table. A consequence of this approach is the destruction of the notion of a process-wide address space, since a process will change address space according to the domain in which it is executing. Some difficulties are also encountered in parameter passing: for example, a recursive procedure requires a separate segment table for each level of call, the successive tables giving access to the parameters appropriate to each level.

An alternative approach is that adopted in the Plessey 250 computer (Williams, 1972; England, 1974). We shall describe this implementation in some detail since it illustrates the way in which memory addressing schemes based on capabilities can be expected to some extent to replace the more traditional schemes discussed in chapter 5. (See Fabry, 1974, for strong advocacy of such a development.)

A capability in the Plessey 250 consists of the access indicator, base address and limit address of a particular segment. The capabilities of the current process are held in a set of program accessible processor registers known as *capability registers*, and program addresses are specified by giving the number of a capability register and an offset. The desired memory location is obtained by adding the offset to the base address held in the capability register. The limit address and access indicator are used to check memory and access violations.

The reader might wonder at this point whether the set of capability registers is not conceptually the same thing, apart from differences of speed, as the traditional segment table. The distinction is that the allocation of capability registers is under local program control and the programmer, or compiler, is free to reallocate the registers as he sees fit. By contrast, segment table entries are allocated by an operating system on a global basis, and once allocated they remain fixed.

Since it is economically feasible to provide only a small number of registers, the capabilities of a process are also stored in a capability segment in memory and loaded into the capability registers as required. Thus the capability segment currently accessible to a process represents its capability list and defines its domain of execution. Access privileges 'read capability' and 'write capability', which are distinct from the normal 'read' and 'write' and which apply only to the capability segment, are used to prevent ordinary data items being treated as capabilities. This prevents capabilities being manufactured in data segments and then loaded into capability registers. By convention capability register C(6) is used to address the capability segment of the current process, and register C(7) is used to address the segment containing the code being executed.

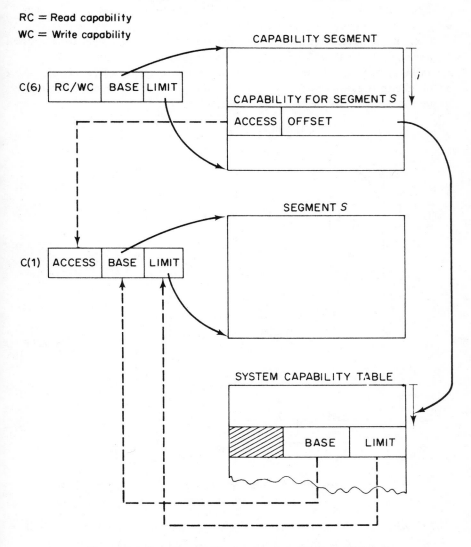

Figure 9.5 'Load capability' operation (C(1): = C(6) + i)

A further refinement is necessary in order to facilitate the sharing of segments among processes. In the scheme as described the relocation in memory of a shared segment would involve a change to the corresponding capabilities in the capability segments of all the processes concerned. To avoid this the base and limit addresses of all segments in memory are contained in a *system capability table*, and all stored capabilities refer to segments individually through this table. Relocation of a segment thus involves an alteration only to the system capability table and not to the entries in the individual capability segments. Figure 9.5 illustrates the process of loading capability register $C(1)$ with a capability for segment S which is contained in the ith entry of the capability segment.

It should be noted that the system capability table is itself a segment, addressed by a special capability register, and is accessible only to certain parts of the operating system which are concerned with memory management. It is invisible to all other processes, which can regard the capabilities in the capability segments as pointing directly to the segments concerned.

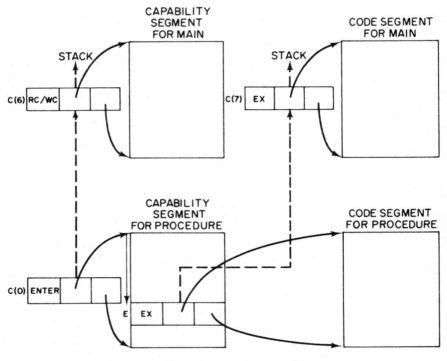

Figure 9.6 Changing the domain of execution
(CALL C(0) + i)

A process may change domain (that is, change its capability segment) only if it possesses a special 'enter' capability for the capability segment of the new domain. Figure 9.6 illustrates the way in which a process executing a program MAIN calls a procedure SUB in a different domain. Initially $C(6)$ addresses the capability segment for MAIN and $C(7)$ holds an 'execute' capability for the segment containing the program code of MAIN. The process possesses in $C(0)$ an 'enter' capability for the capability segment of SUB, which in turn contains in its ith location an 'execute' capability E for the code segment of SUB. A procedure call specifying C(0) and offset *i* results in C(6) being replaced by the 'enter' capability in C(0), and C(7) by the 'execute' capability E. Thus C(6) and C(7) now point to the appropriate capability and code segments in the new domain. A 'read capability' privilege is added to C(6) to enable the called procedure to read its own capabilities, and the previous values of C(6) and C(7) are placed on a stack for retrieval on the subsequent return. Neither the caller nor the called procedure have access to each other's capabilities, except for those capabilities which may be passed as parameters in registers C(1) to C(5). The scheme therefore affords complete protection between mutually suspicious procedures.

9.5 CONCLUSION

We have seen in this chapter that the need for protection is a natural consequence of a multi-user environment. With the advent of large scale data bases and a growing concern over privacy, security and reliability, this need is likely to become more pressing. Although protection has traditionally been provided, to a greater or lesser extent, by a variety of mechanisms at various points in the system it is now becoming possible to take an integrated approach. Given suitable hardware we would wish to include in our paper operating system a protection scheme similar to one of those described above.

10 *Reliability*

In section 2.3 we stated that one of the desirable features of an operating system is reliability; indeed, an unreliable system is of very little use. In this chapter we examine more closely what is meant by reliability, and discuss ways in which the reliability of an operating system can be increased. We shall see that reliability is not an 'add-on extra', but a requirement which must be considered from the earliest stages of system design.

10.1 OBJECTIVES AND TERMINOLOGY

It will be apparent from the preceding chapters that an operating system is a complex piece of software which is expected to perform a variety of functions for a diverse set of users. It is important to the users that these functions are performed correctly, and one of the principal objectives of the system designer is to ensure that this is the case. The task of the designer is made more difficult in that the finished product will not be operating in a perfect world: it is likely to be subjected to a large variety of circumstances which could adversely affect its functioning. Such circumstances include malfunction of the hardware of the host computer, errors in procedure by the computer operators, and illegal or meaningless requests supplied by the user. An operating system should continue providing service, possibly of a degraded nature, even in the face of such adverse circumstances.

These remarks lead us to define the *reliability* of an operating system as the degree to which it meets its specifications in respect of service to its users, even when subjected to unexpected and hostile conditions. This definition emphasises that reliability is a relative rather than an absolute concept: no system can be totally reliable since, to take an extreme example, it would be impossible to provide service in the face of the simultaneous failure of all hardware components of the computer. A highly reliable operating system will continue to meet its specifications even under great pressure from hardware malfunction or user error, a less reliable system may depart from its specifications when subjected only to a single meaningless request.

The level of reliability which should be achieved by an operating system depends, of course, on the reliance its users place on it. Heavy reliance, as in a system which controls a space capsule or monitors the condition of hospital patients, demands high reliability; lesser reliance, as in a system for document preparation and retrieval, requires less reliability. Since (as we shall see later) high reliability often incurs high costs, the system designer should aim at a level of reliability which is commensurate with the reliance of the users. (It is interesting to note, however, that the reliance of users may be influenced by the reliability of the system.)

The concept of reliability should not be confused with that of *correctness*: the notions are related but distinct. An operating system is *correct* if when running in a a specified environment it exhibits a specified (desired) behaviour. Correctness is certainly a desirable attribute of an operating system, but it is an insufficient condition for reliability. This is because demonstrations of correctness, whether by testing or formal proof, rely on assumptions about the environment which are generally invalid. Such assumptions typically concern the nature of inputs and the correct functioning of hardware, and may be quite unjustified in practice. Putting it another way, the environment in which a system operates rarely matches that which is assumed in the demonstration of correctness.

Correctness is not only an insufficient condition for reliability, but, perhaps more surprisingly, it is also an unnecessary one. Parts of an operating system may be incorrect in that the algorithms governing particular processes may not produce the required effect, but the system can still operate reliably. As an example, consider a filing system in which the *close* routine in some circumstances omits to record the length of a file in the corresponding directory entry. Provided that the file terminates with a recognisable 'end of file' mark, the I/O routines can still read the file successfully, and the system will perform reliably even in the face of the incorrect operation of one of its components. This example illustrates the use of redundant, or superfluous, information to conceal and recover from errors, a technique to which we shall return later.

The reader should not assume from this that correctness is unimportant. It may be neither a necessary nor a sufficient condition for reliability, but it certainly helps. An operating system which is correct is likely to be more reliable than one which is not. It would be bad practice indeed for a designer to depend on reliability mechanisms to conceal the effects of known deficiencies, or even to justify lack of effort towards achieving correctness. The proper course is to attempt to produce a system which is correct with respect to specified assumptions about the environment, and at the same time to design reliability mechanisms to cater for those occasions on which the assumptions are invalid. We shall examine these complementary approaches in later sections.

At this point we introduce three more items of terminology. We define an *error* to be a deviation of the system from its specified behaviour. Thus an error is an event; examples are the allocation of an unsharable resource to two processes, or the deletion of the directory entry for a file which is still being used. An error may be caused by a hardware malfunction, by the unanticipated action of a user or operator, or by a deficiency ('bug') in one of the programs within the system. In all cases we use the term *fault* to mean the cause of an error. When an error occurs it is probable that some items of information within the system are corrupted. We refer to such corruption as the *damage* caused by the error; damage can of course result in faults which lead to further errors. We shall see that one of the means of achieving high reliability is to limit the damage that can be caused by an error, and hence limit the propagation of errors throughout the system.

From the foregoing discussion we can see that efforts toward producing a highly reliable operating system should be concentrated on the following areas:

(a) *fault avoidance*: elimination of faults in the design and implementation stages; that is, production of a correct system.

(b) *error detection*: detection of errors as soon as possible in order to reduce the damage caused.

(c) *fault treatment*: identification and elimination of any fault which produces an error.

(d) *error recovery*: assessment and repair of the damage resulting from an error.

In the following sections we shall deal with each of these in turn.

10.2 FAULT AVOIDANCE

As we have seen, faults in a computer system may stem from the hardware, from operator or user incompetence and ignorance, or from 'bugs' in the software. Ways of avoiding each of these types of fault are discussed below.

(1) Operator and User Faults

We shall say little about operator and user generated faults other than that they can never be eliminated: all that can be hoped for is a reduction in their number by means of appropriate training and user education programmes.

(2) Hardware Faults

The most obvious way of reducing the incidence of hardware faults is to use the most reliable components which can be obtained within the overall cost constraints. Hardware designers use several methods of enhancing reliability, ranging from the obvious – using individually reliable components – to more complex techniques which incorporate some form of error detection and recovery within each subsystem. Error detection is usually based on the recording or transmission of redundant information, such as parity bits and checksums; recovery is often attempted by repeating the operation which gave rise to the error. Examples of this technique are magnetic tape and disc drives which are designed to repeat operations a limited number of times if either parity or checksum errors occur. Retrying operations is of course useful only for transient faults (that is, faults which are due to temporary conditions such as interference or dust particles); permanent faults will still result in errors.

Another technique which is often used in data transmission is the use of error detecting and correcting codes, in which redundant information transmitted with the data provides a means of recovery from certain transmission errors. Yet another technique is that of *majority polling*, in which several (usually three) identical components are supplied with the same inputs and their outputs are compared. If the outputs differ the majority verdict is taken to be correct, and the component producing the minority verdict is noted as being suspect. A component which is repeatedly in the minority is assumed to be faulty and can be replaced. Majority polling is an expensive reliability technique since it relies on replication of components and it is normally used only when really high reliability is essential.

The aim of all the techniques discussed is to *mask* the hardware faults from the software which runs on it. That is, faults may be present in the hardware but their effects are concealed from the software, so that as far as the software is concerned the hardware appears fault free. We shall see in section 10.6 that the notion of masking can be extended into the operating system itself, so that errors which occur in one level of the system are hidden from the levels outside it.

(3) Software Faults

There are several complementary approaches to reducing the incidence of software faults. We discuss three of the principal ones below.

The first approach is to adopt management practices, programming methodologies and software tools which are a positive aid towards producing a fault free product. In the mid 1960s it was believed in some quarters that the larger the piece of software to be produced the more programmers should be assigned to it. IBM's experience with huge armies of programmers on OS/360 exploded this myth, and it is now realised that indiscriminate application of manpower is likely to create more problems than it solves. The grouping of programmers into small teams, popularly known as 'chief programmer teams', is now considered a better way of organising software production. Each team is responsible for a module of software which has precisely defined external specifications and interfaces, and within the team each member has a well defined function, such as coding, documentation, or liaison with other teams. Detailed consideration of such organisational practices is beyond our present scope: a revealing and entertaining account of various pitfalls is given by Brooks (1975).

The way in which programmers actually go about writing programs can have considerable influence on the quality of the finished product, in terms of coherence, comprehensibility and freedom from faults. Several programming methodologies have been advocated during the last few years, the most widely known being *structured programming* (Dahl *et al.*, 1972; Wirth, 1971) and its various derivatives (for example, Yourdon, 1975; Jackson, 1975). Structured programming has been sufficiently publicised elsewhere for us not to go into detail here: the reader who wishes to know more is referred to the accounts above, or to Alagic and Arbib (1978).

The software tools which are of most help in creating a fault free product are probably an editor, a macro-assembler, and a compiler for a suitable high-level language. We have already remarked in section 4.2 that the only parts of an operating system which need to be written in assembly language are those which are intimately bound up with the host hardware, namely parts of the nucleus and the I/O device handlers. The use of a high-level language for the rest of the system speeds up the production of useful code and facilitates the elimination of faults. It is sometimes said that high-level languages are unsuitable for writing operating systems since the object code produced is less efficient in execution than the corresponding hand-written code. There are at least three counters to this view: first, that a good optimising compiler can often produce better code than a good assembly language programmer; second, that areas of residual inefficiency can if necessary be optimised by hand; and third, that reliability is at least as important a goal as efficiency.

The second general approach to reducing the incidence of software faults is to attempt to prove, by more or less formal means, that all programs in the operating system, and all their interactions, are correct. This is a formidable task, which for large systems is beyond the current state of the art. However, pioneering work by Floyd (1967), Hoare (1972), and Dijkstra (1976) has opened up the possibility of such proofs being possible in the not too distant future. Even now, a great deal of confidence in the correctness of a system can be inspired by proofs of correctness of some of its component programs.

The most popular approach to proving program correctness (Alagic and Arib, 1978; Hantler and King, 1976) is to formulate assertions (usually expressed in predicate calculus) which are to be true at various stages of program execution. The proof then proceeds inductively from the assumption of the initial assertion to verification that execution of the program statements does indeed make the subsequent assertions true. The chief difficulties encountered are the formulation of appropriate assertions, and the rather laborious step by step proof of their truth.

The third approach to eliminating software faults is by means of systematic testing. Testing has always been a prime method of detecting faults, but there is surprisingly little agreement on an appropriate methodology. Ideally, one would like to test a program on all possible inputs, but this is clearly impractical; all one can hope for is that the test data chosen will reveal all remaining faults. There is no general way of selecting test data to do this, though several pragmatic guidelines have been proposed. One such guideline is to select data which will exercise all possible paths through a program. Another is to select data which lie at the extremes of the allowable ranges: for example, zero is an obvious choice in any situation where the inputs can range over the positive integers.

The difficulty of testing is compounded when a large number of programs are to be executed by several interacting processes, as is the case in an operating system. Not only must each program be tested, but so must the interfaces between different programs and processes. The only hope of doing this at all successfully is to keep the interfaces as simple as possible.

We can summarise this discussion by saying that none of the approaches outlined above — programming methodology, formal correctness proofs, and testing — can be relied on to yield a fault free product. The techniques are still evolving, but it is fair to say that a combination of the three approaches can even now substantially raise one's confidence in the correctness of the software produced.

10.3 ERROR DETECTION

The key to error detection is *redundancy* — that is, the provision of 'superfluous' information which can be used to check the validity of the 'main' information contained within the system. The term 'redundancy' reflects the fact that the information used for checking is redundant as far as the main algorithms of the system are concerned. We have already seen in the last section how redundant information such as party bits and checksums can be used for error detection in the hardware sphere. Coding is also a useful means of error detection, and in some cases can be used for recovery as well. As mentioned before, errors detected by the hardware may be masked by the hardware itself, or they may be reported to the operating system by means of traps into the first level interrupt handler (section 4.4). Examples of the latter type of error are arithmetic overflow, memory violation, and protection violation. The actions which can be taken by the operating system in such cases will be described later in this chapter.

Error detection may also be undertaken by the operating system itself. A common form of checking is for processes to check the consistency of the data structures they use. An example of this might be for the processor queue to be held as a doubly linked list and for the scheduler to trace the links both forwards and backwards wherever it accesses the queue. The redundant information provided in this case is the set of backward links: only the forward ones are required for the main scheduling and dispatching algorithms. Another example is the checking of table modifications by maintaining in the table a checksum of all its entries. When an entry is modified the effect on the checksum can be predicted by calculation. If the checksum after modification does not correspond to that predicted then an error has occurred during modification.

A generalisation of this form of checking (Randell, 1975) is to associate with each major action of a process an *acceptance test* which can be used as a criterion of whether the action has been properly performed. The acceptance test is a Boolean expression which is evaluated (as part of the process execution) after the action is completed. If the result is 'true' the action is considered to have been performed correctly; if it is 'false' an error has occurred. The acceptance test can be as stringent as deemed necessary; it will be formulated to check for those errors which the designer feels are most probable. As an example consider the action of the scheduler in periodically modifying process priorities and re-ordering the processor queue. The acceptance test for this operation may be simply that the process descriptors in the re-ordered queue are indeed in priority order. A more stringent acceptance test contains the additional constraint that the number of descriptors in the queue is the same as before, thus guarding against the inadvertent detachment or duplication of a descriptor. There is of course usually a trade-off between the stringency of an acceptance test and the overhead of performing it, a trade-off which applies to all error detection mechanisms. The designer must weigh the costs, in capital equipment or performance degradation, against the benefits accruing. Unfortunately, it is often the case that neither costs nor benefits can be accurately measured.

So far we have dealt only with errors which occur within a single hardware or software component. Errors which occur at the interfaces between components are more difficult to detect, but some advantage can be gained from checking the credibility of any information passed across an interface. For example, some procedure parameters can be checked to see that they fall within an appropriate range, and it may be possible to check that messages passed between processes conform to some established protocol.

We conclude this section by noting that early detection of an error is the best way of limiting the damage which may be caused, and of limiting the wasted processing which may result. The capability of an operating system to react to errors soon after they occur can be greatly enhanced by the provision of suitable hardware protection mechanisms. Thus the protection mechanisms discussed in chapter 9 can make an important contribution not only to the security of an operating system but also to its reliability. (See Denning, 1976 for greater elaboration of this point.)

10.4 FAULT TREATMENT

Treatment of a fault first involves its location, and then its repair. As any systems programmer will testify, detection of an error and location of the corresponding fault are not at all the same thing. An error may have several possible causes, located in either the hardware or the software, and none of them may be apparent. One of the main aids to fault identification is the detection of errors before their cause is obscured by consequent damage and further errors. Thus the early detection of errors, as indicated at the end of section 10.3, is of prime importance.

In some cases it may be possible to take the easy option of ignoring the fault altogether, but this involves assumptions about the frequency of the errors it can cause and the extent of their damage. For example, it may not be considered worthwhile to attempt to locate a transient hardware fault until the frequency of errors it causes crosses some threshold of unacceptability (Avizienis, 1977). Usually, however, it is important that a fault be located and dealt with. The search for a fault will generally be directed by the investigator's understanding of the system structure. If this is incomplete, or if the fault has affected the structure, then the investigator's task is difficult indeed.

One way of helping the investigator is for the system to produce a trace, or log, of its recent activity. Events recorded in the log might be process activations, procedure entries, I/O transfers, and so on. Unfortunately the amount and detail of information recorded must be very large if the log is to be of practical value, and the overhead of recording it can be very high. Some advantage can perhaps be gained from making the trace optional, so that it need be switched on only when there is reason to believe that the system is malfunctioning. It is also worth while making the trace selective, so that only those parts of the system which are suspect need log their activities. This of course requires a subjective judgement, itself prone to error, of which are the suspect parts.

Once a fault has been located its treatment involves some form of repair. In the case of hardware faults repair usually comprises the replacement of a faulty component. This may be done manually or automatically, depending on the ability of the hardware to locate its own faults and 'switch out' a faulty component. Manual replacement may involve taking the entire system out of service for a time, or, preferably, it may proceed in parallel with continued service, possibly at a degraded level. Repair of a disc drive, for example, should not interrupt normal service if other drives are available, but replacement of a printed circuit board in the central processor of a single CPU system will probably require a complete shutdown and restart.

Faults in software components arise from deficiencies in design and implementation, or from corruption caused by previous errors. (Unlike hardware, software does not suffer from faults due to ageing.) Removal of a design or implementation fault usually involves the replacement of a (hopefully small) number of lines of program, while a corrupted program can be replaced by a backup copy held elsewhere. The repair of corrupted data is a topic we shall leave to the next section, which deals with error recovery generally. As with hardware, one would hope that software components can be replaced without the need to close down the entire system, and the system should be designed with this in mind.

10.5 ERROR RECOVERY

Recovery from an error involves assessment of the damage which has been caused, followed by an attempt to repair it. Damage assessment may be based entirely on *a priori* reasoning by the investigator, or it may involve the system itself in performing a number of checks to determine what damage has occurred. In either case, assessment (like fault identification) will be guided by assumed causal relationships defined by the system structure. An error in updating a file directory can, for example, be expected to damage the filing system but not the process structure or the device descriptors. There is of course a danger that the system structure, and hence any assumed relationship, will itself be damaged, but the probability of this happening is greatly reduced if appropriate hardware protection mechanisms are employed (as suggested in section 10.3).

The usual approach to repairing damage is to back up the affected processes to a state which existed before the error occurred. This approach relies on the provision of *recovery points* (or *checkpoints*) at which sufficient information is recorded about the state of a process to allow it to be reinstated later if necessary. The information required is at least the volatile environment and a copy of the process descriptor; it may also include a copy of the content of the memory space used by the process. The interval between recovery points determines the amount of processing which is likely to be lost when an error occurs. The loss of information after an error can be reduced by *audit-trail* techniques, in which all modifications to the process state are logged as they occur. Error recovery then consists of backing up to the last recovery point and then making the state changes indicated by the audit log. Audit-trail techniques are analogous to the incremental dump of a file system, described in section 7.5; in fact the incremental dump can be viewed as a particular audit-trail mechanism.

Recovery points and audit-trails imply the recording of all state information and all modifications to it. An interesting alternative (Randell, 1975) is the *recovery block* scheme, in which the only state information recorded is that which is actually modified. Since the scheme also includes elements of error detection and fault treatment we feel it is worthy of brief description.

A recovery block is a section of program with the following structure

       ensure   *acceptance test* **by**
                          primary alternate
       elseby
                          secondary alternate
       elseby
                          other alternate
       elseby   .
          .   .
          .   .
          .

The primary alternate is the program fragment which is normally executed; the other alternates are used only if the primary alternate fails. Success or failure of an alternate is determined by execution of the acceptance test (see section 10.3) associated with the block. Thus execution of the recovery block first involves execution of the primary alternate, followed by execution of the acceptance test. If the test passes, which is the normal case, the entire block is deemed to have been executed successfully. If the test fails, the process state is restored to that which existed before the primary alternate was executed, and the secondary alternate is then executed. The acceptance test is again used to determine success or failure, and further alternates are invoked as necessary. If all alternates fail then the block as a whole is said to fail, and recovery has to be made by invoking an alternate block if there is one (recovery blocks may be nested to any depth), or by restarting the process if not.

The alternates within a recovery block can be viewed as software spares which are automatically utilised whenever the primary alternate fails. Unlike hardware spares the alternates are not of identical design, and usually employ different algorithms. The primary alternate employs the most efficient or otherwise desirable algorithm for fulfilling the function of the block; the other alternates employ less efficient algorithms, or algorithms which fulfil the desired function in only a partial, but still tolerable, fashion. Failure of an alternate is regarded as an exceptional occurrence (akin to an error due to a transient hardware fault), and the alternate is replaced only for the current execution of the block. It is wise, however, to log all failures, so that residual design and programming faults can be recognised and eliminated.

The recovery block scheme relies for its operation on the ability to restore a process state whenever an acceptance test fails. The ease of doing this depends on whether or not the process concerned has interacted with other processes during execution of the block. If it has not, restoration of its state reduces to restoring the prior values of all program variables and registers which have been changed. This can be effected by means of a 'recovery cache' (Horning *et al.*, 1974), a portion of memory in which values are stored before being modified. Only those values which are modified need be stored in the cache, and values which are modified several times need be stored only once. Failure of an alternate causes the restoration of values from the cache before the next alternate is tried; success of an alternate leads to the deletion of values from the cache, since the modifications can now be regarded as valid. The nesting of recovery blocks is catered for by organising the cache in a manner similar to a stack.

The case of process interaction within a recovery block is more difficult to handle. A possible approach (Randell, 1975) is to regard any interaction between two processes as a 'conversation' between them. If one of the processes has to be backed up during a conversation then so must the other, since the information transmitted in the conversation may have been erroneous. Thus neither process may proceed beyond the end of a conversation until both have passed acceptance tests at its conclusion, and failure of either acceptance test results in the backup of both processes to the start of the conversation. The idea can be extended to simultaneous conversations between several processes.

This description of the recovery block scheme has been necessarily brief, but the reader will recognise that it combines several aspects of fault tolerance discussed earlier. Error detection is achieved by means of the acceptance tests; fault treatment is effected by the provision of alternates; and recovery is based on the cache mechanism. A more detailed description of the scheme is given in the quoted references.

10.6 MULTILEVEL ERROR HANDLING

In the previous few sections we have described various error handling techniques. In this section we suggest how these techniques can be incorporated into the layered structure of our paper operating system.

The principal aim is to mask from each level of the operating system the errors which occur at levels below it. Thus each level of the system is to be as far as possible responsible for its own error recovery, so that to levels above it appears fault free. The idea is an extension into the operating system of the hardware error masking discussed in section 10.2. In cases where masking is impossible, errors in a lower level which occur while performing some function for a higher level should be reported to the higher level in an orderly fashion (for example, by a specific error return). The higher level may itself then be able to perform some kind of recovery, thus masking the error from higher levels still. Those errors which cannot be masked at any level must, of course, eventually be reported to either the user or the operator. At the lowest level of the system, errors which are detected by the CPU hardware, but cannot be masked, are reported to the nucleus by means of error traps into the first level interrupt handler (section 4.4).

As an example of what we mean, consider a user process which wishes to open a file. The process invokes the filing system by calling the *open* routine (section 7.6), which in turn invokes the I/O system by calling the DOIO procedure (section 6.2) to read the user directory from disc. The required I/O transfer is eventually initiated by the disc device handler. In the event of a parity error a first level of masking may be provided by the hardware of the disc controller itself, which is probably designed to detect such an error and re-read the corresponding block. If a few retries fail to correct the situation the error will be reported to the device handler by means of the device status register, which is set by the controller at the end of the transfer. The device handler may attempt to mask the error by re-initiating the entire operation, but if this is unsuccessful the error must be reported back to the *open* routine in the filing system (by means of an error return from DOIO). Within the filing system recovery is possible if another copy of the directory exists elsewhere: the I/O system can be requested to read the backup copy. If for some reason this also fails, or if the filing system is not sufficiently well designed to maintain backup directories, then the error can be masked no longer and must be reported to the user.

Another error which could occur during the file opening operation is the corruption of a queue pointer in the disc device request queue. This may be due to hardware malfunction or to a programming fault. If, as suggested in section 10.3, the queue is organised as a doubly linked list and the queue manipulation routines trace both forward and backward links, then loss of the IORB for the directory transfer can be avoided. Damage to the pointer is repaired by the queue manipulation routines themselves, thus masking the error from the device handler and hence from the filing system and the user process.

By contrast it is interesting to note what will probably happen if the request queue is only singly linked, so that the queue manipulation routines cannot detect the error, let alone mask it. In this case the IORB will become detached from the queue, and the value of the semaphore *request pending* (section 6.2) will be inconsistent with the number of requests in the queue. One of two things will happen next. The first possibility is that the device handler will assume that a successful *wait* operation on *request pending* implies the existence of an IORB in the queue. It will then remove a non-existent IORB from the queue, interpret the resulting garbage as a valid I/O request, and provoke untold further errors. The other possibility is that the device handler will check that the request queue does indeed contain at least one valid IORB and, finding that it does not, will report this fact back to the DOIO procedure. In this case the error will have been successfully masked from the user, since the IORB can be regenerated. The lesson, however, is to include as much error detection and recovery capability as possible at each level, thus avoiding the potential of serious damage. Further examples of multilevel error handling along these lines are given in a description of the reliability mechanisms of the HYDRA system (Wulf, 1975).

Some errors, of course, should not be masked, since they are indicative of a gross fault in a user program. These errors are not system errors, but user errors: the operating system's responsibility is to do no more than report them to the user. An example is arithmetic overflow, which is detected by the processor and reported to the system nucleus via the first level interrupt handler. The interrupt routine in the nucleus can readily identify the culprit as the current process for the processor concerned, and the process can be aborted with an appropriate error message. (It can be argued that masking of arithmetic overflow is possible, for example, by setting the affected location to the largest representable number. However, we consider such action to be undesirable, since it is likely to lead to further errors which will obscure the original fault.) Other errors which should not be masked are memory and protection violations resulting from execution of user programs. The latter could, however, be logged, since they may be indicative of deliberate attempts to break down system security.

10.7 CONCLUSION

In this chapter we have described techniques for enhancing the reliability of an operating system. As computers intrude into many more areas of human activity, and as reliance on them increases, reliability will be of paramount importance. The techniques we have described, although still subject to considerable refinement, form a basis for achieving the reliability required. As far as our paper operating system is concerned, we note that its layered structure is well suited to the multilevel error handling suggested in section 10.6, and that we therefore expect, by using the techniques described, to achieve high reliability.

Finally, we refer the reader who wishes to make a more detailed study of reliability to the excellent surveys by Denning (1976), Randell *et al.* (1978) and Kopetz (1979).

11 *Job Control*

In the preceding chapters we have described how a large scale general purpose operating system can be constructed. At present our operating system exists somewhat in a vacuum since we have not yet specified how we can inform it about the jobs we want it to do. The next step is to manufacture an interface between the user and the operating system so that the user can tell the system what he requires of it. The interface can also be used to present information, such as resource requirements, about each job so that the system can optimise performance in the ways described earlier. Of course communication between user and system is not all in one direction; we must also construct a complementary interface by which the system can tell the user what it has been doing.

11.1 SOME GENERAL REMARKS

The interface between user and system implies the provision of a language, however primitive, in which communication can take place. The nature of the language is heavily dependent on the type of operating system concerned; languages for multi-access use often differ widely from those used in batch systems. The reason for this is that the interactive nature of multi-access working allows a user the opportunity to direct the course of his work in person, and to respond to system actions as they happen. In a batch system, on the other hand, once the user has submitted his job he has no further control over it. Hence he must give explicit instructions in advance as to what course of action is to be followed, possibly specifying alternatives in cases where he cannot foresee precisely what eventualities may occur.

A consequence of the two styles of working is that languages used for batch operation tend to be more complex and more powerful than those used in multi-access. Indeed in the latter case the language may be no more than a set of commands which can be used as directives to the operating system. Such a language is often termed a *command language*, as opposed to the more general *job control language* used in a batch environment. Many operating systems, such as ICL's VME and IBM's MVS, attempt to provide both batch and multi-access control in a single language. In these cases multi-access users usually find themselves employing only a subset of the complete job control language.

```
                                                    Notes
. LOG                                                (1)

USER# 2167,2167

PASSWORD:                                            (2)

LOGGED ON AT 15.39 5 MAY 74

. EX PROG.ALG                                        (3)

ALGOL:PROG

        ERROR AT LINE 3
        UNDECLARED IDENTIFIER

EXIT

. EDIT PROG.ALG                                      (4)

        editing commands terminating with EXIT

. EX                                                 (5)

ALGOL:PROG

        NO ERRORS

EXIT

LOADER 5K CORE

EXECUTION

        user types any data for program;
        results of execution typed out

END OF EXECUTION    1.26 SECS

. KJOB                                               (6)

LOGGED OFF USER 2167,2167 at 15:54

RUNTIME = 2.18   CONNECT TIME = 15:10

.
```

Figure 11.1 Example terminal session. Notes: (1) request to log on; (2) echoing of password is suppressed; (3) compile and execute program in previously created file PROG.ALG; (4) edit program; (5) compile and execute same program; (6) log off

A common desirable feature of both command and job control languages is that they should be easy to use. We shall say more about this later.

11.2 COMMAND LANGUAGES

The example in figure 11.1, loosely based on the DEC System-10 multi-access monitor, illustrates several points which should be borne in mind when designing a command language. The example is the record of a short terminal session; responses typed by the system have been underlined to distinguish them from commands typed by the user. The figures in parentheses refer to the explanatory notes.

Points arising from the example are

(1) To avoid unnecessary typing, sensible abbreviations should be allowed wherever possible (for example, LOG and EX are abbreviations of LOGON and EXECUTE respectively). The full command can be typed whenever the user is unsure of a particular abbreviation.

(2) Commands should preferably be mnemonic, so that they are easy to remember and easy to guess at if forgotten (for example LOGON, EXECUTE and EDIT).

(3) In commands which take parameters defaults should be supplied whenever sensible (for example in the EXECUTE command the default file name is the name of the file used last time; the default I/O device during execution is the terminal). The judicious choice of defaults can save a lot of tedious typing.

(4) It should be possible to perform commonplace activities with very little effort. (EXECUTE is a single command which causes the compilation, loading, and execution of the named file.)

(5) A sensible set of conventions can reduce the typing load. (A file whose name has ALG as its second component is recognised as an Algol program.)

(6) The format of commands should be as free as possible (for example the number of spaces between the command elements is arbitrary).

(7) It should always be obvious whether or not the system is ready to receive another command (this is signified by the dot at the beginning of each line)

(8) The system should give sufficient information to the user to indicate what is happening, but not so much that he is drowned in verbiage.

We shall not dwell further on command languages except to note that many of the points above are also applicable to job control languages.

11.3 JOB CONTROL LANGUAGES

In early batch operating systems, such as the IBSYS system for the IBM 7090 series, job control was achieved by the insertion of *control cards* at various points in the program and data. The control cards had some particular identifying feature (in IBSYS a '$' in column 1) and were interpreted by the operating system as instructions as to what to do with the cards which followed. The disadvantages of this arrangement are threefold.

(1)   The sequence of operations to be performed cannot be altered in the light of the success or failure of previous steps.
(2)   Control information is scattered throughout the input, which is logically unappealing and renders it prone to error.
(3)   The control cards need some special combination of characters to identify them; this combination must therefore never occur in programs or data. (One way round this restriction is to provide a special control statement which alters the identifying feature for all subsequent control cards to some other combination of characters. This option is available in OS/360 JCL.)

In some systems (for example DEC System-10 batch) this type of job control still persists. However, many systems, following Atlas, require that all job control information should be located in a *job description* at the start of a job. The job description is effectively a program written in a job control language which controls the passage of the job through the computing system.

   The control information to be specified in a job description can be classified as follows.

(1) Accounting Information

This usually consists of the job name and the user identity. The latter can be checked against the list of bona fide users in the accounting file, and any chargeable resources used by the job can be debited against the corresponding account.

(2) Scheduling Information

This generally consists of a specification of the maximum amounts of various resources which the job will use. Systems such as OS/360 and its successors, where jobs are broken up into separate job steps, may require resource specifications for each step. The information required is that which can be used by the scheduler for (a) deciding which job to start next, (b) allocating priorities, (c) avoiding deadlock, and (d) terminating jobs which exceed their resource limits. Typical resource specifications will include memory occupancy, processor time, and output limits.

   Other scheduling information that might be included is a request that the job have a certain priority, or a requirement that the job be run after some other job. Sequencing specifications like this are useful in cases when a job is dependent on a file left by some other job.

(3) I/O Information

This is the information used in stream based systems to associate streams with physical I/O devices (the reader who wishes to remind himself about streams should refer to section 6.1). In non-stream systems this section of the job description is used to request the assignment of I/O devices for the job. Specifications of character codes and block size may also be included under this heading.

(4) Procedural Information

This part of the job description actually tells the operating system what the user requires it to do. Some job control languages may allow nothing more than a simple sequence of directives; others may provide more powerful facilities as discussed below.

As an example, figure 11.2 shows an Atlas-style job description, in which the four kinds of information can be readily distinguished. Other job control languages, such as those in some IBM systems, mingle different kinds of information in a single statement.

```
                                        Notes

    JOB AML123 SAMPLE          job header and accounting
                               information

    CORE 15 PAGES 25      ⎫
                          ⎬    scheduling information
    TIME 200              ⎪
                          ⎭
    AFTER AML123 SORT

    INPUT 1 = CDR         ⎫
                          ⎪    I/O information.  Quotes used to
    INPUT 2 = 'MYDATA'    ⎬    distinguish file names from
                          ⎪    device names
    OUTPUT 1 = LPT        ⎭

    COMPILE FORTRAN       ⎫    procedural information.  File
                          ⎬    name for the compiled program
    EXECUTE               ⎭    supplied by default

    END

        program cards

    ****                       job terminator
```

Figure 11.2 Atlas-style job description

The power of a job control language is largely determined by its facilities for expressing procedural information. Some of these facilities are discussed below.

(1) *Macros.* A macro facility allows users to specify complex actions by single commands. Any sequence of job control statements may be defined as a named *macro* (or *catalogue procedure*), and invoked simply by quoting the macro name with appropriate parameters. For example, the sequence of statements necessary to compile, load and execute a Fortran program might be defined as a macro called FORTRAN; this macro might be used with parameters specifying the file name of the source program and the destination of the output. Expansion of a macro and substitution of para-

meters is performed by the job description interpreter before the job runs; the mechanism is similar to that used in an assembler. Most operating systems provide a library of macros for common activities; many also allow users to build up their own libraries to suit individual needs.

(2) *Control structure*. Job control languages which allow only simple sequences of statements are inadequate for jobs in which the actions to be performed may depend on the outcome of previous steps. Several languages include some form of '*if*-statement', so that parts of a job description can be executed only if certain conditions occur. The conditions which may be tested for are generally the result of some previous step; typical examples are the occurrence of an error, the output of a particular message, or the occurrence of a particular value left in a machine register. Some languages also include a looping facility, so that parts of a job may be executed more than once. The provision of conditional and repetitive constructs makes job control languages increasingly similar to high level programming languages, and there seems no reason why they should not progress even further in this direction by including such features as variables, block structure and procedures. This high level language approach has already been adopted on a few systems (such as the ICL 2900 series).

(3) *Parallelism*. Some job control languages (for example, that in UNIX) include a facility for specifying that various parts of a job may be run in parallel. Such information can be used by the scheduler to initiate a job as a set of processes running in parallel rather than in sequence. The advent of multi-processor systems, in which real gains can be made by parallelism, will perhaps make this facility more widespread.

A possible future development lies in pursuing the analogy with high level programming languages by introducing job control languages which can be compiled or interpreted on any system. This would constitute a significant advance towards machine independence in running jobs; at present the machine independence gained at the programming level is undermined by the different ways jobs must be submitted to different machines. Obstacles to such a development arise from the difficulty of giving widely differing systems the same external interface (Dakin, 1975).

As far as our paper operating system is concerned we shall not attempt to design a particular job control language. Instead we simply remark that any job control language we adopt should contain the features described above, and be designed so as to incorporate those characteristics listed in section 11.2 as desirable from the user's point of view.

11.4 THE JOB POOL

We remarked in section 8.4 that jobs awaiting initiation by the scheduler are held in a *job pool*. Each entry in the job pool represents a single job, and contains information about it which is derived from the job description. This information is in fact an encoded form of that contained in the job description, except that in a spooling system all input device names are replaced by the names of the files into which the input has been spooled. The spooling may be performed by the job description interpreter itself, or the interpreter may delegate the task to separate input spoolers (see section 6.6) which it sets in motion by signalling the appropriate semaphores. In either case the interpreter signals to the scheduler whenever a new job pool entry is complete.

The job pool may be structured as a single list or as a number of lists each of which contains jobs with particular characteristics. The latter structure can be a help to the scheduler in choosing which job to run next.

The size of the job pool may prohibit its storage in main memory. However, storage on disc may involve the scheduler in heavy overheads when it comes to search for the best job to run. A possible compromise is to store abbreviated versions of the job pool entries in memory, while the complete entries reside on disc. The abbreviated entries will contain only such information as the scheduler needs to choose the next job; information about input files, for example, can be omitted.

11.5 SYSTEM MESSAGES

The relationship between the user and the operating system depends not only on how easily the user can tell the system what he wants it to do, but also on the quality of the information he receives from it about what it has done. The information supplied by current systems, particularly when job errors have occurred, varies widely in quantity, detail, relevance, and intelligibility. Ideally the degree of detail should depend on the fate of the job; if it terminates successfully then a brief account of the chargeable resources used is probably sufficient, but if it fails then a full statement of the cause is necessary. In all cases system messages should be couched in normal English in such a way as to be easily understood by a general user. All too frequently the user is presented with a mass of apparent gibberish, or, in the case of failure, with a hexadecimal dump!

In a multi-access environment a user should be able to request information about the current state of the system in terms of how many users are logged on, what resources are available, and so on. This information enables him to assess what kind of response he can expect and to decide whether or not it is worth while starting or continuing the session.

11.6 PASSAGE OF A JOB THROUGH THE SYSTEM

Figure 11.3 summarises the stages by which a job progresses from submission to termination through our paper operating system. The solid lines represent the

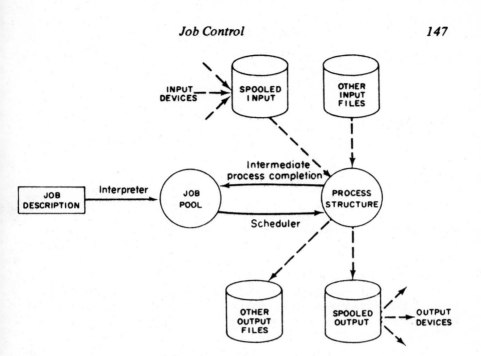

Figure 11.3 Progress of a job

various metamorphoses of the job from job description to job pool entry to
sequence of processes; the broken lines represent the flow of data and programs
associated with the job. If spooling is not employed then the input and output
queues can be removed from the diagram and the data transfers shown as being
direct to or from the peripheral devices. The circular motion between job pool
and process structure is intended to emphasise that it may require the invocation
of several processes to execute a single job. Within the process structure itself
processes move between the three states blocked, runnable, and running, as
previously shown in figure 8.4.

Conclusion

In the last chapter we completed the construction of our paper operating system by providing it with an interface with the outside world. We also gave an overview of the system by describing the progress of a job from start to finish. It is probably appropriate at this stage to stand back a little and examine what we have achieved.

The purpose of building and describing the paper operating system has been twofold. The primary objective has been to use it as a vehicle for illustrating the mechanisms by which an operating system can fulfil the functions expected of it by its users. The secondary objective has been to support the increasingly popular view that operating systems can become reliable, easily maintained, and relatively error-free only if they exhibit a logically coherent structure. We shall return to this point in a moment.

As far as the primary aim is concerned it is hoped that the reader who has reached this point will have a good idea of what operating systems are, what they do, and how they do it. He should understand the nature of the problems posed in operating system design, and the techniques used for overcoming them. In a book as short as this it is of course impossible to give a comprehensive catalogue of all the problems and all the solutions; all one can do is describe those most frequently encountered or adopted. There will inevitably be systems which, because of different user environments or hardware constraints, present problems not covered here; similarly, there will be many systems in which the problems we have mentioned are solved in different ways. However, it is hoped that the material we have presented will provide an adequate basis from which the reader can broaden his knowledge according to his interests. The ground should be sufficiently well prepared for seeds from elsewhere to flourish.

The second point mentioned above, concerning the logical structure of operating systems, is one which merits further discussion. We have constructed on paper a system which is neatly layered, with each layer dependent only on the layers below it. However, it must be admitted that when we constructed the system the dice were loaded in our favour. First, we were not distracted by the problems of working in a large team, and second, we were not obliged by customer demand to add new features after the initial design stage. Third, and perhaps most important, we did not have to make the system work on a real machine. The question must therefore be asked: how far is it possible to translate the structure of the paper system into real life?

The first two obstacles — those of large project teams and changing specifications — can be avoided by judicious management. The third obstacle — that of intransigent machine architecture — is more difficult to overcome, particularly in the short term. Machine architecture impinges on the system at many levels, but the areas most directly influenced are interrupt handling, I/O, and memory protection. It is worth looking at each of these in turn.

As indicated in chapter 4, the complexity of the interrupt handler can vary greatly according to the amount of help given by the hardware. This help is particularly important in interrupt identification and in the determination of priorities. For example the DEC System-10, which provides a hardware priority interrupt mechanism in which devices may be assigned to any one of seven levels, gives more help than the IBM 370, in which priority is largely predetermined and can be modified only partially by selective software masking. Both machines do however provide adequate information for the source and nature of an interrupt to be readily determined.

The framework for I/O handling established in chapter 6 can become severely distorted by the constraints of a particular I/O architecture. The framework is well suited to architectures based on a simple bus system, but may have to be modified in cases (such as the IBM 370) involving a hierarchy of channels, control units, and devices. In the large CDC machines I/O functions are distributed among special peripheral processors, and the device handlers are executed by the peripheral processors rather than by a CPU. Terminals, because of their special control function, are treated as special cases in most systems. On the DEC System-10, for example, terminal buffers are allocated from space belonging to the operating system, rather than (as is the case for other devices) from space belonging to individual user processes. The reason for this stems from the fact that a process which is performing I/O cannot be swapped out of main memory as its buffers might be overwritten. Since terminal buffers are always potentially in use it follows that if they were allocated from user space the corresponding user processes could never be swapped out.

The architectural feature which most seriously affects the structure of an operating system is probably the mechanism for memory protection. The total realisation of the layered structure of our paper operating system implies the existence of a protection system that can be made to mirror it. It seems that the segment, being the logical unit of address space, should be the natural unit for protection, and that what is required is the ability to create an arbitrary number of protection domains. One machine which departs far from the ideal is the IBM 370. Here protection is applied not to segments but to 2K byte blocks of physical memory; the confusion between logical and physical divisions of memory is made even worse by allowing the page field of an address to overflow into the segment field. Several machines, including the Burroughs 6700 and the Honeywell 645 apply protection to segments, but very few have more than two or three protection domains. The most common arrangement is the two-domain 'supervisor-user' system, typified by the IBM 370 and many microprocessors. Multiple domains exist in the CYBER 180 and ICL 2900 series, but there are only a fixed number and they carry a high operational overhead. The problems of implementing multiple domains at low cost are by no means yet solved; the use of capabilities as described in chapter 9 is perhaps the most promising approach. However, despite the deficiencies of current architectures, we can expect that new protection mechanisms will soon provide the means for facilitating layered system structure. In the meantime we can regard structure as a legitimate objective while lacking the means to enforce it.

What other developments can be expected? Crystal ball gazing is a hazardous occupation in such a rapidly changing field, but we shall indulge in it briefly at the risk of being proved wrong by events. Short term developments are likely to be concentrated on improving the reliability of operating systems, on making them more easily portable between different machines, and on making them easier to use by means of more powerful and flexible job control languages. In the longer term the two factors we consider will most influence the nature and role of operating systems are the advent of microprocessors and the provision of improved telecommunications facilities.

Microprocessors offer a new form of processing power — small, discrete units of very low cost, in contrast to the large, monolithic, expensive units of the last 30 years. The challenge presented by microprocessors is to exploit this power to best advantage. One trend is already apparent: the dispersal of computing facilities to the places they are most needed, rather than their concentration in a central location. The rapidly decreasing cost of processors, memory, and secondary storage devices, has made it economically feasible to dedicate a complete computing system to a single application, be it payroll, process control, teaching, home budgeting, or whatever. Resource allocation, which is one of the chief functions of the traditional mainframe operating system, becomes trivial in such a dedicated system, since the resources required are always available.

Dedicated systems may be completely independent, or they may be linked by means of data transmission lines. In the latter case, information stored at one site can be transmitted for use at another, or work which is beyond the capacity of a single installation can be passed elsewhere for processing. The ability to link semi-independent installations into a large network gives the potential of delivering enormous computing power and information accessing capability to widely dispersed individuals or groups. The function of an operating system in such an environment includes message transmission and validation, load sharing, and the maintenance of the consistency of information which may be held in several forms at different sites.

Another possible development, in areas where large amounts of concentrated computing power are still required, is to replace the mainframe CPU by a collection of interconnected microprocessors. One advantage of doing this is that each process can have its own processor, thus increasing the parallelism in the system and eliminating the need for process switching. Another advantage is the potential increase in reliability which comes from the replication of processors. There are, however, several problems which must be overcome before such a system can be realised. One of the principal ones concerns memory organisation:

should each processor have its own private memory, should they all share a common memory, or should there be a combination of the two? Common memory brings problems of contention for access, while private memories imply a requirement for easy transmission of data between them. Mixed memory requires solutions to both types of problem, as well as that of devising and implementing an appropriate address map. Other architectural problems are the direction of external interrupts to the appropriate processor, and the provision of a mechanism for communication between processors. At the operating system level there are problems concerned with the recognition of potential parallelism, the allocation of processes to processors, communication between processes which may share no common memory, the sharing of resources, and error detection and recovery. All these problems are being vigorously tackled, and one can expect viable multi-microprocessor systems to become a reality within the next few years.

Finally, I would urge the reader not to regard this book as in any way a definitive study of operating systems. There are many excellent papers and books which will give fresh insight to the material covered here, or which will introduce the reader to new ground. It is hoped that the references given on the following pages will provide an adequate starting point.

Appendix: Monitors

The general structure of a monitor (Hoare, 1974), using a Pascal-like syntax, is

var *m: monitor*;
begin
    declaration of local variables representing the shared object;
    declaration of procedures accessing the local variables;
    initialisation of local variables
end

The local variables are inaccessible outside the monitor; after initialisation they may be operated on only by the monitor procedures themselves. To prevent simultaneous manipulation of the local variables by several processes the monitor procedures are implemented as mutually exclusive critical sections. Mutual exclusion is guaranteed by the compiler, which generates appropriate synchronisation operations (such as *wait* and *signal* operations on semaphores) in the compiled program. (For the reader familiar with abstract data types, a monitor can be regarded as an abstract data object which can safely be shared by several processes.)

Although mutual exclusion of monitor procedures is guaranteed by the compiler, other forms of synchronisation remain the responsibility of the programmer. The synchronisation operations suggested by Hoare, and adopted in most monitor implementations, are not *wait* and *signal* operations on semaphores, but similar operations on objects called *conditions*. Like a semaphore, a condition has two operations which can be applied to it — one is used to delay a process and the other to resume it. We shall refer to these operations as *cwait* and *csignal* respectively to distinguish them from the *wait* and *signal* operations on semaphores.

The definitions of *cwait* and *csignal* are

cwait (condition):   suspend execution of the calling process
csignal (condition):   resume execution of some process suspended after a *cwait*
                        on the same condition. If there are several such processes
                        choose one of them; if there is no such process do nothing

The *cwait* operation releases exclusion on the monitor — otherwise no other process would be able to enter the monitor to perform a *csignal*. Similarly, *csignal* releases exclusion, handing it to the process which is resumed. The resumed process must therefore be permitted to run before any other process can enter the monitor.

Although conditions and semaphores are used for similar purposes, the following differences are significant.

(a) A condition, unlike a semaphore, does not have a value. It can be thought of as a queue to which a process is added on performing *cwait* and from which it is removed when some other process performs a *csignal*.

(b) A *cwait* operation *always* causes the executing process to be delayed. This contrasts with the *wait* operation, which causes delay only when the semaphore value is zero.

(c) A *csignal* operation has an effect only if a process is suspended on the same condition. A *signal* operation, on the other hand, always has an effect — that of incrementing the semaphore value. Thus *signal* operations are 'remembered' (in the value of the semaphore), whereas *csignal* operations are not.

As an example of the use of conditions for synchronisation, we give details of the buffer monitor referred to in section 3.4.

```
var buffer: monitor;
begin
    var B: array [0 ... N - 1] of item;          {space for N items}
        nextin, nextout: 0 ... N - 1;             {buffer pointers}
        nonfull, nonempty: condition;             {for synchronisation}
        count: 0 ... N;                           {number of items in buffer}

procedure deposit (x: item);
begin
    if count = N then cwait (nonfull);            {avoid overflow}
    B [nextin] := x;
    nextin:= (nextin + 1) mod N;
    count:= count + 1;                            {one more item in buffer}
    csignal (nonempty)                            {resume any waiting consumer}
end;

procedure extract (var x: item);
begin
    if count = 0 then cwait (nonempty);           {avoid underflow}
    x:= B[nextout] ;
    nextout:= (nextout + 1) mod N;
    count:= count - 1;                            {one fewer item in buffer}
    csignal (nonfull)                             {resume any waiting producer}
end;

    nextin:= 0; nextout:= 0;
    count:= 0                                     {buffer initially empty}
end
```

References

Alagic, S., and Arbib, M.A. (1978), *The Design of Well-Structured and Correct Programs*, Springer-Verlag, New York

Andrews, G. R., and Schneider, F. B. (1983), Concepts and notations for concurrent programming, *Computing Surveys*, **15**, 3–43

Avizienis, A. (1977), Fault-tolerant Computing: Progress, Problems and Prospects, *Proceedings IFIPS 77*, North-Holland, Amsterdam, p. 405

Brooks, F.P. (1975), *The Mythical Man-Month*, Addison-Wesley, Reading, Mass.

Coffman, E.G., and Denning, P.J. (1973), *Operating System Theory*, Prentice-Hall, Englewood Cliffs, N.J.

Coffman, E.G. and Kleinrock, L. (1968), Computer scheduling methods and their countermeasures, *Proceedings AFIPS Spring Joint Computer Conference*, **32**, 11–21

Coffman, E.G., Elphick, M. and Shoshani, A. (1971). System deadlocks, *Computing Surveys*, **3**, 67–78

Colin, A.J.T. (1971), *Introduction to Operating Systems*, MacDonald-Elsevier, London and New York, p. 36

Corbató, F.J., Merwin-Dagget, M. and Daley, R.C. (1962), An experimental time sharing system, *Proceedings AFIPS Spring Joint Computer Conference*, **21**, 335–44

Courtois, P.J., Heymans, R. and Parnas, D.L. (1971), Concurrent control with "readers" and "writers", *Comm. ACM*, **14**, 667–8

Dahl, O.J., Dijkstra, E.W., and Hoare, C.A.R. (1972), *Structured Programming*, Academic Press, London and New York

Dakin, R.J. (1975), A general control language: structure and translation, *Computer Journal*, **18**, 324–32

Daley, R.C. and Dennis, J.B. (1968), Virtual memory, processes, and sharing in MULTICS, *Comm. ACM*, **11**, 306–12

Daley, R.C. and Neumann, P.G. (1965), A general-purpose file system for secondary storage, *Proceedings AFIPS Fall Joint Computer Conference*, **27**, 213–29

Denning, P.J. (1968), The working set model for program behaviour, *Comm. AC.* **11**, 323–33

Denning, P.J. (1970), Virtual memory, *Computing Surveys*, **2**, 153–89

Denning, P.J. (1971), Third generation computer systems, *Computing Surveys*, **3**, 175–216

Denning, P.J. (1976), Fault-tolerant operating systems, *Computing Surveys*, **8**, 359–89

Dennis, J.B. and Van Horn, C. (1966), Programming semantics for multi-programmed computations, *Comm. ACM*, **9**, 143-55

Digital Equipment Corporation (1973), *DEC System-10 Assembly Language Handbook*, 3rd edition

Dijkstra, E.W. (1965), Cooperating sequential processes, In *Programming Languages* (ed. F. Genuys), Academic Press, New York (1968)

Dijkstra, E.W. (1968), The structure of the T.H.E. multiprogramming system, *Comm. ACM*, **11**, 341-6

Dijkstra, E.W. (1976), *A Discipline of Programming*, Prentice-Hall, Englewood Cliffs, N.J.

England, D.M. (1974), The capability concept mechanism and structure in System-250, *IRIA International Workshop on Protection in Operating Systems*, Rocquencourt, 63–82

Evans, D.C. and Leclerc, J.Y. (1967), Address mapping and the control of access in an interactive computer, *Proceedings AFIPS Spring Joint Computer Conference*, **30**, 23-32

Fabry, R.S. (1974), Capability based addressing, *Comm. ACM*, **17**, 403–12

Floyd, R.W. (1967), Assigning meanings to programs, *Proc. Symposium in Applied Maths*, **19**, American Math. Soc.

Foster, C.C. (1970), *Computer Architecture*, Van Nostrand Reinhold, New York, pp. 146-52

Frank, G.R. (1976), Job control in the MU5 operating system, *Computer Journal*, **19**, 139–43

Fraser, A.G. (1969), Integrity of a mass storage filing system, *Computer Journal*, **12**, 1-5

Graham, G.S. and Denning, P.J. (1972), Protection – principles and practice, *Proceedings AFIPS Spring Joint Computer Conference*, **40**, 417-29

Graham, R.M. (1968), Protection in an information processing utility, *Comm. ACM*, **11**, 365-9

Habermann, A.N. (1969), Prevention of system deadlock, *Comm. ACM*, **12**, 373-7

Habermann, A.N. (1972), Synchronisation of communicating processes, *Comm. ACM*, **15**, 171–6

Hansen, P.B. (1970), The nucleus of a multiprogramming system, *Comm. ACM*, **13**, 238-50

Hansen, P.B. (1972), Structured multiprogramming, *Comm. ACM*, **15**, 574-8

Hansen, P.B. (1973), *Operating System Principles*, Prentice-Hall, Englewood Cliffs, N. J.

Hansen, P.B. (1975), The programming language Concurrent Pascal, *IEEE Trans. Software Engineering*, **1**, 199–207

Hantler, S.L., and King, J.C. (1976), An introduction to proving the correctness of programs, *Computing Surveys*, **8**, 331–53

Hartley, D.F. (1970), Management software in multiple-access systems, *Bulletin of the I.M.A.*, **6**, 11-13

Havender, J.W. (1968), Avoiding deadlock in multitasking systems, *IBM Systems Journal*, **7**, 74-84

Hoare, C.A.R. (1972), Proof of correctness of data representation, *Acta Informatica*, **1**, 271–81

Hoare, C.A.R. (1974), Monitors: an operating system structuring concept, *Comm. ACM*, **17**, 549–57

Horning, J., Lauer, H.C., Melliar-Smith, P.M., and Randell, B. (1974), A program structure for error detection and recovery, in *Lecture Notes in Computer Science*, **16**, Springer-Verlag, New York

Huxtable, D.H.R., and Pinkerton, J.M.M. (1977), The hardware/software interface of the ICL 2900 range of computers, *Computer Journal*, **20**, 290–5

IBM Corporation, *IBM System 360/ Operating System Concepts and Facilities*, Manual C28-6535

ICL (1969), *Operating Systems George 3 and 4*, Manual 4169

IFIP (1969), *File Organisation*, Selected papers from File 68, IFIP Administrative Data Processing Group, occasional publication number 3, Swets and Zeitliger

Jackson, M. (1975), *Principles of Program Design*, Academic Press, London and New York

Judd, D.R. (1973), *Use of Files*, MacDonald-Elsevier, London and New York

Keedy, J.L. (1976), The management and technological approach to the design of System B, *Proc. 7th Australian Computer Conf.*, Perth, 997–1013

Kernighan, B. W., and Ritchie, D. M. (1978), *The C Programming Language*, Prentice-Hall, Englewood Cliffs, N.J.

Knuth, D.E. (1968), *The Art of Computer Programming*, vol. 1 Fundamental algorithms, Addison-Wesley, Reading, Mass.

Kopetz, H. (1979), *Software Reliability*, Macmillan, London and Basingstoke

Lampson B. W., and Redell, D. (1980), Experience with processes and monitors in Mesa, *Comm. ACM*, **23**, 105-17

Lister, A.M. (1974), Validation of systems of parallel processes, *Computer Journal*, **17**, 148–51

Martin, J. (1977), *Computer Data-Base Organisation*, 2nd ed., Prentice-Hall, Englewood Cliffs, N.J.

Randell, B. (1975), System structure for software fault tolerance, *IEEE Trans. Software Engineering*, **1**, 220–32

Randell, B., Lee, P.A., and Treleaven, P.C. (1978), Reliability issues in computing system design, *Computing Surveys*, **10**, 123–65

Richards, M. (1969), BCPL: a tool for compiler writing and systems programming, *Proceedings AFIPS Spring Joint Computer Conference*, **34**, 557–66

Ritchie, D.M., and Thompson, K. (1974), The UNIX time-sharing system, *Comm. ACM*, **17**, 365–75

Schroeder, M.D. and Saltzer, J.H. (1972), A hardware architecture for implementing protection rings, *Comm. ACM*, **15**, 157–70

Stone, H.S. (ed.) (1975), *An Introduction to Computer Architecture*, SRA, Chicago

Svobodova, L. (1976), *Computer Performance Measurement and Evaluation*, Elsevier, New York

Watson, R.W. (1970), *Timesharing System Design Concepts*, McGraw-Hill, New York

Welsh, J., and Bustard, D. W. (1979), Pascal-plus – another language for modular multiprogramming, *Software Practice and Experience*, **9**, 947–57

Williams, R.K. (1972), System 250 – basic concepts, *Proceedings of the Conference on Computers – Systems and Technology*, I.E.R.E. Conference Proceedings number 25, 157–68

Wirth, N. (1971), Program development by stepwise refinement, *Comm. ACM*, **14**, 221–7

Wirth, N. (1977), Modula: a language for modular multiprogramming, *Software Practice and Experience*, **7**, 3–36

Wirth, N. (1983), *Programming in Modula-2*, 2nd ed., Springer-Verlag, Heidelberg, Berlin and New York

Wulf, W.A. (1975), Reliable hardware-software architecture, *IEEE Trans. Software Engineering*, **1**, 233–40

Wulf, W.A., Russell, D.B. and Habermann, A.N. (1971), BLISS: a language for systems programming, *Comm. ACM*, **14**, 780–90

Yourdon, E. (1975), *Techniques of Program Structure and Design*, Prentice-Hall, Englewood Cliffs, N.J.

Index

A COLONIAL LEGACY

The Dispute Over the Islands of Abu Musa, and the Greater and Lesser Tumbs

Farhang Mehr

University Press of America,® Inc.
Lanham • New York • Oxford

Copyright © 1997 by
University Press of America,® Inc.
4720 Boston Way
Lanham, Maryland 20706

12 Hid's Copse Rd.
Cummor Hill, Oxford OX2 9JJ

Library of Congress Cataloging-in-Publication Data

Mehr, Farhang.
A colonial legacy : the dispute over the islands of Abu Musa and the
Greater and Lesser Tumbs / Farhang Mehr.
p.   cm.
Includes bibliographical references and index.
1. Abu Musa--International status. 2. Tumb Islands--International
status. 3. United Arab Emirates--Boundaries--Iran. 4. Iran--
Boundaries--United Arab Emirates. 5. Persian Gulf Region--
Foreign relations--Great Britain. 6. Great Britain--Foreign relations-
-Persian Gulf Region. I. Title.
DS247.T85M44   1997   341.2'9'095357--dc21   97-25739 CIP

ISBN 0-7618-0876-0 (cloth: alk. ppr.)
ISBN 0-7618-0877-9 (pbk: alk. ppr.)

TO PARICHEHR

with Love and Admiration

Contents

Preface

This book deals with the legal status of the three islands of Abu Musa, and the Greater and Lesser Tumbs. In December 1971, the sixty-seven years of the Anglo-Iranian dispute over the islands transformed itself into Irano-UAE conflict - a conflict which Iran considers a colonial legacy inherited by the United Arab Emirates.

The alliance of convenience between Iran and Britain cemented under Shah Abbas in the early seventeenth century had faded away by the mid-eighteenth century, after the collapse of the Safavid Dynasty. During the nineteenth century, the Anglo-Iranian relationship evolved into mutual distrust and resentment.

For the British, Iran and Afghanistan were the first lines of India's defense, and the Persian Gulf was the gate to India. During the nineteenth century, British hegemony in the Gulf was threatened primarily by European powers (France and Russia), by regional powers (the Ottoman Empire, Egypt, the Wahhabi Saudis and Iran), and by piratical Arab tribes. France coveted the Indian sub-continent, Russia desired access to warm water, and the Ottoman Empire craved possession of the Arab territories.

Meanwhile, Iran wanted the restoration of her sovereignty over the Gulf islands, the Saudis sought the conversion of Muslims to the Messianic Wahhabi faith, and local Arab tribes employed their maritime skill to assail and plunder the merchant shipping in the Persian Gulf. With the Iranian governments increasingly fragile following the assassination of Nader Shah in 1750, the bases and privileges which had been granted to the British and the East India Company under Shah Abbas were no longer of any practical value, weakening Britain's clout.

The invasion of Iran in the early nineteenth century and the annexation of Iranian Caucasian territory gave Russia an advanced post towards India, while the failure of the British to assist Iran under the 1801, 1809, and 1814 treaties intensified Iran's mistrust. Furthermore, the British change of policy towards the Irano-Afghan conflict over Herat -- from inciting Iran to attack Herat in 1798, to pledging neutrality in 1814, to seizing the island of Kharaq and Bushehr in 1851 in order to force Iran to retreat from Heart -- all had deepened Iran's indignation. The Irano-British war of 1856-57, the proclamation of Jihad by Naser al-Din Shah against the British in 1857 heightened the mutual animosity. The British suspected Iran to be playing into the Russians' hands, and Iran believed that Britain was fortifying her interests in the region at the expense of Iran's sovereignty and territorial integrity. By the nineteenth century, the problems of Iran, Afghanistan, and the Persian Gulf were entangled, and the British wanted the region to be either under her influence or completely neutralized. In 1847, the protection of British interests in Iran and Afghanistan was transferred from London to Bombay, reflecting the sensitivity of the region to the security of India.

There was an additional reason for British uneasiness with Iran, related to the British desire to acquire a military base in the Gulf. Local pirates had long endangered the safety of trade routes in the area. The British speculated that the acquisition of a military base would enable them to launch immediate retributive military expeditions against the perpetrators whenever a maritime crime was committed. Iran adamantly denied cooperation.

The British preference was directed towards the three Persian islands of Qishm, Hanjam, and Khark. Having failed to obtain Iran's consent, the British tried to forge evidence in favor of Oman's ownership of Qishm and the alleged "inherited rights" of the Imam of Muscat. In the meantime, the British adopted the carrot-and-stick policy toward Iran. The British emissary in Teheran told the Shah that, should Iran allow the British to have a base in Qishm, the British government would, in return, use her influence to restore Iran's suzerainty over Bahrain; but if Iran still denied their request for the base, the British might question the rights and title of the Shah to the islands in the Gulf. Indeed, this was the same policy that Britain pursued in 1904 with regard to the three disputed islands of Abu Musa, and the two Tumbs.

The acquisition of a military base seemed so important to Britain that the Governor-General of India said "Britain should retain Khark at any cost, the island could become the Singapore of the Persian Gulf".[1] At the same time, Britain's enhanced mistrust of Iran prompted Palmerston, the British Prime Minister to state that "Persia for many years was deemed our barrier of defense for India against Russia. We

---

[1] J.B. Kelly, Britain and the Persian Gulf 1795-1880 (Oxford: 1968) p. 347

must now look upon Persia as the advance guard for Russia"[2].

As an alternative to a military base, the British devised a plan to broker a "Treaty of Maritime Peace in Perpetuity" between the Arab sheikhs after a retributive military expedition against the piratical Qawassim in 1853. Britain forced the sheikhs to sign "Exclusive" and "Non-alienation". Agreements in her favor, thus depriving the sheikhs of their ability to engage in international relations and to grant mining rights or other concessions to any outside agents. This is how the Trucial States, as British protectorates, emerged. By the end of the nineteenth century, Britain had already tightened her grip on the Trucial States and Oman.

In 1898, Iran hired Belgian administrators to modernized Iran's customs offices; and in 1901 used the customs revenue as collateral for several large loans obtained from Russia. Thus, the Russians gained the privilege of influencing tariffs and working closely with the Belgian officers, who gradually became "Protegés and agents of the Russian government"[3]. Hence, in 1903 when Iran decided to establish customs offices in Abu Musa and the Tumbs, the British, as guardians of the sheikhs' rights, prevented Iran's exercise of sovereignty over the islands and claimed that the Qawassim Sheikhs of Sharjah and Ras al-Khaimah had "inherited rights' in the islands. At this juncture the overt Anglo-Iranian conflict erupted.

Iran has always considered the dispute over the three islands of Abu Musa and the Greater and Lesser Tumbs a "colonial issue" -- the British colonial legacy inherited by

---

[2]Ibid. p. 90

[3] W. Morgan Shuster, "The Strangling of Persia", (New York: 1912) p. 313

the British wards (the Sheikhs of Sharjah and Ras al-Khaimah) and now by the United Arab Emirates. Before the British military withdrawal from the Persian Gulf in December 1971, Iran exerted every effort to resolve the conflict peacefully, in order to avoid an Arab-Iranian polarization in the Gulf. Iran argued that an imperial power should not be allowed to allocate parts of Iran's territory to her colonial wards. Iran bases her claim on historical facts and map evidence. The Sheikhs of Sharjah and Ras al-Khaimah base their claims on tribal patrimony.

Both parties have also resorted to the rules of International Law on acquisition of land. Currently Iran regards the issue as purely an internal matter, rejecting the jurisdiction of the International Court and has no intention of submitting the case to arbitration. However, she has agreed to open dialogue on the subject with the United Arab Emirates, within which federation the two sheikhdoms have been integrated since December 1971. The United Arab Emirates prefers to submit the issue to the International Court at Hague.

The matter is complex, particularly because material facts and evidence, relating to a very short span of time in the nineteenth century, are ambiguous and debatable. British Colonial interests and past interventions have marred the evidence. Hence, clarification of the material facts and the choice of applicable law form the crux of the present study. This is a multi-disciplinary study, dealing with geography, history, economics, politics, international relations and law.

In the preparation of this work, my graduate student Maryam Khodadoust rendered valuable assistance in collecting materials, and typing the manuscript, with great care, and my former student Amin Ashrafzadeh with much dexterity helped me in compiling the index and formatting the book. To both of them I express my deep appreciation and gratitude. Finally, I dedicate this work, with love and admiration, to my wife in recognition of her unfailing support, dedication and sacrifices.

Boston University
December, 1996

Introduction

The sixty-seven years of the Anglo-Iranian dispute over the four islands of Bahrain, Abu Musa, and the Greater and Lesser Tumbs ended in 1971, marked by Iran's recognition of Bahrain's independence, a British withdrawal from the region, and Iran's occupation of Abu Musa and the two Tumbs.

The recognition of Bahrain's independence was expediently explained by the Iranian government as a manifestation of Iran's deference to the principle of self-determination sanctified in the charter of the United Nations. It came soon after an opinion pole done by representatives of the U.N. Secretariat in which the people of Bahrain allegedly chose independence. The occupation of the three islands of Abu Musa and the two Tumbs was proclaimed by Iran as the restoration of her sovereignty over the lands, the exercise of which had been temporarily obstructed by the British in conjunction with the Sheikhs of Sharjah and Ras al-Khaimah. In reverse, the Sheikhs, whose sheikhdoms have since been federated in the United Arab Emirates (U.A.E.), regard the occupation of the islands as an act of aggression committed by Iran, in collusion with Britain.

Iran bases her ownership rights to the islands on historical facts, her continuous protests to the British over the latter's encroachment upon Iran's sovereignty since 1904, and the British political and military backing of the Sheikhs' trespasses during the period of 1904-1970. The Sheikhs base their proprietary rights on tribal patrimony, claiming that the islands belonged for over a century and a half to their forefathers, the Sheikhs of the Qawasim, and that the recent seizure of the islands by Iran was the result of an Irano-British conspiracy. The British, on their part, denying any conspiracy, assert that months before their military withdrawal from the region, they had alerted the Sheikhs to the likelihood of Iran's retake of the islands after the British departure from the region on 1 December, 1971. The British also state that they had advised the Sheikhs to use available diplomatic channels to resolve their territorial disputes with Iran peacefully, before it was too late.

For the three years prior to the British withdrawal, sovereignty over the islands was a topic of discussion between Iran and Britain. The long-disputed islands are located at a strategic "choke point" near the Strait of Hurmoz. Apart from her historical claim, Iran, during the negotiations, had emphasized the vital importance of the Strait of Hurmoz to Iran; save the Strait of Hurmoz, Iran has no outlet or pipeline to transport its oil to the global market. For Iran, the dispute was a colonial one which concerned only Iran and Britain. Iran argued that, for eighty years, Britain, by force and under duress, had prevented Iran from the exercise of sovereignty over the islands; and it would not be fair that a *colonial power* on its departure from the region, would cede Iran's property to the sheikhdoms, thereby perpetuating its *colonial legacy*.[1] Iran wished to regain the islands without an Irano-Arab polarization in the Gulf, for which reason, Iran thought, the occupation of the islands before Britain's withdrawal would be advisable.

While endeavoring to pacify Iran, Britain did not want to betray the Arab's confidence and thereby endanger her oil interests in the region. Hence, she brokered, however in vain, several plans for resolving the issue. These included the renting of the islands to Iran on mutually agreeable terms[2] or the Sheikhs' leasing the islands for 99 years to Iran if the latter recognized the Sheikhs' sovereignty over them.[3] Also explored was the stationing of a joint Irano-Arab garrison on the islands to allay Iran's security concerns, the permanent demilitarization of the islands, and finally an equal division of the islands between the claimants.[4] Needless to say, none of these solutions were acceptable to Iran.

Likewise during this period, Iran attempted to provide an incentive for the Sheikhs to withdraw their claims voluntarily. In April 1970, Iran promised increased economic assistance to the sheikhdoms and the Shah said that "(The Sheikhs) could count all the more on Iran's economic aid"[5]. In July 1971, Iran suggested to compensate the Sharjah Sheikhdom for Abu Musa, without having the payment of compensation affect Iran's sovereignty claim to

---

[1] The Times (London), 11 May,1971; Blitz (India), June 1971.
[2] The Economist, 6 March, 1971; Financial Times (London), 1 October, 1970.
[3] The Guardian (Manchester), 9 November, 1971.
[4] The Times (London), 2 November, 1971.
[5] Keyhan International, 13 April, 1970.

this island in any way.[6]   However, these efforts were aborted.

At first, there seemed to be a quid pro quo understanding between Britain and Iran, which later events proved to be false. Iran had dropped her claim to Bahrain, expecting Britain to change her stand on the matter of Iran's claim to the other three islands, but Britain proffered to act instead as an honest broker.

Prior to Iran's occupation of the islands, during the period of 1969-1971, the attitude of most Arab countries towards Iran on the issue was mild and non-confrontational. Egypt called on all Arabs for moderation, arguing that Arabs should focus their attention on Israel alone.[7]   Saudi Arabia remained silent on the issue. The Deputy Ruler of Ras al-Khaimah had stated that Iran would certainly never harm the sheikhdoms.[8]

After this event, the sheikhdoms of the Gulf were astonished to the point of incredulousness. Several Arab states like Iraq and Kuwait criticized Iran harshly for her claim to the islands, which they asserted were Arabian and, in November 1971, in a disapproving diplomatic gesture, the Kuwaiti Minister of Foreign Affairs, canceled his scheduled visit to Iran.[9]

Following the occupation, Egypt and Saudi Arabia still reacted mildly and did not join the radical Arab States in imposing sanctions against Iran. The situation was different in the sheikhdoms of Sharjah and Ras al-Khaimah, where anti-Iranian demonstrations took place, and the properties of Iranian residents were damaged. In Sharjah, the Deputy Ruler of the island was assassinated, allegedly for his

---

[6] Daily Telegraph (London), 21 July, 1971.
[7] New York Times, 7 November, 1971.
[8] The Guardian (Manchester), 30 July, 1971.
[9] Keyhan International (Weekly), 19 June, 1971.

collaboration with Iran, and in Ras al-Khaimah, several people were killed.[10]

On 2 December, 1971, the United Arab Emirates was formed and on 9 December, 1971, she filed a protest against Iran with the United Nations. Iraq and Libya severed their diplomatic relations with Iran and, charging Britain with collusion with Iran, Libya nationalized the British Petroleum Company, and Iraq severed her diplomatic relations with Britain.

On 9 December, 1971, the four radical Arab States (Iraq, Libya, Algeria, and the People's Democratic Republic of Yemen) requested the U.N. Security Council to consider "the dangerous situation arisen from the occupation of the three islands by Iran's armed forces".[11] The representatives of Kuwait and the U.A.E. requested to be present in the Security Council when the issue was being discussed. Following a low-key debate, the U.N. Security Council opted to adopt a proposal, tabled by the Somali delegate, deferring consideration of the issue, in favor of the use of diplomacy and some third party efforts.[12]

Iran rejected the jurisdiction of both the Security Council and the Arab League to entertain the dispute, arguing that the question of the three islands of Abu Musa and the two Tumbs was purely a domestic matter for Iran. She also rejected the Security Council's recommendation "for third party efforts". Regarding the island of Abu Musa, Iran maintained that the Agreement of 29 November, 1971

---

[10] Sharham Chubin and Sepehr Zabih, "The Foreign Relations of Iran: A Developing State in a Zone of Great Power Conflict"; (California:1974), pp.228-231.
[11] U.N. Security Council Official Records, 26th year, Doc3/10409.
[12] ibid.

amounted to the recognition of Iran's sovereignty over the island by the Sheikh of Sharjah and thus the question was closed by mutual consent. This claim was supported neither by the Sheikh of Sharjah nor Britain. Obviously, the Irano-Sharjah Agreement was a cover for Iran to restore her sovereignty over the island, and a face-saving device for the Sheikh to let Iranian troops occupy the island. The British maintained that, in the agreement, the question of sovereignty was not discussed. But Amir Abbas Hoveyda, the Prime Minister of Iran, said in Majlis on 3 December, 1971,that, after 80 years, Iran had re-established her suzerainty over the islands.[13]

Whilst, during the post-occupation years, Irano-Arab relations were generally tranquil, the rage of Arab radicals persisted and, inter alia, was translated into the toppling of the Sheikh of Qatar in February 1972 while he was vacationing in Iran.[14] On 18 July, 1972, fifteen Arab states, in a joint letter addressed to the President of the U.N. Security Council, reiterated that "the islands are Arab and continue to be an integral part of the United Arab Emirates and of the Arab homeland." The Signatories to that letter were Algeria, Bahrain, Egypt, Iraq, Kuwait, Liberia, Libya, Morroco, Oman, People's Democratic Republic of Yemen, Sudan, Syria, Tunisia, the U.A.E. and Yemen. Saudi Arabia did not sign the letter.

On the whole, the resolution of the Security Council on 3 December, 1971 constituted a victory for Iran. The non-joinder of the moderate Arab states with the radicals and their endorsement of the Somali proposal, the support of the British and the United States for the resolution and the

---

[13] Keyhan International, 4 December, 1971; Iran's Foreign Relations (1971-71) pp. 412-413.

[14] New York Times, 23 February, 1972.

U.S.S.R.'s acquiescence worked all in favor of Iran. The motives of the various protagonists in this political drama will be analysed in the last chapter.

The Soviet reaction was unexpectedly helpful. Iran established normal relations with the U.S.S.R. without abandoning its ties with the U.S. In 1969, the Shah, in an interview, said "(The relationship between Iran and the Soviet Union) is based on mutual respect. We are not asking them what they are doing in the Warsaw Pact, so why should they ask us what we are doing in other places". At the same time, the normal relations with the Soviets gave Iran the leverage necessary to reduce its dependence on the U.S.

Iran also wanted the littoral states to have a greater voice on the future of the Gulf. On his return from Egypt in September 1968, Amir Abbas Hoveyda, the Prime Minister of Iran stated, in connection with Iran's policy in the Gulf, that the future of the Gulf region should be determined by the littoral states alone.[15] And, in a move to display her earnest intention in this policy, during the period of March-July 1970, Iran unrealistically sought a defense agreement with Saudi Arabia and Kuwait.

An ebullient charge launched by certain radical Arab states immediately after Iran's occupation of the islands was that of Irano-British collusion -- a charge which has not been corroborated by any evidence. The fact is that, after Bahrain's independence, Britain did not show any resolve to solve the three islands issue in favor of Iran. The British proposal for the division of the islands between Iran and the sheikhdoms can hardly be labeled as collusion or conspiracy. There are positive indications that Britain pressed Egypt to

---

[15] Keyhan International Weekly, 1 October, 1968.

use its influence in favor of the sheikhs.[16]   In the Security
Council, Britain's representative said "under the agreement,
neither party has given up its claim to the island, nor
recognized the other's claim".[17]

In the circumstances, Iran played her hand very well.
She decidedly threatened to use force, if necessary, to
regain the islands or to prevent oil drilling off the shore of
the islands.   She assumed the right to fire upon British
aircrafts hovering over the islands or harassing the Iranian
Navy.   Above all, she declared she would not recognize the
United Arab Emirates prior to the resolution of the dispute
over the islands.   Finally, Iran occupied the islands on the
eve of British withdrawal and before the emergence of the
U.A.E., thus sending the message that the dispute was of a
colonial nature between Iran and Britain, and had nothing to
do with the Arabs.   In an attempt to further justify her
seizure of the islands before the world, Iran argued that the
risk of a blockade to the Strait of Hurmoz by militant Arabs
existed, as had been demonstrated by the attack by the
P.F.L.P on an oil tanker bound for Eilat through Bahr al-
Mandel in June 1971.[18]   Thus Iran declared that she ensures,
for all nations, freedom of passage through the Strait of
Hurmoz.

In the last twenty years, no noteworthy Irano-U.A.E.
tension, no serious diplomatic initiative, no third party effort
has occurred to resolve the Irano-U.A.E. territorial dispute.
Indeed, the issue had been relegated to oblivion for two
decades. It has been only since liberation of Kuwait that the
conflict has gained momentum.

---

[16] The Times (London), 30 June, 1971.
[17] U.N. Security Council, 9 December, 1971, p.91.
[18] New York Times, 16 June,1971.

The dramatic changes in the political equations in the Middle East have been responsible for the revival of the territorial claims to the islands. The collapse of communism and the disintegration of the Soviet Empire, the fall of the Shah and establishment of an anti-Western Islamic government in Iran have rendered otiose the role of this country as gendarme of the Gulf. Both the Irano-Iraqi war of the 1980's, and the Iraqi invasion of Kuwait in 1990, which prompted the military intervention of the United States and its allies under the auspices of the United Nations, have demonstrated the need for a new political design for stability in the Middle East and the security of the oil supply from the region.

As recent as on 26 May 1994, the President of the U.A.E., Sheikh Zayid Bin-Sultan al-Nahayan urged Iran to have the dispute referred to the International Court of Justice. The U.A.E.'s claim to the three islands has been supported by the Gulf Cooperation Council (G.C.C.) in its Ministerial Council held in Riyad on 3 April 1994, when the G.C.C. reviewed the new developments and reinstated its firm stance supporting the U.A.E. in its claim against Iran.

In Iran, two years earlier on 25 December, President Hojat al-Islam Rafsanjani, articulating his major foreign policy positions, had taken a hard line on Iran's claim towards the three islands by stating that: "The U.A.E. will gain nothing from such claims; its forces will have to cross a sea of blood in order to reach these islands."[19] Nevertheless, while reaffirming his conviction of the legality of Iran's stand, President Rafsanjani indicated that he was willing to negotiate with the U.A.E. over the islands without spelling out the scope and purpose of such a negotiation.

---

[19] Reuters, 27 December, 1992.

With the categorical denial of the possibility of any compromise on the sovereignty question, and with firm assertion that the U.A.E. would not gain anything by pursuing their claim, the purpose of an invitation to negotiate remains murky. In the past, Iran has intermittently hinted to the resumption of negotiations on Abu Musa, but never on the two Tumbs.

Any future bilateral Irano-U.A.E. negotiation, or any ruling by the international Court of Justice, requires the willingness of the conflicting parties to start a dialogue, or the consent of Iran to submit to the jurisdiction of the International Court on the matter. Should Iran decide to negotiate on the sovereignty of the islands, or to submit to the jurisdiction of the International Court, the dispute will necessarily revolve around the two following questions:

1. The validity of Iran's claim of a continuous exercise of sovereignty over the islands before British intervention in 1904; and

2. The validity of the U.A.E. claim to the ownership of Abu Musa by the Sheikh of Sharjah and the two Tumbs by the Sheikh of Ras al-Khaimah, as heirs to the Qawasim Paramount Sheikh.

Under international law, political sovereignty over a particular territory is subject to change; and succession does not follow the inheritance principles in the municipal laws. Thus, legal resolution of the dispute presupposes an investigation into the material facts immediately relevant to the claims, and the application of the relevant international rules to the factual situation. Hence, this treatise will be concerned with the historical facts and pertinent legal issues. The problem is complex and the material data, at some time junctures, scanty.   In the new world order, interstate conflicts should be resolved by negotiations and through diplomatic channels and not by military confrontations. This study focuses on the issues that would be addressed if the parties were to enter a bilateral negotiation or resort to the judicial process .

I

Iran: A Historical Overview

A Geographical Sketch

The islands of Abu Musa, and the Greater and Lesser Tumbs stand near the Strait of Hurmoz, where the Persian Gulf joins the Gulf of Oman. The Persian Gulf is surrounded by the Persian plateau to the north and the Arabian desert to the south.

According to the widely accepted geological theory, the greater part of the region known today as the Persian plateau and Central Arabia, was, during the Cretaceous period, submerged in water, except for a strip of land which is now called the Strait of Hurmoz.[1] At the close of the Miocene period, a shake-up in the earth's crust in Central Asia gave birth to the Persian plateau. With a reverse process, a synclinal depression in tertiary times (Cenozoic era), produced the Persian Gulf.[2]

The earth is a dynamic planet and its surface has been in a process of continuous change and violent upheavals. Over a billion years ago, the continents and seas had different shapes and positions. Weathering, erosion, volcano,

---

[1] Sir Percy Sykes, "A History of Persia," two volumes first edition 1915, third edition 1951 (London , 1951) Vol.   I, p. 4.

[2] Sir Arnold T. Wilson "The Persian Gulf," (London: 1928) p. 3.

mountain buildings and other natural forces have contributed to both constructive and destructive processes, altering the landscape of the earth. Orogenesis has been associated with enormous forces which have folded, faulted and generally deformed large sections of the earth.

In early Pliocene times, the last epoch in the Cenozoic era, "the Persian Gulf was confined to a narrow strip along the present coastal plain of Persia, extending as far as Laristan."[3] The powerful folding movements which led to the formation of the Zagros mountain ranges occurred during the Pliocene period and displaced the depressed zone to the northwest of Laristan to the southwest. Those changes gave rise to the formation of the present Persian Gulf. The great pressure that caused mountain formation in Western Persia during the Pliocene era left the well-secured Arabian plateau basically untouched. Oman had its strong folding and mountain-building process millions of years before in the mid-Cretaceous period. The extreme pressure, caused by the mountain-building processes, squeezed thick deposits of metamorphosed sedimentary rocks out of the deep and remote parts of the earth, which formed many islands and islets when they reached the surface of the Gulf. The islands of Hurmoz, Hanjam, Larak, Abu Musa and the Tumbs are the result of such processes. The emergence of Mesopotamia out of the waters was the result of earth's shake-up in Persia and Arabia, while the delta in the south was formed by silt deposits contributed by the rivers Tigris, Euphrates, and Karun.[4]

---

[3] ibid. pp. 18-19.

[4] ibid. p. 9.

The Persian Gulf which once extended from Hit and Samara to the mountain barrier of Musandan, currently covers an area of about 96,000 square miles, extending from the mouth of the Tigris-Euphrates rivers in the west to the Strait of Hurmoz in the east. Its length, from the head of the Gulf to the coast of Oman, is about 500 miles, and its breadth varies from 180 miles at the widest point to a minimum width of only 29 miles at the Strait of Hurmoz. Presently, on the Persian side, the land edges seaward about 159 feet annually. Should the present trend continue, within two millenium the three islands of Abu Musa and the two Tumbs will become annexed to the mainland.

The geological structures in the region reveal that the *Arabian peninsula is the continuation of East Africa, and the Persian Gulf is an extension of the Persian plateau.* Before the mountain formation in Western Persia, the coast of Muscat ran along the coast of Mukran, and Oman mountains were a continuation of the range of Minab and Zendan.[5] The implication of the "plate tectonics" theory in geology, developed in the 1960's, confirms the foregoing hypothesis: The Persian Gulf is part of the Eurasian plate and the Arabian peninsula is part of the African plate.

The Persian Gulf is a shallow sea, 40 to 50 fathoms (about 250 feet or 76 meters) throughout the Gulf and about 80 fathoms (480 feet or 146 meters) in the Strait of Hurmoz. Therefore, the sea floor lowers rapidly to an extreme depth of approximately 1800 fathoms (10,800 feet or 73-90 meters) midway through the Gulf of Muscat. The thalweg line is nearer to the mountainous site of the Gulf. The water in the Gulf is generally saline due to an almost

---

[5] Ahmad Mostofi; "Khalij-e Fars: Its Geological Structure and Formation," in proceedings of Khalij-e Fars Seminar (Tehran: 1962) Vol. I, p. 5.

lack of currents from the ocean. Only during the season of the southwest monsoon is there a slight inflow from the Gulf of Oman and, during the rest of the year, a slight outflow into the Gulf of Oman. The habitual flows of water into the Persian Gulf are supplied by the Tigris, Euphrates, Karkheh and Karun, which receive water from tributaries running down the Zagros mountain ranges in Persia and Mount Ararat in Turkey.

Because of the shallowness of the Gulf, some 130 isles appear in the basin. The majority of the islands are located near the shore in the western portion of the Gulf, and they differ in structure. Those nearer to the Persian coast such as Hurmoz, Qishm, Sheikh Shuaib, Abu Musa, the Greater and Lesser Tumbs, Larak, and Hanjam are rocky with steep slopes, having physical features similar to the Persian coast.

The three islands of Abu Musa and the Tumbs are in close proximity to Persia, and lie between the mainland and the median line of the Persian Gulf. The islands of the Greater and Lesser Tumbs are situated about 26 miles (42 kilometers) off the Persian Coast while Abu Musa island is located about 30 miles (48 kilometers) off the Iranian island of Sirri. The nearest point from the Arabian side to the islands is Jazirat al-Hamrah in Ras al-Khaimah which is 46 miles (74 km.) away from Greater Tumb.

Greater Tumb is situated 23 miles (37 km.) off the Persian coast, 17 miles (27 km) away from the Iranian island of Qishm, to the north of the median line. It is about 2.5 miles (4 km) in diameter with sandy beaches and low rocky cliffs. It is an infertile land with a small number of trees, mostly palm and ganyan. The island is sparsely inhabited. It has little or no cultivation. Scarce grass and shrubs on the island feed the few gazelles, goats, horses and cattle kept by the inhabitants, who live in mud huts. The island lacks fresh water; it has a small amount of bitter water and is infested with venomous snakes.

Lesser Tumb is located a few miles away to the southwest of Greater Tumb and 20 miles (32 km.) from the port of Lingeh. The island is one mile (1.6 km.) long and 3/4 mile (1/2 km.) wide. It is waterlogged and uninhabited and, like Greater Tumb, is infested with venomous snakes.

Abu Musa is the largest of the three islands, almost rectangular in shape and three miles (4.8 km.) in diameter. About fifty families regularly reside there. Half of the inhabitants are of Persian and half are of Arab origin. Abu Musa, unlike the two Tumbs, has fresh water, plantations of date trees, deposits of red oxide-iron, and proven oil reserves. Abu Musa is located on the median line of the Persian Gulf.[6]

The three islands, like other islands in the Gulf, have a hot and humid climate with limited rainfall. There are nine months of hot summer and three months of cool winter. The annual average temperature ranges roughly from 10 to 32 centigrade (50-90 Fahrenheit) and the average rainfall ranges from 7 to 25 centimeters (3-10 inches), depending on the island. Treacherous winds, from south to north in summer and from east to south in winter, are frequent in the area.

The Persian Gulf is rich in marine life; more than 200 species of fish and shellfish have been identified, among which the Gulf shrimp is world-renown. The pearls of Bahrain were once the most famous and precious sea product of the Gulf. With the discovery of oil, the economy

---

[6] As we shall see these facts are "material" in determination of the exercise of sovereignty by Iran before 1904. In Palmas case (1928), the Arbitrator stated that manifestation of sovereignty over a small island inhabited only by natives (small population) need not be frequent.

of the littoral states currently revolve around the exportation of oil, which constitutes the main, and for some states the sole, source of revenue.

The three islands of Abu Musa and Tumbs, together with the four islands of Hurmoz, Hanjam, Qishm and Larak, form a curved line, which is considered by Persia of great strategic defensive value.

The Nomenclature Of The Persian Gulf

Since the fifth century BC, except for insignificantly brief intervals, the geographical designation of the landlocked sea of the Persian Gulf has remained almost unchanged.

The Early Historical Period

The region's early history is comprised of the Assyrian, Akkadian, and Sumerian periods, and Babylonian interactions with the Elamites. During this time, the sea separating the Persian plateau and the Arabian desert was already an active maritime route. The names of the sea and certain of its seaports have been preserved.[7] Assyrians called it "Nar Marratu" meaning "bitter river", and perhaps this is the Persian Gulf's most ancient name.[8] The Akkadians called it "Tâmtu Spalïtu" meaning the lower sea

---

[7] Amongst many recorded names for various ports, the names of "Niduk-ki" in Akkadian and "Dilmun" in Assyrian seem to refer to the present day Bahrain.

[8] Atlas Historique L'antiquite Carte II, Presses Universitaire, Paris, 1955.

versus "Tâmtu Elënïtu" meaning the upper sea, which was used for the Mediterranean.[9] Sennacherib (705-681), son of Sargon, King of Assyria, describing the route of his naval expedition across the Gulf of Elam, called it "The Great Sea of the East."[10]

Some Greek writers, inter alios, Herodotus in the fifth century BC, called all the seas in the southwest of Asia, including the Persian Gulf, Arabian Sea, Gulf of Aden and the Red Sea, en masse, "hë Erythra Thalassa, or the Erythraen Sea".[11] In Latin, it is Mare Erythraeum. As to the origin of the name, some have suggested that it refers to the red clays in those seas, which is doubtful. Others believed it was the name of the son of a Greek notable, or a Persian prince, which is again unverifiable. We may also mention here that for some unknown reasons Chau-ju-kua, a medieval Chinese writer, has called the Persian Gulf the "Green Sea."[12]

The Second Period

This era starts with the establishment of the Achaemenians, who created a strong navy and merchant shipping for Persia.

---

[9] First appears on a tablet of Sargon of Akkad (2872 B.C.). See Sir Arnold Wilson "The Persian Gulf" (Oxford: 1928). The "Gulf is specifically named in the historical text of Lugal Zagesi; King of Uruk (2340-2316 B.C.) where it is said that then from the Lower Sea by the Tigris and Euphrates, as far as the Upper Sea [the god Enlil] provided him with clear routes", C. Edmund Bosworth, "The Nomenclature of the Persian Gulf" in *The Persian Gulf States: A General Survey*, G. Ed. Alvin J. Cottrel, (Baltimore:1980), p. xviii.

[10] Edmund C. Bosworth op. cit., p. xviii.

[11] Herodotus iv, 40.

[12] Edmund C. Bosworth, op. cit. p. xviii.

In the fifth century BC, Darius the Great of the Achaemenian Dynasty called the Persian Gulf "Draya: tya: hacá: pársa: Aitiy," meaning, "The sea which goes from Persia."[13] In this era, some of the Greek writers continue to call it either "hë Erythia Thalassa" or "Kolpi;" meaning gulf, and others preferred to call it "Persikonkaitas", meaning the Persian Gulf. Claudius Ptolemaeus, the celebrated Greco-Egyptian mathematician/astronomer in the second century, called it "Persicus Sinus" or Persian Gulf.[14] In the first century AD, Quintus Curticus Rufus, the Roman historian, designated it "Aquarius Persico" -- the Persian Sea.[15] Flavius Arrianus, another Greek historian, called it "Persiconkaitas"[16] -- Persian Gulf. Strabo, the renown Greek geographer/historian in the fifth century AD used the same denomination.[17]

During the Sassanian Dynasty, the Gulf was invariably called the "Persian Sea". After the Arabian conquest of Iran, for eight centuries the Persian Gulf was called "Bahre Farsi", meaning Persian Sea. *This was the term used during the time of the prophet Mohammad and the four Right Guided Caliphs, which constitutes a "sunna".* The designation of "Persian Gulf" was also used during the

---

[13] Roland G. Kent, "Old Persian Texts" *Journal of Near Eastern Studies*, Vol. I, Oct. 1942, no. 4, p. 419.

[14] See geography of Claudius Ptolemy translated by Edward L. Stevenson; Sir Arnold Wilson, op. cit., p. 43.

[15] Histoire d'Alexandre le Grand par Quinte Curce, traduction en Français, Tom II (Paris: 1834), p. 184.

[16] Flauvius Arrianus, "History of Alexadndre and Indica" with an English translation by E. Lliff Robinson (London: 1949), The Loeb Classical Library vol. II, pp. 414-417.

[17] The Geography of Strabo" English translation by H.C. Hamilton and W. Falconer (London: 1857), vol. III, p. 187.

Umayyads and the Abbassids.[18] The Ottomans regularly called it either "Persian Gulf" or "Persian Sea"; however, occasionally they also used the names "Khalij Basra" or the "Basra Kurfuzi", meaning the Basra Gulf.

The leading historians and geographers, both Arab and Persian, who wrote mostly in Arabic from 9th to the 17th century AD have used the term "Bahr Farsi" or "Khalij Pars" for the Persian Gulf. The most notable among them are Abu al-Qassim Obaidalläh ibn Khordadbeh Khorassani,[19] Abu Bakr Shahab al-Din Ahmad ibn Mohammad ibn Ishaq Hamadani (Ibn al-Faqih),[20] Abu Ali Ahmad ibn Omar ibn Rasteh,[2] Sohrab,[3] Nakhoda Bozorg ibn Shahriyar Ramhormozi,[4]Abu Ishaq Ibrahim Mohammad al-Farsi al-Istakhri,[5] Abu' al-Hassan Ali ibn al-Hussein ibn Ali Massudi,[6] Ibn al-Mottahar al-Moqadasi al-Taher ibn al Mottahar,[7] Abu al-Qässem Mohammad ibn Hawqal,[8] Shams al-Din Abu Abdallah Mohammad ibn Ahmad ibn Abu Bakr

---

[18] *Given the Sunna, one may question the permissibility of any change in the name of the "Persian Gulf" as it would constitute an innovation or Bed'a which is Harām.*

[19] "Al-Massalek Wa al-Mamalek," Leyden edition: 1889, p. 233.

[20] The abridged "al Boldan" Leyden 1885, p. 8.

[2] al-Álaq al-Naffssiya, vol. VII ed.: De A.J. Goeje, Leyden 1891, p. 84.

[3] AJayeb al-Aqalim al-Saba ila Nehayate al-Mara, (Vienne: 1929), p. 59. Sohrah was a Persian geographer who lived in the 9th century A.D.

[4] "AJayeb al-Hind" ed.: M. Davis, Leyden 1886, p. 41.

[5] "Massalek al-Mamalek," ed.: De M.J. Goeje, Leyden 1927, p. 28.

[6] "Muruj al-Dhahab," English translation by Aloys Sprenger, Vol. I, (London: 1841), p. 259.

[7] "Al-Bod' Wa al-Tarikh" (Paris: 1907) Tom IV, p. 58.

[8] "The Oriental Geography of Ebn Hawkal," Translated by Sir William Ouseley (London: 1800) p. 62; 'Surat al-Arz," (Leyden 1938), Vol. I, p. 42. Ebn Hawqal was an Arabian traveler in the tenth century.

(Shami Moqadassi),[9] Mohammad ibn Najub Bekiran,[10] Abu
Reyhan Mohammad ibn Ahmad al-Biruni al Kharazmi,[11]
Abu Abdallah Mohammad ibn Mohammad ibn Abdallah ibn
Edris (al-Sharif al-Edrissi),[12]Shahab al-Din Abu Abdallah
Yaqut ibn Abdallah Hamawi Rumi,[13] Abu Abdallah Zakariya
ibn Mohammad ibn Mahmud Qazvini,[14] Abu al-Feda Emad
al-Din Ismail ibn Ali Amir Homat,[15] Shams al-Din Abu
Abdallah Mohammad ibn abu Taleb al-Ansari al-Dameshqi
al-Sufi,[16] Hamadallah ibn Abu Bakr Mostowfi Qazvini,[17]
Abu Hafs Zein al-Din Omar ibn Mozafar (Ibn Alwardi),[18]
Shahab al-Din Ahmad ibn Abd al-Wahab ibn Mohammad al-
Nobari,[19] Sharaf al-Din abu Abdallah Mohammad ibn

---

[9] "Ahsan al-Taqassim fi Ma'refat al-Aqalim' ed.: De A.J. Goeje,
(Leyden 1906), p. 17.

[10] "Jahn Nameh" quoted by M.J. Mashkour in an article entitled
"Nam-e Khalij-e Fars" in the proceeding of the "Seminar on Khalij-e
Fars" (Tehran: 1964), Vol. I, p. 44. Bekiran lived in the eleventh
century A.D.

[11] "al-Tafhim Beavaele Sana'at al-Tanjim" ed.: Jallal al-Din Homai
(Tehran: 1318 Hijri Solar Year), p. 167; also "Qanun Masudi,"
(Heydarabad: 1955), Vol. II, p. 558.

[12] "Géographi d'Edrisi" traduite de l'Arabe en Français par P. Amedée
Jaulert (Recueil des voyages et des memoires publiées par la Societé de
Géographie), (Paris: 1840), Vols. V and VI. "Nuzhat al-Moshtaq fi
Ekhtraq al-Afaq," (Rome: 1878), p. 9.

[13] "Mo'jam al-Buldan," (Cairo: 1906), Vol. 2, p. 68.

[14] "Athar al-Belad" (Gutingen: 1848), p. 104.

[15] "Taqwim al-Buldan," Géogrphie d'Aboulfeda traduite de l'Arab par
M. Reinaud, 2 Vols., (Paris: 1848), Vol. 1, p. 23.

[16] "Nokhbat al-Dahr," quoted by M.J. Mashkour op. cit., p. 46.

[17] "Nuzhat al Qulub" ed.: Muhammad Dabir Siyaqi, (Tehran: 1336
Hijri Solar Year), p. 164.

[18] "Kharida al-Ájayeb" quoted by M.J. Mashkour op. cit. p. 47.

[19] "Nehayat al-Erb fi Fonoon al-Árab" cited by M.J. Mashkour, op.
cit., p. 46.

Abdallah Tanji (Ibn Batuta),[20] Ahmad ibn Ali ibn Ahmad al-Qolqoshandi,[21] Mustafa ibn Abdallah Kateb Qostantini,[22] and Sharaf al Zaman Taher Marvazi.[23]

The Third Period

The third period started when the Ottomans, without abandoning the nomenclature "Persian Gulf" altogether, opted to use as alternatives the terms "Khalij Bassra" and "Bassura Kurfuzi" for political reasons. Following the change of regime in Turkey by Ata Turk, the term "Persian Gulf" has exclusively been used.

However, in recent years a new development has taken place. In 1958, after the overthrow of the monarchy by Abd al Karim Qässem, the new revolutionary regime in Baghdad changed the name of the "Persian Gulf" to "Arabian Gulf", in 1960, for political aims. The newly coined nomenclature was taken up by Gamal Abdul Nasser of Egypt after the severance of Irano-Egyptian diplomatic relations. Soon the term was in vogue for Arab states in the Gulf. It has been used as a psychological tool in their war of rhetoric with Iran. In 1966, Sir Charles Belgrave, a former British commissioner in the Persian Gulf (1926-1957), used in his book the term "Arabian Gulf" interchangeably with the term "Persian Gulf". He seemingly maintains that, since the two denominations, "Khalij-e- Arabi" and "Khalij-e- Farsi", are being used by Arabs and Persians respectfuly, both should be acceptable to outsiders.[24]

---

[20] "The Travels of Ibn Batutah," translated from the abridged Arabic MSS of Cambridge by the Rev. Samuel Lee (Cambridge: 1824), p. 56.
[21]

[22] Ibid., pp. 47-48.
[23] "Tabaye al-Hayvan," quoted by Mashkoor ibid., p. 44.
[24] Sir Charles Belgrave, "The Pirate Coast," (London: 1966), p. 3.

With the escalation of bickering between Iran and its Arab neighbors over the islands, and the emergence of more radical Arab states, the wrangle over the name intensified and became problematic for the foreign companies, oil and others, operating in the region. To come out of the deadlock, a majority of the companies chose "the Gulf," equivalent of "Kolpi" used by some Greek writers in antiquity. But history cannot be changed. The authentic and historical name of the landlocked sea between Iran and Arabia will remain the Persian Gulf. However, if the British and the French can live in peace with their separating sea being called the "English Channel" and "La Manche", shouldn't the littoral states of the Persian Gulf feel comfortable with either of the terms "Persian" or "Arabian" Gulf, and not allow the row over the name to strain their relations, causing embarrassment to foreigners trading with them?

A Brief Historical Survey of the Persian Gulf

The Pre-Islamic Period

The Persian Gulf, since the dawn of history, has been a passage of maritime trade. Its coastline inhabitants have paddled the shallow waters of the Gulf for fishing, its local navigators have transported and traded merchandise between the Gulf ports and islands. The seafarers of all nations, on their routes to India, China and East Indies, have called on the ports of the Persian Gulf and the Gulf of Oman.[25]

Although the origin and ethnicity of the early inhabitants of the Gulf coasts remain a matter for conjecture, the current hypothesis recognizes several ethnic groups including the Davidians, Semitic people, and the pro-Elamites as the initial settlers of the areas along Mokran, Bandir, and the head of the Persian Gulf respectively.[26] The Davidians were the aborigines; the Semites were comprised of Assyrians, Babylonians, Arabs, Phoenicians, Hebrews and Moabites; the pro-Elamites were the Elamites who had migrated to the Iranian Plateau, Syria and Egypt earlier than 4000 BC[27]

During the time of the Achaemenians (559-330 BC), the Persian Gulf was under Persian sovereignty. The Achaemenian Empire extended from India in the east to Egypt and Libya in the west, from the Aral and Black Seas in the north to the Arabian coast of the Persian Gulf in the south. The number of Persian vessels in the sea battle of Salamis (480 BC), as narrated by Greek historians, suggest that, during this period, Persia had a large fleet. Cyrus the Great (559-529 BC) could not have produced such a vast empire without a mighty army and an effective naval force. "Persians were notable seagoing people with a strong navy and renown admirals, uniting the whole Western Asia and Egypt into an enduring empire" writes Roger Savory.[28] In

---

[25] G.F. Hourani, "Arab Seafaring in the Indian Ocean in Ancient and Early Medieval Times," (Princeton: 1951), pp. 3-4.

[26] Sir Arnold T. Wilson, "The Persian Gulf," (London: 1928), p. 25.

[27] ibid., pp. 26, 29, 33.

[28] Roger M. Savory, "The History of Persian Gulf," in "The Persian Gulf States" G.E. Alvin J. Cottrell (Baltimore: 1980), p. 8. Savory rejects Lord Curzon's assertion that Iranians had an aversion to the sea. Lord Curzon had based his assumption on instances from some

the Iranian fleet, the services of citizens of integrated nations such as Phoenicians and Egyptians were enlisted.

For promotion of international trade, Darius the Great (521-486 BC) constructed a canal linking the Nile with the Red Sea. That project was accomplished twenty-four centuries before the advent of the Suez Canal. An inscribed memorial, the Stele of Shaluf, discovered during the excavation of the modern Suez Canal by Ferdinand de Lesseps, reads:

> The Great God is Ahura Mazda, who created yonder sky, this earth, man and welfare for man, who made Darius King . . . . I am Darius, the Great King of kings, King of the countries containing all [kinds of] men, . . . an Achemenian, a Persian from Fars; I seized Egypt; I ordered the canal to be dug from the river by name Nile, which flows from Egypt, to the sea which goes from Persia. Afterwards this canal was dug, thus as I commanded, and ships went from Egypt through this canal to Persia, thus as was my desire.[29]

Through maritime expeditions along the Persian Gulf to areas north of the Indies, Darius conquered West India and incorporated it into the Hindukush Satrap (province).[30] Herodotus writes that Darius set up an expedition, under the Greek Scylax of Caryanda, from Caspatyrus (Upper Indies) to the Red Sea. They "sailed down the river

---

Iranian literary tradition in the tenth century onward which has no bearing on the historical realities in Pre-Islamic Iran.

[29] Roland G. Kent, "Old Persian Texts," Journal of New Eastern Studies, (Chicago) vol. I, No 4, October, 1942, p. 419.

[30] Roger M. Savory, op. cit., p. 9; Ismail Ra'in, "Daryanavardi-e Iranian," (Tehran: 1952), vol. I, chapter 2.

towards the east and the sunrise till they came to the sea; then they turned towards the west till they arrived at the head of the Arabian Gulf (Red Sea)." Herodotus also states that "Darius subdued the Indians and made use of this sea."[31]

The Achaemenians retained their control over the Persian Gulf and beyond, until Alexander the Great of Macedonia defeated them and captured Iran in 330 BC Alexander and his successors ruled Iran for eighty years until they were destroyed by the Parthians around 250 BC The journal of the voyage of Nearchus, the Admiral of Alexander the Great,[32] shows the persistence of Iran's sway over the seas in the south of the Iranian Plateau.

The Parthians who came from Northeastern Iran, ruled the country for 476 years (250 BC to 226 AD). The Parthians too controlled the Persian Gulf. Mithradates I (174 BC) stretched his authority from the Euphrates to India. They came in contact with the Romans, who vied with Iran for territory and trade, in the early first centuries AD Both the Romans and the Persians used the waterways of the Tigris, Euphrates, and the Persian Gulf as maritime channels of communication to India and China. Iran, alarmed with the expansion of Roman trade, frequently interfered with the Romans' free passage in the Gulf. As the result, by the middle of the second century AD, the Romans shifted their trade routes to the Red Sea, at the expense of the Persian Gulf, and the Red Sea trade route flourished thereafter.

The Sassanians (226-617 AD), who replaced the Parthians, conscious of the preeminence of trade, strengthened their merchant fleet and vigorously

---

[31] Sir Arnold T. Wilson, op. cit., p. 36.

[32] ibid., p. 37.

encouraged the Iranians to engage in seafaring. Ardashir Papakan, the founder of the dynasty, constructed many ports including Hurmozd Ardashir (Ahvaz), Veh Ardashir (Seleucia), Vahishtabadh Ardashir (Basra), Astrabadh Ardashir (Karkh Maysen), Vahman Ardashir (Bahmanshir), Riv Ardashir (Rishahr), Ram Ardashir, and Bith Ardashir.[33] Under the great Sassanian king, Khusrow Anushiravan (531-79), the Persian influence extended far beyond the river Indus. Some Muslim sources mention that Anushiravan even sent a fleet to Ceylon[34]

In the third century AD, the Romans built a highway from the Gulf of Aqaba to Damascus, and for a short time occupied Mesopotamia, thereby gaining access to the Persian Gulf. The Roman fleet was regularly on the Red Sea.[35] As a result of the increase in maritime trade, the ship building industry on the coast of Oman prospered in the fourth century.

A noteworthy event during the Sassanian era was the migration of Arab tribes to the southern coast of Iran, some of whom subsequently became a threat to peace and order in the region. Shahpur II suppressed the marauding Arab tribes effectively. One of the reasons for confrontation between the Arabs and Iranians might have been mounting competition in maritime activities in the Persian Gulf. Supported by the State, the number of Iranians taking up trade was on the rise, embittering Arabs engaged in similar

---

[33] Hadi Hassan, "A History of Persian Navigation," (London: 1928), op. cit., p. 12.
[34] Roger M. Savory, op. cit., p. 12.
[35] G.F. Hourani, "Arab Seafaring in the Indian Ocean in Ancient and Early Medieval Times," (Princeton: 1951), p. 35.

the plundering of villages. In 570, Anushiravan severely punished them, conquered Yemen, and controlled the Red Sea trade. Having reestablished Iran's authority over Bahrain and Oman, Anushiravan greatly undermined the Arabs' maritime operations in the Persian Gulf.[36] The Arab-Persian animosity in the region continued until the defeat of the Sassanians by the Arabs in 633 AD, when a new era in Persian history began.

The Iranians' impact on maritime trade in the pre-Islamic era is undeniable and can be traced to the pre-Achaemenian times. The building of the Rishahr port, to the south of Bushehr Peninsula, has been ascribed to Lohrasp of the Keyanian Dynasty; the port was rebuilt by Shapur I of the Sassanian Dynasty in the third century AD The construction of Bushir on the littoral of Fars is traced to the Elamites; it was renovated by Ardashir Sassani. Siraf, the modern village of Taheri, located on the slope of the Siri mountains, is said to have been erected by Kaykavous of the Keyanian Dynasty; Ubulla, on the western slope of the estuary of the Tigris, was founded by Ardashir Sassanian in the third century AD In the port of Tahiri, archaeologists have unearthed the ruins of a Zoroastrian Dakhma, the place for the disposal of the dead body, which bears witness to its antiquity.[37] The Farsi names of the ports which were in usage in the time of Achaemenians, such as Karmama (Kerman), Anamis (Minab), Organa (Hurmoz), Odakta (Qishm), and Kataria (Kish), are preserved for us by Greek classical writers. These were ports of call and centers of maritime trade at the dawn of Persian history.

---

[36] Roger M. Savory, op. cit., p. 13.
[37] Sir Arnold T. Wilson, op. cit., p. 93.

The Islamic Era

After the Arab conquest of Iran in the seventh century, the Iranian territories including Mesopotamia, the southern coast of the Persian Gulf, Bahrain, Oman, Mahra and Hadharmaut, became parts of Dar al-Islam, the Zone of Islam. Inhabitants of all the conquered lands acquired a new identity, Muslim, replacing their former identity based on nationality. The capitals of the Arab empire under the Umayyads (666-750 AD) and Abbassids (750-1258 AD) were Damascus and Baghdad respectively.

During the Abbassids, fragmentation occurred both in the religious and state leadership. The concurrent rule of the Umayyads of Spain, Fatimids of Egypt, and autonomous principalities in Iran eroded the solidarity of Umat (the Islamic nation). In 1258, Hulagu, the Mongol conqueror, sacked Baghdad, and slew the last Abbassid Caliph.

Under the reign of the two Arab dynasties, particularly in the time of Abbassids, maritime trade to China and India via the Persian Gulf continued[38] with the Iranians still at the helm. The Arab historian, writing about seafaring in this era, calls the Persian "masters" in maritime craft. He further states that during the Caliphs, the majority of inhabitants of Aden and Jedda as well as their ruling classes were Persians who spoke Arabic.[39]

Persistence of the use of Persian marine vocabulary, despite the universality of the Arab language under the Islamic-Arab regimes, testifies to the lasting supremacy of the Iranian navigators during the six centuries after the fall

---

[38] Roger M. Savory, op. cit., p. 16.

[39] G.F. Hourani, op. cit., pp. 65-66; Hadi Hassan, op. cit., pp. 144-145.

the Iranian navigators during the six centuries after the fall of Iran to the Arabs. Hadi Hassan in his scholarly work in "The History of Persian Navigation," remarks that many Arabic maritime terms, such as Rahnamaj (Rahnema in Persian and Rahnameh in Pahlavi), Nakhoda, and Bandar are of Persian origin, which proves the predominance of Persian mariners in the Gulf.[40] One may add that it also proves that Iranians preceded the Arabs in seafaring and lent them their maritime terms.

One of the reasons for the persistence of Persian predominance may be the fact that at the dawn of Islam, the Arab leaders were not supportive of marine military expeditions, the long seafaring tradition of the Arabs notwithstanding. It is related that Omar, the second Caliph, had an aversion to the sea. This is evident in his response to Muáwiya, the Governor of Syria, who had asked the Caliph's permission for a sea expedition. Unlike Omar, Muáwiya considered naval strength vital for the pursuance of the Arab conquests. In his response, Omar, wrote:

> The sea is boundless expanse, whereon great ships look tiny specks, nought but the heavens above and waters beneath; when calm, the sailor's heart is broken; when tempestuous, his senses reel. Trust it little, fear it much. Man at sea is an insect on a splinter, now engulfed, now scared to death.[41]

Under the Caliphs, Iranians not only maintained their dominance over the Persian Gulf and its maritime trade, but also managed to extend their influence far and wide in the Zone of Islam. Colonies of Iranian merchants established

---

[40] Hadi Hassan, op. cit., p. 129.
[41] Sir William Merir, "The Caliphate: Its Rise, Decline, and Fall," (Edinburgh: 1924),p.205.

themselves in "Calicut on the Malabar coast, at Bengala in Bengal, at Cambay, and as far east as Malacca. At many places in East Africa, Iranians became the ruling princes, for instance in Pemba, Zanzibar, Brava, Mogadishu, and Kilwas."[42] The use of the Persian word "bandar" for "port", and the use of Persian suffix "bar" in such names as Malabar and Zanzibar, further reveals the Persian influence in South Africa. This influence was associated with a change in the population mix and demographic structure of the region, affecting the geopolitical status of certain areas on the southern coast of the Persian Gulf.

A significant phenomenon under the Caliphs was the disappearance of the traditional rivalry between the Red Sea and the Persian Gulf as the main trade routes between the West and the East. Both seas had become integrated parts of Dar al-Islam. However, the rivalry resurfaced during the Fatimids of Egypt (909-1171 AD) when Cairo became more prosperous than Baghdad and the Red Sea again surpassed the Persian Gulf as a trade route. Consequently, the geographical importance of Basra, Siraf, Kish, Tiz and Hurmoz alternated with the political and economic vacillation in the region.

Another important development in the Persian Gulf that lingered into the nineteenth century was the increase in piracy. The Arabs, accustomed to the nomadic traditions of attack and plunder, introduced piracy at sea. George Hourani defined the maritime activity of the Arabs in terms of trade and piracy. According to Hourani, the Arabs extended to the oceans the Bedouin principle of the Ghazwas: Tribal raid. Hourani has pointed out that in Arabic, the verb "Rakaba," meaning "to ride a camel," also

---

[42] Roger M. Savory, op. cit., p. 16.

means "sailing a ship."[43]   And writing on the significance of the lingual usage, Roger Savory notes: "It is not by chance, therefore, that piracy became a way of life for many maritime Arabs from Bahrain to Oman."[44]

With the waning of the Caliph's control over Dar al-Islam, the Persian Gulf region turned into a field of continuous strife between local rulers, tribal chiefs, and outside invaders, at times intensified by ethnic, racial, and religious differences.   Such conflicts often led to violent confrontations, population dislocation, and damages to life and property.   For instance, in the early tenth century, during the Abbassids, the Sheikh of Oman rebelled, and the Governor of Bahrain, at the behest of the Abbassid Caliph, attacked Oman.   The Sheikh of Oman was defeated and with his people fled to the city of Hurmoz, on the Persian coast, where they founded an Arab colony, becoming vassal first to the Saljuq (1041-1073), and then to the Ghuzz (1186-1200) rulers of Iran.   Likewise, in 1203, a conflict broke out between the rulers of Kish Island and the city of Hurmoz; both integrated parts of Iran, with each ruler claiming authority over the other.   Both Kish and Hurmoz were legally subordinate to the governor (Atabeg) of the province of Fars.   The Governor of Fars, at the request of Abu Bakr, the ruler of Hurmoz, sent his army to Kish and Bahrain, restoring Iran's sovereignty over the islands.   For the following two hundred years, that is until the Portuguese invasion of Hurmoz, the two islands were under Iranian rule.

The Post-Arab Period

---

[43] G.F. Hourani, op. cit., pp. 52-53.
[44] Roger M. Savory, op. cit., p. 15.

After the collapse of the Caliphate in Baghdad, the Mongols sacked Oman in 1272. The lawlessness in the Persian Gulf escalated and the piratical tribes pursued this turn of events, preying on the ships that sailed in the Gulf. The rampant violence even impelled some Arab tribes to seek safer places for residence. The choice was always a difficult one, and the following serves as an illustration. Seeking a sanctuary, in 1302 Ayaz moved his people from Hurmoz to the island of Qishm, only to find it more vulnerable due to its proximity to the coast. Thirteen years later, Ayaz moved his people from Qishm to the island of Jarun.[45] Ayaz was one of the influential tribe chiefs in Hurmoz. He was neither the owner of any of those islands, nor had any assignment from the Governor of Fars. His movements from one island to the other were motivated by a sense of better security and a greater freedom in collecting booties. The tribesmen owed their loyalty to the chief. There was no bond between them and the occupied land per se.

The Portuguese Invasion

The arrival of the Portuguese in the Persian Gulf in 1505 altered the geopolitics of the region. The Portuguese aimed at monopolization of the lucrative East-West trade and dominion over the strategic points on the trade route. This was a great design set out by General Alfonso de Albuquerque, the prime targets of which were the ports of Hurmoz, Aden, and the Straits of Malaca.

---

[45] ibid., p. 19.

Proceeding along the coast of Southeastern Arabia, the Portuguese captured "Qalhat, a dependency of Hurmoz," and forced its governor "to become a Portuguese tributary."[46] Thereafter, General de Albuquerque pillaged Quryat, Muscat, Khor Fakkan, and seized Suhar and, finally, Hurmoz in 1507. On that occasion, the occupation of Hurmoz did not last long. A rebellion broke out in 1508 in Hurmoz, and the Portuguese retreated. However, seven years later the Portuguese Navy returned and reoccupied Hurmoz. Iran protested. In 1515, General de Albuquerque forced a treaty on Shah Ismail Safavi, whereby the latter acknowledged the ruler of Hurmoz to be a Portuguese vassal. In return, the Portuguese General promised to assist Iran to recover Bahrain and Qatif from mutinous Sheikh Jabrid, to quell the revolt in Mukran, and to repel Ottoman aggression in the northwest of Iran. The Portuguese not only failed to honor their promise, but also captured Bahrain and Qatif for themselves.

In 1523, the Portuguese General compelled Iran to sign the Minab Treaty, under which the Portuguese vessels calling at Hurmoz became exempt from port charges. The General also assumed the authority to appoint a new Governor and impose new taxes within the Hurmoz jurisdiction. Furthermore, the people of Hurmoz were forbidden to own or carry arms, except for a small number of soldiers engaged in guarding the Governor's residence. This was a device used to forestall any future uprising like the one which had occurred in 1508. The Portuguese dominion over Hurmoz and Bahrain lasted for 107 years.

The Portuguese sway in the Gulf remained unchallenged until 1534, when the Ottomans, having retaken Basra from Iran, consolidated their position to confront the Portuguese

---

[46] ibid., p. 22.

in the Gulf. The Ottoman-Portugese armed confrontation for the seizure of the key ports of Hurmoz, Qishm and Bahrain took place intermittently for 30 years, causing human and material losses to both sides without affecting the status quo.

The change came about in the early 1600's from new political developments, both in Iran and in England. In Iran, Shah Abbas ascended the throne and he was resolute to regain Iran's lost territories. In England, Queen Elizabeth I was equally determined to expand the English eastward trade. She issued a charter to the newly formed English East India company, granting it and certain other corporate bodies exclusive rights to trade east of the Cape of Good Hope and west of the Strait of Magellan. Access to the Persian Gulf was crucial to the British design.

The commonalty of interests in the Persian Gulf brought England and Iran together. Iran lacked a strong navy to exercise her sovereignty on the islands and Britain needed a foothold in the Gulf for achieving her trade ambitions. Shah Abbas provided the incentive.

In 1615 Iran granted preferential rights to the English East India Company against other foreign traders. These rights included the right for its vessels to call at all Iranian ports in the Gulf, for its members to establish factories at any city, and for its traders to export Iranian silk to Europe. Furthermore, Shah Abbas accorded the English the right to bear arms for self-defense and be exempted from Iranian court jurisdiction for crimes committed by them on Iranian soil. The latter privilege, which was an extraterritorial right, afforded the English nationals the required security to stay and work in Iran without anxiety of being subjected to the harsh Islamic punishments.

The grant of preferential treatment to the English convinced the Portuguese of an Irano-English plot against them. Five years later, in January 1620, a naval clash broke out between Portugal and Britain, from which the latter emerged victorious. In 1622 the Portuguese occupied Qishm Island, only to be ejected by the Iranians with the backing of the naval force of the English India Company. The last blow to the Portuguese came in April 1622 when the Iranian military, with the support of the English East Indian Company, attacked Hurmoz, crushed the Portuguese resistance, and restored Iranian sovereignty over Hurmoz after 107 years. The Portuguese still retained their control of Muscat, Ras al-Khaimah, and Suhar in the south of the Gulf until 1643 when the Imam of Muscat seized those ports and evicted the Portuguese from Oman.

British Intrusion

With the ouster of the Portuguese from the region in the seventeenth century, the stage was set for devastating intervention by the British. In the following two centuries, the Persian Gulf became the scene of rivalry between Britain, the Netherlands, France and the Sa'udis. The Dutch East India Company, established in 1602, and the French East India Company, formed in 1664, posed a potential threat to British interests in the region. The Sa'udis, pursuing the Messianic Wahhabi mission, sought supremacy in the Arabian Peninsula, including the southern coast of the Persian Gulf. However, none of these competing forces could produce a lasting political impact on the region or hamper British expansionism. The future of the region was to be shaped by the declining influence of Iran and the rising dominance of Britain.

Following his triumph over the Portuguese, Shah Abbas reconstructed the city of Gombran, renamed it Bandar Abbas, and moved the residents of Hurmoz to the new city. He extended to the British in Bandar Abbas the privileges they had enjoyed in Hurmoz. They were also allowed to share the spoils of the Irano-Portuguese war and to occupy the forts erected by the Portuguese. The British also obtained exemption from import-export duties.

The Decline of Iran

The gradual decline of the Safavids in the succeeding years, prompted the Afghans' invasion of Iran, culminated in the total collapse of the Safavid Dynasty. Iran faced disintegration in the chaos that ensued from the occupation of the Afghans (1722-1734). In 1734, Nader, the chief of the Afshar tribe, rose to evict the invaders and reunite the country. After succeeding, Nader proclaimed himself Shah of Iran.

During the reign of the Safavids, Iran exercised sovereignty over the northern coast of the Gulf and intermittently controlled the islands of Bahrain, Qishm, Abu Musa and the Tumbs. Nader Shah was determined to suppress the breakaway local rulers, to wipe out foreign interventions, and to establish Iran's hegemony anew over the southern coast of the Persian Gulf. Despite initial success, Nader Shah failed in his attempts, mainly due to the infighting of two of his military commanders and treacherous acts of a number of the Arab sheikhs in the south, Ottoman aggression in the north, and British intrigues in the Gulf. The assassination of Nader Shah in 1750 put an end to his plans.

After Nader Shah, the central authority of the government of Iran was further eroded by the power struggle between the two tribes of Zand and Qajar, vying for the kingship. The result was 32 years of Zand and 135 years of Qajar reign in Iran. During this period of increasing anarchy, certain Arab tribes migrated to Iran, weakening the country and furthering her decline. The maundering Arab tribes in the Persian Gulf were solely interested in piracy, plundering, and accumulating booties. Notable among them were the two tribes of Bani Ka'b and Bani Lamb.

The Bani Ka'b, operating across the borders of Mesopotamia and Persia, were more powerful, unbridled, and callous. They owned over eighty small and large boats that "preyed on the ships plying to or from Basra".[47] In the southern coast of the Persian Gulf, other Arab tribes, particularly the two tribes of the Qawasim and Bani Yas, were engaged in the same adventures as their fellow Arab tribesmen in the north.

The severity of savagery in the Gulf and the threats posed by the Arabs to the British interests in the area prompted the British to act. They could no longer rely on the government of Iran to restore order in the Gulf, or to keep rival foreign powers, namely the French, Dutch, Ottomans and Sa'udis, out. Hence the British adopted a two-pronged policy: Make an alliance with the most stable government in the area (considered by the British to be Oman) and, work to directly control unruly Arab pirate sheikhs in the Gulf. Thus the English East India Company initiated direct negotiations with the tribal sheikhs, obtaining pledges from them to refrain from attacking the vessels of the English East India Company. In the Company's

---

[47] ibid., p.37.

negotiations with the sheikhs, representatives of the India Office were present who gave recognition to the sheikhs as autonomous rulers within specified territorial jurisdictions. The first agreement of this type was concluded with the Imam of Muscat in October 1798. This was a prudent move on the part of the British.

After the downfall of the Ya'riba Dynasty and the establishment of the Al Bu Sa'id Dynasty in Oman, the Imam of Muscat was the most powerful ruler in the Gulf. He also had expansionist aspirations. In the course of the Oman civil war (1742-1743), Nader Shah of Iran, supporting one of the warring parties, conquered Muscat and Suhar. In 1744, while Nader, was engaged in a newly erupted war with the Ottoman Empire, Ahmad ben Sa'id, the Governor of Suhar, rebelled against Nader, seized Muscat, and founded the Al Bu Sa'id Dynasty in Oman. In 1794, the Imam of Oman extended his control over northern coast of the Gulf, occupied Gwadar, Chahbahar, the islands of Qishm and Hurmoz, and leased Bandar Abbas from the Bani Ma'in, an Arab tribe, who had already settled in that city and assumed a certain degree of autonomy.[48] A few years later, the Imam of Muscat and Oman leased Bandar Abbas from Iran, [49] thereby admitting Iran's sovereignty over the port.

Under the 1798 agreement between the Imam of Muscat and the East India Company, the Imam pledged to keep the French out of his realm. At this time, Napoleon, having won a victory in Egypt, was building an alliance with the Russian Tsar with a view to invade India. Subsequently, by

---

[48] Lockhart, Nader Shah, (London: 1938) p.219-220.
[49] Sir Arnold T. Wilson op. cit., p. 232; Alvin Cottrel op. cit. pp.53-54.

a supplementary arrangement, the Imam (Sultan) of Muscat obligated himself to conduct all his foreign relations through the English Resident designated by the English East India Company. The Imam also recognized and reaffirmed the privileges that the British had enjoyed under Shah Abbas in Bandar Abbas including the right "to establish factory, fortify it with guns, and to station military in that part for the protection of the English subjects."[50]

For the defense of India, both against the French (who controlled Egypt at that time), and the Russians (who nurtured ambitions to reach the warm waters of the Indian ocean), control of the Persian Gulf was vital to the British. So was the safety of the British shipping routes against the attacks of the local Arab maritime tribes in the Gulf.

To punish the pirate sheikhs, the East India Company sent out three naval expeditions in 1806, 1809, and 1819 after which events the sheikhs submitted to the British request to refrain from assailing British vessels.[51] Despite their individual pledges to the East India Company, the sheikhs often resorted to arms in intertribal conflicts, causing instability and putting British interests at risk. To stop this practice, the British, first in 1835 and then in 1892, compelled the sheikhs to make use of British arbitration in the case of future intertribal conflicts, and to refrain from armed confrontation. Thus, the power vacuums created by the gradual decline of both Iran in the Persian Gulf and the Ottoman Empire in the Arabian Peninsula, were being filled by the bilateral arrangements between the East India Company and the Arab sheikhs. The British recognized

---

[50] J.C. Hurewitz, "Diplomacy in the Middle East", (New York: 1951) pp i,64

[51] This implies that Britain was more concerned with her own interests and not with enforcing the international covenants against piracy in the Sea.

each piratical tribe as a separate, legal entity, required them to confine their maritime operations to littoral areas, and forced them to enter into bilateral agreements with the English East India Company. Consequently, they obligated themselves to the company (and to the British) and through it, to each other -- a process tantamount to a collective agreement. By 1892, these littoral Emirates delivered letters of covenant to the British, thereby relinquishing their rights to establish any contact with foreign powers, to sell or lease land, and to grant any concession to any foreign country or their citizens without the prior approval of the British.[52]

In the case of the Trucial States, these concessions, which have been labeled as "Exclusive Agreements" and "Non-Alienation Agreements or Bonds", gave the British a legal basis for the exclusive exploration of natural resources and the exclusive use of the naval bases in the lower Gulf. The Exclusive Agreements were political, economic and military in nature. In broad terms, these agreements gave Britain a free hand on the Arabian shore of the Gulf, enabling her to perform a regulatory role in the area, and authorizing her to intervene for the protection of the sheikhs against external threats whenever they saw fit. In 1890, France opened a consulate in Muscat, Germany and Russia obtained concessions from the Ottomans to build a railway through Asia Minor to Kuwait, and the Russians continued to nourish the aspiration of an outlet to the Persian Gulf. All of these were considered a threat to British interests. The Exclusive Agreements, which at the initial stage were

---

[52] J.B. Lorimer, "Gazetteer of the Persian Gulf, Oman and Central Arabia", (Farnborough: Gregg Internation/Irish University Press, 1970) Vol. 1

limited in scope, were extended to include every aspect of foreign relations.

In essence, Britain was thus able to dictate the Sheikhs' foreign policy. Under the Bahrain-British agreement of 1880, Sheikh Isa of Bahrain covenanted "to abstain from entering into negotiations or making treaties of any sort with any state or government other than the British without the consent of the said British government, and to refuse permission to any other government than the British to establish diplomatic Consular agencies or coal depot in (his) territory, unless with the consent of the British government".[53]   In June 1899, the British Political Resident obtained from Sheikh Mubarak of Kuwait, a covenant whereby he, on behalf of himself, his heirs, and his successors, undertook not to receive any representative or agent of other governments or "to alienate any portion of his territory to the government or subjects of another power, without the previous consent of the British government".[54]

The Arab sheikhdoms did not gain their independence before 1960. Hence, whatever was done in their name was effectively done by the British and for the protection of British interests in the region. Under the Exclusive Treaties, the sheikhs could not grant any economic concession to foreign entrepreneurs without the prior consent of the British. This became particularly important in 1920's when, the American Oil Companies, with the backing of the U.S.

---

[53] J.B. Kelly, "Britain and the Persian Gulf: 1795-1880", (Oxford, 1986) p. 825.

[54] J.B. Kelly op. cit., p.836; from the text of the treaties see Aitchison, Treaties (15th ed.) xi., pp. 258-261

government, were vying for oil concessions in the Middle East.[55]

After W.W.I, with the partitioning of the Ottoman Empire and the emergence of Turkey, the Ottoman aspirations in the Arab territories evaporated. The only state that continued to voice its claims over the islands of Bahrain, Abu Mussa and the two Tumbs was Iran.

In order to protect their mounting colonial interests against external and local threats, the British assumed the task of the gendarme of the region. At the turn of the nineteenth century, Russia seized the greater part of Iran's transcaucasian territory, and tried to make Northern Iran a zone of Russian influence. To foil the Russian plan, the British, in 1801, signed a treaty with Iran promising to supply the latter with military equipment and technicians in return for an Iranian pledge to support British efforts should the Russians move towards Iran or India. That treaty was followed by two other treaties of 1809 and 1814. Iran hoped that, through British aid, she would be able to recapture the territories lost to Russia in the 1804-1813 war. Iran's hopes were dashed when she did not receive any military or political backings from Britain in the 1926-1928 war with Russia. At the end, under the Turkomachai Treaty of 1828, Iran lost even more land and had to forgo all claims to her transcaucasian territory.

In 1856, Iran attempted to retake Herat from the newly established state of Afghanistan. The city of Herat had a large Persian speaking population and was, until 1747, part of Iran. In that year Ahmad Khan Abdali, a general in charge of the Treasury under Nader Shah, defected to

---

[55] Edward W. Chester "United States Oil Policy and Diplomacy" (Connecticut: 1983) Ch. 5 on the Middle East and North Africa.

Afghanistan, proclaimed that country independent, and himself Shah; thus he established the Durani Dynasty in Afghanistan.[56]   In 1856, while the Iranian army was marching towards Herat, the British troops in the north of Afghanistan intervened and the British fleet in the Persian Gulf landed troops in Bandar Bushehr, threatening to invade the country unless Iran withdrew her troops. Subsequently in 1857, the British forced Iran to sign the Treaty of Paris and to abandon her claim to Herat. However, in the same year, Iran managed to occupy Chahbahar, eradicate the influence of the Arab tribes over Baluchestan, and restore full control over that province. "By 1872, the Arab influence in the coast of Iranian Baluchestan had disappeared."[57]

During the nineteenth and twentieth centuries, the British and the Russians had many interests at stake in Iran. Their policies leaned towards dividing the country into zones of influence (as occured in the 1907 Anglo-Russian Agreement) , or maintaining a positive (or active) equilibrium by extracting as many concessions from Iran as possible. (This was the case in the second half of the nineteenth century.)

The ruling Qajar kings, not having a national populace base for the survival of the dynasty, relied on both the British and the Russians, from whom they had received a tacit guarantee of patronage. The Qajar kings were also anxious to have the presence of both powers in Iran lest one power try to completely colonize the country. This policy came   to   be   known   as   "equilibrium" or   "positive

---

[56] Vartan Gregorian "The Emergence of Modern Afghanistan" (Stanford, California: 1969) p. 46

[57] Malcom Yapp "British Policy in the Persian Gulf" in "The Persian Gulf States" g. ed.: Alvin J. Cottrell (Baltimore: 1980) p. 53

equilibrium".[58] If for any reason Iran made a special concession to one power, the other would react with hostility. This was illustrated by the reaction of the British towards Iran, after the latter hired Belgian customs officers who, in furtherance of their fiduciary position towards the Russians, soon tilted towards them.

In 1898, the Chief Minister, Amin al-Dawleh hired Monsieur Joseph M. Naus, a Belgian administrator, to reorganize the Customs Offices, which had for many years been farmed out by the government. In 1900 and 1902, Iran obtained large loans from Russia, and the customs revenue served as collateral for the loan. Hence, the Russians became directly interested in the tariffs and custom management and, through the Belgian officers, monitored the revenues. Although the improvement of efficiency in the customs management was undeniable, Naus was blamed for favoritism towards Russia, both by Iranian merchants and the British. The Persians, who were used to low tariffs and even non-payment, were unhappy with the Belgian takeover of the Customs Offices and the raising of the tariffs. The British, apart from the economic disadvantages, did not want the pro-Russian Belgians to establish themselves in the Persian Gulf islands and thus gain a foothold closer to India.

In 1902, Nause was appointed Minister of Customs. This further displeased the British and, in 1903, they prevented the Belgian officers from establishing customs offices on the islands of Abu Musa and Tumbs. This was the first time that the British claimed to be acting on behalf of the Arab sheikhs of the southern coast of the Persian Gulf

---

[58] Rouhollah K. Ramazani "The Foreign Policy of Iran, 1500-1914" (Virginia: 1966) p. 65

under the Exclusive Agreements. The demands of the constitutionalists in the uprising of 1905-1906, in which the British too were involved, included the removal of Naus and the Belgian custom officers. When Mozafar al-Din Shah was pressured by the constitutionalists to dismiss Naus, the Russians threatened to take the necessary measures to insure that the customs did not pass out of "secure hands".[59] Likewise, the British in the south did not wish to see the islands fall into the "insecure hands".

The British policy in Iran during the second half of the nineteenth century and early twentieth century evolved from that of a gunboat policy to the creation of a buffer state, to the division of Iran (with Russia's complicity) into zones of influence, and finally to the plotting of a de facto colonization of Iran. The Anglo-Russian Agreement of 1907 divided Iran into two zones of influence: Northern and Central Iran, including Tehran and Isphahan, fell in the Russian sphere, the southeastern part of Sistan and Baluchestan in the British sphere, and the area in between the two zones remained for Iran. The Iranians were neither consulted before, nor advised after the signing of the treaty, which also settled the Anglo-Russian disputes in Tibet and Afghanistan.

With the October 1917 Revolution in Russia, the change of the ruling dynasty in Iran in 1925, and the mounting might of Britain as the sole political arbiter in the Gulf, the geopolitics of the region changed. The Soviet Union, in the Friendship Treaty of 1921, relinquished all Russian vested rights in Iran which had been acquired during the time of the Tsars, short of giving back the territories that the Russians had annexed under the Turkmanchai Treaty of 1828.

---

[59] Ervand Abrahamian "Iran Between Two Revolutions", (Princeton, NJ: 1982) p. 81

Meanwhile, the British tried to transform Iran into a protectorate through the 1919 Treaty -- an attempt which was foiled by the Majlis. Failing to colonize Iran, the British were determined to keep the Trucial States in the southern coast of the Persian Gulf under their sway, as well as the islands of Bahrain, Abu Mussa, and the two Tumbs, to which Iran had always laid claims. These claims had been intensified under the nationalist regime of Reza Shah Pahlavi. The British obstruction of Iran's exercise of sovereignty over the islands was due to profound mistrust by the British of Iran. The islands were of economic and strategic significance to both countries. However, with the superpower status of the British in the region, the Irano-British dispute had to wait until the 1970's for resolution, by which time British hegemony in the region had faded away.

The hundred and fifty years of gradual decline in Iran's influence, and the stealthy rise in British power in the Gulf (significantly since the introduction of *Pax Britanica*) gave birth to new political entities in the Gulf. National identity was unknown to the pirate population of the area; their loyalties scarcely extended beyond the family, clan, and tribe. The British, in a furtive and painstaking manner, forged the Trucial States at the expense of Iranian and Ottoman traditional rights and interests. Several decades of almost absolute British hegemony as the single superpower in the region curtailed the exercise of control by Iran over her territories, be they Iran's southern provinces or the islands in the Gulf. As the exclusive oil concessionaire in Iran, Britain was also in a position to manipulate the central government in Tehran by its economic leverage. The unequal relationship between Britain and Iran gave the British an unfair bargaining power and an abiding ability to coerce Iran into conceding to Britain's terms.

The independence of the subcontinent of India in 1947, the nationalization of the Iranian oil industry in 1950 and of the Suez Canal in 1956, the loss of the British military bases in Egypt in 1954 and of Kenya and Aden (in 1960 and 1967 respectively), the rising Arab and Iranian nationalism in the Middle East, and finally the drastic deterioration of the British economy, forced this country out of the Persian Gulf by the end of 1971. The geopolitical vacuum, created by the British withdrawal from the Middle East, had to be filled by an American client state, either Iran or Saudi Arabia. The final choice was Iran. Nevertheless, the British maintained a foothold in the region. The British client state in the process of formation, the United Arab Emirates, was to remain a political base for the British.

The unexpected, though inevitable, withdrawal of the British Forces from the region posed new security issues for the West. The hasty creation of a federation amongst the seven frail sheikhdoms (the United Arab Emirates), the selection of Iran as the gendarme of the Persian Gulf, and the resolution of territorial disputes amongst the littoral states were components of a security package in the Gulf against Soviet potential danger.

The main territorial dispute related to Bahrain; Iran had never waived her sovereign right to the island. Three years after the conclusion of the Paris Treaty in 1857, by which Iran relinquished her claim to Herat, Iran repeated her claim to Bahrain in 1860 and again in 1869 and took some measure to restore her control over the island.[60] But, due to British intervention Iran's actions did not bear fruit. In 1889, Iran made her first attempt, although in vain, to oust British influence from the southern coast of the Gulf, Abu

---

[60] Malcom Yapp, op. cit., p. 53

Dhabi and Dubai.[61] This attempt was repeated in 1900 with regard to Dubai.[62] Encountering the British protest, Iran had to deny her involvement.

After arduous diplomatic efforts by Britain Iran consented to forgo her claim to Bahrain, in 1969, with a tacit understanding that Britain, in return, would support Iran's claim over the three islands of Abu Musa and the Tumbs. To achieve the first objective, a face-saving formula had to be found for the Shah. Up to this point, the Shah had insisted that Bahrain was the fourteenth province of Iran.[63] As a signatory to the Charter of the United Nations, Iran agreed to a sort of plebiscite (or pole taking), to be conducted in Bahrain, by the representative of the United Nations' Secretary General, to ascertain the political aspiration of the Bahrainis. The result had been predetermined. The findings, made public on 2 May, 1970, were for the independence of Bahrain.[64] The conclusion was unanimously endorsed by the United Nations Security Council on 11 May and approved by Iranian Majlis on 12 May, 1970.

Having removed the main obstacle to a carefully worked-out security arrangement, the British proceeded to

---

[61] J.B. Lorimer, op. cit., pp.737-744

[62] ibid. p. 745

[63] "On 23 March, 1934 the U.S. Minister to Iran, William H. Hornibrook, informed Secretary of State Cordell Hull, that the government was maintaining that Bahrein belonged to Iran, and that under these circumstances the British and American oil interests desiring a concession in Bahrein had to obtain it from the Iranian government. Edward W. Chester "United States Oil Policy and Diplomacy" (Connecticut: 1983), p. 249

[64] Shahram Chubin and Sepehr Zabih, "The Foreign Relations of Iran: A Developing State in a Zone of Great-Power Conflict";(California:1974), pp. 218-219.

broker a satisfactory ordering between Iran on the one hand, and the sheikhdoms of Sharjah and Ras al-Khaimah on the other. In February 1971, the Sheikh of Sharjah, recognizing the strategic imperatives of Iran, consented to Iran's troops being stationed on the island. In return, Iran recognized the Sheikhs' rights on the island of Abu Musa. Ostensibly such rights, in Iran's view, were confined to the rights of citizens of Sharjah on the islands, though some British newspapers construed it as the recognition of the right of sovereignity for Sharjah.[65]

Evidently, in 1971 it was not feasible for Britain to completely abandon the region. After fifty years of grooming and patronization, towards the end of the nineteenth century the British government conferred upon the sheikhdoms the status of "Trucial States" as protectorates of the mighty British Empire; and required them, as well as Bahrain and Kuwait, to deny concessions of their valuable natural resources to other states.

Up until 1960, while she was still master of the region, Britain made no attempt to enter into a serious dialogue with Iran to resolve the dispute. Since the establishment of the Constitution of 1906 in Iran, the Iranian Majlis (parliament) had taken measures to curb the British influence. Among these were the employment of Morgan Shuster (the American financier) and a team of American experts by the second Majlis in 1910 for the overhaul of the Iranian financial system, the invitation to the American oil companies in 1920-21 to seek concessions in Iran, and the annulment of the 1919 Anglo-Iranian Agreement. Likewise, the cancellation of the Anglo-Iranian oil concession in 1933, the rescission of the concession of the (British) Imperial Bank in 1928, which enjoyed the right of issuing Iranian

---

[65] The Times (of London) February 15, 1971.

bank notes, and a bundle of other measures adopted by the Iranian government during the three decades before W.W.II convinced the British of the deep resentment of Iranians towards the British presence. Hence, Britain adamantly refused Iran's claims to Bahrain, Abu Musa and the two Tumbs.

It is noteworthy that Mohammad al-Khalifa, the Sheikh of Bahrain, had asked for Iran's protection in 1851 to crush the Wahabbis' attack and was ready to become Iran's protectorate. As we have seen, the pressure of Britain in 1880 and 1892 forced the Sheikh to relinquish his rights to establish relations with other states, and thus Bahrain was instead officially reduced to a protectorate of the British. In the post W.W.II era, Iran proclaimed that Bahrain had never been independent and, before British intervention, owed allegiance to Iranian rulers. Thus, in 1949, Iran proclaimed the island her fourteenth province.

Iran has been equally unyielding in her claims over the three islands of Abu Musa and the two Tumbs. Iran argued that historically these islands were parts of Iran. After a period of decline, Iran established full sovereignty over the north coast of the Gulf by 1856.[66] The fact that the ruler of Muscat, who had leased Bandar Abbas from the Bani Ma'in Tribe, chose subsequently to lease it from the government of Iran, confirms Iran's sovereignty over the northern coast. Under the new lease, Iran obtained a higher rent and imposed more stringent conditions on the lessee state. The lease was canceled by Iran in 1868.

In 1798, Iran reconquered the islands of Kish and Hurmoz, which had been previously seized by Muscat.[67]

---

[66] Roger M. Savory, op. cit., pp. 53-54.
[67] ibid.

Her authority over Bandar Lingah was reasserted by 1887.[68]
The consolidation of Iran's power started in 1856, when she
regained control over Baluchestan and Chahbahar and, by
the middle of the 1870's, the influence of the Arab tribes on
the Iranian coasts had been completely eliminated.

The Irano-British Conflict Over Certain Islands

As already mentioned, in 1904 Iran proceeded to set up
customs houses in Abu Musa and the Tumbs, under the
reorganized administration by the Belgian advisors. The
British prevented this, arguing that the islands belonged to
the Arabs of the southern coast. The British Navy also
removed all Persian flags from the islands.[69] Iran protested
in vain; lacking a naval force, Iran was not in a position to
force the issue. However, Iran's diplomatic protest against
the British continued; the matter was also raised in the
Majlis (the Iranian parliament) in 1910.[70] Even with the
change of dynasty from Qajar to Pahlavi in 1925, Iran
neither abandoned her claim nor ceased protesting through
diplomatic channels.[71] Iran's complaints ranged from the
unlawful removal of the Iranian flags, to the exploitation of
the natural resources of Abu Musa without Iranian license,
and the prevention of Iran's fledgling coastal patrol boats
from exercising Iran's sovereign rights over the islands.

In W.W.II, British and Soviet forces occupied Iran,
during which time Iran's territorial claims had to be

---

[68] Lorimer, op. cit., pp.2063-65

[69] "Gozideh Asnade Khalij'e Fars"; published by the Bureau of
International and Political Studies (Tehran: 1368 solar year), Vol. I,
p.264.

[70] ibid. pp. 268, 272.

[71] ibid. pp. 268, 272.

relegated until 1948 when Iran resumed her claims to the islands, at which time Bahrain was declared her fourteenth province. The Irano-British disputes that followed entered a new phase in 1960's. In May 1961, an Iranian helicopter carrying Iranian Naval officers landed on Greater Tumb, and the Iranian officers gathered information from the Arab sentries guarding the lighthouse built by the British. The British government filed a protest with the Iranian government while asserting that the Tumbs have, since 1887, been a part of Ras al-Khaimah territory, and that the rulers of Ras al-Khaimah have governed the island since 1921, when Ras al-Khaimah became independent of Sharjah.[72]

In the mid 1960's, the issue came up again in connection with the partitioning of the Gulf's continental shelf between the littoral states.[73] Before 1968, the claims and counterclaims by Britain and Iran over the island had been a private exchange in bilateral correspondents. But in mid-1968, it became public. Mohammad Reza Shah, in his interview with A.M. Rendel, said: "As regards to the Arab countries we really do not have any problem with them...the only difficulty is that certain of these Arab countries that presently exist or are about to be created, believe that they must become the successors and heirs of Britain's ancient imperialism."[74]

In April 1970, Iran informed the sheikhs that they could count on future Iranian economic aid, should they consent

---

[72] F.O. 371/11464 British Residency, Bahrain, 10 November, 1954 to the Foreign Office.

[73] Husain M. Albaharna; "The Legal Aspects of the Arabian Gulf States: A Study of Their Treaty Relations and Their International Relations", (New York:1968) p.67

[74] The Times (London), 13 April, 1970; Ayandegan, 14 April, 1970.

to a peaceful settlement of the issue.[75]   This was the first
time Iran formally addressed the sheikhs concerning the
islands.   In October 1970, Iran formally informed Britain
and the sheikhs that she would not recognize the federation
of Trucial States, proposed by Britain, until and unless the
matter of the islands was resolved.

In the following months, the Shah, in interviews with the
editor of the Indian Newspaper *Bliz* on 26 June, 1971[76], and
with Dennis Walters, the British M.P. on 11 May, 1971[77],
repeated the sentiments of Mohammad Reza Shah.   He
stated that, up to eighty years before, the islands belonged
to Iran.   Britain then interfered with Iran's exercise of
sovereignty over the islands, and subsequently claimed that
they belonged to the Qawassim sheikhs.   In Iran's view, the
issue concerned Iran and Britain and not Iran and the
sheikhs; the question was a "colonial one".   The Shah
argued that an imperialist country (Britain) should not be
allowed to perpetuate its colonialist legacy by ceding Iran's
islands to other states.   The British had seized the islands by
force.   Meanwhile, in February 1971, the Shah publicly
announced that, if necessary, Iran would use force to retake
the islands.   In May 1971, in a move to appease Iran and
prevent armed intervention, the British persuaded the
Occidental Petroleum, an American Oil Company, to
postpone a drilling operation offshore of Abu Musa.
Despite this, on 30 November, 1971, Iranian troops
occupied Abu Musa by agreement and the Tumbs by force,
to stress the nature of the disagreement between the British
and Iran, and to occupy the islands before the British
departure.

---

[75] Keyhan International, 13 April, 1970.
[76] Keyhan International, 26 June, 1971.
[77] The Times (London), 11 May, 1971.

The occupation of Abu Musa followed bilateral arrangements between Iran and Sharjah. Under the mutually agreed set-up, Iranian troops were stationed on the island to maintain order and defend it. Iran further agreed to protect the rights of Sharjah citizens residing there. The issue of sovereignty seems to have been shunned expediently by the parties. Though it remained undiscussed, each presumed the issue closed; Iran considered the occupation the restoration of her sovereignty while Sharjah considered it a bilateral arrangement made for strategic considerations, short of abandoning her claim.

The occupation of the two Tumbs eventuated without the consent of the Sheikh of Ras al-Khaimah. As previously mentioned, the reaction of the Arab world to Iran's occupation of the three islands generally was mild, except for a request by radical Arab states (Iraq, Libya, Algeria, and the People's Democratic Republic of Yemen) to the U.N. Security Council on 9 December, 1971 to consider "the dangerous situation arisen from the occupation of the islands by Iran's armed forces."[78] On this occasion, the U.N. Security Council adopted a resolution, proposed by the Somali delegate, to defer consideration of the issue in favor of using diplomacy and third party efforts.[79]

For a decade, the dispute was assigned to abeyance until after the establishment of the Islamic Republic when, in September 1980, the U.A.E. submitted its claim to the three islands to the United Nations.[80] This was the first time that the U.A.E. raised the issue, ten years after its creation. At

---

[78] UN Security Council records, 26th year (Doc. s/10409), 3 December, 1971.
[79] ibid., 9 December, 1971.
[80] Inter-Press Service, 10 September, 1993.

the time of the occupation of the islands by Iran, the U.A.E. had not been formed. Immediately after her birth, she filed a protest with the U.N.

Since 1980, the hostile rhetoric in relation to the three islands, between Iran on the one side and U.A.E. and G.C.C. on the other, has been recurrent. Iran rejects the U.A.E. petitions as "illusions and repetitive claims", declaring that "these islands have always belonged to Iran and will always do so."[81]   Furthermore, Iran ascribes the agitation in the Arab Gulf states to the "mischief-making" of Washington, attempting to isolate Iran. The U.A.E.-Iranian dispute flared again in April 1992 after Iran tightened its security grip on Abu Musa.

For years, both Iranians and Arabs from Sharjah have had a presence on Abu Musa. However, since its seizure, Iran has constructed a port on the north side of the island; Sharjah has not. Iran has also built a runway for aircrafts on the island.   Hence, travelers have had to conform to the Iranian entry procedure. The crisis in April 1992 started when oil workers from Sharjah were refused entry by Iranian authorities. In May, the Supreme Council of the U.A.E. lent its full support to Sharjah in its claim against Iran. In August 1992, Iran provoked the issue of Abu Musa again by allegedly encroaching on the area under Sharjah's jurisdiction when she prevented Egyptian teachers from returning to Abu Musa, under the pretext that they did not have the correct Iranian visa.

By November 1992, in a move to reduce tension, Iran allowed foreigners who had been working on Abu Musa operating a school, the power station, and the clinic, to return to the island. They had been expelled from Abu

---

[81] ibid., 7 September, 1993.

Musa by Iranian authorities in March 1992.[82]   The U.A.E. now demands that Iran observe the 1971 agreement. Iran meanwhile asserts that nothing has happened in Abu Musa to justify such a charge.

Iran's appeasement of the U.A.E. has not worked. According to the Egyptian Al-Ahram, "Tehran is bent on turning Abu Musa into a fortress, complete with enormous naval, air and missile base...This is part of Iran's drive for regional ascendancy."[83]

On 1 December, 1992, in response to Iran's military build-up in Abu Musa, the U.A.E. Chief-of-Staff of the Armed Forces, Lt. General Mohammad Sa'id al-Badi, said, "We still have a lot of responsibilities and the challenges and threats that still face us are great. We are determined to strengthen our country and stand fast to achieve security and peace".[84]

In her official reaction, Iran has charged the U.S. with provoking the Arabs as well as the Europeans and Japanese to cripple Iran militarily, as well as in economic and industrial areas. Otherwise, Iran's rearmament would not go beyond her legitimate defense needs.[85]

Regarding the U.A.E. claim that Iran is trying to annex Abu Musa, the official Iranian reaction has been "Abu Musa is an Iranian island", a matter which has been reaffirmed by President Hashemi Rafsanjani time and again.[86]   President Rafsanjani, during his Friday prayer on 26 December, 1992, with reference to the U.A.E. claim to the three islands,

---

[82] Reuter from Nicosia, 26 November, 1992.

[83] Guardian, (Manchester), 28 November, 1992.

[84] APS Diplomat Recorder, 7 December, 1992.

[85] Middle Eastern Economic Digest, 4 December, 1992

[86] ibid.

stated: "Iran is surely stronger than the likes of you (the Gulf States). To reach these islands, one has to cross a sea of blood".[87] *Tehran Times*, believed to be close to the Foreign Minister Velayati, wrote: "(The) U.A.E. should be aware that Iran's self-restraint has certain limits."[88]

In these years of hostile political and military rhetoric, occasionally a suggestion for a peaceful resolution of the disputes through diplomatic channels has been made by third parties. Syria, the only major Arab state with close ties with the Islamic Republic of Iran urged an amicable settlement of the dispute in January 1993, recalling that the U.A.E. was one of the first states to recognize and establish relations with the Islamic Republic of Iran after the 1979 Revolution. Syria also reminded Iran that during the Iraqi-Iranian war of 1980's, the U.A.E. remained neutral and, unlike most Arab states, did not side with Iraq. Although the statement was essentially in favor of the U.A.E., Iranian officials responded positively in the interest of reducing tensions between Arabs and Iran.[89] However, Iran did not show any change of attitude on the substantive aspect of the claim. In September 1992, there had been exploratory talks between the U.A.E. and Iran that collapsed because of Iran's unwillingness to include the Tumbs on the agenda. In February 1993, Sheikh Zaid, referring to Iran's declared desire to develop friendly ties with the U.A.E., stated that "the continued occupation of Abu Musa and Greater and Lesser Tumbs is a violation of its declared desire (to establish a closer bond) and a threat to regional stability".[90]

Another third-party attempt for the resolution of the U.A.E.-Iranian dispute came from Sir Michael Burton,

---

[87] ibid., 15 January, 1993.
[88] Tehran Times, Saturday, 26 December, 1992.
[89] Middle East Mirror, 6 January, 1993.
[90] Reuter, 6 February, 1993.

Britain's Undersecretary of State for Foreign Affairs. On 18 September, 1993, he urged Iran's Director General of the Ministry of Foreign Affairs, who was visiting the U.K., to settle the U.A.E.-Iranian dispute by peaceful means.[91] Whilst Iran seriously wants the dispute to be resolved through political negotiation, there can be little doubt but that the existing political and military ambiance in the Gulf is not condusive to a mutually agreeable settlement.

Iran considers the security agreements (signed between Kuwait, Bahrain and Qatar separately with the U.S., the U.K., and France) a threat to Iran's security. Iran tries to exploit the Islamists' anti-colonial and anti-Western sentiments to undermine these Western-oriented security arrangements. Iran is also sensitive to the G.C.C.'s refusal to admit Iran into its security systems for the region: Iran considers her own participation in the region's security organization more justified in the defence of the Gulf than, for instance, Egypt and Syria, as addressed under the Damascus Declaration.

Iran's stringency in 1992 to expel the Egyptians teachers from Abu Mussa was prompted by the fear of threats to her security by unfriendly Arab states. The Irano-U.A.E. relationship reflects the climate of mistrust, apprehension, and acrimony. The growing Islamic fundamentalism in the Gulf State poses challenges to the ruling regimes; and the sheikhs suspect Iran of sponsoring radical Islamic movements in the emirates.

Suspicion of Iran is not limited to the G.C.C. States. The governments of Egypt and Algeria have charged Iran with fomenting Islamist rebels in their countries, producing

---

[91] The Press Association Ltd., 18 September, 1993.

evidence to show that anti-government plots in those countries have been stirred up by Iran. At the same time, Iranians make no secret of their support for the fundamentalist groups that advocate the rule of Sharia and opposition to the U.S.-sponsored Middle East peace process. While admitting her backing of Islamic movements, Iran categorically denies any involvement in terrorist activities; Iran considers the militancy of the Palestinians an exercise of liberation and not a terrorist offensive. Iran cannot abandon her revolutionary rhetoric, which is the main source of its legitimacy at home. Likewise, it cannot ignore the imperative of rebuilding its economy for which it needs Western capital and technology. This is a dilemma that Iran has to resolve if she is to pursue a true reconciliation with her neighboring Arab-states.

Iran's post-revolutionary phase has been more successful than has been admitted by the West. Working with the IMF and the World Bank, trying to join the GAAT agreement, allowing inspection of its nuclear facilities, and welcoming outside investment and arbitration have certainly taken Iran a long way out of isolation. Iran considers herself the victim of venomous propaganda by Washington, Tel Aviv, and Cairo, the purpose of which has been political isolation and her economic destruction.

Unable to resolve the dilemma of adhering to revolutionary rhetoric and attracting international goodwill, Iran has followed a policy of damage limitation. While paying lip service to the start of a bilateral dialogue with the U.A.E., she has unequivocally and repeatedly asserted that the three islands are an integral part of Iran and Iran's sovereignty over the islands cannot be a matter for discussion. When the late Shah reclaimed the islands for Iran in 1971, an ambiguous arrangement had been made between the Sheikh of Sharjah and the Shah, which nevertheless worked for almost a decade. The uneasiness started after the establishment of the Islamic regime in Iran in 1979. It flared up when Iran, worried over security matters, expelled a number of residents of Abu Mussa, and then refused to permit a boatload of third-country nationals to disembark on the islands. It was then that Iran unequivocally reminded the world that Abu Musa was exclusively an Iranian island. This aggravated the issue and no subsequent attempt to diffuse it has changed her image in the eyes of the U.A.E.

In a softer approach, Iran's Minister of Defense and Logistics, Akhbar Trokan, spoke in March 1993 of "Iranian responsibility for maintaining security in the island under the 1971 agreement." He further stated that it was "in this regard that Iran banned entry of foreign materials to the island" in mid-1992.[92] Although an intermittent easing of U.A.E.-Iranian tension is felt, Iran's occupation of the islands remains on the agenda of G.C.C. Council. Iran calls the G.C.C. stance on the Gulf islands "unprincipled, unrealistic, and one-sided", and "welcomes continuation of talks for the removal of doubts without any preconditions." The Foreign Minister of the G.C.C. declared Iran's conditions unacceptable for the resumption of talks over Abu Musa and the Tumbs.[93]

In the meantime, the mutual high-level visits by the ministers of Iran and the U.A.E., the participation of scholars in the seminars held in the two countries, and the exchange of delegates for negotiations on trade as well as allusions to the Gulf islands continue.[94] The relationship

---

[92] Middle East Economic Digest 12 March, 1993.

[93] Reuters, Nicosea 6 April, 1993.

[94] Agence France press, 26 June, 1993.

between G.C.C. states and Tehran remain generally amicable at least on the surface. Iran's policy towards the G.C.C. has been a blend of pragmatism and toughness. Both presidents Hashemi Rafsanjani and Sheikh Zayed al-Nahayan, have been sensible enough to prevent the dispute from taking a military dimension.[95]

In a new initiative, 'Ali Akbar Nateq Nouri, the Speaker of the Majlis on 18 August, 1993 announced that "Tehran has fresh proposals for resolving its row with the U.A.E. about Abu Musa and two other Gulf islands", and promised "to relay the proposals through visiting Kuwaiti Parliament Speaker Ahmed al-Saadoun".[96]

Two days earlier, the Deputy Speaker of the Majlis, on his visit to Kuwait, had expressed his delight at the liberation of Kuwait and reminded the speaker of Kuwaiti Parliament, that Iran had overlooked Kuwait's stance in the Irano-Iraqi war and had objectively condemned Iraq's invasion. He also criticized the Gulf littoral states who every now and then raise the issue of the Gulf islands, an act which undermines the interest of all countries in the region.

The nature of the new proposals from Tehran has never been disclosed. In the meantime, Abu Dhabi has repeated its disapproval of Iran's seizure of the three islands in September 1993. Despite all the ups and downs in the Iranian-U.A.E. relations, armed confrontation over the islands seems unlikely. Economic relations between Iran and the U.A.E. are expanding, trade volume between the two states is multiplying, and Arab investment in Iran is growing.

---

[95] APS Diplomat Strategic Balance in the Middle East, 5 July, 1993.

[96] Middle East Economic Digest, 23 August, 1993.

While Iran is downplaying the dispute as a minor side issue, the Arab League foreign ministers, on 20 September, 1993, reconfirmed their support for the U.A.E.'s claim over the island. In response, Iran's naval commander threatened to use force should the islands be attacked.[97] On Thursday, 23 December, 1993, a foreign ministry statement read on Tehran Radio said: "An Iranian invitation to the U.A.E.'s State Minister for Foreign Affairs to discuss the row without preconditions still stood."[98] However, it reiterated that "Iranian sovereignty over the islands was unchangeable".

In September 1994, the Abu Dhabi newspaper, *Al-Ittihad*, wrote in its editorial:

> Iran remains negative towards reaching a peaceful solution...the islands were and will continue to belong to the U.A.E. despite the efforts to improve a fait accompli...we have evidence and documents which confirm our possession of these islands...The U.A.E. repeatedly called on Iran to resolve the islands issues, but all these calls were in vain. Our only choice is to resort to the International Court of Justice to maintain our rights and interests.[99]

Three days later, Ayatollah Mohammad Yazdi, head of Iran's Judiciary Branch said that "before the U.A.E. became independent, these islands were Iranian, belonged to Iran, and were under Iran's sovereignty. And so they are to-day, and so they shall remain. No one can have the right... to do its slightest thing that might undermine this sovereignty."[100]

---

[97]Middle East Mirror, 27 September, 1993.

[98] Renter Nicosia, 23 December, 1993.

[99] Al-Ittihad, 22 September, 1994.

[100] Iran-Times, 26 September, 1994.

The repetitive game of claims and counterclaims and invitations to direct negotiation over the islands by the contesting states continued during 1994. A G.C.C. communiqué on 18 September, 1994 urged Iran "either to accept the U.A.E.'s call for direct negotiations or to accept taking the issue to the International Court of Justice."[101] This is how the matter stands at present.

---

[101] Deutsche Presse-Agent, 18 September, 1994

II

The Qawasim: A Historical Perspective

Introduction

The claim of United Arab Emirates to the three islands of Abu Musa and the two Tumbs rests on the alleged hereditary rights of the Qawasim Sheikhs of Sharjah and Ras al-Khaimah, the nature and legality of which call for an historical investigation.

The designation of Qawasim may have derived from the name of a prominent sheikh of the tribe-family, Sheikh Qasim, who was the grandfather of the Sheikh Rashid ibn Mattar.[1] Sheikh Rashid ibn Mattar attained power in 1727.

The original home of the Qawasim tribes is shrouded in mystery. Najd, Muscat and Ras-al Khaimah on the Arabian Peninsula, and Siraf (Tahiri) on the Persian coast, have been mentioned as their probable homes.[2] Colonel S.B. Miles, an acclaimed authority on the Persian Gulf, maintains that the

---

[1] S.B. Miles, "The Countries and Tribes of the Persian Gulf" (London: 1919) Vol. II, p. 269.

[2] J.B. Kelly, "Britain and the Persian Gulf: 1795-1880" (Oxford: 1968) pp.17-20.

Qawasim, who were a branch of the Huwailla, migrated from Persia to Muscat and Ras al-Khaimah on the Arabian coast during the eighteenth century. Huwailla was an appellation used for Arab émigrés who had originally settled on the Persian coast and later, particularly in the eighteenth century, migrated to the Arabian shore.[3] If Colonel Miles' assumption is correct, the Qawasim were members of one of the tribes that had settled in Iran and, as such, they were *Iranian subjects*, before migrating to the southern coast of, or to some Iranian islands in, the Persian Gulf. In certain regional dialects, wherein the letter "Q" is pronounced "J", the Qawasim were called *Jawasim*.

Based on the information contained in India Office records, the Qawasim of Ras al-Khaimah encroached upon the Iranian shore for the first time in 1727and seized Basidu.[4] This coincided with the downfall of the Saffavid Dynasty. In 1730, Tahmasp Quli of the Afshar tribe, who had expelled the Afghans from Iran, proclaimed himself Nader Shah, and resolved to restore Iran's sovereignty over the lands previously possessed by the Safavids. He was merciless towards unruly tribes, regardless of origin. In 1737, he evicted the Qawasim from Basidu and captured their stronghold, Ras al-Khaimah. He also conquered Oman and invaded India. Nader Shah's rule was too short to allow him to consolidate his empire and an outburst of irresolute warfare among petty chiefs followed his assassination. After ten years of anarchy, Karim Khan Zand took the reign. In his struggle for power, he rallied the support of some Iranian Arab tribes; "Karim Khan's leaning towards the Arabs helped the Qawasim achieve prominence in the coasts

---

[3] S.B. Miles, op. cit. vol ii, p 268.
[4] L/P&S/18 B397 J.G. Laithwaite, "Status of Tumb, Little Tumb, Abu Mussa and Sirri", 8 pp., confidential.

of the Persian Gulf during the second half of the Eighteenth Century."[5]

Another incident that brought the Qawasim into the limelight was the strife between Mulla 'Ali Shah, the Governor of Bandar Abbas and Hurmoz, and Nasser Khan, the Governor of Lar. Mulla 'Ali sought the Qawasim's aid and gave his daughter in marriage to Rashid ibn Mattar, the Sheikh of Qawasim. This alliance proved very costly to Mulla 'Ali Shah.[1] Mulla 'Ali Shah and his Qawasim allies invaded and plundered Bandar Abbas but were ousted. Subsequently Karim Khan Zand ejected the Qawasim from Lingeh in 1767, but they returned after Karim Khan's death in 1779.[6]

At this time, the Qawasim who came to Iran submitted to the Iranian government and became Iranian citizens. The Iranian government appointed the Qawasim sheikh, who was now an Iranian subject, Governor of Lingeh. Thereafter, for nearly one hundred years (until about 1887), the Governorship of Lingeh was assigned by the Iranian government to the Qawasim sheikhs and the Sheikhs regularly paid due taxes to the government of Iran. During this period, the islands of Abu Musa, the Tumbs, and Sirri were located in the jurisdiction of Bandar Lingah.[7]

The realization of the true nature of the Qawasim's settlement in Lingeh (since 1779) is of crucial importance. All the evidence indicates that they intended to make Iran their permanent home. There was little cohesiveness

---

[5] Donald Hawley, "The Trucial States" (London: 1971) p. 92.

[1] ibid. cit. p.93.

[6] J.B. Kelly, op. cit. p.19.

[7] F.O. 371-13010 "Status of Islands of Tunb, Little Tunb, Abu Mussa and Sirri", 24 August, 1928.

amongst various sub-groups in the tribe. The Qawasim settlers in Iran might have kept some relations with other Qawasim in the Lower Gulf, but their political identity after settlement, became, at least nominally, Iranian.

The following statement by Sir John Malcolm, quoting a descriptive narrative by his Persian servant, explains the nature of activities and loyalties of the Qawasim of the Lower Gulf: *"Qawasim occupation is piracy, and their delight (is) murder, and to make it worse, they give you the most pious reasons for every villainy they commit."*[8] They were fishermen and pearl hunters in summer, pirates and plunderers in winter. The Qawasim had no inclination for farming and, as such, had no tie to the land. They were nomadic tribes, looking for places where the authority of the central government was at its ebb, migrating to a different location when the central government attempted to restore control over the area. Thanks to the Qawasim's way of life, the coasts of the Persian Gulf came to be known as the Pirate Coast.

During this period, the societal structure in the southern coast of the Persian Gulf was exclusively tribal and the tribes were scattered all over the islands. As J.B. Kelly indicates "all the islands off the Persian coast, from Kharku and Khark in the north to Hurmoz and Larak in the south were *rightly Persian, though many were in the hands of Arab tribes.*"[9] The Sheikhs were distrustful of each other and "guarded their independence jealously. Some like *the Qawasim of Lingeh, were directly related to the tribes on the opposite coast"*. Others did not have any affinity except that all were Arabs. *"Whenever the Persian authorities attempted to bring them into subjection they took their*

---

[8] Sir John Malcolm "Sketches of Persia", (London: 1845) p. 15.

[9] Kelly, op. cit. p. 40, emphasis added.

ships and retired to one of the islands off-shore, where they waited until they could safely return to their homes."[10]

About two hundred large and a greater number of small tribes roamed the region. The tribes were loosely grouped in two camps: Hinawi (Bani Hinah) and Ghafiri (Bani Ghaffir). The deep enmity between these two camps often transpired into armed conflicts between the two tribes of Bani Yas (Hinawi) and Qawasim (Ghafiri), who were the most powerful in their respective camps.[11] The jurisdiction of Qawasim extended form Ras al-Khaimah to Dubai, comprising of Umm al-Qaiwain, Ajman, and Sharjah; the jurisdiction of Bani Yas extended from Dubai to Qatar, comprising of Abu Dhabi.

The tribal conflict was not only over the division of booties, it was also related to religious and sectarian differences. The Hinawi belonged to the "Ibadi" sect, an offspring of Khawarij, whilst the Ghafiri were Sunni; The Bani Yas were a land power, whilst the Qawasim were skilled sailors; The Bani Yas had their headquarters in Qatar, whilst the Qawasim were scattered in many places including Sharjah, Ras al-Khaimah, Shamailiyah (on the Gulf of Oman), and Hurmoz.

The Bani Yas reached the apex of their power under Zayid bin Khalifah (1855-1909) of Abu Dhabi, who extended his authority over a number of inland tribes previously loyal to the Qawasim. In the tribal world, power was measured by the number of tribes recognizing the authority of the prominent sheikh and not by acquisition of the new lands. Amongst the sheikhs subdued by Sheikh Zayid were the Sheikhs of Sharjah and Ras al-Khaimah.

---

[10] ibid., p. 40, emphasis added.
[11] ibid. pp. 17 et seq.

As there was no law of succession or primogeniture in the tribes, there was no legal process to determine the smooth transfer of power from one ruler to the other. Following the death of Sheikh Zayid in 1909, a state of anarchy ensued in the sheikhdom. The struggle for power between the many male offspring of the sheikh lasted until 1928, in which year Shakhbut bin Sultan, the grandson of Zayid, seized power and kept a tight rein on the tribe, restoring the Bani Yas' predominance in the area.

Our knowledge of the Qawasim tribes is murky for many reasons. The term Qawasim itself, in the proper sense, was originally used for the Sheikhly family itself, though in an extended, or rather loose sense, it was employed to denote the tribes subordinate to the Qawasim Sheikhs of Sharjah and Ras al-Khaimah.[12] Unfortunately, the number of such tribes, their geographical distribution, their extent of power and degree of their subordination to the Qawasim Sheikhs, are uncertain matters. The Qawasim were also called, "Bani Siraf", referring to their origin in Iran. J.B. Kelly, relying on a few shreds of evidence and the present geographical distribution of the Qawasim, suggests that the Qawasim confederacy comprised of Khawatir (Na'im), dwelling in Ras al-Khaimah, Bani Qitab in Sharjah, Za'ab in Jaziral al-Hamra, Al'Ali in Umm al-Qaiwain, Al Bu Khuraiban (Na'im) in Ajman, Shihu (in league with the Qawasim) in Rams, and Mazari' and Habus in the hills. [13]

Furthermore, Kelly states that,

> *The authority wielded by the Qawasim Sheikhs over all these tribes was limited.* In the politics of Southeastern Arabia, the balance of power was held by the Bedouin tribes, whose support might be transferred from one

---

[12] ibid., p. 17.
[13] ibid., p. 18.

Sheikh to another, according to his liberality or parsimony, while the Sheikhs on their side were restrained from an arbitrary exercise of their authority by a fear of alienating the Bedouin."[14]

The Qawasim were a keen migrating people, roaming between Iraq, Iran and the Arabian Peninsula.

Both the Bani Yas and Qawasim were Bedouin tribes. The tribal way of life did not lend itself to the formation of a civil society, socio-political structures, or the rule of law. The extent of each sheikh's authority was a function of his personality, tribal stature, and the awe he inspired in his followers and neighboring tribes. The concepts of nation, defined territory, and a legally established government were alien to their nomadic way of life; no permanent administration and no system of peaceful succession to chieftanship existed. The tribal alignments were indeterminate and fluid. Loyalties changed for immediate gains. Tribes split as frequently as the clans rejoined. As nomadic tribes, the Bani Yas and Qawasim owed allegiance neither to Iran nor Oman, the only other stable government in the region. The Bani Yas, however, were more aligned with the Abu Sa'id rulers of Muscat, whilst the Qawasim were hostile to both.

By 1763, the Al Bu Sa'id rulers of Muscat had subjugated the Qawasim Sheikhs except for the Sheikh of Ras al-Khaimah. This was also the year in which Karim Khan Zand expelled the Qawasim from Lingeh and Qishm,[15] leaving them for two decades with self-rule only in Ras al-Khaimah. From here, in 1780, Sheikh Saqr ibn Rashid ibn Mattar, taking advantage of the decline in Oman's power,

---

[14] ibid., p. 18.
[15] ibid., p. 20.

raided the Shamailiyah tract in the Northern Musandam Peninsula. The interests of the Qawasim in Shamailiyah lay in its strategic position from which they could attack vessels sailing through the Strait of Hurmoz. Thus, piracy and not the land per se constituted the motive. For the next two decades, frequent armed clashes over the control of Shamailiyah took place between Oman and Qawasim piratical tribes.

In the absence of a cohesive social, economic, and political system, and in the absence of a body of unified people through the bonds of common interests and loyalties, no nation-state in the southern coast of the Persian Gulf could possibly have emerged. The scanty existing data on the number, name, identity, and alignment of the multitude of Arab tribes in that era indicate that the peoples of Ras al-Khaimah, Sharjah, Umm al-Qaiwain, and Ajman, all members of the present United Arab Emirates, whether Khawatir (a branch of the Na'im), Bani Qitab, Za'ab, Al'Ali, Al Bu Khuraiban (another branch of the Na'im) or Shihu, had associations with Qawasim sheikhs, although the sheikhs did not wield much authority over those tribes. Furthermore, these tribes individually posed a serious threat to British shipping operations in the Gulf. This was the reason for British insistence to make bilateral arrangements with each sheikh separately; had the Qawasim sheikh in Ras al-Khaimah exercised full authority on all the sheikhs, there would not have been a need for the British to obtain the consent of each tribe individually. The ties amongst these tribes were too loose to amount to a unified front, or one body of people. By the same token, no sheikh, by mere fact of being a Qawasim sheikh at the time, could claim succession to other sheikhs in the Qawasim camp.

On the Persian shores, the sheikhs, in an attempt to increase their illicit gains whenever and wherever feasible, would charge occasional arbitrary duties on the exports-imports. This was in addition to the legal duties traders had to pay the Iranian authorities.[16]

Another event that somewhat strengthened the position of the Qawasim was Wahhabi expansionism. In early 1800, a Wahhabi detachment of 700 cavalry and camel riders under Sa'udi General Salim al-Hariq advanced towards Oman. Although initially a movement of religious reform, the Sa'udi Wahhabis adopted the same tactics that had been employed by their ancestors in the dawn of Islam. Plundering, brutality and destruction were practiced indiscriminately wherever they went. These were the cardinal attributes of the Qawasim as well. In Ras al Khaimah, Salim al-Hariq solicited the Qawasim's aid in attacking Oman. Proceeding to Shamailiyah, the Sa'udis encountered adamant resistance by the Omani army under the Sultan. Salim al-Hariq retreated and the Qawasim, who were always after their immediate gain, made peace with the Sultan.

After several years, having consolidated his power, Salim al-Hariq invaded Dhahirah, populated mainly by Khawatir -- a branch of the Na'im tribe under the Qawasim. Conquered Dhahirah, the Wahhabi army advanced towards Wadi al-Jizzi, subduing the Bani Qitab, the Shawamis and other tribes of the Qawasim confederacy. A large number of the Qawasim gladly embraced Wahhabism, since Wahhabism did not frown at their custom of rampage and pillage. However, the conversion of the Qawasim into the Wahhabi branch of Islam displeased Saqr ibn Rashid, the Paramount Sheikh of the Qawasim, who saw it as an

---

[16] I. O. "Persia and the Persian Gulf", Vol 21, Manesty and Jones' Report, 18 December, 1790.

erosion to his authority. This was particularly bitter as Salim al-Hariq also levied Zakat, the alms tax, on new Wahhabis on behalf of the Sa'udi authorities, thus depriving Sheikh Saqr from one of his sources of revenue.

Except for in Oman and the Bani Yas confederacy, the Wahhabi's influence in the region was spreading fast. The Sa'udi Sultan ordered Salim al-Hariq to seize Oman in 1803. He also asked the Sheikhs of Qawasim, Bahrain and Kuwait to launch piratical attacks against Omani shipping. The Qawasim, while willing to buccaneer for material wealth, were reluctant to engage in warfare for religious or political reasons. Fortunately for them, the Sa'udi Ruler, was soon assassinated and the Qawasim's new prominent sheikh, Sultan ibn Saqr, preferred to make peace with the Sultan of Oman.

Following the assassination of the Sultan of the Sa'udis, Abdul Aziz, the Persian Gulf became the scene of a power struggle for maritime hegemony, between Oman and the piratical sheikhs. At that time Iran was engaged in war with Russia, and was not in a position to address issues in the Persian Gulf.

In 1805, the Qawasim seized Lingeh, Qishm, Hurmoz, Bandar Abbas and Minab. Thus, they were in a superb strategic position to assail all ships sailing through the Strait of Hurmoz. This constituted a serious threat to British maritime interests in the Persian Gulf.

The Qawasim and the British

The first Qawasim confrontation with the British occurred in 1759 in Bandar Abbas, when Qawasim bandits attacked the British factory in this port and seized a large quantity of lumber. The East India Company sought redress from the Iranian government, since the offense had been committed in Persian territory. The local Iranian governor did not act in earnest, since the Qawasim perpetrators had family relations with Mulla 'Ali Shah, then Governor of Bandar Abbas and Hurmoz.[17] The British appeal to Iran's central government too, was of no avail; the central government was too weak to act. Iran's failure to render justice damaged her external image, and the East India Company realized that, in future, it could not rely on Iran for protection. However, Britain had too much at stake to treat the incident casually. So the British looked for alternative security arrangements to safeguard their vital interests in the Gulf.

The following year witnessed a futile clash between Nassir Khan, the Governor of Lar, and the Qawasim of Ras al-Khaimah. Nassir Khan attacked the Qawasim in Lingeh and Ras al-Khaimah. The Qawasim of Ras al-Khaimah, probably in support of Mulla 'Ali Shah, the Governor of Bandar Abbas and Hurmoz, landed in Bandar Abbas. Neither of the two expeditions proved successful, though the inability of Iran to subdue the Qawasim, further damaged her credibility, lending support to those in British India, who advocated the expediency of seeking allies other than Iran in the Persian Gulf.

The second Qawasim-British confrontation occurred in 1778. For Britain, it was an alarming event. After three days of warfare, the Qawasim of Ras al-Khaimah captured a small ship belonging to the Bombay Marines, demanding a ransom for its release. A month later, in January 1779, *Success*, another boat flying the English flag, was attacked by eight Qawasim dhows. She managed to repel them. In

---

[17] Donald Hawley, op. cit. p93.

February that same year, a similar incident occurred and the English boat *Assistance* was also unsuccessfully attacked by the Qawasim dhows. A fifth incident took place in 1790, when the vessel *Beglerbeg*, was seized by the Qawasim near Bushehr. The sixth blow came in 1797 when the Qawasim of Ras al-Khaimah captured *Bassein*, a British dhow en route to Bassrah. The ship was released three days later. The British preferred to turn a blind eye to the event and not file a protest.

These incidents emboldened the Qawasim. In October 1797, Sheikh Saleh of the Qawasim confederacy, while preying on Omani ships near Bushehr, fired on *Viper*, a 14-gun cruiser of the Bombay Marines, killing thirty-two members of its crew before withdrawing. This was a serious event. Prior to the attack, Sheikh Saleh had fooled the commander of the British cruiser by calling on, and expressing his friendship to the British Political Resident in Bhushehr. In that meeting the Sheikh had requested the Resident to refrain from providing commercial or military support to the Omanis. He had also asked for balls and powder, which were supplied to him from the cruiser. A few days later on an early morning, when the commander and a number of his crew were ashore, Sheikh Saleh attacked the ship. The cruiser fired back and the Qawasim fled. The Resident in Bassrah protested to the Paramount Qawasim Sheikh, Sheikh Saqr of Ras al-Khaimah, who happened to be Sheikh Saleh's uncle. Sheikh Saqr, while reassuring the Resident of his friendship and respect, accused the British cruiser of having fired first. He also charged Sheikh Saleh with betrayal, in that he had married a woman of the infamous Beni Khalid tribe of Lingeh, thereby distancing himself from the Qawasim tribe. Finally, Sheikh Saqr put all the blame on the Qawasim of Lingeh, thereby implicitly admitting that the Qawasim of Lingeh did not owe any loyalty to him. Although those pretexts did not satisfy the Resident, he did not consider military retaliation a wise option, and the matter was relegated to abeyance until 1804.

British policy in the Gulf continued to be one of noninvolvement unless British interests were severely threatened. Also, the British did not want to provoke the Qawasim's allies. The Qawasim and Omanis, although traditional enemies, had temporarily united to fend off the Wahhabi Sa'udi threat. By the time the Wahhabis dominated trucial Oman, the Qawasim who had embraced Wahhabism, broke away from the Omanis, focusing all their attention on piracy.

In the beginning of the nineteenth century, the government of Muscat was divided into two: The Sultanate of Muscat and the Immamat of Oman. The government of Muscat received support from the British whilst the Qawasim were backed by the Wahhabis. Under the Wahhabis' influence, the Qawasim escalated their plundering, one-fifth of which, as tribute, went to the Sa'udis.

In 1804, a sudden and violent attack by a Qawasim tribe on a chartered dhow carrying the salvaged merchandise of *Fly*, a cruiser of the East India Company, revived the memory of the attack on *Viper* in 1797 and put the British on the defensive. The Company's cruiser, *Fly*, had been sunk by a French privateer near Qais Island, but the crew of the *Fly* had salvaged part of the precious merchandise, put it on board a dhow, and managed to dispatch it to India. En route to Bombay, the dhow was seized by the Qawasim and escorted to Ras al-Khaimah, where its merchandise and treasures were displayed for the view and pleasure of the Qawasim ladies. The Qawasim were hoping for a handsome ransom from the British. Since no ransom was forthcoming, the Qawasim threatened to massacre the entire crew. Before carrying out the threat, the Qawasim forced the crew to accompany them to the exact location where the Fly had been sunk, and to help them salvage the remainder of the treasures. Thus, the British crew led the Qawasim to Qais. Recovering the rest of the treasure, the Qawasim murdered the entire British crew[18] except two, who managed to escape to Bushehr and inform the Resident. Again, no direct retaliatory measure was taken by the British. This further encouraged the Qawasim to expand their piratical attacks on the British fleet.

After some deliberation, however, Britain planned to act through her protégé, the ruler of Oman. Politically, Britain looked to Oman as an ally. Saiyid Sultan of Oman who nurtured the hope of one day controlling navigation in the Gulf and making Muscat the sole center of international trade in the Arabian Peninsula, seized the opportunity to suppress the Qawasim, his main rival in the region, with British help. In 1804, he launched an attack on the Qawasim but due to strategic errors, the expedition failed and Saiyid Sultan was shot and buried in Lingeh.

In the same year, the Qawasim struck two brigs, the *Trimmer* and the *Shannon*, both of which were owned by Samuel Manasty, the East India Company's Resident in Bassrah. They amputated one arm of the Captain of the *Shannon*, murdered the Indian crew members, and deported the European crew members to Arabian shores. The *Shannon* was taken to the Lingeh port in Iran and the *Trimmer* was taken to Ras al-Khaimah. The only action taken by the Resident was the issuance of an appeal sent to the Wahhabis to intervene and have the British ships released. This too proved to be futile. A month later, in

---

[18] ibid., p.98.

January 1805, forty Qawasim vessels tried to capture the 24-gun cruiser, *Mornington*, but they were repelled by the latter's gunfire.

In the meantime, the British established good working relations with Saiyid Badr ibn Saif, the Saiyid Sultan's successor. Saiyid Badr, on his part, improved relations with the Wahhabis, and sought and received military assistance from the Sa'udis against the contestants to Oman's throne. This was a welcome situation for the British, who were contemplating an all-out assault on the Qawasim pirates without provoking any third party in the region. British policy was reflected in the following instructions issued to the Resident in Muscat: "In your proceedings against the pirates (meaning the Qawasim), you're...to be particularly cautious to act with the greatest moderation, to aim at pacification by means of negotiation, and to avoid hostilities at all events...you are likewise...to keep clear of all disputes with the Wahhabis, or either of the two governments of Turkey or Persia."[19] It was a policy of non-interference that the British pursued.

The first British expedition against the Qawasim pirates was launched in 1805. With British military aid, Badr invaded Bandar Abbas and crushed the Bani Ma'in tribe, the Qawasim allies who, after the death of Saiyid Sultan, had seized control of the city. Although the Bani Ma'in were Persian subjects, Bandar Abbas had been given, on lease by Iran, to the Omani ruler. In this expedition, Saiyid Badr's fleet, backed by the British cruiser *Mornington*, occupied Qishm and obstructed the passage of some thirty ships in the Qawasim fleet under the command of Sheikh Sultan ibn Saqr. Since 1803, Sultan ibn Saqr, the presumed

---

[19] Kelly, op. cit., p. 107.

fleet, backed by the British cruiser *Mornington*, occupied Qishm and obstructed the passage of some thirty ships in the Qawassim fleet under the command of Sheikh Sultan ibn Saqr.   Since 1803, Sultan ibn Saqr, the presumed "Paramount Sheikh of the Qawassim", had headed the Qawassim confederacy from Ras al-Khaimah.   Recognizing the superiority of the British military equipment, Sheikh Saqr offered peace, which was accepted by the British Resident, Seton.   This concession by Seton was in accord with his original instructions to act cautiously, resort to negotiations, and avoid confrontation with the Sa'udis, Turks and Persians. The reason for this was that, in 1805, the Qawassim "*at times claimed the Persians or the Wahhabis as their overlord.*"[20]   At the same time Seton imposed the following pre-conditions for peace: observance of a seventy-day truce, the return of *Trimmer* within 25 days, and restoration of the ship's cargo or   payment of compensation. *It is noteworthy that the return of Shannon was not a pre-condition, because the British realized that the Paramount Sheikh, Sultan Saqr, had little or no authority on the Qawasim Sheikh of Lingeh.*[21]

Having agreed to make peace, the Paramount Qawassim Sheikh, Sheikh Sultan Saqr, through his representative, signed a Qawlnameh (a Memorandum of Accord) in Bandar Abbas on 6 February, 1806, whereby the Sheikh solemnly promised to respect the property and the safety of the crews of vessels of the East India Company. In return, the British agreed to allow the Qawassim dhows to call at Indian ports -- a right that had been denied the Qawassim since the *Shannon-Trimmer* incident. The East India Company also relinquished its claim to the Trimmer's cargo and payment

---

[20] Donald Hawley, op. cit. p.100.

[21] J.G. Lorimer, op. cit., pp 181 et seq.

In the course of negotiations, the Sheikh indicated that in the past the Wahhabis had compelled the Qawasim to engage in piracy and, in all likelihood, they may do so again. It was mutually agreed that in such an eventuality, the Sheikh would inform the British at least three months in advance, of their intention to terminate the accord, of their own will or due to pressure from the Sa'udis. The 1806 accord held for slightly over two years. During this time a strong British squadron patrolled the Gulf to thwart any hostile French initiative.

The British-Qawisim Accord of 1806, however , did not bring total peace to the region. The Omani- Qawasim armed clashes continued and reached their height during the rule of Saiyid Sa'id, who succeeded his father, Badr. Badr, who had embraced Wahhabism, was assassinated (perhaps to the delight of the British) in 1805. The Wahhabis were extending their influence to the coast of India, eliminating their opponents. Sheikh Sultan Saqr, who was weary of the Wahhabis' interference in the region, was deposed in 1809 by the Wahhabis and replaced by Hussain ibn Ali, the Sheikh of Rams. It was also evident to the British that the Wahhabis encouraged the Qawasim in their pursuit of piracy ,as they received a share of the loot.

Despite the 1806 accord, the Qawasim in 1808 made three attacks on the British vessels: In April on *Lively*, in September on *Minersva*, and in October on *Sylph*. The last was most savage and daring. Sir Harford Jones, the Minister Plenipotentiary to Iran, had traveled aboard H.M.S. to Bushehr, and *Sylph*, an East India Company 8-gun schooner, was the vessel in the squadron which had escorted him. On her return to Bombay, *Sylph* was attacked and seized by the Qawasim. "After the ship had been ceremonially purified with rose water, the Qawasim

cut their victims' throats one by one in the name of God."[22]
The slaughtered victims were mostly Sepoys (Indian)[23] ; the
Europeans and a Persian diplomat on board were
unharmed.[24]   There is a discrepancy on the time of the
incident between Hawley and Kelly; the former states that
this happened when *Sylph* was on her way to Iran, the latter
states that this happened on the return voyage.   Kelly,
quoting from an account given by the Captain of *Nereide*,
states that the victims were mostly Sepoy. If all the victims
were indeed Indian, religion must have been a factor in the
act of savagery committed by the Qawasim.

Again on this occasion, no punitive action was directed
by the British against the Qawasim.   The continuing
Napoleonic threat to British interests in the Gulf, the
exhaustion of East India Company military resources, and
the British indisposition to antagonize the Wahhabi Sa'udis
who were supporting the Qawasim, were contributing
factors to the British inaction.   In the meantime, the
Qawasim stretched the range of their piratical activities to
the Indian coasts, and Hussain ibn Ali, the Qawasim Sheikh
who enjoyed the Wahhabi's support, required British ships
passing up the Gulf to pay a tribute to him.

At this juncture, the British, in conjunction with the
Omanis, decided to act.   A joint naval and military
expedition was organized in November of 1809. Its military
objective was the destruction of all vessels and crafts in Ras
al-Khaimah, and other Qawasim bases on the Persian coast,
including Luft, the Qawasim stronghold at Qishm Island,
and Lingeh.   The British were careful not to enrage the
Persians by encroaching upon their sovereignty over Lingeh.

---

[22] ibid., p. 101.

[23] Kelly, op. cit. p.112.

[24] Donald Hawley, op. cit. p.101.

In the instructions issued to the commanders of the British Navy it had been emphasized that: *"The Prince-Governor of Fars was to be informed of the attack, and if no word of protest had been received from him by the time the squadron was off the Persian coast, the attack on the Persian ports was to go forward."*[25] During 11-17 November, in a fierce battle, the British fleet burned over fifty Qawasim vessels in the Ras-al-Kharah harbor, bombarded their fortresses on land, destroyed naval stores, freed some Indian prisoners found in the town, and then withdrew. The purpose of the expedition was not to occupy land or ouster the ruling sheikhs, but to strip them off their maritime capabilities, and thus to forestall future acts of piracy and savagery. Also, the British hoped to impose another agreement, similar to that of 1806, on the Qawasim. The British fleet then sailed towards the Persian coast, attacked Lingeh on 17 November, and destroyed twenty vessels there. Then the expedition sailed to Qishm to assail Luft which was held by the Qawasim and Bani Ma'in. There, eleven vessels were burned and Mulla Hussain, the Sheikh of Bani Ma'in, surrendered after obtaining a guarantee for his personal safety. From there, the fleet proceeded to Rams, Jazirat al Hamra and Sharjah, and destroyed all the vessels they could put their hands on. Despite the destruction of a large part of the Qawasim war fleet during the British-Omani expedition of 1809-1810, no pledge of refrainment from piracy was forthcoming from the Qawasim who still possessed many undetected vessels.

This was an embarrassment to the joint commanders of the expedition; the imposition of the agreement was the mission's ultimate goal. (The instructions of the government

---

[25] Kelly, op. cit. p. 117.

in Bombay to the joint commanders read: "On the termination of operations (the joint commanders) were to endeavour to impose a treaty upon the Qawasim, embodying a guarantee of their future good behavior at sea."[26]) The main obstacle to the attainment of this objective was the Sa'udi's influence on the Qawasim. In response to a request by the British for the abandonment of piracy, the Sa'udi Amir had said that he had no quarrel with the Christians, nor with the British; and that he had issued orders not to attack the British vessels, but he would not abandon war against religious dissenters.[27] By "religious dissenters", he meant Muslim heretics who would not join the Wahhabi sect and the non-Muslims such as Hindus who were designated as "idolatrous Hindus".[28]

The Qawasim began preparing for retaliation against the British and by 1812, they already had a strong fleet. In 1813, their dhows reappeared off the coasts of India and in 1814 they seized several East India Company crafts. The British Resident in Bushehr promptly demanded the Sheikh of Ras al-Khaimah to stop harassing the merchant shipping off the Indian coast. The Sheikh, while promising noninterference with British ships, contended that the Indian ships were not British and that non-British ships would be attacked by Qawasim. A few weeks later, the Qawasim dhows again attacked ships off the Indian coast.

The piracy question for British authorities had become a complex issue. They had accepted the Qawasim Sheikh's pledge to spare British ships, thus expressing their indifference towards the plundering of non-British vessels. On this issue, the Governor-General of India wrote:

---

[26] ibid., p.117.
[27] Donald Hawley, op. cit., p.104.
[28] ibid., p.108.

The systematic and constitutional profession and practice of piracy (by the Qawasim) ...might perhaps be deemed a solid ground of justification for every regular and civilized state to attack and destroy them on the admitted principle of self-defense...but whether this be or be not so on general grounds, the British government has deprived itself of the right of acting upon it, since by taking engagements from the Qawasim to respect its own British trade it has to that extent recognized them as a power capable of maintaining the ordinary international relations with other states.

Kelly rightly argues that: *"The inference was that the government of Bombay had purchased immunity from attack for British shipping by tacitly recognizing the Qawasim's right to plunder the shipping of other states."*[29]

Facing new Qawasim threats, the British sought a solution. By this time Sheikh Sultan ibn Saqr had fled from Wahhabi custody. Saiyid Sa'id, the ruler of Oman, devised a plan that he, in alliance with the Bani Yas tribe of Abu Dhabi and with British support, would reinstall Sultan ibn Saqr in Ras al-Khaimah and make him sign a treaty with the British in line with that of 1806. The Resident in Bushehr endorsed the plan and a British vessel accompanied the expedition.

However, the plan largely failed. The ruler of Oman jointly with the Sheikh of the Bani Yas tribe attacked Ras al-Khaimah and extracted a pledge from Hassan ibn Rahmah, the de facto ruler of Ras al-Khaimah, to respect the safety of Oman's coasts and the security of its residents. In return he persuaded Sheikh Sultan ibn Saqr to drop his

---

[29] Kelly, op. cit. pp.1311-32.

claim to Ras al-Khaimah and be content with being Sheikh of Qawasim for Sharjah. These pledges did not satisfy the British, whose main concern was the safety of maritime trade. They had to rely on the Qawasim promise to keep away from British ships, whatever this meant – It was a promise that more often had been dishonored than kept.

Soon after the signing of the Oman-Ras al-Khaimah Accord, *Ahmad Shah*, a vessel belonging to the East India Company was seized by the Qawasim and the booties were carried to Ras al-Khaimah. In reply to a written protest by the British Resident, Sheikh Hassan Rahmah, as well as the Sa'udi Amir, denied the charge and promised to return the cargo of the vessel, should it be found. Despite all the friendly gestures and repeated assurances, the attacks on merchant shipping by the Qawasim were escalating. In 1815, the ship *Baghalah*, belonging to Oman, and six Indian crafts off the coast of Sind were seized; in 1815 a British-Indian ship, and in 1816, a British armed ship named *Deriah Dowlat*, and an American ship, *Persia*, were captured by the Qawasim. This list is not exhaustive. Piracy had become such a lucrative business that the Sheikhs of Charak and Bahrain also joined the enterprise. Even close relatives of Sheikh Hassan ibn Rahmah, the most recent signatory to the Accord, were identified as having been directly engaged in capturing Indian vessels flying the British flag.

The situation became intolerable for the British. The Resident of Bushehr went in person to visit Sheikh Rahmah and present him with an ultimatum. The Resident was snubbed, and the Qawasim's contempt for the British increased. Between Rams and Sharjah on the southern coast, and between Lingeh and Luft on the northern coast of the Persian Gulf, the Qawasim possessed 100 large dhows carrying 400 cannons. It constituted a considerable naval force. At this juncture most, if not all, of the

Qawasim tribes were under the Wahhabi influence, allied with the Sheikh of Ras al-Khaimah and resentful of the British.[30] *It should be emphasized that it was the religious bond of the Wahhabi faith, rather than tribal affiliation that held the tribes together.*

In 1817, two British cargo ships and an Arab ship (*Mustapha*) flying the British flag, were seized by the Qawasim in Indian waters. In the same year, a number of sea battles were fought by the Qawasim fleet against British and Omani ships. The Qawasim had withdrawn the privilege of safe passage previously granted to the British. Also, they no longer differentiated between European and non-European crew members in their butchery. It was an ominous situation. The British authorities in India concluded that punitive measures against the Qawasim were imperative, and that the time was propitious; the Wahhabis, the main supporters of the Qawasim, were involved in a war with Egypt and their intervention in the gulf seemed unlikely. In February 1817, the Governor-General of India ordered an investigation into the form and intensity of the required punitive action and the following three options were considered: A retributive military expedition against Qawasim followed by withdrawal, the establishment of a permanent base in the Gulf where sufficient troop and military equipment could be kept for an indefinite time (enabling the British to act as soon as a crime occurred), and the providing of a supply of arms to Oman to subdue the Arab tribes of Bahrain and the Arabian Coast (thereby suppressing piracy).

After careful consideration, the Governor-General of India came out in favor of the first suggestion. The second

---

[30] ibid. p. 134.

option required continuous British involvement in the future politics of the region, which would prove burdensome and costly. The third option, too, was rejected because the Governor-General considered Saiyid Sa'id, the ruler of Oman, inert and unsuitable for the task: His claim to the overlordship of the southern coast of the Persian Gulf and Bahrain was untenable, his claim to sovereignty over Qishm unfounded, and Iran would certainly not allow him to occupy Bahrain.[31]

The British punitive expedition began in November 1819 with a strong military and naval force under Major General Sir William Grant Keir. This constituted the third military expedition against the Qawasim.[32] Ras al-Khaimah was the first target which fell on 9 December, and all vessels and naval equipment in the port were destroyed. Then the expedition sailed to Rams, Dhayah, Jezirat al-Hamra, Umm al-Qaiwain, Ajman, Fasht, Sharjah, Abu Hail, Dubai, and lastly Bahrain, where many piratical vessels had taken refuge. In all these places, the fortresses, vessels, and military equipment were demolished. Finally General Grant Keir sailed for Lingeh, where he found and burned a few boats. Then he proceeded to Mughu and Kangun.

Before attacking the Persian ports, General Keir wrote to the Governor-General of Fars and the Governor of Bushehr explaining the aim of the expedition, whilst the British Chargé d'Affaires in Tehran informed the Shah of the forthcoming events, clarifying the aim and scope of the operations. He assured Iran that the expedition was directed solely against the pirates, particularly against the Sheikhs of Lingeh and Charak and that the territorial integrity of Iran would not be encroached upon.

---

[31] Donald Hawley, op. cit. p.110.
[32] J.G. Lorimer, op. cit. pp.197 et seq.

Neither the Shah nor the Governor-General of Fars acquiesced. The Iranian government firmly responded that no news of piracy by Iranian subjects had been received and, should such acts be committed by Iranian subjects, the government would take the necessary measures to punish them; foreign governments have no right to resort to hostile activities on the Iranian Coasts. Furthermore, the Governor of Fars emphatically told General Keir that the port of Lingeh belonged to Iran and that it was the government's responsibility to watch over the safety of its residents. The General, having thus been rebuked, tried to produce evidence to incriminate the Iranian Qawasim. He commissioned William Bruce, the Resident in Bushehr to travel along the coast and collect all helpful data to that end.

The result of the investigation, however, corroborated Iran's claim. Bruce reported that he had not observed any wrongdoing committed by Iranian subjects. He had seen only a wrecked vessel near Kish Island, which had been robbed by the people of Charak. On this occasion, the Sheikh of Charak had gone to the scene, assisted the crew of the vessel, and punished the perpetrators. He saw another vessel which had been plundered by the Qawasim under Sheikh Saqr of Sharjah but done without any involvement by Mohammad ibn Qadhib, the Sheikh of Lingeh. He concluded that the Iranians had never cooperated with the Qawasim pirates.[33] As a result, General Keir not only avoided landing his troops on Persian soil; but also paid compensation to Iran whenever a place was attacked erroneously, without any proof of the pirates having sought shelter there.

---

[33] J.B. Kelly, op. cit. p.162.

During the siege of towns, the British commander bid the sheikhs to surrender while guaranteeing them personal safety. Those who surrendered included Sheikhs Qadhib of Jezirat al-Hamra, Hassan ibn Rahmah of Ras al-Khaimah, Sultan ibn Saqr of Sharjah, and Muhhamad ibn Hazza of Dubai. Sheikh Hussain ibn Ali of Rams, who had been arrested, was released sometime later.

The protection and security of British trade, without the acquisition of any territorial base and with minimum involvement in the regional politics, remained British policy in the nineteenth century. Temporary modifications of the policy were necessitated by Wahhabi threats, French provocation, and Qawasim greed, which called for military operations. At the final stage, the British realized that the forging of a new relationship between the Arab tribes, and a change in the traditional way of life in the Persian Gulf were inescapable. The mighty British sea power on the one hand, and the declining power of its rivals in the region (namely the Wahhabi Sa'udi, the Ottoman Empire, Persia and France) on the other, helped the realization of the British dream and the transformation of the power balance in the region.

The Qawasim and the Wahhabis

The extent of the Sa'udi's political dominion over the Qawasim confederacy, during the eighteenth and nineteenth centuries, was generally a factor of the Wahhabi faith.

Promulgated in the middle of the eighteenth century by Mohammad ibn Abdul Wahhab, Wahhabism expanded rapidly in the eighteenth and nineteenth centuries. Mohammad ibn Abdul Wahhab had been born and raised in Arabia, studied in Madinah, traveled in Mesopotamia to

Basra and Baghdad, and to Hamadan, Isphahan, and Qumm in Persia both to study and to preach. He advocated a return to the simplicity of early Islam and a strict observance of the Shari'a law.

The British, in their encounters with the Qawasim were sensitive coming into open conflict with the Sa'udis. Following the British humiliating retreat from Ras al-Khaimah in the 1817 incident, the Sa'udi Amir stated in a letter to the Resident in Bushehr concerning the Qawasim's piracy: *"I declare myself responsible for the demeanour of all Muslims towards English subjects. The people, however, of Egypt, of Jedda, of Yemen, of Shoher and Makella, of Muscat, of Bussora, of Irak, and the Persian subjects of Sa'id bin Sooltan, all these are our enemies, and by the Almighty aid, whenever we may find them or their property, we will assuredly slay the one and seize the other, in pursuance of the commands of that God whose praise is great."*[34] Evidently the Amir's statement is inspired by the Qoran. The Amir considered Wahhabism as true Islam, and himself as the only ruler and protector of Islam. He considered the Turks under the Ottoman Khalifs, the Egyptians under the Mamluks, and the Omanis, as well as the Persian subjects of Sa'id ibn Sultan, infidels. He called the Ottoman subjects, "Turkish dogs who wish to sow discord among us (Muslims)". And finally he advised the Resident in the following terms: "All those who are of your tribe we will respect, and not allow our subjects to molest them in the slightest degree; but you must not use my enemies with your people or give them papers (meaning

---

[34] I.O. Bombay Secret Proceedings, Vol.41, Consuln. 29 of 21 July, 1819, quoted by Kelly op. cit. p.135.

passes)."[35]   It is interesting to note that the Sa'udi Amir perceived allegiances only in terms of tribal loyalties, and considered the British a tribe. The concept of nation-state was generally alien to the Arab tribes.

From the outset, the religio-political movement of Wahhabism was marked by rampage, plunder and cruelty. In traditional Islam, no distinction is made between politics and religion. For the Wahhabis, the Qoran contained all the rules governing policy and morals. It was "thus that the right of conquest over infidels, the promulgation of the faith by fire and sword, and the right to dispose of the lives and properties of their prisoners, were preached, not as admissible, but indispensable duties binding on all adherents of the true faith, which it was both cowardly and criminal not to carry into execution."[36]

At the turn of the nineteenth century, a religio-military expedition towards Oman was launched. Following the pattern set by the prophet and the Guided Caliphs, he first sent an invitation to Saiyid Sultan ibn Ahmad, the ruler of Muscat, to embrace the true Islamic doctrines as defined by Mohammad ibn 'Abdul Wahhab, and also accept the religious and secular suzerainty of the Sa'udi Amir 'Abdul 'Aziz. In his letter, al-Hariq labeled "Ibadiya" the sect to which Saiyid Sultan belonged: heretic.

The Saiyid Sultan's reaction was one of scorn and fury. He headed his army to confront al-Hariq at Buraimi. The Wahhabi General retreated to Ras al-Khaimah to seek the help of Qawasim, the traditional foe of the Al Bu Sa'id family. The Wahhabis and Qawasim in alliance advanced to Shamailiyah where the armed collision took place. Having seen the Omanis' superiority, the Qawasim separately asked

---

[35] Kelly op. cit., p.132.
[36] Sir Arnold Wilson op. cit. p. 197.

for peace, which was granted to them. Al-Hariq retreated to Buraimi, and the Sultan agreed to let him keep Buraimi. This was indeed a strategic blunder by the Sultan.

Al-Hariq used Buraimi as a base, and, during the following two years, managed to win over the support of certain Qawasim tribes who had embraced Wahhabism. The Dhawahir tribe, a Hinawi faction who were traditionally loyal to the Al Bu Sa'id family, too embraced the new creed. Al-Hariq also levied Zakat, the Islamic alms tax, on the Qawasim which was collected and sent to the Sa'udi Amir.[37] Likewise, the Qawasim were demanded to observe the Wahhabi practice of remitting one-fifth of all booty taken in war to the Treasury in the capital of Najd.[38]

In the meantime, having consolidated his forces, al-Hariq decided on another invasion of Oman. Several factors reinforced his decision with respect to its timing. Sultan ibn Ahmad of Oman was involved in both stamping out the rebellious Sheikh of Bahrain and in helping the Sheikh of Hejaz to halt the Sa'udi's offensive. In retaliation, the Sa'udi Amir ordered the Sheikhs of Qawasim, Kuwait and Bahrain to increase their piratical operations against Oman. In the summer of 1803 in an armed collision between al-Hariq and the Sultan's troops, the latter was defeated. The Sultan signed a three-year peace treaty, and thereby agreed to the payment of an annual tribute to the Sa'udi treasury. He also agreed to allow the Wahhabi preachers in Muscat to convert the Omanis into the reformed Islam of Wahhabi.

The imposition of the peace treaty on Oman was a device to allow al-Hariq time to fortify his position for the

---

[37] Kelly op. cit., p.103.
[38] ibid., p.106.

final blow to the Sultan: Al-Hariq laid siege to Sauhar.
Luckily for the Omani Sultan, Amir Abdul Aziz of Sa'udi
was assassinated at this time and, following the confusion in
the Sa'udi's army, al-Hariq abandoned his plan and retired to
Birami.   Immediately, the new Paramount Sheikh of
Qawasim, Sultan ibn Saqr, as well as the Sheikh of Bahrain
and Kuwait made peace with the Sultan of Oman.

These events reveal the vulnerability of alignments
amongst the sheikhs and the frailty of their religious beliefs,
when pecuniary interests were at stake.   Even the solidarity
and hierarchical authority of the tribal system was extremely
volatile.   On the renewal of piratical operations in the Gulf,
encouraged by the Sa'udis, the Paramount Qawasim Sheikh
Saqr ibn Rashid, disclaimed any responsibility to the British
Resident in Bushehr by indicating that the piratical activities
under discussion had been conducted not from Ras al-
Khaimah, but from Bushehr in Iran, over which he had no
control.[39]   Yet the overlordship exercised by the Sa'udi
Amir over the Qawasim confederacy continued.   For the
recovery of his towns from the Qawasim, the ruler of Oman
had to resort to the Wahhabi Vice-Regent in Ras al-
Khaimah.   Likewise, the British who had defeated the
Qawasim Sheikh in the 1809-10 military expedition could
not make the latter sign a non-aggression treaty without the
consent of the Sa'udi Wakil (representative).   The Wahhabi
Sa'udis were in a position to demand tribute from the British
vessels passing up the Gulf; and the Sa'udi Amir still
appointed a Wahhabi *Wakil* to supervise the Sheikhs of
Bahrain and Qatar.[40]   In 1820 even the Sheik of Bani Bu 'Ali
tribe, who, in 1818, had given up his allegiance to Saiyid

---

[39] I.O. Bombay Selection xxiv, p.302; Miles, Countries and Tribes,
ii,pp 275-76,288; quoted by Kelly p.106.
[40] Kelly op. cit. p.121.

Sa'id, the Sultan of Muscat, and had embraced Wahhabism, captured a Karachi vessel and massacred its crew. Captain Thompson, the commander of the British detachment, sent a letter by the courtesy of Sheikh of Ras al Hadd, to the Sheikh of Bani Bu 'Ali asking for redress. The latter killed the emissary on his arrival. The indignation was too much for the British to swallow. A retaliatory expedition was organized but that, too, met a humiliating defeat.

The Wahhabi movement began to decline in 1818, when Ibrahim Pasha of Egypt defeated Sa'udi Amir, Abdullah, and sent him to Cairo as a prisoner.[41] The British took advantage of the situation, and launched the third major military expedition against the Qawasim in 1819. The Qawasim's power was crushed and the ground was paved for the establishment of a new order in the Gulf.

The Qawasim and the Persians

Encouraged by Mulla 'Ali Shah, the Governor of Bandar Abbas and Hurmoz, the Qawasim turned more aggressive on the Persian coast after Nader Shah's death in 1747 by intensifying their piratical activities -- ravaging the coast and plundering caravans. In 1760 the Qawasim established bases on the island of Qishm, the home of Bani Ma'in tribe, and in the ports of Lingeh and Shias. Those intrusions took place at a time when internal struggle between the Zend and Qajar tribes had reduced Iran to a state of complete chaos. Having secured his position as Shah of Iran, Karim Khan Zand expelled the Qawasim from Lingeh, Qishm and Shias in 1763.

---

[41] Lorimer, op. cit. p.190.

In 1777, the Qawasim Sheikh, Saqr, married the daughter of the Sheikh of Qishm, and thus a closer tie emerged between the two tribes.[42] During this period, the Qawasim, by adherence to the Wahhabi religious sect had accepted a de facto Sa'udi overlordship which stemmed from the Islamic principle of the unity of religion and politics. At the same time those Qawasim who resided in Iran were, in theory, citizens of Iran. In addition to the dual identity, namely religious and political, the members of the Qawasim and Bani Ma'im tribes held a loyalty (identity) to their membership in their respective tribes. The three loyalties or identities (tribal, religious, and political) were distinct. The most important was loyalty to the tribe, or more accurately the sub-tribe (clan) to which the tribesmen belonged.

The Persian coast and *all the islands off the Persian coast, from Kharku and Khark in the north to Hurmoz and Larak in the south belonged to Persia,*[43] though many of them were inhabited by nomadic tribes who lived on fishing, pearling and trade. Occasionally some tribesmen who had become sedentary engaged themselves in farming of grain and date.

Notwithstanding the obscurity of the extent of Iran's control over the Southern part of its Empire during the last two decades of the eighteenth century, it is clear that the scattered Arab enclaves did not constitute anything resembling a nation-state. Before his death, Nader Shah had a project to transplant the entire population of the Gulf coast to the shores of the Caspian and to replace them with Caspian tribes.[44]

---

[42] Sir Arnold Wilson op. cit. p. 201.

[43] Kelly op. cit. p.40.

[44] ibid. p. 40.

In 1789, after the death of Karim Khan Zend, some of the coastal tribes gave up their loyalty to Karim Khan's successors. The internal struggle of power in the Zend tribe itself reduced the Zend's territorial jurisdiction to half of a dozen cities in the south. Bushehr, the main trade center at the time, remained under de jure jurisdiction of the Zend Dynasty: Duties on exports were levied and collected by the government agency, though the Sheikh of Bushehr occasionally imposed and collected arbitrary dues.[45] In Lingeh, the Qawasim exercised greater influence. In addition to their usual involvement in piracy, they engaged in trade, particularly with India. After the Afghans' occupation of Iran, Bandar Abbas lost its importance as a center of trade. Subsequently Iran leased the port to Al Bu Sa'id, the Sultan of Muscat, who consented to be treated, for the purpose of the lease as an Iranian subject. The lease lasted over a century, during which time it was once revised and certain terms were changed in favor of Iran.

In 1700, the Persian Governor of Fars encouraged the Sa'id Sultan to attack the shipping in Bahrain with the intention of weakening the Sheikh of Bahrain's authority and restoring Iran's suzerainty over the island. Sa'id Sultan welcomed Iran's encouragement because of his own aspiration to seize Bahrain. At this juncture, the Sheikh of Bahrain, induced by the Sheikh of Bushehr, placed himself under Iran's protection. In retaliation, Sa'id Sultan, who had sensed foul play by Iran, occupied Khark Island, which was under Sheikh of Bushehr's administration.[46]

---

[45] ibid. p. 41.
[46] J.G. Lorimer;"Gazeteer of the Persian Gulf, Oman, and the Central Arabia"; Vol.I Historical Part (Calcatta:1915) p. 180.

The Qawasim's hopes for maritime supremacy in the Gulf were enhanced with the assassination of the Sultan of Oman by one Qawasim. The Qawasim wished to assume the position previously held by Oman in the Gulf. To achieve this objective, an alliance was struck between Ras al-Khaimah, of the Bani Ma'in tribe of Qishm (recently united with Qawasim by marriage), and the Qawasim of Lingeh. In February 1805, the Qawasim and Bani Ma'in occupied Lingeh, Qishm and Bandar Abbas, and laid siege on Minab. They also seized the island of Khark. Thus, the Qawasim controlled the Strait of Hurmoz and the passage up and down the Gulf. They were in a position to strike at any vessel entering or leaving the area. It was at this time that they attacked the British cruiser *Mornington* and the brigs *Shannon* and *Trimmer*. To curb Qawasim activities, the British in June 1805 assisted the Sultan of Muscat to recover Bandar Abbas, which they had leased from Iran. The cruiser *Mornington* also blockaded the Bani Ma'in in Qishm. Finally, the representative of Sultan ibn Saqr of Ras al-Khaimah signed a pledge not to further attack the British ship. The most difficult task for the British was the detection of the exact location of the pirate ports.[47]

Despite the 1804 Qawasim attack, Lingeh and Qishm remained Persian. This was tacitly acknowledged by the Governor General of India who, in the late 1809 military expedition against the Qawasim, instructed the British Resident in Fars and Chargé d'Affairs in Teheran to assure the government of Iran of the British respect for the sovereignty and territorial integrity of Iran.[48]

---

[47] ibid., p. 117.

[48] I.O. Bombay Political and Secret Proceedings, Range 383, Vol. 9, pol. Consuln. of 8 September, 1809, cited by Kelly, p. 117.

In his presentations to the Government of Iran, the British Chargé d'Affairs, Willock, declared formally his expectation that Iran would not want the pirates, who had established bases in certain ports in Iran, to remain unpunished because *they dwelt on the Persian soil..* The Shah categorically denied the commitment of such crimes in the sea by *Persian subjects.* He reproached the British for not having brought the matter to his attention earlier, so that he could have ordered an investigation and the perpetrators, if Iranian subjects, would have been brought to justice. Notwithstanding his initial displeasure with Willock's request, the Shah permitted the British operation on Persian soil. However, the Governor of Fars would not cooperate. First, he expressed his delight in the decision to punish the Qawasim offenders and promised cooperation hoping that the Shah would not agree to the British request. Later, having learnt of Shah's favorable reply to Willock, the governor turned hostile to the British. Given the Shah's acquiescence, he could not have opposed the expedition per se. So the governor registered his opposition in a subtle way. In a letter to General Keir, he warned him to make sure that, while in the Gulf, none of the inhabitants of various ports of Fars province, particularly those in Lingeh would be molested. He further rebuked the General by stating that Lingeh belongs to the province of Fars, and that its inhabitants are dutiful Persian subjects.[49]

---

[49] I.O. Persia and Persian Gulf (HM Consuls and Consulates in); Vol. 34, Hussain Ali Mirza, (Rabi'i a; Awal, 1235/January 1820, enclosed in Keir to Warden, 10 February, 1820), cited by Kelly, p. 161.

III

The Persian Gulf, Iran and the British

Introduction

The warm and mutually rewarding Anglo-Iranian relationship that developed in the course of the seventeenth century ended in 1722, with the downfall of the Safavid Dynasty. The following seventy tumultuous years in Iran did not allow the development of a meaningful foreign policy. The nineteenth century, however, ushered into the Gulf region numerous international issues with their attendant intricacies and intrigues. The weak and unpopular Qajar Kings, who ruled Iran throughout this period, were not in a position to exercise full sovereignty over the country, to safeguard its territorial integrity, or to protect its economic interests. From the turn of the century onward, Britain consequently assumed a major role in Iran's political affairs.

During this period, the focus of British policy in the Persian Gulf and Iran was the security of the subcontinent of India and the safety of maritime trade routes. The potential threats to such interests came primarily from the European powers of France and Russia, the regional powers of the Ottoman Empire, Egypt, the Sa'udis, and Iran, and the piratical Arab tribes of the Qawasim and Bani Yas. France coveted a part of the Indian subcontinent, and Russia aspired access to the warm-water ports. Meanwhile, The Ottoman Empire desired all Arab territories, Iran claimed sovereignty over the islands of the Gulf, the Sa'udis sought the conversion of Muslims to the Masonic Wahhabi faith, and local Arab pirates stooped to unruliness to test their maritime skill and ruthlessness in the service of their insatiable greed for pillage and buccaneering. The only local power that remained loyal to the British almost throughout was the Al Bu Sa'id Dynasty of Oman. All British activities in the region during the nineteenth century were directed towards the exclusion of these foreign powers and the subordination of regional powers.

In 1796, Russian invaded the Persian territory in Transcaucasia and annexed Georgia. An accord was also reached between Napoleon and the Russian Czar for an expedition towards India. The British were alarmed. In 1801, the Governor of Bombay commissioned Sir John Malcom to go to Iran, buy the Shah's favor, and sign a treaty, promising Iran assistance. In return, Iran covenanted to attack Afghanistan if the Afghans invaded India, and not to allow France to acquire a foothold within her borders[1]

The 1801 Anglo-Iranian Treaty, although a failure at the end, marks Iran's first alliance with a European power, which soon was followed by the treaties of 1809 and 1814. The futility of this first treaty was brought home to Iran in 1803 when Britain stopped short of giving military assistance to Iran after a rapprochement with Russia. This induced Iran to respond favorably to several French

---

[1] Rouhollah K. Ramazani, "The Foreign Poliy of Iran: A Developing Nation in World Affairs, 1500-1941", (Virginia: 1966)p. 40

attempts to form an alliance. The Finkenstein Treaty of
1809 was the outcome. Under this treaty, France
recognized the legitimacy of Iran's claim to Georgia, which
had been ceded by Russia, and pledged to help Iran with a
supply of military equipment and a reorganization of the
Iranian army, to retake her lost territory. In return, Iran
granted the French army a right of passage through Iran to
India. Iran also promised to sever diplomatic relations with
Britain and to encourage the Afghans to invade India.

France demonstrated immense interest in having Iran on
her side by immediately dispatching a military mission,
under General Gardène, for the modernization of the Iranian
Army and by commissioning Napoleon's brother to serve as
Ambassador.[2]   However, the Franco-Persian political
honeymoon was short-lived.   A Franco-Russian
rapprochement in the same year, and Iran's military
ineptitude retarded French enthusiasm to proceed with their
promises. This came as a blow to Fath Ali Shah who was
already wondering at the inscrutable behavior of the
Europeans, instantly changing their allegiances, switching
allies and enemies, and making or breaking treaties.

At this juncture, the British approached Iran for a new
treaty which was made in 1809 and complemented by three
other agreements, culminating in the 1814 Treaty. By virtue
of the new treaty, Britain was obligated to assist, financially
and militarily, should Iran be attacked by any European
power, and to remain neutral in the eventuality of an Irano-
Afghan war. In return, as in the Treaty of 1801, Iran
promised to terminate her alliance with France, to deny the
French free passage through Iran, and to fight Afghanistan if
the latter invaded India.

---

[2] Ruhollah K. Ramazani op. cit. p. 41.

Also, the 1809 Treaty included a provision that the occupation of any Persian port or island by the British forces without the prior knowledge of the Persian Government would not constitute a right of possession. When, with the prior permission of the Shah of Iran, British troops landed on the island of Khark or any other Persian island or port, they would be subject to the command and instructions of the Shah of Iran; the maximum number of such troops would be decided in the final treaty.[3] However, in 1810, the Shah rejected the British suggestion of ceding Qishm or other islands to the British in lieu of a subsidy or rent.[4] The 1814 Treaty provided that, should Iran require naval and military assistance in the Persian Gulf, the British government would supply it, if the assistance requested by Iran was convenient and practical. The expenses entailed were to be paid by Iran and British vessels were to use only the ports named by Iran.[5] It is ironic that Iran's undertaking regarding Afghanistan in the 1814 Treaty with Britain directly contravened that in the 1807 Treaty with France. Perhaps Fath Ali Shah was imitating the inscrutable maneuvers in which Europeans had used in their dealings with Iran.

The 1814 Treaty, too, proved to be a failure. In the 1826-28 Irano-Russian War, the British did not honor their promise under the 1814 Treaty to support Iran in the war against Russia. However, in an attempt to appease Iran,

---

[3] Mahmood, Mahmood ,"Tarikh-e Ravabet-e Iran va Engylis", p. 138; Kelly p. 941.
[4] Kelly, op. cit., p. 94.
[5] Kelly, op. cit., p. 97.

Britain offered to assist Iran with the payment of the indemnity due under the Turkmanchai Treaty.[6]

Fath Ali Shah's interest in an alliance with Britain might have been aroused by practical expediency and a historical precedence. Iran did not possess a strong navy and had to rely on British naval aid to suppress Qawasim piracy against Iran. This historical precedent went back to the time of Shah Abbas. During the Portuguese occupation of Iranian ports and islands in the seventeenth century, Shah Abbas of the Safavid Dynasty had wooed the British in the hope of rallying their naval backing towards expelling the Portuguese aggressors. The British, too, sought a foothold in Iran for the expansion of their trade. At that time, friendly relations proved mutually advantageous.

Shah Abbas granted preferential rights to English subjects against other foreigners. Those rights included the carrying arms for self-defense, and the establishment of factories at all cities. Furthermore, vessels of the East India Company could call freely at any Iranian port. With such extensive privileges, the British never considered establishing a military base in the Gulf region. All had gone fairly smoothly for the British in the Gulf until the early nineteenth century and the breakout of horrifying piracy.

While pondering how to combat this piracy, Henry Willock, the British Chargé d'Affairs in Tehran, proposed to the Viscount Robert S. Castlereagh, the British Foreign Secretary, in 1817 that the acquisition of a base in Iran would be advisable and would serve a dual purpose: It would enable the British to suppress the piracy and also restrain the Russians from eroding British influence in the

---

[6] Sir Henry Rawlinson, "England and Russia in the East", (London: 1875) p. 37.

Persian Court.[7] On that occasion, no decision on the matter was taken by the British Foreign Office.

In the course of planning for the third military expedition against the Qawasim pirates in 1819, the British authorities in Bombay re-examined the question of establishing a military base in the Gulf so that quick and effective retaliatory actions against the pirates would be possible. They even discussed the location for such a base and came up with the suggestion that it should be within easy access to the Pirate Coast, preferably on an island commanding the Strait of Hurmoz. On those two grounds, the island of Qishm was thought to be the most suitable location.   Sir Evan Nepean, the Governor of Bombay, instructed General Keir to investigate both the suitability of, and the title to, the island.

As to the title, Nepean, on the basis of a statement by Captain G. F. Sadlier, advised Keir that Saiyid Sa'id of Muscat considered Qishm his own property. According to Sadlier, Sa'id claimed that he had inherited the island from his father, Sultan ibn Ahmad, who had acquired the island by conquest from Iran. Sa'id also claimed that he had never remitted any tribute to Iran.[8]

Contrary to Captain Sadlier's statement, Captain Taylor reported in 1818 that Qishm had been farmed to Saiyid Sa'id

---

[7] J.G. Lorimer, op. cit., pp199,200; I.O. Persia and the Persian Gulf, Vol.33, Willock to Castlereagh, Tehran 16 Apr. 1817; Kelly, op. cit. p.167.
[8] I.O. Bombay Secret Proceeding Vol. 41, Consuln. 29 of 21 July, 1819, Sadlier to Governor in Counil, Muscat, 17 May, 1819; Kelly op. cit. p.168.

by the Shah of Iran.[9] Furthermore, Sir John Malcolm, who was an emissary to the court of Iran, had suggested to the Iranian government during his first mission of 1800-01 that it either cede or lease the two islands of Qishm and Hanjam to the British.   The Shah declined the offer.   After his second mission, Malcolm discarded Qishm and Hanjam in favor of the island of Khark.   It is also remarkable that, in his fervor for a British military base, Malcom recommended the acquisition of the island by military force should Iran reject the offer.[10] It is clear that Sir John Malcolm, who had visited Iran several times during the first two decades of the nineteenth century, recognized Qishm, Hanjam, and Khark as parts of Iran's territory.

The combined policy of distortion of facts and intimidation proved successful tools in politics and the British politicians employed these tools extensively.   The British did not want to admit that the failure or refusal to pay tribute to Persia did not give title to the lessee or the person to whom the land had been farmed out, per se.   The British were determined to control Qishm in one form or another.   In the meantime, they were looking for a plausible excuse for their soon-to-be illicit actions. Ignoring the views of Captain Taylor and Sir John Malcolm on the title to the island, Francis Warden, the Chief Secretary to the Bombay government, ordered General Keir to occupy the island on the basis of a statement by Captain Seton, the former Resident at Muscat.[11]

---

[9] I.O. Bombay Secret Proceedings Vol.41, Consuln 37 of 20 September, 1819, Minute by Warden, 12 August, 1819; Kelly op. cit. p.168.

[10] I.O. Persia and Persian Gulf, Vol. 33, Willock to Castlereagh, 16 April, 1817; Kelly op. cit. p. 166.

[11] I.O. Bombay Secret Proceeding, Vol.45, Consuln 5 of Feb. 1820, Warden to Keir, 29 Jan. 1820; Kelly op. cit. p. 168.

Simultaneously, the British Chargé d'Affairs in Tehran was instructed to inform the Shah of the British decision and, if required, offer him favors and inducements to consent. One of these was an offer of mediation to restore Iran's sovereignty over Bahrain and other islands whose sheikhs had defected. The Shah was also told that the British were even ready to use compulsion, if necessary, in favor of Iran. Furthermore, the British Chargé d'Affairs insisted that the establishment of peace and security in the Gulf would benefit Iran and that this could only be achieved with Iran's cooperation, by letting Britain acquire a military base in the Gulf. In conclusion, Willock "showed the stick" by warning Iran that, *in the case of a rejection of the offer, "it was possible that the right and title of the Shah to all the islands in the Gulf might be questioned"*.[12] Willock also said, "If the invasion of Bahrein was attempted and proved unsuccessful and our mediation was declined, I could not assert that the British government might not hereafter mediate its occupation."

Fath Ali Shah did not concede to the British request. His minister, in conveying the Shah's response to Willock, reminded him that Qishm belonged to Iran and that Saiyid Sa'id held the island of Qishm on lease as a dependency of Bandar Abbas, implying that the British could not negotiate on Qishm with Saiyid Sa'id. This was the start of the deterioration of Irano-British relations.

It is more than a coincidence that, in disputes over the islands of Abu Musa and the Tumbs, the British resorted to similar arguments of the "inherited rights of the Qawasim Sheikhs" of Sharjah and Ras al-Khaimah over these islands

---

[12] I.O. Persia and Persian Gulf, Vol.34, Willok to Keir, 10 March 1820; Kelly op. cit. p. 170.

seventy years later. Like Qishm, they command the Strait of Hurmoz. The British certainly kept their resolve and challenged Iran's title to the islands when that policy suited their security and economic interests.

In July 1820, the British detachment in Ras al-Khaimah was transferred to Qishm with the prior approval of Saiyid Sa'id. It was soon called upon to engage in a retributory action against Banu Bu Ali tribesmen, who had captured a Karachi ship and murdered its entire crew. The expedition sent from Qishm proved a disaster and thus called into question the wisdom of having a military base in the Persian Gulf.

In December 1820, the Iranian Government protested the occupation of Qishm and, through the British Embassy in Tehran, demanded prompt evacuation.[13] In his letter, the Minister of Iran rejected Saiyid Sa'id's claim of title to Qishm, objected to the British occupation of the island, rebuked the British claim of past success in restoring peace and security in the region, and stated unequivocally that the responsibility of combatting piracy remained with the province of the Governor of Fars. Also, the Minister had asked for the recall of Captain Bruce, the British Resident in Bushehr, charging him with complicity against Iran.[14] In a more comprehensive letter to the British Minister of Foreign Affairs, the Iranian Minister warned the British Government that the military occupation of an Iranian island in the south could provide the Russians with an excuse to demand a similar concession in the north, and that this would not be in the interests of either Iran or Britain.

Iran's protest served the purpose of reopening, in the British circle, a discussion on the whole issue of a base.

---

[13] Lorimer op. cit., pp. 199-203.

[14] ibid., p. 202.

The Indian military was viewing the base for a detachment (an absolute necessity) and their choices were Qishm, Qais, or Hanjam -- all Iranian islands. Facing unrelenting Iranian opposition, the British decided to stop the payment of the subsidy provided for in the 1814 Treaty. They also commissioned an investigation into the history of the island, in the hopes of finding some evidence that would corroborate Saiyid Sa'id's title. It was found that, after Nader Shah's assassination in 1747, the Governor of Qishm had refused to acknowledge the authority of the new King and that, since 1764, the island had been ruled intermittently by the Qawasim, Bani Ma'in, and Al Bu Sa'ids of Oman -- some of whom did and some who did not pay tribute to the Shah of Iran. The evidence was not conclusive. At the end, the decision was for evacuation of the island, and transfer of the supply depot to Muscat. However, soon they realized that Muscat was not a suitable location for the depot, and hastily decided to transfer it to Mugha Bay on the Persian coast. Iran immediately filed a protest, and the British moved their depot from Mugha Bay to Basida, a location on Qishm. This may have happened through a covert accord between the Governor of Fars and the British Resident, as it was incorporated in an agreement that came to be known as the Treaty of Shiraz.

The Treaty of Shiraz was signed by Captain William Bruce, the Resident in Bushehr, and Mirza Zaki Khan, the Minister to the Prince Governor-General of Fars, in August 1822. The preamble contained regrets for some unfortunate acts by the British officials which had harmed Anglo-Iranian relations. The three major provisions of the treaty related to the recognition of Iran's sovereignty over Bahrain,[15] the payment of compensation to the Iranians who had suffered as the result of the British expedition of January 1820, and the permission for British troops to stay at the Qishm base for a maximum of five years, during which time Iran would construct her navy and be able to preserve peace and order in the Gulf independently.

Although the British considered the treaty invalid, saying that Bruce did not have authority to negotiate on Bahrain, Iran insisted that the provision on Bahrain in the treaty was as valid as other provisions that had been implemented by the British. The British troops left Qishm in January 1823, but the depot remained in Basidu until the end of the nineteenth century. Moreover, the British Resident of the Lower Gulf was stationed in Qishm.

After the departure of the British detachment, Hussein Ali Mirza, the Governor of Fars, Saiyid Sa'id, the ruler of Oman, and Sultan ibn Saqr, the Sheikh of Sharjah conspired to dislodge the Sheikh of Bahrain. Again, the British intervened and the plan was forestalled.

The Irano-British disputes were not confined to the islands nor to the question of a military base in the Persian Gulf. Herat was another unresolved issue. After Nader Shah, Iran had lost Herat, a city with a majority of Persian speaking, Shi'a Iranian. Fath Ali Shah twice, in the years 1799 and 1800, and his son Abbas Mirza in 1832, had sent military expeditions to Herat. The outbreak of Irano-Russian War in 1804 halted Fath Ali Shah's plans, and British countermeasures in 1837 thwarted a similar attempt by Mohammed Shah, Fath Ali Shah's successor. The

---

[15] Lorimer, op. cit., pp.202-203.F. Adamiyat, "Bahrein Islands: A Legal and Diplomati Study of the Irano-British Controversy" (New York: 1917); Gholami Reza Tadjbakhsh "La Question des Iles Bahrein", (Paris 1960).

preservation of Afghanistan's status quo as a buffer state between India and Russia was part of the British imperial policy in the Near East. The Anglo-Iranian confrontation over Herat recurred in 1837 when Mohammad Shah marched to Herat with his army. The British Ambassador had warned the Shah against such an attempt, a warning which the Shah did not heed. In order to halt Iran's advancement towards Herat, British troops seized the island of Khark in the Persian Gulf and were ready to land in Bushehr. Mohammad Shah ended the expedition and returned to Tehran and the British evacuated the island of Khark. The confrontation ended but mutual mistrust and resentment were enhanced.

With the evacuation of Qishm, the idea of holding a military base in the Gulf was temporarily set aside. In future, Britain intended to rely on her navy (a patrolling cruiser squadron) in the Gulf, as well as on contractual arrangements with the sheikhs. Mountstuart Elphinstone, who had replaced Nepean as Governor of Bombay, believed that sovereignty over the Pirate Coast and the sheikhs, as well as the task of patrolling the Gulf, should be assigned to the Sultan of Muscat, to act as a surrogate for Britain.[16]

In the meantime, neither Iran nor Oman had given up their hopes for subduing the Sheikh of Bahrain. For many years, the Prince Governor of Fars and Saiyid Sa'id of Muscat toyed with the idea of jointly occupying Bahrain and then deciding on how to run it. To cement the alliance, in 1827 the Prince-Governor of Fars gave his daughter in marriage to Saiyid Sa'id. In the meantime, the British Resident persuaded the Sheikh of Bahrain to become a

---

[16] I.O. Bombay Secret Proceeding Vol. 43, Consuln 53 of 15 December, 1819; Kelly op. cit. p. 156.

signatory to the General Agreement, signed by the Trucial Sheikhs, so that if Bahrain were attacked, the British could step in on the basis of a contractual undertaking for the maintenance of peace and order in the Gulf. At the same time, the British warned Iran that, should Iran attack Bahrain, the British would have to reconsider the issue of a military base in the Gulf. In 1827, the lease of Bandar Abbas and Qishm to Saiyid Sa'id was renewed and Iran succeeded in securing more favorable terms, including a higher rent in the lease agreement.

The Russian Factor in Anglo-Iranian Relations

In the late 1820's, sporadic piracy and tribal uprisings re-emerged and periodic political disturbances in Bushehr caused anxiety to the British Resident. The policy of non-involvement came under scrutiny in British circles. Sir John Malcolm, now the Governor of Bombay, was entertaining the idea of establishing a new base in the Gulf that could also accommodate the Residents' offices, as well as becoming a trading center. Amalgamation of the two Residencies of Bushehr and Bassrah in one place could also reduce the cost.

The Residents were responsible for maintenance of peace in the Gulf and for the protection of British subjects. They reported not to the Ministry of Foreign Affairs in London or the British Legation in the country concerned, but directly to the Indian Office. The locations under consideration by the British for the base were the islands of Basidu, Kung, Lingeh, Asalu, and Khark, all part of Iranian territory. The use of any of these islands necessitated prior negotiation with Iran, unless the British chose to occupy them by force, and past experience showed that the employment of force would backlash.

There was another parameter in the political equation, the Russian factor, that the British could not ignore. After the defeat of Napoleon, the major external threat to British India came from Russia. This threat was exacerbated by the Irano-Russian War which culminated in the Gulistan Treaty of 1813. As a result of this treaty, the Russians annexed large parts of Iranian territory in Caucasia, thus acquiring an advanced post towards India. If Russia decided to attack India, the probable routes would be either Khivah, Bokhara, and the Oxon River, or Iran, Herat and Khandhar in Afghanistan. Evidently, the British were sensitive to any Russian advancement into Iran or Afghanistan as they wanted both to remain as buffer states between India and the European states. As Malcolm had viewed, India's first line of defense lay in Persia.

Britain commanded the Persian Gulf, which constituted the gate to India. Communication lines between England and India went either overland via Egypt, Syria, Iraq and the Gulf, or through the Red Sea. Hence, the British were determined to arrest any further Russian advancement into Iran. For this reason, the Tehran Treaty of 1814 had been signed, in which the British promised support to Iran should she again be attacked by Russia. As previously mentioned, British credibility in Iran had seriously been impaired after 1828 when, in the course of the Irano-Russian War, Britain did not honor her promises under the 1814 Treaty. Also the fact that Britain since 1823 had transferred the control of the British mission in Tehran from England to India, indicated the importance of Iran to the security of India.

After the conclusion of the Turkmanchai Treaty of 1828, and the imposition of its harsh, humiliating conditions

on Iran, the British came to their senses. The cession of
more Iranian territory to Russia had brought the latter's base
nearer to India. The economic and judicial capitulation had
increased Russian clout in the Persian court at the expense
of the British. This Russian ascendancy in Tehran could
prove costly to Britain. Perhaps Britain had fallen victim to
the improvement of her relation with Russia after 1815, and
to her involvement in Balkan. Whatever the reason, at this
stage the British were making every effort to encourage
greater intercourse with Iran, with a view to enhance their
own influence and diminish that of the Russians. But it was
not easy. Fath Ali Shah died in 1834 and his grandson,
Mohammad, with the help of the British and the Russians
ascended to the throne. Although the British lent much
support to suppress other contenders, they did not win the
favor of the new Shah.

Mohammad Shah, who had been raised in Tabriz and
witnessed the Russo-Iranian Wars and the defeat of the
Iranian army under his father's command, feared the
Russians and distrusted the British. He was patriotic at
heart and, had it not been for the ignorance, fatuity,
jealousy, vanity, insolence, and indolence of his Chief
Minister, he might have made some achievements.
Mohammad Shah aspired to restore Iran's sovereignty over
the territories that Iran had lost during his grandfather's
reign. In an endeavour to divert his attention from
Caucasia, the Russians encouraged him to proceed to, and
capture, Herat. In return, Russia agreed to advance him a
loan and offered other financial concessions, once Herat
was conquered. Such an expedition, the Russians thought,
would also weaken the British stand in Afghanistan. The
British, on the other hand, tried to dissuade the Shah from
proceeding to Herat, lest it give the Russians a greater
opportunity to incite the Afghan tribes against Britain. After

all, Herat was the eastward gate to Kabol, Khandhar, and ultimately India.

The British Ambassador to Iran, Sir John McNeill, at the instruction of the Prime Minister Viscount Henry Palmerstone, approached the Shah and requested him to let Britain mediate in the Irano-Afghan dispute. The pretext was the prevention of loss of life and property. The Shah would not concede to the request. Despite McNeill's oral protest, Mohammad Shah, having allied himself with the rulers of Kabol and Khandhar, who had a personal rivalry with the ruler of Herat, marched his army from Tehran towards Herat in March 1837.

The British reaction was instantaneous. The Ambassador traveled to the Persian Camp near Herat, handed over his government's protest in writing and warned the Shah that Britain would retaliate by seizing the island of Khark and invading Bushehr. The Ambassador, in a meaningful tone, indicated that the British had reason to believe that the military campaign against Herat had been instigated and planned by Russia and, if the Russians knew the way to India, the British army knew the way to Isphahan and Tehran.[17] The British had already started causing insurrection in the cities near Bushehr in order to divert the attention of the Shah to the south. Obviously the British did not intend to keep Southern Iran, lest the Russians occupy part of the northern province of Gilan. They intended only to send a message to the Shah to withdraw.

In the meantime, in an attempt to reinforce their position in Afghanistan, the British conspired to remove Dost Mohammad from Kabol and replace him with Shah Shoja' of Herat and confirm Ranjit Singh in Peshawar. Their efforts

---

[17] Kelly op. cit. p. 297.

were in vain. At the end, the British army was entrenched in Kabol.

Having captured Khark and landed in Bushehr, McNeill was instructed to hand an ultimatum to the Shah to withdraw from Herat, and to evacuate Ghorian. He also was to require the Iranian government to extend the British all the privileges enjoyed by the Russians under the Turkmanchai Treaty. Once the Shah had conceded to those terms, then the Ambassador was to renew the request for the retention of Khark as a military base. George Auckland, the Governor-General of India had recommended the retention of Khark at any cost. He believed "the island could become the Singapore of the Persian Gulf".[18]

Both Russia and Iran were outraged. Russia protested the occupation of Khark, called it a gross violation of Iran's territorial integrity, and demanded the immediate withdrawal of the British troops from the island and the recall of their naval squadron from the Gulf. In November 1838, a mob in Bushehr attacked the British Residency. The government of Iran imposed an embargo first on the supply of grain, and later on all supplies to the British garrison on Khark.

At this time, Anglo-Iranian relations were at their nadir, and mutual distrust stood at its highest level. The improvement of relations with Iran seemed farfetched so the British tried their luck with the Arab sheikhs. If necessary, they were ready to forge the title to several islands for the sheikhs. The confrontation between Iran and Britain came to a head in March of 1839, and Britain broke off diplomatic relations. A sequel of attacks on the British Residency led to the dispatch of H.M.S. *Wellesley Cruiser*, carrying 74 guns, and HM brig *Algerine* to the Gulf. They

---

[18] ibid. p. 347.

arrived off Bushehr on 20 March. The Shah was perturbed, lest he lose part of Southern Iran to the British. Under duress, the Shah therefore conceded to the British demands: Ghorian was evacuated. The Anglo -IranianTreaty, signed on 28 October, 1841recognized freedom of trade for the subjects of each contracting party in the territory of the other, and the British were permitted to open consulates in Tehran and Tabriz.

The British now were looking for a base on the Arabian coast. Falarka, in Kuwait, was the best of several bad choices, but it was eventually abandoned. Their attention was again directed towards Iran. The British suggested the lease or purchase of the island of Khark, which Iran again refused.

The British could not afford another showdown with Iran. She was deeply engaged with suppressing the dissidents in India who opposed the gradual piecemeal annexation of their country to the British realm, and in alleviating the hostility of the Afghans to the presence of the British garrison in Kabol. The British mission in Kabol had already been massacred. Hence, the British were not in a position to engage in an armed clash with Iran.

The Emergence of the Trucial States

By the 1830's, piracy at sea had been largely suppressed but warfare and piracy on land persisted. The claims of Iran, Oman, and the Wahhabi Sa'udi to certain islands or territories lingered. The direct real or perceived Russian threat to India continued, and Iran and Afghanistan remained immediate victims to Russo-British rivalry.

In November 1834, a clash between the Al Bu Sa'id family of Oman and the Qawasim triggered an upheaval in the Gulf, providing a new opportunity for the Qawasim and Bani Yas tribes to re-embark on piracy. Colonel Samuel Hennell, Resident in the Gulf, to whom the credit of introduction of "the Trucial System" has been attributed, succeeded in arranging a five-month Maritime Truce Pact for the pearling season through negotiations with the pirate sheikhs. He first negotiated the pact with the Paramount Sheikhs of the Qawasim and Bani Yas, Sultan ibn Saqr, and Shakhbut ibn Dhibya. Then he dispatched a cruiser to fetch the Sheikhs Ubaid ibn Sa'id of the Al Bu Falasah (Dubai) and Rahsid ibn Hamad (Na'im). The pact, which was signed on 21 May, 1835 in Basidu, Qishm, proscribed maritime warfare for five months, provided for the payment of compensation by maritime aggressors, and stipulated that any violation of the pact could be directed to the British Resident for redress. The sheikhs wanted a guarantee from the Resident which he could not oblige. The pact also granted the signatories the option to give notice of their intention to renew it, four weeks before its expiration.

The preference of Hennel's pact of 1835 to Malcolm's agreement of 1828 lay in the fact that the latter forbade piracy and the former proscribed warfare in general. Moreover, in the new pact, the sheikhs recognized the shipping route along the Persian coast, which was the main maritime channel, as a neutral highway. Consequently, no war dhow was allowed to cruise along this stretch of water. A line was drawn between the islands of Sirri and Abu Musa to delimit the southern boundary of the highway. The boundary line was subsequently drawn between Sha'am, Abu Musa and Abu Nu'air. At the outset, Sultan Saqr complained that the new line would deprive him from defending his possessions in Khaur Fakhan, only to be reminded by the British Political Resident that "he had got possession of Khaur Fakhan by exploiting the troubles in Oman at the close of 1834".[19]

In 1836, the pact was extended for eight months with one more signatory, the Sheikh of Umm ul-Qaiwain. In the previous year, Sultan Saqr had opposed a British invitation to the Sheikh of Umm ul-Qaiwain to join the pact, arguing that he was not an independent Sheikh but a Qawasim dependent. This proved to be false. Thus, all the signatories of the General Treaty of 1820, except the Sheikh of Bahrain, joined the truce pact.

The Resident succeeded in renewing the pact each year by inducement or intimidation. In 1843, a ten-year truce was signed. Under the new treaty, the sheikhs covenanted to preserve peace on sea; each Sheikh accepted responsibility for the wrongdoing of his tribesmen; and all agreed that, should any violation of the terms of treaty occur and the parties to the dispute be unable to settle the claims satisfactorily amongst themselves, the wronged party would seek redress only through the good offices of the British Resident and refrain from direct retaliation.

Although the truce pacts worked smoothly and the number of piratical attacks and acts of warfare on sea were drastically reduced, warfare on land was still rampant. In addition, if the rampage on sea was committed by a Persian or a Turkish tribe of pirates, no immediate retribution was available since Turkey and Iran were not parties to the pact. For instance, in 1841 during a clash between the Qawasim and Bani Yas when Sultan Saqr was demanded to punish the perpetrators, he pleaded that he could not enforce the rules against the Persian Qawasim who stayed outside his

---

[19] ibid. p. 359.

jurisdiction. Iran would not voluntarily agree, or allow the Persian Qawasim tribe to sign the pact. The British could not force Iran, lest the Russians seek similar authority in the Caspian Sea. The only plausible way to circumvent the impediment was to proceed under the requirement of the Law of Nations against piracy and leave the Bombay government to deal with the problem.

In March 1845, an expedient channel was found to deal with the acts of piracy committed by the Persian Qawasim. The British schooner, *Emily*, was wrecked off the island of Qais and was plundered by the Qawasim inhabitants. Britain asked for redress. As Iran did not have the naval capabilities to catch the culprits, the Governor-General of Fars requested that the Resident in Bushihr aid him by sending a cruiser with a Persian officer on board to chase the culprits, arrest them, and hand them over to the Iranian government. This practice was repeatedly employed by virtue of an oral understanding between the Governor-General of Fars and the Resident in Bushehr and it worked well. In November, two cruisers with a Persian officer aboard were dispatched to Asalu, Chiru and Nakhilu on the Persian coast to reclaim from the sheikhs, who were Iranian subjects,[20] the cargoes that had been depredated from British vessels. By using this device, the British were in effective control of the Gulf from 1846.

Despite sporadic cooperation, the tension and mistrust in Irano-British relations persisted. Prevented from the exercise of sovereignty over certain islands considered her own, and the control over the northern coast of the Persian Gulf, the Iranian government feared a gradual piecemeal annexation of Iranian territory by the British, following their

---

[20] I.O. Persian and Persian Gulf, Vol.85, Hennel to Malet 3 August, 1846.

pattern of operations in India. The presence of the British Resident in Bushehr was a source of bitterness and suspicion for Iran.

There were good reasons for Iran to doubt the intentions of the British in the Gulf. In a letter sent to the Resident in Iran concerning Iran's alleged preparation to regain its control over Bahrain, the Governor of Bombay stated: "In the event of the Persian government sending out any force of armed vessels, or vessels carrying armed men, such vessels should be watched and any actual attempt to possess themselves of *territory belonging to Arab Chiefs in friendly alliance with the British government* should first be remonstrated against, and then, if persevered in, resisted."[21]

Apart from historical evidence, Iran's suzerainty over Bahrain had been recognized by the British in the Treaty of Shiraz. Subsequent denial of the treaty did not change Iran's conviction of the validity of its claim. But Britain was mindful of its friendship with the Arab sheikhs who, unlike Iran, were not exposed to Russian influence. And the British knew that they would never be fully trusted by Iran.

May, 1853 was the time for the renewal of the truce pact. The Resident's invitation to the sheikhs to assemble in Basidu coincided with the Sa'udi Amir's invitation for them to gather in Burial. This turned into a test of authority between the Amir and the Resident. The sheikhs opted for the Amir. As a reason for his preference, Sultan ibn Saqr mentioned that he stayed with the Wahhabi Amir hoping to regain his control over Umm ul-Qaiwain and Ajman.

In this assembly, the Sa'udi Amir compelled the sheikhs and Saiyid Sa'id to reimburse the Zakat in arrears to his

---

[21] I.O. Bombay Secret Proceeding Vol. 192, Consuln 38 of 7 September, 1842, letter 2740; Kelly op. cit. p. 382.

treasury. He also established the overlordship of Amir
Faisal of Sa'udi over Inner Oman, from Wadi al-Jizzi to
Bahlah and Ras al-Hadd.[22] In a letter to the Resident, the
Sa'udi Amir qualified the Sheikhs as his "dependents" who
were "connected" with him. All this constituted a serious
challenge to the British. Hence, the order was issued for the
British cruisers *Clive* and *Tigis* to patrol the Trucial coast
and watch the movements of the sheikhs.

It seems that, finally, the Sa'udi Amir had acquiesced to
the sheikhs' visit to the Residency and the renewal of the
truce treaty. Thus, during the first week in May, Sheikhs
Sultan ibn Saqr of Sharjah and Ras al-Khaimah, Abdullah
ibn Rashid of Umm al-Qaiwain, Hamid ibn Rashid of
Ajman, Sa'id ibn Buti of Dubai, and Sa'id ibn Tahnun of Abu
Dubai assembled at the Residency and signed the "Treaty of
Maritime Peace in Perpetuity" on 4 May, 1853. The treaty
provided for the complete cessation of hostilities at sea, the
punishment of perpetrators by their respective ruling sheikh,
redress for injured parties and the return of property, and
recourse to the Resident in case of a failure by the parties to
arrive at a satisfactory arrangement. The endurance of the
trucial system, undoubtedly, was a credit to the vision,
patience, perseverance and skill of Samuel Hennell. The
trucial system eradicated the rampant piracy and plunder
and entrenched the hegemony and control of Britain in the
region through the Sheikhs for the next one hundred years.

The Irano-British War of 1856-57

Irano-British relations after the 1837-41 crisis vacillated
between indifference and suspicion. Both parties nursed

---

[22] ibid. p. 407.

grudges against the other. The British under the 1841 Commercial Treaty could open consulates only in Tehran and Tabriz, whereas the Russians under the Turkmanchai Treaty of 1828 could have consulates in all cities in Iran. The British did not enjoy the extraterritorial immunities to which the Russian subjects were entitled; they feared that Iran may play into the Russian hands to the detriment of the British interests in India. Iran was resentful of British support for the Sheikh of Bahrain and the obstruction of Iran's operations to recover Herat. With the amelioration of Russo-British relations after 1838, Iran lost Russia's backing for her designs on Afghanistan.

Before 1747, the greater part of Afghanistan belonged to Iran. In that year, after Nader Shah's assassination, one of his Afghan generals, Ahmed Khan, defected, seized Herat, and laid the foundation for an independent Afghanistan. In 1798, with the encouragement of the Indian Muharageh, Zaman Shah of Afghanistan invaded India and reached Lahore. The British sent an emissary to Iran with instructions to urge Iran to attack Afghanistan and recapture Herat. The British even promised to reimburse the cost of this expedition. Fath Ali Shah led his troops to Khorassan and dispatched the army to Afghanistan under the command of Mahmood Shah and Firuz Shah, brothers of Zaman Shah who had taken refuge in the Persian Court. Zaman Shah returned from India to deal with his brothers' insurgence. He was captured and blinded by his brother Mahmood.

Afghanistan, for a long time, was grappling with civil war; thus the threat to India was averted without any gain for Iran.[23] The Anglo-Iranian Treaty of 1801 contained a

---

[23] Kelly, op. cit. pp. 68-69.

provision whereby Iran undertook to invade Afghanistan should the latter decide to attack India, and would refrain from concluding a peace treaty with Afghanistan, unless the latter acknowledged that India was an integral part of the British Empire, thereby renouncing Afghanistan's claim to the subcontinent.[24] As previously mentioned, Iran's undertaking, vis-à-vis Britain with regard to Afghanistan and the invasion of India, was also incorporated in the 1814 Anglo-Iranian Treaty.[25]

In 1837, Afghanistan still was not a united state; Herat, Kabol and Kandhar were autonomous. The British favored the status quo while Dost Mohammad of Kabol intended to unite the three cities. Khandhar was governed by his half-brother and thus did not present any obstacle to Dost Mohammad's ambitious plan. The Governor of Herat was, however, from a different clan and a rival. Iran was distrustful of Dost Mohammad and opposed any attempt by the latter to annex Herat.

In the nineteenth century, the problems of Iran, Afghanistan and the Persian Gulf became further entangled. Britain now considered them vital for the protection of India. Hence, she wanted the two countries to be under her influence or completely neutralized. The importance of the two countries to the security of India was such that, in 1847, the protection of British interests in Iran and Afghanistan was transferred from London to Bombay.

Mohammad Shah was fearful of the Russian and resentful of the British. He had witnessed Iran's defeat from the Russian army, both in the 1805-1813 and 1826-1828 wars, as well as the British betrayal -- failing to honor her

---

[24] Mahmood Mahmood, "Tarikh-e Ravahet- e Syassy Iran va Inglis", (Tehran:) p.33; Kelly pp. 72-73.
[25] Kelly, op. cit. p. 97.

undertakings under the 1814 Treaty and supporting Iran. Thus, Mohammad Shah's foreign policy tilted more towards Russia and, at the latter's instigation, he launched a military attack against Afghanistan. As previously mentioned, this was thwarted by British intervention in 1838.[26] Mohammad Shah died in 1848 and his teenage son, Nasser al-Din, became Shah.

In 1851, the Governor of Herat, apparently threatened by Dost Mohammad (the Governor of Kabol), appealed to Iran for military assistance. In the summer of the same year, Iran organized a military maneuver near Afghanistan's border in anticipation of the future attack on Herat. The British warned Iran against it. After a lengthy negotiation, the British extracted a pledge from Iran not to invade Herat, and in return they agreed not to interfere in the internal affairs of Afghanistan in the future. The only beneficiary of this understanding naturally was Russia.

In 1853, with the Russian invasion of the Ottoman principalities in Europe, the British policy towards Russia turned hostile. Three months later, the Ottomans declared war on Russia. In Tehran, Nasser al-Din Shah came out in support of Russia, and the British reacted by suspending diplomatic relations with Iran. Iran was contemplating invading Iraq and seizing Basra and Baghdad. The Resident in Bushehr alerted the Governor of Bombay to be prepared to use the reoccupation of Khark as leverage against Iran, should the Shah venture to invade Iraq.

The government in London, in collaboration with the government in Paris, decided to dispatch the Anglo-French fleet to the Black Sea to repel any attack by the Russian Navy. At the same time, they resolved to instruct Bombay

---

[26] Kelly op. cit. pp.298,299.

to occupy Khark if Iran did not change its policy of aggression against the Ottomans. However, in the meantime, Irano-British diplomatic relations were resumed, and the British put the occupation of Khark on hold.

Iran was determined to capitalize on the Russo-British conflict. The Chief Minister of Iran, approached the British Ambassador in Tehran, to inform him of an attractive offer made to Iran by the Russians: to enter the war against the Ottoman Empire. The offer included a grant of 10,000,000 pounds sterling to Iran, remission of the remaining indemnity of 5,000,000 pounds (owed by Iran to Russia), under the Turkmanchai Treaty, and permanent annexation of any part of the Ottoman territory that Iran should conquer. The Chief Minister also intimated that, despite the Russians' generous offer, Iran preferred to ally herself with Britain and fight against the Russians if Britain could offer Iran equal financial inducement and promise to help Iran to recover territories ceded by Russia in 1828. The British Response was negative. They preferred Iran to remain neutral, and suggested that this would be Iran's best policy option.

Russo-Iranian relations in the second half of 1855 further improved at the expense of the British. Mirza Malcolm Khan, who acted as interpreter both to the Russian Embassy and to the Iranian Royal Court, seemingly played a role in this. Likewise, Irano-French relations improved upon the conclusion of the 1855 Commercial Agreement, which was more generous towards the French than that of 1841 was towards the British. Obviously, this was deliberate on Iran's part, used as a political gesture to gain France's friendship. Iran even tried to woo the U.S.A. by sending a generous draft Commercial Agreement to the United States of America, in return for which Iran expected the U.S.A. to come to Iran's defense should a third party attack any of the Persian islands of Khark, Hurmoz, Qishm, or Bahrain. Obviously, it was to be a guarantee against the probable attack by the British. The U.S.A. declined to sign the agreement. The following year, in December 1956, a standard commercial agreement with the U.S.A. was concluded.

In the meantime, Nasser al-Din Shah received information that Dost Mohammad, in connivance with the British, was cogitating the annexation of Herat. Iran precipitated this by assisting Prince Mohammad Yusef, a pro-Iranian contender of the governorship of Herat, who staged a coup d'état and ousted Saiyid Mohammad Khan, the incumbent governor. Nasser al-Din Shah was also anxious to see the British Ambassador, Murray, temporarily leave the country so that, in his absence, the Shah could organize an expedition to Herat.

This expectation materialized in November when the Ambassador sent an Iranian subject by the name of Hashem Khan on a mission to Shiraz. Iran objected to this, arguing that under the Commercial Treaty of 1841, Britain was permitted to have representatives only in Tehran, Tabriz, and Bushehr. Since the Ambassador failed to comply with the Persian request, the government arrested Khan's wife and took her to the Royal court. The Ambassador protested, demanding her release. The Chief Minister informed him that Khan's wife was the sister of one of the Shah's wives and had gone to the court to stay with her. Murray, unconvinced, left Iran on 5 December. Nasser al-Din Shah demanded an apology from the Queen of England for the insolence of her Ambassador and Irano-British relations were again ruptured.

In December, Dost Mohammad launched his attack against Herat. The Governor, Mohammad Yusef, repeated his appeal to the Shah for military support. Iran's expedition marched towards Herat and occupied Ghorian. The commander of the Iranian army indiscreetly ordered the coins to be struck and Friday prayers be read, in the name of Nasser al-Din Shah. This infuriated the Afghan patriots and an uprising was led by Isa Khan against Mohammad Yusef, who fled to Iran.

The news of Iran's invasion of Herat was received in England with dismay and anger. Palmerstone, the Prime Minister of Britain, said: "Persia for many years was deemed our barrier of defense for India against Russia. We must now look upon Persia as the advanced guard for Russia."[27] The British received the news of the fall of Herat on 2 June and sent an ultimatum demanding immediate withdrawal.

As later revealed, the news of Herat's fall was premature. Iran sent Mirza Malcom Khan to London for negotiation, wanting Dost Mohammad's pledge with a British guarantee that Herat would never be attacked, as a precondition for the evacuation of the city. Iran, in fact, was buying time for the final assault on Herat, which fell to the Iranian army on 26 October. The British declared war on Iran on 1 November, and the British Resident in Bushehr left on 16 November.

Anti-Christian sentiments, which had broken out in September in Bushehr were mounting. A British strong expedition consisting of 45 vessels sailed for Iran in the second week of November. The British plan was to capture Khark and Bushehr, and then proceed to Isphahan via Mohamareh and Shushtar. The island of Khark was captured without any confrontation; the Iranian garrison had already retreated to the mainland. Bushehr put up a gallant defense for three days and suffered many casualties in the

---

[27] ibid. p. 464.

light of enemy's superior firearms.   Finally, the town surrendered. Having confronted a brave resistance by the Iranian army, and fearing the dangers of the tortuous roads ahead, the British were anxious to secure Iran's withdrawal from Herat and end the hostilities.   Consequently, the British announced their conditions for a truce.   These included Iran's withdrawal from Herat, the payment of compensation, the relinquishment of all claims to Herat, the recognition of Afghanistan's independence, the reference of all future disputes with Afghanistan to British mediation, the renewal of the lease of Bandar Abbas with favorable terms to the ruler of Muscat, the reimbursement of debts to the British subjects in Iran, an extension to the British of all the privileges granted to the Russians under the Turkmanchai Agreement of 1828, an offer of apology for the insult to the British Ambassador, and the dismissal of the Chief Minister. After three weeks Iran agreed to withdraw from Herat on the condition of a simultaneous withdrawal of British troops from Iran and the withdrawal of Dost Mohammad's troops from Kandhar. The other conditions were unacceptable to Iran.

In the meantime, rumours spread that the Russians had seized Strabad on the Iranian coast of the Caspian Sea. On 8 January, 1857, the Shah, reminding people of the atrocities committed by the British in India against their Muslim brothers and sisters, proclaimed *Jihad* (holy war) against the British.   The British asked Bombay for reinforcement troops, which arrived on 27 January, 1857. At the same time, British agents in Iran intensified their instigation of Persian tribes against the government in Tehran. With the mediation of the French Ambassador, Iran sent a negotiating team to Paris.   Finally, the British dropped the demands for compensation, a formal apology, the dismissal of the Chief Minister, and the leasing of Bandar Abbas to the ruler of Muscat. The other conditions were incorporated in the Paris Treaty of 1857 with a Most Favored Nation clause, enabling the British to enjoy the economic, political, and judiciary privileges embodied in the Turkmanchai Agreement, pari passu with the Russians.

Iran evacuated Herat in September, 1857; the British troops stayed on Khark until October. Afghanistan became a united independent country on 27 May, 1863 and the Anglo-Iranian war of 1856-57 ended. Yet, Iran's bitterness towards Britain, and British suspicion of Iran had escalated.

Russo-British Economic Rivalry: Iran's Policy of Positive Equilibrium

Having failed in his policy of irredentism, Nasser al-Din Shah turned to piecemeal economic, social, and administrative reforms. Granting concessions to foreigners topped his economic policy. Due to intense rivalry between Russia and Britain, he pursued a policy of equilibrium.

The first concession to the British for an overland telegraphic line from Khaneqin to Karachi via Kirmanshah, Hamadan, Tehran, Isphahan, Shiraz and Bushehr was followed in 1865 by the construction of a domestic line for use only in Iran. Iran received a fixed annual rent fee for English messages sent through the international line. The most extensive concession was granted in 1872 to Baron Julius Reuter, a naturalized British subject. It embraced the construction of railways, canals, and dams, the exploitation of mines except for gold and silver, the formation of banks and establishment of industries throughout the country. In the words of Lord Curzon, it was "the most complete and extraordinary surrender of the entire industrial resources of the Kingdom into foreign hands".[28]   This irritated the Russians as well as nationalists and mullahs in Iran. As it proved, Reuter did not have the backing of the British government. The concession was canceled in 1873 and the 40,000 pounds caution money was forfeited.

In the following years, the Russo-British competition for concessions intensified. In 1888, the British obtained the exclusive rights of commercial navigation on the Karun River, the only navigable river in Iran.   In 1889, the Russians asked for a railway concession. At this juncture, the British raised the question of the Reuter concession of 1872, contending that while Reuter's claim was not met, no concession with regard to railway could be granted to anyone else. While considering the British complaint, the Shah promised that once the matter was settled, he would give the railway concession to the Russians.[29]   In the meantime, a concession for fishery and caviar on the southern shore of the Caspian Sea was given to Russia as an appeasement.

With the intervention of the British government in 1889, Reuter was accorded the right to establish a bank in Iran. The Imperial Bank of Persia had the exclusive right to issue bank notes for sixty years.   In return, the Russians were given the 1891 concession to establish "Banque d'Escompte de Perse", which was a branch of the Russian Ministry of Finance and the Central Bank.   Although by this time

---

[28] George N. Curzon "Persian and the Persian Question", (London: 1892), p.408

[29] F. Kazemzadeh, "Russia and Britain in Persia: 1864-1914", (Newhaven: 1968) p. 127

Reuter's claims had been settled, a railway concession to Russia was not forthcoming.

The two concessions that caused the British much loss of prestige and aroused immense public resentment were the 1889 lottery concession to an English syndicate and the 1890 tobacco concession to Major G. Talbot for fifty years. The first was criticized by the religious leaders as being a form of gambling and was as such forbidden in the Qoran. The second was assailed as being detrimental to the interests of Persian farmers, traders, and consumers, in as much as it gave a British company the monopoly to tobacco and cigar sales, at home and abroad. The tobacco concession led to an outburst of public fury, culminated in the issuance of Fatwa by, or in the name of, a paramount religious leader, forcing the Shah to annul it. By the end of the nineteenth century, the Russians and the British had weighty economic interests in Iran, amounting to total control in some sections.

The most important concession, was granted to William Knox D'Arcy in 1901 by Mozzafar al-Din Shah for the exploration and exploitation of oil throughout Iran, excluding the five northern provinces. This concession proved to be the single most important factor determining the domestic and foreign relations of Iran for the next half of the century. Also, Mozzafar al-Din Shah signed a new commercial treaty with Russia, which gave lower tariffs to the Russians at the expense of Iranian merchants.

For modernization of communication and administrative reforms, finance, customs, and military foreign advisors were employed. The result in most cases was the full domination of foreigners over the Iranian administration. The exception was the modernization of the post office in 1874 by Austrian advisers. This was a politics-free decision.

In 1898, Belgian experts were hired to modernize the custom offices in Kermanshah and Tabriz. The customs offices for many years, had been farmed out by region; the customs bidders underbid each other to attract more trade and to collect more than what they had paid to the government to obtain the job. In 1900 and 1902, two large loans were floated from Russia, and the customs revenue was made collateral for the loans. Thereafter, Iran's foreign trade was closely tied to the two Russian loans. Under the new treaty, the tariffs were revised with Russian approval and each Belgian officer became a "protégé and agent of the Russian government".[30]   Indeed, the Russians, by virtue of the new Irano-Russian Commercial Treaty, secretly dictated to the Belgian officials the terms of the tariffs and thereby Iran's foreign trade policy.[31]

Discrimination against British commercial interests and increased Russian control over Iran's fiscal policy alarmed the British. Iran was no longer allowed to take foreign loans without Russia's prior approval. *The extent of the British mistrust of the Belgian customs officers and Iran manifested itself in 1903 when the British prevented the Belgian officers from establishing custom offices in Abu Mussa and the Tumb Islands.* During the Constitutional Revolution of 1905-1907, in which the British, unlike the Russians, supported the movement, one of the demands of the constitutionalists was the dismissal of Naus and other Belgian officers. At the turn of the century, the Russians had greater clout than the British with the royal court and, for that reason, suffered greater popular resentment. When

---

[30] W. Morgan Shuster, "The Strangling of Persia", (New York: 1912) p. 313.
[31] Ramazani, op. cit. p. 44.

the constitutionalists asked for sanctuary in the British legation in Qulhak, the British Chargé d'Affairs gave a favorable reply and in August 1906, 14,000 people stayed in the legation for several days.

The Russo-British Rapproachment of 1907

In 1907, a drastic change of policy took place between Russia and Britain over Iran: rapprochement replaced rivalry. Kaiser Wilhelm of Germany had been challenging the British rule of the sea and was interfering with British supremacy in the Middle East. He had obtained a concession from the Ottoman Empire to construct a railway from Tripoli in Syria in 1902, through Baghdad to Kuwait.[32] In those days, a concession for the construction of railways was a vehicle for access to minerals and thus Germany became a threat to the commercial interests of both Britain and Russia.

In order to reduce confrontation, the old rivals, Britain and Russia, decided to divide Iran into zones of influence. By succeeding in suppressing piracy, brokering the "Treaty of Maritime Peae in Perpetuity" amongst the Arab sheikhs in 1853, and delivering the "Trucial System", Britain had already tightened her grip on the sheikhdoms in the region. Her next policy was to reduce them to protectorships. This was achieved through bilateral British-Trucial State "Exclusive" and "Non-Alienation" agreements, signed between 1879 and 1916. The Exclusive Agreements required the sheikhs to deny other foreign states and their subjects the right to establish coal depots or a consular office in the sheikhdoms without prior British approval.

---

[32] Sir Arnold Wilson, op. cit. p. 252, 259.

The Non-Alienation Treaties obligated the sheikhs to delegate, irrevocably, their foreign relations to Britain. Under the Non-Alienation Treaties, the sheikhdoms surrendered their rights to engage in relations with any foreign power or to dispose of any part of their territory without British consent.[33]

With respect to these agreements, the British were quite successful. The first Exclusive Agreement was signed by Saiyid Sultan of Muscat, whereby the Sultan covenanted to always take the British side in international disputes, to deny the French and the Dutch a foothold on his territory, to dismiss all French employees, and to stop French vessels from calling on Muscat for privateering operations.[34] Under the British-Bahrain Exclusion Treaty of 1880, Sheikh Isa of Bahrain covenanted

> ...to abstain from entering into negotiations or making treaties of any sort with any state or government other than the British without the consent of the said British government, and to refuse permission to any other government than the British to establish diplomatic or consular agencies or coal depots in (his) territory, unless with the consent of the British government.[35]

In June 1899, the British Resident obtained a non-alienation covenant from Sheikh Mubarak of Kuwait in which the Sheikh pledged on behalf of himself, his heirs and successors, "not to receive any representative or agent of

---

[33] J.G. Lorimer, "Gazetear, of the Persian Gulf, Oman, and Central Arabia" reprinted from an original in the India Office Library, (Farnborough: Gregg International/Irish University Press, Vol. i) p. 309.

[34] Sir Arnold Wilson, op. cit. p. 232.

[35] Kelly, op. cit. p. 825.

other governments or to alienate any portion of his territory to the government or subject of another power without the previous consent of the British government".[36] Under the Non-Alienation Treaties, the sheikhs could not give mining concessions to other governments or the citizens of foreign governments without prior British approval.   This particularly became an important issue in the 1920's when U.S. oil companies were barred from the Middle East until the matter was resolved at the highest political level between Britain and the U.S.[37] Similar treaties were signed with other trucial sheikhs in and after 1887. The last of such treaties was signed with Qatar in 1916.

By the end of the nineteenth century, Britain had already tightened her grip on Muscat and the trucial sheikhs, and could afford more leniency towards the Russians, not for Russia's sake but for that of having a new ally against the Germans.   The change in British foreign policy is well-reflected in Sir Edward Grey's statement: "Firstly, we should protect and promote British trade in the Gulf. Secondly, we should not exclude the legitimate trade of others.   Thirdly, we should regard the establishment of a naval base or a fortified port in the Gulf by any other power as a very grave menace to British interests, and we should certainly resist it by all means at our disposal."[38]

The 1907 Anglo-Russian accord proved to be also in Russia's interest. By the turn of the century, the Russians, despite having opened consulates in Basra, Bushehr, and Bandar Abbas, had failed to establish a commercial foothold in the Gulf. In 1902, the hopes of having their subordinate

---

[36] Kelly, op. cit. p. 836.

[37] Edward W. Chester, "United States Oil Policy and Diplomacy", (Connecticut: 1983), Ch. 5.

[38] Sir A. W. Ward and G.P. Gooch, "The Cambridge History of British Foreign Policy", (New York: 1923) iii, p. 320-21.

Belgian custom officers in the Persian island of Abu Mussa were dashed. Their defeat in the Russo-Japanese war of 1905 was humiliating. The conclusion of the Franco-British Entent Cordiale of 1904 further strengthened the British hand in Europe. Under the circumstances, the 1907 convention was a welcome event for Russia.

Negotiations between the two countries had secretly started in June 1906 and the convention was signed on 31 August, 1907. The convention delimited the zones of influence in Iran, Afghanistan and Tibet. Without Iran's knowledge, the convention amounted to a de facto partitioning of the country and, as a result, the line of defense of India was moved up to the middle of Iranian territory. The British zone of influence was defined by a line extending from Qasr-i Shirin to Isphahan, Yezd, and Kakh, ending at a point on Iran's frontier at the intersection of the Russian and Afghan borders. The towns on the line were not included in the British zone. The line delimiting the Russian zone extended from Gazik, Birj, and Kerman, ending at Bandar Abbas. Again, the towns on the line were excluded from the Russian zone. Thus, Tehran and Isphahan fell in the Russian zone; the southeastern part of Sistan and Baluchestan fell into the British zone. The remainder of the country constituted the neutral zone, in which no concession could be sought by either contracting party. Russia, by signing the convention, thereby acknowledged British interest and hegemony in the Persian Gulf and the Russo-British policies in Iran remained harmonized until the establishment of the Communist regime in Russia.

The 1907 convention caught both nationalists and constitutionalists by surprise. The British withdrew their support from the constitutionalists. In May 1908, when

Mohammad Ali Shah was plotting against the fledging democracy, the Russian and British Ambassadors jointly visited the Shah, pledged their support, and confirmed the justifiability of measures taken against the constitutionalist who had endangered the safety of the Shah.[39]

On 13 June, 1911, the second Majlis hired Morgan Shuster, an American financier, as Treasurer-General of Iran to reorganize the financial system. Shuster proposed bringing the customs revenue under the Treasury; the Russians announced that the Belgian customs employees should not be subject to the control of an American Treasurer-General. They even threatened to have Russian troops seize the custom houses in the north.[40] Another confrontation occurred when the government, having confiscated the properties of Mohammad Ali Shah (the architect of the coup d'état who had taken refuge in the Russian legation), instructed the Treasurer-General to seize the Shah's property. The Russians intervened and gave an ultimatum to the Iranian government demanding the dismissal of Shuster, indemnification for the expenses of the Russian troops on their way to Tehran, and refrainment from employing any foreigner without prior consent of the British and Russians. The British supported the ultimatum and the American financier was dismissed.[41]

As the result of Russo-British cooperation in Iran, the presence of the Russian Cossack brigade in the north (created in 1879) headed by Russian officers, the South Persian Rifles (created in 1917) headed by the British officers, the gendermeri (created in 1911), headed by the Swedish officers, and the lack of an effective national army,

---

[39] Brown, "Persian Revolution 1905-1909", (Cambridge: 1910) p. 201.
[40] Shuster, op. cit. p. 53.
[41] Ramazani, op. cit. pp. 100-101.

the economy and politics of Iran were at the mercy of Russo-British imperialist aspirations, carried out through the intimidation and manipulation of Iranian politicians. Throughout all, Britain remained the master of the Persian Gulf.

With the October 1917 Revolution in Russia, and the mounting might of Britain, the geopolitics of the region changed. The Irano-Soviet Treaty of Friendship of 1921 relinquished all Russian vested interests in Iran. The rejection of the Irano-British Treaty of 1919, which would have transformed Iran into a British protectorate, forced the British to support a centralized national government capable of resisting the possible penetration of communism. The British policy towards Iran and Afghanistan reverted to that of a buffer state policy, supporting the established governments in those countries. Her policy of control of the Trucial States continued at the expense of Iran. The Sa'udi state, too, had become a British protectorate until she gained independence in 1927. Britain continued to rule the Gulf while a national awakening was growing and anti-colonial sentiments began to challenge British hegemony in the Middle East.

IV

The Legal Status of the Three Islands of Abu Musa And the Greater And Lesser Tumbs[1]

Introduction

The British departure from the Persian Gulf in December 1971 created a political vacuum in the region which was filled by Iran with the tacit support of Britain and the United States. In the new power structure of the region, Iran relinquished her long-standing claim to Bahrain, occupied Abu Musa with the consent of the Sheikh of Sharjah, and seized the two Tumb Islands under the protest of the Sheikh of Ras al-Khaimah. The United Arab Emirates also emerged as the federation of the seven coastal sheikhdoms of the Lower Gulf, the Trucial States. Thus, Iran assumed the role of gendarme of the region, mainly for monitoring, and preventing communist activities in the neighboring states of the Lower Gulf.

Apart from a cursory discussion on the dispute over the three islands in the United Nations, no major complications

---

[1] For the clarity of legal arguments, certain material facts mentioned in the previous sections have been repeated.

arose during the 1970's immediately after the aforementioned geopolitical changes. However, with the establishment of the anti-western Islamic Republic in Iran and the disintegration of the Soviet Union, the political vista in the region changed. The notion of the regional gendarme became obsolete, and the new regime of Iran posed a threat to Western interests in the region. Hence the old dispute between Iran and the United Arab Emirates resurfaced.

Iran considers the occupation of the three islands the restoration of her sovereignty over lands that belong to her, the exercise of which was previously obstructed by the British in collusion with the sheikhs. She bases her ownership on historical facts, and the legal evidence produced from both Iranian and British archives. The Sheikhs of Sharjah and Ras al-Khaimah, too, assert historical claims and draw evidence from British India Office records. In 1928, in relation to the Iranian claim on the islands, the British had stated that: "it is not clear whether any effective dominion had been exercised by Persia in the islands of Tumbs, Abu Musa, and Sirri prior to 1750."[2] The Iraqi representative in the United Nations in 1973 went so far as to suggest that "these islands have always been under Arab Jurisdiction."[3] Thus both claims to the title of the islands should be examined in the light of historical facts, political documentations and reliable evidence in order to come up at least with certain *prima facie* presumptions, if not conclusive results.

---

[2] I.O. L/P&S/18 B397, P4512/28 Laithwaite, "The Status of the Islands of Little Tunb, Abu Mussa and Sirri", August 1928, Part II, para.7.

[3] Security Council, Official Records, 9 December, 1971.para174.

Iran's Historical Title

On 2 December, 1991 in the Security Council, entertaining the complaint against Iran's occupation of the islands, Iran's representative said "Iran's claim to the islands was long-standing and substantial; both maps, hundreds of years old, and modern, highly authoritative encyclopedias have treated the territories as belonging to Iran."[4] This was reiterated in the following terms by Mohammad Reza Shah Pahlavi, in an interview given to the editor of the Indian magazine, *Bliz*: "The islands were ours; but some eighty years ago, Britain interfered with the exercise of our sovereignty and grabbed them and subsequently claimed them for her wards Sharjah and Ras al-Khaimah."[5] Four months later, in another interview, the Shah said: "What we are demanding is what has always belonged to our country throughout history."[6]

Iran's historical claim of title has persisted with the government of the Islamic Republic of Iran. On 14 March, 1993, the Islamic Majlis of the Islamic Republic, with reference to the three islands, declared that "Iran's territorial integrity is inviolable and Iran's geographical map has a clear historical and proven record."[7] In September 1993, Iran's naval commander reaffirmed that claim by saying: "The disputed Gulf islands of Abu Musa and Greater and Lesser Tumbs were an indivisible part of Iran."[8] President Akbar Hashemi Rafsanjani, elaborating on his foreign policy, has on several occasions emphasized Iran's historical

---

[4] UN Security Council, S/PV 1610, para 211, 9 December, 1971.

[5] Bliz, 24 June, 1971.

[6] Kayhan International, 23 October, 1971.

[7] Reuter, 15 March, 1993.

[8] Mideast Mirror, 27 September, 1993.

rights and has threatened that "to reach these islands one has to cross a sea of blood."[9]

Iran's claim to the historical title can be traced to antiquity, although the names of Tumb or Abu Musa do not appear in the works of the classical historian. These islands were too small and relatively insignificant to be specifically named in the vastness of the Iranian Empire from the sixth century BC to the seventh century AD.[10]   Nevertheless, there are certain references in the classical history books and memoirs, which have been assumed to relate to the Tumbs. The reference of the Greek admiral, Nearchus, to *another island* near the island of Qishm in his diary (the Register) is believed to be the Greater Tumb.[11]   During the Greek's rule (330-150 BC) Iran kept her predominance in the Gulf. Pliny, in 79 AD, writes that the Parthians had dominion over Batrasables, all ports of the Persian Gulf, and Oman Athana.[12]   Petolemy, in his geography (which was written in 168 AD) refers to *Tabiana Island*, as an island adjacent to Iran. This is also assumed to be Greater Tumb.

The intensive interest of the Sassanian Kings in maritime trade was well-reflected in the construction of at least seven new ports on the Euphrates and the Persian Gulf.[14]   This, coupled with Iran's documented influence extending beyond the river Indus, renders the suzerainty of Iran over the Lower Gulf unquestionable. In the Pre-Islamic era, Persians were notable seagoing people, had a strong navy, renown

---

[9]   Reuter, 20 December, 1992.

[10]   Supra pp. 16-18.

[11]   William Vincent, "The Voyage of Nearchus from India to the Euphrates", (London: 1807), Vol.I, pp. 356-57.

[12]   Pliny, "Historia Naturalis", Book VI, Chapter XXII.

[14]   Supra p. 18

admirals,[15] and had dominion over the Lower Gulf During the Sassanian reign, the Persian fleet regularly sailed as far as Ceylon.[16] The nomenclature of the Gulf, "Persian Sea", corroborates the said statement, and indicates that the landlocked Persian Gulf was considered a Persian lake, with its islands part of the Iranian Empire.[17]

Islamic Iran

The conquest of Iran by Muslim Arabs in the middle of the seventh century brought the littoral coast of Iran, the Persian Gulf, and its islands, under the suzerainty of the Arab Caliphs.   At the dawn of Islam, nationalism, as a political identity, was replaced by religious identity. The Muslims formed the *Umma*, and the territory under the Caliph's rule was Dar al-Islam.   Thirty years after the prophet's death, a split erupted among the Umma, and the *Ummayyads* prevailed.   They ruled the Umma from Damascus for over eighty years, during which time the Persian Gulf region remained a part of Dar al-Islam. In 750 AD, the Ummayyads were overthrown by the Abbassids and the capital was moved to Baghdad. During the Abbasids, Dar al-Islam split into three parts: The Eastern Capliphat, which comprised inter alia, Iran, the Persian Gulf and the Arab Penninsula, was ruled by the *Abbasids*; Spain remained under the Ummayyads; Egypt and North Africa were ruled by the *Fatimids*.

Thanks to eminent historians and geographers, both Persian and Arab, who lived during the Abbasids, accurate

---

[15] Supra pp. 16, 19.
[16] Supra p. 17.
[17] Supra p. 18.

information on the status of the islands of the Persian Gulf in that era is available. For nearly one hundred and fifty years, the Abbassid Caliphs were leaders, both spiritual and temporal, of the Eastern Caliphat. In 945 AD, the Iranian *Buyids* conquered Baghdad, allowed the Caliph to continue as a spiritual leader on the condition that temporal responsibilities would be delegated to the Buyids. Thus the Buyids controlled the office of the Regent of the Abbassid Empire, and the Viceroy of Persia. *This may be the first case of separation, though in an atmosphere of cooperation, between the clergy and the government.* This was much the way Pre-Islamic Iran had been managed. This was a Muslim Iranian government in the guise of Arab supremacy. Thereafter, the names of the Buyid Kings entered Friday prayers and were struck on the coins. The Buyids (945-1055) crushed the Karmatians of Hasa and Bahrain, and seized and annexed Julfar (Ras al-Khaimah) and Oman to their territory.[18] Thus, the Buyids controlled the Upper and Lower Gulf, and the Persian Gulf became an Islamic Iranian Gulf for over a century, its islands under Iranian dominion. This fact is confirmed by ibn Balkhi,[19] Istakhri,[20] and ibn Hawkal,[21] who lived in the tenth and eleventh centuries.

---

[18] Salil ibn Razik, "History of the Imams and Seyyids of Oman from 661-1856", translated into English by George Percy (London:1871); pp. 29-34; S.B. Miles 'The Countries and Tribes of the Persian Gulf (London:1919) Vol. 1 pp. 102-128.

[19] Ibn al-Balkhi, Fars Namah; (London:1921) p 279.

[20] Al-Istakhri, "Al-Masalik Wal-Mamalik" (Leyden:1927) pp. 96-113.

[21] Ibn Hawkal, "Surat al-Ardh", (Leyden:1939) Vol. II pp. 260-315; "The Oriental Geography, William Ousely's translation (London:1800) p. 62.

The Buyids were ousted by the Saljuqs of Northwest Iran in 1055 AD. The Saljuqs conquered Baghdad and made a bargain similar to that of the Buyids with the Abbassid Caliph. They were made Regent of the Abbassid Dar al-Islam and Viceroy of Iran.[22] With regard to the Persian Gulf, Saljuqs were almost in the same position as the Buyids. They had dominion over the littoral coast of Iran as well as over the Lower Gulf. They conquered Oman and thus completed their hold on the islands of the Persian Gulf.

The Saljuqs were overthrown by the Kharazmshahian from the northeast of what then constituted Iran. During the reign of the latter dynasty, Banu Qais, the ruler of Qais (Kish) Island who had attained prominence in the Gulf, controlled the Tumbs and several other islands.[23] However, he was a tributary to the Governor of Fars of Iran.[24] Ibn Battuta, the famous Arab traveler-writer who had visited the area wrote: "The city of Qais is rekoned as one of the districts of Fars, and people are Persians of noble stock and among them is a body of the Arabs of the Banu Saffaf."[25] The Abbasid Dynasty was destroyed by the Mongols, but Iran's dominance in the Gulf persisted. Hamdolla Mostowfi, the eminent geographer and historian of the fourteenth century, wrote that "the inhabitable and known (islands) that belong to Iran are: Bahrain, Khark, Khasal (Kharku), Amus (Hangam), Kand or Gand (Shitavar), and Qais ."[26] In the

---

[22] John Malcolm, "The History of Persia" ,(London:1829) vol. I pp. 175-208.

[23] John Malcom, op. cit. pp. 234-235.

[24] Arnold T. Wilson, "The Persian Gulf", op. cit. pp. 99-100.

[25] "The Travels of Ibn Battuta", translated into English by H. A. R. Gibb (London:1959) Vol. II pp. 403-404.

[26] Hamdullah Mustowfi, "Nuzhat al-Qolub"edited by Muhammad Dabir Siyaqi (Tehran:1336 Hijri) p. 276, translated into English by

fifteenth century, Jahan Shah of Kara Koyunlu of Iran reigned undisputedly over the whole Azerbayejan, the two Iraqs and Kerman as well as over the coast of Oman.[27] The continued supremacy of Iran over the Persian Gulf evinces the Iranian historical title to the islands until the sixteenth century, the dawn of European colonialism in the region.

Circumstantial evidence also corroborates the above conclusion. During the time of Abbasids, maritime trade to China and India via the Persian Gulf continued. Persistence in the use of Persian marine vocabulary, despite the universality of the Arab language in Dar al-Islam, testifies to the lasting supremacy of Iranian navigators in the Gulf during the six centuries of Arab rule.[28]

Under the Caliphs, the Iranians extended their maritime supremacy beyond the Persian Gulf in the Zone of Islam, and established colonies of Iranian merchants on the Malabar coast -- in Bengal, at Camby, and as far as Malacca. At many places in East Africa, Iranians became the ruling princes.[29] Iran's influence was accompanied with a change in population mix and demographic structure of the region which is noticeable in the Lower Gulf even today.

The Era of European Colonialism in the Gulf

Portuguese Dominance

Guy Le Strange (Leyden: E.J. Brill:1919); The Enccyclopaedia of Islam (London:1927) Vol. III pp. 844-845.
[27] C. Huart "Kara Koyunlu" Vol. II (London: 1927); p. 741.
[28] See Supra p. 22.
[29] Roger M. Savory, op. cit. p.16.

The sixteenth century ushered several colonial powers into the Persian Gulf. This was five years after the establishment of Safavid Dynasty in Iran. On the eve of the arrival of the Portuguese General, Alfonso D'Albuquerque, in August 1507, the entire northern coast of the Gulf belonged to Iran;[30] the southern coast, extending from Hasa to the interior of Oman, was controlled by the Bani Jaber Sheikhs of Rustaq.[31]   The Portuguese dreamt of monopolizing the lucrative East-West trade through the dominion over the strategic points on the trade route. Their initial targets were the ports of Hurmoz, Aden and the Straits of Malaca. Proceeding along the coast of Southern Arabia, the Portuguese captured Qalhat, a dependency of Hurmoz, and turned it into a Portuguese tributary.[32]   Then they pillaged Quryat, Muscat, Khor Fakkan and Suhar. Finally, the Portuguese General captured Hurmoz in 1508.

The occupation of the city, however, did not last long. A rebellion broke out in the same year and the Portuguese retreated.   Seven years later, the Portuguese Navy recaptured Hurmoz. Iran protested, but in vain. In 1514, in an attempt to persuade Iran to recognize the Portuguese dominion over Hurmoz, General de Albuquerque promised military assisstance to Shah Ismail Safavi, enabling Iran to repel Ottoman agression, quell insurgence in Mukran, and regain Bahrain and Qatif. Under duress, the Shah agreed to the General's request and recognized the ruler of Hurmoz as a Portuguese vassal.   This oral recognition was later formalized in the Minab Treaty of 1521, whereby the General was granted the right to appoint the governor of the port, and to exact taxes on the inhabitants. The treaty also

---

[30] Malcolm, op. cit. Vol I pp.320-326,348.
[31] Miles, op. cit. Vol. I p.144.
[32] Savory, op. cit. p.19.

exempted Portuguese vessels from port dues. Thus, the Portuguese military commander became the de facto ruler of Hurmoz and its dependencies.[33] In 1521 and again in 1526, two abortive uprisings against the Portuguese forces took place in Hurmoz, which were supressed. In 1516, the Portuguese captured Bahrain and Qatif and kept them for 107 years.

In the meantime, the Ottomans, having recovered Basra from Iran, challenged the Portuguese ascendancy in the Gulf and its hold over Bahrain in 1777. The Ottomans considered the lands occupied by the Arabs part of Dar al-Islam. The Ottoman-Portuguese armed clashes persisted intermittently for thirty years, with the Portuguese retaining the upper hand.

In 1600, Shah Abbas Safavid ascended to the Persian throne. Regaining Iran's lost territories stood on the top of his agenda yet Iran did not have the required naval force. Fortunately for him, in the same year Queen Elizabeth I too ascended the throne. The first item on her agenda was the expansion of British trade, for which purpose she granted a charter to the newly-formed East India Company for exclusive trading rights east of the Cape of Good Hope and west of the Strait of Magellan.[34] Shah Abbas granted special trade privileges to the East India Company with the hope of gaining future favor with the British. Iran had never relinquished her rights and sought an opportunity to retake the islands.[35]

---

[33] Supra p. 22.

[34] Supra p. 23.

[35] George N. Curzon, "Persian and the Persian Question"; (London:1892), VolII p. 415.

In an attempt to further and strengthen the Irano-British alliance, Shah Abbas granted additional advantages against other foreigners to the British in 1615. In 1622, the Portuguese, who had occupied Qishm Island, were ejected by Iran with the help of the English East India Company's navy. In April 1622, Iranian forces, with the backing of the British, attacked Hurmoz, crushed the Portuguese resistance and, after 107 years of Portuguese rule, restored Iranian sovereignty over Hurmoz and its dependencies. Thus, the cities of Kung, Lingeh, Ughu, Charak, Nakhilu and the Tumb Islands, again came under Iranian control. In 1623 and 1625, the Portuguese made military bids for Hurmoz, but were defeated.

Forced out of Hurmoz, Qishm, Bandar Abbas and other islands, the Portuguese,"...by the Treaty of 1625 restored to Iran all her coastal possessions, retaining only the pearl banks of Bahrain, and a moiety of the customs of Kung".[36] "Restoration of possessions", according to Curzon and Lorimer, meant coastal and offshore islands. During all this time, Iran kept a garrison in Julfal (Ras al-Khaimah).[37] This indicates that, at that time, Iran's influence extended to the Lower Gulf as well.

In 1633, the Imam of Oman, Nasir ibn Murshid al-Yaariba, a rising power in the Gulf, expelled the Persian garrison from Ras al-Khaimah and annexed the area to his territory.[38] In 1670, he attempted to capture Hurmoz but failed.[39]

---

[36] George N. Curzon "Persia and the Persian Question"; (London: 1966) Vol. II p. 419; Roger Savoy op. Cit., p. 29.

[37] Lorimer, "Gazetteer of the Persian Gulf, Oman and the Central Arabia"; (Farnborough: 1970) Vol. I pp. 31-37.

[38] ibid., p. 39

[39] S.B. Miles, "The Countries and Tribes of the Persian Gulf"; (London:1919) p. 215.

In 1684, a Dutch squadron in the Gulf blockaded Bandar Abbas and the islands of Hurmoz, Qishm, Qais, and Khark.[40] This was an attempt to compel Iran to renew an expired silk concession granted by Shah Abbas. Since the Tumbs are located between Qishm and Qais, the reasonable inference is that they belonged to Iran at that time and were blockaded as well.

With the decline of the Safavids, the Imam of Oman captured Bahrain in 1718, ending a century of Iranian rule over the island. The Imam also seized the islands of Larak, Hurmoz, Qishm and Qais. In 1719, the Portuguese squadron in the Gulf defeated the Omani fleet at Kung. A year later, they captured Bandar Abbas, but were expelled by Iranian forces.

In 1720, both the Safavids and al-Yaariba of Oman lost their preeminence in the Gulf. However, it is clear that, up to the end of the Safavids' reign, Iranians had paramountcy in the Gulf and controlled the islands in the proximity of their coast. *Thus the historical claim of Iran to the islands, until 1720, is hardly deniable,* and any claim of title from that date to 1970, the year of the withdrawal of British troops from the Persian Gulf, must be discussed in the context of British intervention in the region since the middle of the eighteenth century.

British Intervention

An investigation into the nature and reality of the Irano-U.A.E. dispute requires an inquiry into a similar Irano-British dispute, from the middle of the eighteenth century up to the withdrawal of the British army from the Gulf in

---

[40] Lorimer, op. cit. Vol. I p. 66.

December 1970, during which time Britain acted as a guardian and protector of the Qawasim Sheikhs of Sharjah and Ras al-Khaimah.

Reference has already been made to the uncertainty of the origin of the Qawasim, and that a majority of historians now concur that the bulk of the Qawasim, now residing in the Lower Gulf, migrated from Iran sometime in the eighteenth century.[41] This is corroborated by the fact that the Qawasim were also called "Huwailla", which comes from the word "Mutahawwilt", a designation for people who change their original dwelling.[42] Hence, the Qawasim were Arab migrants from neighboring lands and Africa to Iran, very much like immigrants from Latin America and European countries who come to the United States. The Qawasim, Bani Ma'in, Bani Ka'b and other tribes who migrated to Iran were not of the same stock. They spoke the same language, Arabic, and were Muslim (though belonging to different denominations), but their motivation to settle in Iran differed. They were mostly nomads. Some had fled the despotism of the local rulers, seeking a new home. Others had migrated simply following their nomadic lifestyle.

These groups roamed from one place to another, hunting for locations where authority was weak, migrating to a different area when control became strict. They were skillful sailors, engaged in fishing and pearling in summer, and piracy during the winter. The Qawasim were reputed for carnage, plundering and brutality, in which they took

---

[41] S.B. Miles, op. cit., p. 269.

[42] Muhhamad Morsy Abdullah, "The United Arab Emirates" (London: 1978), p. 284; Salik ibn Razik, "History of the Imams and Seyyids of Oman from 1601 to 1850:, translated into English by George Perry Badgi (London: 1871, pp. 110-112)

delight.[43] Thanks to the Qawasim, the Lower Coast of the Persian Gulf acquired the ignominious designation of "the Pirate Coast".[44]

In 1719, having been pounded by the Portuguese, the Qawasim migrated in large number to Julfar (Ras al-Khaimah) and acquired a distinct status vis-a-vis other Arab immigrants.[45] In 1720, aligned with the Omanis, the Qawasim attempted to seize Bandar Abbas, but failed.[46] During the 1720's, the Qawasim backed Imam Mohammad Nasir, the ruler of Oman, during a civil war. It is reasonable to assume that, during the 1720's when the authority of both Iran's Saffavid Kings and Omani al-Yaariba Imams was on a decline, the Qawasim moved to capture more land and enhance their power. In 1724, while Iran was fighting the invading Afghans and Oman was grappling with internal conflicts, Rashid ibn Matar, the brother of the Qawasim Sheikh of Ras al-Khaimah, established a settlement at Basidu on the island of Qishm, where ships had started to call, following the fall of Bandar Abbas to the Afghans. In 1729, the British, who used to receive a moiety of the revenue and customs of Bandar Abbas, demanded the Sheikh make good the loss they had incurred as the result of the shift of trade from Bandar Abbas to Basidu.[47]

The Qawasim's occupation of Basidu was short-lived. In 1733, General Nader Gholi, who later became Nader Shah, pursued the rebellious general, Mohammad Khan Baluch, through Shiraz, Lar, Charak and Qais. He captured

---

[43] Supra p. 44.
[44] ibid.
[45] S.B. Miles, op. cit., Vol.II pp. 199-237.
[46] I.O. B397, p. 451, 28.
[47] Lorimer, op. cit. pp. 97-135.

and executed Baluch as well as Sheikh Madain, the Huwailla Sheikh, who had sheltered Baluch. In this expedition, Nader enjoyed the collaboration of the English and Dutch agents in the Gulf and that of Qawasim Sheikh Rashid ibn Mattar of Basidu and the Huwailla Sheikh Jabreh, who provided vessels for Nader. At the end of the expedition, Nader commissioned Sheikh Jabreh to collect tributes from all Qawasim and Huwailla Sheikhs.[48] *This shows that the Qawasim and Huwailla Sheikhs who resided in Iran were subordinate to Iranian law and jurisdiction. With this last expedition, Nader's authority over the Qawasim and other Huwailla Arabs on the Persian coast was fully established.*

On the Arabian coast, the Qawasim of Ras al-Khaimah, having broken away from the Imam of Oman, were more inclined towards Iran in 1728. Placing the restoration of Iranian territories on the top of his agenda, Nader Shah retook Bahrain and despatched a naval expedition to assist the besieged Imam Saif of Oman in 1736. Such expeditions were repeated during the next eleven years, and on each occasion, the Iranian troops stayed in Julfar (Ras al-Khaimah), where Iran had a permanently stationed garrison.[49] Even when the Iranian army, supporting Imam Saif in the internal war of Oman, was defeated in 1742, the Persian garrison remained unharrassed in Ras al-Khaimah and maintained communications with the Persian ports.[50] On this event, Lorimer wrote: "In 1737, when a Persian force landed at Khor Faklan and began to overrun the territories of the Imam of Oman, the Arabs of Julfar appear to have made submission to the Persian Command."[51] This

---

[48] Lawrence Lockhart, "Nader Shah"; (London:1938), pp. 78-79.

[49] Salih Razik, op. cit. p. 10.

[50] Lockhart, op. cit. pp. 19-221.

[51] Lorimer, op. cit. p. 631.

provides strong circumstantial evidence in favor of the continued dominance of Iran over the Qawasim of Ras al-Khaimah until the middle of the eighteenth century.

Against this background, 186 years later at the height of the Irano-British dispute over the islands, the India Office wrote that, "In 1738, the Qawasim were attacked in their own territory by the Persians and appear to have made submission, but it does not seem that Persians retained any hold on the Julfar". Yet, Lorimer several times alluded to the peaceful submission of the Julfar Qawasim to Iran.[52]

In 1928, the India Office prepared a report on the status of the islands of Greater Tumb, Lesser Tumb, Abu Musa, and Sirri, in which it was claimed that the Qawasim aligned themselves with the Omanis to take Bandar Abbas in 1720.[53] Indeed, this was also a part of British colonial historiography to forge records showing autonomous rule for the Qawasim in the eighteenth century. The mutiny of the Huwailla crew in the Persian fleet in 1738 and 1739 over wages and rations[54] shows that the Huwailla people were in the service of Iranian Navy. Since the mutiny was not political, it did not affect the Persian garrison in Julfar.

In 1740, the Arab crews in Qishm mutinied, and it got out-of-hand. The mutineers defected onto ships and delivered these ships to the Arab sheikhs, one of whom was a Qawasim. In 1741, the Iranian Navy subdued the mutineers and recovered the ships.[55] During all this time, the Persian garrison in Julfar remained unharmmed, showing that the relationship between the Qawasim in Ras al-

---

[52] Lorimer, op. cit. pp. 135-406.

[53] I.O. B397, p. 4512/28.

[54] Lockhart, op. cit. pp. 183-184.

[55] Lockhart, op. cit. pp. 144-147.

Khaimah and the Iranian government remained friendly if not subordinate.

Iran's hegemony in the region is further confirmed by Thomas Salmon who, in 1744, wrote:

> The sea (Persian Gulf) and the islands in it and the coast of Arabia about al-Qatif, was subject to the Persians, and this account I had from a gentleman who came from Gombar (Bandar Abbas) about twenty years ago, and it seems that the Persians were actually masters of them; but the Arabs, taking advantage of the late indolent reign (Note: He is referring to the last Safavid King) have made themselves master of one island after another and even Bahrein itself and the part of the coast of Arabia which the Persians possessed.[56]

The historical title of Iran to the three islands, relating to the period of 1750-1885, has been contested by the U.A.E. The only pieces of documentation presented by the U.A.E. are a few correspondences and reports, extracted from British files in the India office. Iran considers them flimsy, often one-sided, and evidently compiled at the time in the interest of British dominion over the region. Despite all those correspondents and the frequent British denial of Iran's title, it is significant that the British Foreign Office, as late as in 1901, acknowledged in a letter to a British Agent that the ownership of the Tumb Islands has always been dubious.[57]

In the same letter, the said acknowledgement notwithstanding, the British government admitted that, whenever the issue had been raised by Iran, the British had rejected Iran's claim and insisted that the islands of Tumbs

---

[56] Thomas Salmon, "Modern History or the Present State of All Nations";(London:1744) Vol. I p. 327.

[57] R/15/2/625, Political Agency, Bahrein, NO CR-231.

and Sirri belonged to the Qawasim. Iran maintains that the British Foregin Office's admission calls into question the validity of similar documents in the India Office records that are supportive of the claims of the Sheikhs of Sharjah and Ras al-Khaimah.

Since 1747, the Qawasim, taking advantage of the political vacuum created by the decline of the authority of Iran and Oman, have enhanced their power and visibility in the Gulf. Under the administrative procedures set by the Governor-General of Fars, the Governor of Bandar Abbas was responsible for the collection of taxes of the neighboring cities, and remission of the same to Shiraz. In 1747 Mulla 'Ali Shah, the Governor of Lar, failed to remit the tax of his town. Nassir Khan, the Governor of Bandar Abbas, demanded it, and Mulla 'Ali defied him. As explained in the history of Iran, when Nassir Khan pressed Mulla 'Ali, the latter sought the Qawasim's assistance. In a dramatic move, to strenghten the alliance, Mulla 'Ali gave his daughter in marriage to the Qawasim Sheikh, Rashid ibn Mattar. In 1760 Mulla 'Ali and the Qawasim attacked and plundered Bandar Abbas, the seat of Nassir Khan. Later, they were defeated by Nassir Khan and retreated to Qishm Island. Quite independent of this incident, another Qawasim leader, Sheikh Salih, raided Lingeh and occupied Shinaz. This explains how the Qawasim of the Lower Gulf obtained a foothold in Iran.

In January 1761, Karim Khan Zand appointed Sheikh Muhamad Khan Bastaki as Governor of the Persian coast, including the Port of Lingeh and its dependency, the island of Qishm. Having restored law and order in the coastal area, he invited Mulla 'Ali and his Qawasim allies, Sheikh Rashid ibn Mattar of Ras al-Khaimah, and Sheikh Abdullah ibn Main of Qishm to come to Bandar Abbas for reconcilliation.

Their meeting ended in the signing of a four-party accord whereby the signatories recognized Karim Khan's sovereignty over Lingeh and Qishm, and Sheikh Muhamad Bastaki's authority to collect revenues in his entire coastal district, from Bandar Abbas to Gavdani.[58] In return, Bastaki recognized the right of Sheikh Rashid ibn Mattar and his son, Sheikh Saqr, to maintain residencies in Lingeh and Lashtar, the right of Bani Ma'in tribe to stay in Basidu, in Qishm (provided they continue to pay tribute to Iran), and the right of Mulla 'Ali and his Qawasim allies to retain the ship *Rahman* , which belonged to Mulla 'Ali through inheritence.

The spirit of peacemaking brought by Bastaki envigorated in the region. This led the Imam of Oman to sign an accord with Sheikh Rashid ibn Mattar recognizing the independence of Ras al-Khaimah, in return for the latter's recognition of the Imam's sovereignty over the rest of Al-Sir region.[59] The recognition of the independence of Ras al-Khaimah was a notable success for the Qawasim.

However, due to bitter animosity between Nassir Khan and Mulla 'Ali Shah on the one hand, and between the Sheikhs of Bani Ma'in and the Qawasim on the other, the 1761 accord did not last long. To re-establish order and peace in the region, Sheikh Muhamad Bastaki dismissed Nassir Khan, and annexed the province of Lar to his own. The governorship of Bandar Abbas, Qishm, and the island of Hurmoz was assigned to the Sheikh of Bani Ma'in who was a tributary to the Governor of Shiraz. The Qawasim were expelled from Iran by 1767, as were the Bani Ma'in in

---

[58] J. Movahed, "Bastak va Khalij-e Fars", (Tehran: 1970) p. 38.

[59] Miles, Vol. II, p. 269.

1768, because they were plotting with the Sultan of Oman against Iran.

In 1764, two thousand families of the Bani Ka'b under Sheikh Salman migrated to Fallahi in Iran. They had been a tributory to the Ottomans in Baghdad, and had engaged in piracy against Ottoman vessels. Omar Pasha, the Governor of Baghdad, sent an emissary with gifts to the Shah, requesting him to punish the Bani Ka'b and expressed the readiness of Baghdad to pay the cost of the expedition. The Governor of Fars subdued the Bani Ka'b tribe and Sheikh Salman pledged to disengage the tribe from illegal enterprises, to pay tribute to the Iranian government and, in return, prayed to be allowed to stay with his tribe in Iran. His request was granted because of his pledge and the fact that they were Shi'a.[60] This too, Iran argues, is an indication of the re-establishment of the Persian government's control in South Persia and on the Persian Coast in the 1760's.

In the 1770's, the alliances in the gulf shifted continuously. The rivalry between the Qawasim and the Omanis, between the Qawasim and the Bani Ma'in, and between both the Qawasim and the Bani Ma'in (who had been evicted from Iran) and Iran, continued. In 1777, Sheikh Saqr, who had succeeded Sheikh Rashid as the ruler of Qawasim in Ras al-Khaimah, married the daughter of Sheikh Abdulla of the Bani Ma'in, hoping to enhance the Qawasim's prestige and influence in the Gulf.[61] However, this objective was not achieved, since the Bani Ma'in did not

---

[60] Haj Mirza Hossain, Husseini Fassai, "Farsnameh Nasseri", written in 1883, edited by Mansur Rastigar Fassai, (Tehran: 1988) pp. 607-608.

[61] Wikon, op. cit. p. 201.

let the Qawasim re-establish themselves in Qishm.[62]   In
1775, Karim Khan conquered Basra, which remained under
Iranian control for over two years.   The pretext was the
injustice done to the Iranian merchants by Omar Pasha, the
Governor of Baghdad.[63]

In 1776, the Governor of Fars commissioned troops to
Fallahi and Mohammareh, where Sheikh Ghazhan of the
Bani Ka'b, the governor of these two cities, had rebelled.
The Sheikh was subdued and his property confiscated.[64]

It is evident that Iran's sovereignty over the Persian
coast and its dependent islands continued untill 1779, the
year of Karim Khan's death. It has been stated that in the
1780's, the Qawasim were not able to obtain a foothold in
Qishm but did return to Lingeh,.[65]   However, there is no
evidence to prove that, once there, they controlled the port.
There is evidence, however, that Hadi Khan Bastaki, the
Governor of the Jahangireh District, settled a dispute
between the tribes of the Qawasim and the Marazi of Lingeh
in 1788.[66] which can be regarded as an indication of the
continuance of Iran's control over Lingeh. Hadi Khan was
married to a daughter of Sheikh Soleiman of the Mazari
tribe, and stayed most of the time in Lingeh; enjoying good
relations with most of the Arab sheikhs including the
Qawasim sheikhs.[67] Furthermore, Iran argues that even if
Lingeh was governed by a Qawasim Sheikh, the Iranian
government would have had to have assigned him the post.

Evidence also shows that, despite ethnic and tribal
affinity, there was no political connection between the

---

[62] Kelly, op. cit., p. 19.

[63] Farsnameh Nasseri, op. cit., p. 613.

[64] ibid., p. 637.

[65] Kelly, op. cit., p.19.

[66] J. Movahed, op. cit. p. 38.

[67] ibid. p. 39

Qawassim of Lingeh and those of Ras al-Khaimah. The Qawassim of Lingeh, unlike the Qawassim of Ras al-Khaimah, did not participate in the internal Omani conflicts, nor did they join their co-tribesmen from the Lower Gulf in the taking of Sharjah and Rams. In 1797, when the British Resident complained to Sheikh Saqr of Ras al-Khaimah that Sheikh Saleh of Lingeh had fired on the vessel *Viper* and killed 32 members of its crew, Sheikh Saqr shelved the responsibility for the incident on the grounds that Sheikh Saleh was not under his control. Saleh had married a woman of the Bani Khaled tribe of Lingeh (an Iranized Arab tribe) and the boats that had fired on *Viper* belonged to the Qawassim of Lingeh. The two groups were clearly not connected. The Qawassim of Ras al-Khaimah embraced Wahabbism in 1800, whereas the Qawassim of Lingeh were converted much later. The Qawassim of Lingeh, unlike their co-tribesmen of Ras al-Khaimah, seldom engaged in piracy. (The attack on the Omani fleet in 1804 and murder of the ruler of Oman might have been an isolated case, or even a political, rather than piratical, act).

Above all, Iran's contention that the Sheikh of Ras al-Khaimah was not the Paramount Qawassim Sheikh, and therefore did not have control over the profuse sub-tribes, is supported by the process of treaties concluded between the British and the Arab sheikhs of the Gulf.

The first *Qawlnameh* (accord) was signed in 1806 with the representative of Sheikh Saqr, who pledged, on behalf of all Qawassim sub-tribes, to respect the property of the East India Company. As Sheikh Saqr was not, in reality, the Paramount Sheikh, he could not deliver what he had promised. Hence, the British subsequently made all the sheikhs signatories to the "Maritime Truce" and "Maritime Peace in Perpetuity" Agreements. This is a tacit acknowledgment that the British likewise did not consider Sheikh Saqr a Paramount Sheikh. The removal of Sheikh Saqr from his position in Ras al-Khaimah by the Sa'udis in 1808 and the installation of the Qawasim Sheikh of Rams to that position did not meet with any insurrection, or even deprecation from other Qawasim Sheikhs. Obviously, no deep ties of allegiance were felt.

In fact, Captain Seton, the British Resident in the Gulf reported to the Governor of Bombay that "Sheikh Qadhib of Lingeh on the Persian side of the Gulf is a Qawasim by birth... but he calls himself, when it suits his purpose, a Persian subject".[68]

Sheikh Saqr surrendered and offered peace after the British expedition against the Qawasim in 1806. The British Resident in the Gulf, Seton, imposed conditions for a cease-fire on Sheikh Saqr including the observance of a seventy-day truce and the return of the vessel *Trimmer* within 25 days. There was no provision for the return of the vessel *Shannon*, which had been taken by the Qawasim of Lingeh, because Seton knew that the Qawasim of Ras al-Khaimah did not exercise any control this tribe.

The object of the 1809 British-Omani expedition was the destruction of all Qawasim vessels and crafts in Ras al-Khaimah and other Qawasim bases on the Persian Coast, including Lingeh and Luft in Qishm. The British were careful not to enrage the Persians by encroaching upon Iran's sovereignty over Lingeh. One of the instructions issued to the commanders of the British Navy emphasized that "the Prince-Governor of Fars was to be informed of the attack, and if no word of protest has been received from him by the time the squadron was off the Persian Coast, the

---

[68] Kelly, op. cit. p. 106, footnote no. 4, I.O. Board's collections, Vol. 1922, Seton to Duncan, 14 August, 1805.

attack on the Persian ports was to go forward."[69]   This is compelling evidence, in favor of Iran, indicating that, in 1809 at least, the British did recognize Lingeh as an integral part of Iranian territory and the Qawasim as settlers.

The Iranian government had been wary of the Qawasim's unlawful activities in the Gulf.   In September 1809, two months before the British-Omani expedition, the Governor of Fars had informed Seton that he would crush the Qawasim and other "piratical" settlements on the Persian Coast, should they engage in piracy.[70]   In 1809, the British Resident was instructed to explain to the Persians and Wahhabis that their expedition was against piracy and was in response to a unilateral break by Sheikh Saqr of the 1806 Treaty.

Iran wanted neither to shelter pirates, nor to allow such ignominious operations to be carried out on her shores.   Yet Iran did not have a navy to suppress the Qawasim in sea. The 1809 Anglo-Iranian Preliminary Treaty provided that whenever British troops landed in Khark or any other Iranian port with the permission of the Imperial Iranian government, they would be accorded a friendly reception, and such occupation of any Iranian port or island would not be construed as constituting a right of possession.   In the 1812 Treaty, it was provided that, should the Iranian government need any assisstance from the British, the latter, to the extent that it were convenient and practical, would furnish naval and military aid in the Gulf to Iran.   The expenses of this operation would be met by the Iranian government. British ships were to call on any of the ports designated by Iran.   Obviously, Iran wished to eliminate

---

[69] Kelly op. cit., p. 117.
[70] Lorimer, op. cit., p. 1930.

piracy and lawlessness in her waters with British aid and, as events unfolded, the British were looking for a naval base in the Gulf and had their eye on the Iranian islands. The relevant provisions in the Treaties of 1809 and 1812 were intended for the contingency of a British expedition against the Qawassim.

Again, in the course of a military and naval operation of 1819 against the Qawassim, General Keir, the Commander of the British forces, wrote to the Governor-General of Fars and the Governor of Bushehr before attacking the Persian ports of Mughu, Kangee, Charak and Lingeh, explaining the aim of expedition. His goal was the eradication of piracy without encroaching on Iranian sovereignty. At the same time, the British Chargé d'Affairs in Tehran informed the Shah of the forthcoming events, and tried to clarify the aim and the scope of the operations. Since Iran did not acquiesce, British forces did not land on Iranian soil, and even indemnified Iranians wherever they had assailed any island or port and caused damage to Persian citizens. According to the government of Iran, all this proves beyond a shred of doubt that Lingeh at this time was under Iranian sovereignty.

The Iranian government argues that the sovereignty of Iran over Lingeh was never in doubt, and that the Qawassim were only settlers. But political developments and colonial ambitions after 1819 moved the British to call into question the title of Iran to certain islands in the Gulf. After two expeditions, the Qawassim pirates were still operating and disrupting the British trade route. The British were contemplating a more effective means of combatting the lawless sheikhs . In 1817, Henry Willock (the British Chargé d'Affairs in Tehran) proposed to Viscount Robert Stewart Castlereagh (the British Foreign Secretary) that the acquisition of a base in Iran would serve a dual purpose: It would enable the British to control the piracy by enabling swift operations against the offenders. Furthermore, it would restrict the Russians from undermining British influence in Iran and the Persian Court.[71]

In 1819, in the course of planning for the third military expedition against the Qawasim pirates, the question of an Iranian base was again on the agenda.. The British Commissioners in the India Office opined that such a base would facilitate effective and quick retaliatory operations against Qawasim perpetrators. The British had their eye on the island of Qishm, since it was within easy access to the coast of the pirates and also commanded the Strait of Hurmoz. Of course, there was a precedent which suggested this. Sir John Malcolm, an emmissary to the court of Iran in 1800-1801, had suggested to the Iranian government that they either cede or lease the two islands of Qishm and Hanjam to the British. The Shah had declined. In his second mission, Malcolm proposed the cession or lease of the island of Khark to the British. Again, the Shah declined. Then Sir John Malcolm recommended to London the acquisition of the island by force should Iran not consent. It is obvious that the British knew that Qishm, Hajam, and Khark were integral parts of Iran.

With this historical precedent, the British were certain that Iran would not concede to their requests. Hence, by their own admission, they contrived of a vile device: they called into question Iran's basic title to the islands. Thereupon Sir Evan Nepean, Governor of Bombay, initiated a new inquiry on the title to the island of Qishm through General Keir. The General received two contradictory

---

[71] I.O. Persia and the Persian Gulf, Vol. 33, Willock to Castlereagh, Tehran, 16 April 1817.

reports. Captain G.F. Sadlier told him that Sayid Sa'id, the Sultan of Muscat considered Qishm his own property, inherited from his father who had conquered it from Iran; whilst according to Captain Taylor, the island belonged to Iran and had been farmed out by the Shah to Sayid Sa'id. Although Taylor's version corresponded with Sir John Malcolm's opinion that the British had to negotiate with Iran over Qishm, the Governor of Bombay instructed General Keir to occupy the island.

For Iran, this constituted a piratical act which was not entirely unexpected. A few months earlier, the head of the British legation in Tehran had told the Shah that, should Iran refuse to grant Britain a base in the Gulf, "the right and title of the Shah to all the islands in the Gulf might be questioned".[72] This was a vicious plot. At one point, the island of Qais (Kish) was being considered as a substitute for Qishm. On the basis of this report, which exists in the British India Office records, Iran maintains that Britain decided to undermine Iran's title to the Tumbs and Abu Musa in favor of the newly created coastal states solely because of her failure to secure an Iranian base. There exists sufficient historical records to show that Qishm, as a dependency of Bandar Abbas, had been farmed to the Sultan of Oman while the ownership remained with Iran, therefore there should be no doubt with respect to the title. The fact that the lease of Bandar Abbas and Qishm to Saiyid Sa'id of Oman in 1827 was renewed at a higher rent, with more favorable terms for Iran, testifies to Iran's claim to Qishm.[73]

While asserting that the responsibility of combatting piracy in Persian waters remained with her alone, Iran

---

[72] Supra p. 69.

[73] Haj Mirza Hassan Hosseini Fassai, op. cit., p. 806.

protested the occupation of Qishm and demanded a prompt evacuation in December 1820. Furthermore, the Iranian government warned the British that the Russians may use the British occupation of Qishm as an excuse to occupy parts of Iranian territory in the North, and that this would not serve the British interests in India.

After careful consideration, Britain decided to locate its military depot at Basidu in Qishm. This was in accord with the Treaty of Shiraz of August 1822. The British troops left Qishm in January 1823 but kept their depot in Basidu untill the end of the nineteenth century.

By this time, British mistrust of Iran was deep-rooted. The British, who in 1810, had encouraged Fath Ali Shah to take Herat (in the Treaties of 1809 and 1812), warned Muhamad Shah in 1837 to withdraw and keep his army away from Herat. This change of policy was due to the fact that, at the turn of the nineteenth century, the Afghans invaded India and advanced as far as Lahore. The British wanted to create another warfront so that the Afghan King would return to defend his country. In the 1830's, the British established themselves in India, and Muhamad Shah of Iran tilted towards Russia. The British did not want the Russians to establish, through Iran, a foothold in Herat.

Hence, in 1836, when Muhamad Shah (with a Russian blessing) launched a military expedition against Herat, the British occupied Khark and landed their troops in Bushehr, giving an ultimatum to Iran to withdraw their army from Afghanistan. Thereafter, the British withdrew their troops from Bushehr but remained in Khark. George Auckland, the Governor-General of India, recommended the retention of Kharaq at any cost as the British base in the Gulf.[74] Such

---

[74] Haj Mirza Hassan Hosseini Fassai, op.cit. p. 806.

were the ambitions of the British in the Gulf against Iran. Had it not been for the protest of Russia, the mob's assail on the British Residency in Bushehr, and Iran's embargo on the supply of goods to the British garrison in Khark, British troops would not have evacuated the island.

After these incidents, Anglo-Iranian relations were at their lowest ebb, and mutual distrust stood high. The confrontation between the two states came to a head in March of 1839, and Britain broke off diplomatic relations with Iran. The arrival of the British naval squadron off Bushehr intimidated Nasser al-Din Shah, and the Anglo-Iranian Treaty of 1841 was signed securing privileges for Britain. Again the British suggested the lease or purchase of the Khark Island which Iran again denied them.

At this stage, the British were convinced that they could no longer rely on Iran's friendship and support in the Gulf. The good era of Shah Abbas was gone forever. So the British looked instead to the Lower Gulf in search of a base and an alternative to Persian friendship. This is how and why the trucial system emerged.

The 1835 and 1843 Maritime Truce Agreements, and finally the 1853 Treaty of Maritime Peace in Perpetuity provided for a complete cessation of hostilities at sea amongst the sheikhs, gave the sheikhs a distinct identity as wards of the British, and established Britain as the guardian and umpire. As previously mentioned, in December 1887, the government of India obtained undertakings from the Trucial sheikhs not to enter into any negotiations or agreements with the foreign states, and not to allow a foreign state to set up consular offices, commercial agencies, or coal depots on the territories of the Trucial sheikhdoms without the prior knowledge and consent of the British -- what came to be known as "Exclusive Agreements". In 1892, the sheikhs signed another arrangement, whose parts came to be known as "Non-Alienation Agreements" They undertook not to cede, sell, mortgage, or otherwise give for occupation any part of their territories, save to the British government.

The British, having gained full control over Bahrain and the Trucial States, and being in alliance with the Sultan of Oman and Imam of Muscat, were in a strong strategical position in the Gulf. At this point, they wanted control over the Tumbs and Abu Musa, commanding the Strait of Hurmoz, to have complete hegemony in the region.

Another development which strengthened British resolve to control the three islands occured in 1903. For the reasons described below, any control had to be exercised through the British surrogates, the Sheikhs of Sharjah and Ras al-Khaimah.

Iran, in 1898, had employed Belgian experts to modernize its custom offices in Kermanshah and Tabriz. The custom office had, for many years, been farmed out by region to the highest bidders. In 1900 and 1902, two large loans were floated from Russia and the custom revenue was made collateral for the loans. Thereafter Iran's foreign trade was closely tied to the Russian loans and the tarriffs had to be approved by them. Hence Belgian officers ostensibly received their directives from the Russian government.[75] Discrimination against British commercial interests and the increased Russian control over Iran's fiscal policy alarmed the British. In 1903, when the Belgian customs officers visited the Tumbs and Abu Musa to establish new customs offices, they were stopped by the British, who argued that Iran's title to the islands was debatable. Subsequently the British supported the sheikhs' claim that they had inherited

---

[75] Morgan Shuster, Supra., p. 86.

the islands from their Qawasim ancestors in Lingeh. This claim was made despite the fact that in a letter dated 1 December, 1900, addressed to the British Resident in the Gulf, the British Foreign Office admitted that the ownership of the Tumbs had always been questionable. In the same letter, the British Foreign Office had emphasized that, the uncertainty in the legal status of the islands notwithstanding, Britian has always supported the claim of the Qawasim against that of Iranian ownership.

The Status of the Qawasim of Lingeh

Today, Iran rejects the tribal patrimonial claim of the Qawasim sheikhs to the islands.

The Qawasim, as was reported to the India Office in 1820 by Captain William Bruce (the British Resident at Bushehr) were not a *monolithic tribe*. In fact, the Qawasim of Lingeh were a descent separate from their cousins in the Lower Gulf. The monolithic status of the Qawasim was an untruth promoted in the nineteenth century by the British to serve their colonial interests.

The Qawasim of Lingeh were Iranian subjects. Historical facts reveal that the Qawasim sheikhs at Lingeh, who were recognized by the Persians as governors or deputy-governors of the town, were independent from the Qawasim of the Lower Gulf.[76] The material facts corroborating this contention have been mentioned in the historical section. In 1797, Sheikh Saqr of Ras al-Khaimah admitted that he had no control over the Sheikh of Lingeh.[77]

---

[76] George N. Curzon "Persia and Persian Question"; (London:1966) Vol. II, p. 409.

[77] Kelly, op. cit., p. 100.

In 1819, the East India Company recognized the separate political identity of the Qawasim of Lingeh from their fellow tribesmen in Ras al-Khaimah ; therefore it paid compensation to Iran for damages inflicted upon the vessels in Lingeh and Charak.[78] In 1819, Captain Henry Willock, the British Chargé d'Affairs at Tehran, filed a complaint with the Iranian government for the alleged piratical activities of Qawasim in Lingeh.[79] The Qawasim Sheikh of Lingeh, Mohammad ibn Qadhib, did not sign the General Treaty of Peace of 1820, wheras all Qawasim sheikhs of the Arabian coast did.

The idea of the subordination of the Qawasim sheikhs to Sultan Saqr had been promoted by the British to enable Saqr to assume the role of spokesman for the Qawasim. It was only fiction; Sheikh Saqr had become a British ward. The British unsuccessful efforts to reinstate Sultan Saqr in his seat in Ras al-Khaimah, after his deposition by the Wahhabis, was part of the British plan to create a monolithic Qawasim tribe under a Paramount sheikh.

The supposed paramouncy of Sheikh Sultan ibn Saqr helped neither the suppression of piracy, nor the stopping of slavery in the Gulf, aside from the signing of the "Prevention of Slave Trade in the Gulf" by Sultan Saqr in 1839. Colonel Arnold Burrowes Kemball, the British Assistant Political Resident in the Gulf, wrote to the British Minister in Tehran in 1847 that the Agreement of 1839 could not be enforced on the Iranian coast since Bushehr, Asalu, and Lingeh were subject to the authority of the Persian government; Sultan Saqr had no authority over the Qawasim of Lingeh. In the same letter, Kemball had even doubted the enforcement of

---

[78] Kelly, op. cit., p. 161.
[79] Kelly, op. cit., p. 160.

the agreement on the Arabian side,[80] implying that Sheikh Saqr did not have the authority to deliver his promise.

Sheikh Saqr had reached old age when some of the Qawasim sheikhs, such as Sheikh Hamriyah, turned against him. He sought a temporary resting resort in Lingeh, which was provided for him by Sheikh Khalifa ibn Saeed. The myth of the Paramount Sheikh of Qawasim died with his demise in 1866. By 1869, Sharjeh and Ras al-Khaimah had broken their alliance and become two separate political entities ruled by two Qawasim sheikhs.

Iran has always maintained that the Qawasim of Lingeh were Iranian subjects and the Sheikh acted as an official of the Iranian government. In 1856, the Sheikh enforced a new customs tariff that had been approved and ordered by Tehran.[81] On the population mix of Lingeh, Curzon has written that it is partly Arab, partly Persian, partly African, partly that nameless hybrid mixture that is found in every maritime town east of Port Sa'id. The Arab population of Lingeh were Qawasim. For generations, the governorship of Lingeh and of the islands lying off its shore, has been based on hereditary patrimony of the sheikhs of this tribe who were recognized by the Persians as deputy-governors and remained loyal to the Governor of Fars.[82]

The U.A.E.'s contention as to the status of Lingeh, is based on several correspondences, allegedly exchanged between the Sheikhs of Ras al-Khaimah and Lingeh during the 1870's, apparently discovered in 1905 when the Irano-British strife over the status of the islands had reached a peak. Unfortunately, the original documents of some of

---

[80] Report on the Slave Trade of the Persian Gulf: reprinted in British and Foreign States Papers (London: Foreign Office) Vol. 36 (1847-1848) pp. 711-712.

[81] Sir Arnold Wilson, op. cit., p.201.

[82] George N. Curzon, op. cit., Vol. II, p. 409.

these correspondences are non-existent. The issue in those correspondences related to the usufruct of the pasturage on Greater Tumb, which in the nomadic tradition had been enjoyed by both the Qawasim Al-Bu-Sumait tribe of Lingeh and the Qawasim of Ras al-Khaimah. In response to a complaint by the Sheikh of Ras al-Khaimah about the use of pasturage on Greater Tumb by Al Bu Samait, Shaikh Khalifah bin Saeed of Lingeh wrote in November 1872: "Oh brother! Know that the Bu Sumaitis are your followers and are obedient to you, but you should prohibit such people as the Chief of Dubai, Ajman and Ummal-Qaiwain, as all of these go to that place, otherwise, the al-Sumait as mentioned, are obedient".[83]

What does this letter prove? Was the complaint about the proprietorship or the usufruct of the island? According to the letter, even non-Qawasim tribes of other ports crossed over to the island for pasturing. What are the legal connotations of "followers" and "obedient"? Whatever these may be, it appears that Al Bu Samait continued to use Greater Tumb's pastures and the concern of Sheikh of Ras al-Khaimah was not allayed. Hence, most probably the words "followers" and "obedient" had been used as a matter of courtesy. In a follow-up letter on 22 November, 1872, the Sheikh of Lingeh wrote that "the island of Tumb belongs to you just as it was under the authority of your father".[84] Apart from the circumstance, timing, and manner of production of this letter (all of which have been called into question by Iran), the Iranian government argues that Sheikh Khalif's concession in that letter, if at all real, was *ultra vires*; he, as Deputy-Governor of Lingeh, did not have

---

[83] R/15/4/148, 1871.
[84] F.O. 371/1372,1929 Arabia E840/52/91.

the authority to make such statements. Indeed, despite Sheikh Khalif's submissive letter, he completely ignored the demands of the Sheikh of Ras al-Khaimah, which lends credence to the supposition that Khalifa's letter was meant only as a courtesy letter in the best tribal tradition.

As a result, Sheikh Humaid of Ras al-Khaimah took his complaint to the British Residency Agent at Lingeh, Haji Abul Qasem, on 10 February, 1873. Having discussed the matter with Khalifah, Haji Abul Qasem unambiguously asserted that Iran owned the Greater Tumb. Haji Abul Qasem conveyed this to the Sheikh of Ras al-Khaimah,[85] which invalidates the admission in the Califah's letter of 22 November, 1872.

After Khalifah's death, his son, Ali ibn Khalifah assumed the office of deputy governor in Lingeh. Again, letters on the usufruct of Tumbs were exchanged between the Sheikhs of Ras al-Khaimah and Lingeh revealing no new facts, except that Ali ibn Khalif, while reaffirming that the Ali Bu-Sumait tribe of Lingeh had always been using pastures on Greater Tumb, would stop this practice, should the Sheikh of Ras al-Khaimah so desire.[86] The crucial part in the letter of 1877 read: "It has been ascertained by me that the island of Tumb is a dependency of the Qawasim of Oman and we have no property there to interfere".[87] It is noteworthy that "dependency of Oman" is not interchangeable with "dependency of Ras al-Khaimah", particularly so because, at this time, Sheikh Humaid of Ras al-Khaimah did not exercise any control over the Arabian Coast -- Sharjah had already been ceded, while Rams Sha'am and Shimit had become autonomous.

---

[85] Morsy Abdullah, op. cit., pp. 235-236.

[86] F.O. 371-1372/1929 Arabia E982/52/91.

[87] R/15/4/1/148, 1877.

Sheikh Ali, who had acted *ultra vires,* was assassinated a year later in 1878 by Sheikh Yusef, his relative and guardian. The latter was immediately confirmed as Governor of Lingeh by the Iranian government. In the meantime, an administrative shake-up of the Persian Coast region took place in 1879. This was followed by two other reorganizations in 1882 and 1887.

In the 1879 overhaul, Nasir al-Molk, a non-Arab Persian subject, became Governor and Sheikh Yusef was named Deputy-Governor of Lingeh. In 1882, Lingeh, previously under Fars' governorship, was placed directly under the Chief Minister's office in Tehran, and Mohammad Hassan Khan was appointed as the Chief Minister's Deputy in the Gulf. Sheikh Yusef became Mohammad Hassan Khan's Agent in Lingeh.[88] Sheikh Yusef, in addition to letting the Al Bu-Sumait cross over Greater Tumb for pasturing their animals, ordered new date trees to be planted on the island. This further aggravated Sheikh Humaid, who ordered the trees be pulled out. Sheikh Humaid also wrote a complaint to the British Residency Agent, Haj Abul Qasem. It is said that on this occasion, at Haj Abul Qasem's behest, Sheikh Yusef, stated that Greater Tumb belonged to the Qawasim of Oman. Today, Iran contends that Sheikh Yusef's change of attitude was in deference to British policy. Sheikh Yusef was assassinated in April 1885 by Sheikh Qadhib who was soon confirmed as Deputy-Governor of Lingeh by the Governor-General of Lingeh and Bandar Abbas.[89] In 1887, Lingeh, together with the ports of Bushehr, Bandar Abbas and their dependencies, was placed under the jurisdiction of a newly created administrative unit designated "The Persian

---

[88] Lorimer, op. cit., pp. 2056-2064.
[89] Lorimer, op. cit., pp. 2065-2066.

Gulf Ports" which was headed by a high ranking Iranian official, Qawam al-Molk.

These administrative reforms, particularly the last one, was intended to facilitate the formation of an Iranian naval force in the Gulf with Germany's collaboration. The Iranian government was determined to reduce the influence of the Qawasim in Lingeh, and to forge an alliance between Iran and the non-Qawasim sheikhs of Dubai and Abu Dhabi. To achieve the last objective, in September 1887, Naser al-Din Shah commissioned General Haji Ahmad Khan to visit the Sheikhs of Dubai and Abu Dhabi, deliver the Shah's personal letter and explore the prospects of an alliance, against both the British and the Qawasim.[90] The mission failed because of foul play on the part of the Sheikh of Dubai, who informed both the British and the Qawasim of Iran's plans.

On his return to Iran, General Haji Ahmad Khan replaced Sheikh Qadhib, and transferred him to Tehran. Furthermore, General Haji Ahmad Khan ordered that garrisons of regular Persian troops be stationed in the ports of Lingeh, Bandar Abbas and Sirri island, where an Iranian flagpole was planted.[91] Evidently, these measures were taken to ensure Iran's territorial integrity in the face of the British threat through the Qawasim.

Confidential Persian documents trace British intrigue in Lingeh back to 1863, when the British consul in Bushehr consigned one of his agents, Haji Mohammad Bashir, to Lingeh to agitate its Arab residents. He was to focus namely on the Qawasim, encouraging them to become British subjects and rebel against Iran. Nasser al-Din Shah,

---

[90] Muhamad Morsy Abdullah, "The United Arab Emirates", (London:1978), p. 233.

[91] Mosrsy Abdullah, op. cit., pp. 238-239.

in the margin of a report submitted to him by the Minister of Foreign Affairs, wrote: "Discuss this matter with the British Minister in Tehran, and (ask him) why doesn't he prevent his consul in Bushehr from engagement in such (illicit) activities. Instruct Qawam al-Molk to appoint a competent governor for the Port of Lingeh, who need not be an Arab".[92] Despite the Shah's explicit order, the dismissal of the Arab Governor of Lingeh, was delayed until 1887 when Sheikh Qadhib ibn Rashid, the last Qawasim Sheikh of Lingeh, was exiled to Tehran where he died a few years later.   The exchange of letters between the Sheikhs of Lingeh and Ras al-Khaimah over the status of the Greater Tumb are the main documents in the British files in favor of a system of tribal patrimony governing the island.   It is interesting to note that they relate to this period.

Disputes Over Sirri, The Tumbs, and Abu Musa

Following the restoration of Iran's sovereignty over Sirri, Irano-British tensions heightened.   The British Minister in Tehran requested an explanation for the occupation of Sirri. Iran's reply of March 1885, indicated that Sirri was a dependency of Lingeh, governed by Iran, and paid taxes to Iran.[93]   Therefore, Iran was merely exercising her rights. At this point, the British adopted a new line of reasoning, suggesting that the Qawasim Governor of Lingeh was acting in a dual capacity;   while

---

[92] Jahangir, Qaem Maghami, "Bahrein and Khalij Fars",
(Tehran:1350, Islamic Solar Year), p. 122.
[93] Correspondent of the Iran Minister of Foreign Affairs to the British Minister in Tehran, dated 10 March, 1888.

admitting that Lingeh belonged to Iran, that the Qawasim Governor of Lingeh derived his authority from the government of Iran, and that Sirri paid taxes to the Governor of Lingeh. The British argued that the Qawasim Sheikh in Lingeh wore two hats -- one as the Governor of Lingeh, answerable to the government of Iran, and the other as a Qawasim sheikh accountable to the Paramount Sheikh in Ras al-Khaimah. It was in the second capacity, the British argued, that he collected taxes from Sirri. The Qawasim of Lingeh and the Oman Coast were relatives and the residency of the Sheikh of Lingeh in Iran could not destroy tribal traditional rights. The foregoing fallible reasoning has been taken up by Qawasim Sheikhs who, overlooking all historical evidence, claim that Iran in 1887 disposed of the Qawasim Governor of Lingeh and then occupied the island of Sirri. Furthermore, during 1878-1887, the Qawasim Deputy Governor of Lingeh administered the islands of Abu Musa and the Tumbs on behalf of the Qawasim of Oman and not on behalf of Iran.

For Iran, this argument is far-fetched and unacceptable. Mindful of the flimsiness of their arguments, the British took the occupation of Sirri as a fait accompli; yet, in order to warn Iran against any future attempt to occupy the Tumbs, Abu Musa, or Bahrain , she kept sending signals threatening military action should Iran nurture such ambitions.

However emboldened by her success in Sirri, in 1903 Iran proceeded to establish customs offices on the islands of Greater Tumb and Abu Musa. In 1900, Sheikh Humaid of Ras al-Khaimah died and Sheikh Saqr ibn Khalid, the ruler of Sharjah, annexed Ras al-Khaimah to his territory. In January 1903, Sheikh Saqr, directed by Colonel Arnold Burrowes Kemball (the British Resident in Gulf), hoisted his flag over the island of Greater Tumb, in an effort to pre-empt a possible occupation by Iran. Likewise, on 30 April, 1903, the Indian government stressed to the Sheikh of Sharjah the necessity of keeping his flag constantly flying on Abu Musa as a sign of the Sheikh's ownership.[94] At the same time, Kemball warned the British that the hoisting of the flag might provoke the Iranian government to seize the island and thus the India Office should be prepared for military confrontation. Colonel Kemball also had suggested that Abu Musa could replace Lingeh as a port of call because, the traders would like to avoid paying the high tariffs, recently enforced by the Belgian administrators in Lingeh.

The Iranian Customs Officers who landed in the islands saw the flags of Sharjah being flown on the islands guarded by a sentry, and reported the encroachment on the Iranian territory to Tehran. Iran protested to the British. Not having received a reply by April 1904, Iranian custom officers pulled down the flag of Sharjah, and hoisted the Iranian flag nearby, stationing a sentry to guard it.

The British Regent in India intended to send gunboats to the islands and remove the Persian flags but Sir Anthony Herding, the British Minister to the Persian Court, preferred resolution of the dispute through negotiation and the British Foreign office complied. In response to a complaint by Herding, the Belgian administrator, Naus (who at that time was holding the position of Iran's Minister of Customs), admitted that the removal of Sharjah's flag by Dambrain (the Director General of Customs in the south) had been at his instructions. He also had stated that he had received his orders from Moshir al-Dowlah and that Iran was determined to restore its control over the Tumbs and Abu Musa. Naus

---

[94] Lathwaite Memorandum, op.cit., Part I, Para. 17.

also informed the British Minister, that Moshir al-Dowlah had objected to the presence of the British troops on Bassidu, and the island of Qishm as well.

Sir Herding's impression was that all these maneuvers had been conducted by Iran in collusion with the Russians, who were still seeking a foothold in the Gulf. Sir Herding wrote to the British Foreign Office that Naus had confidentially shown him Damberain's report regarding his visit to the islands. In this report, Damberain had spoken about the demands of the merchants of Lingeh to turn Bassidu into an open port, a proposal that had been considered unfeasible by the British Resident in Bushehr as it would harm British trade with Oman and other ports on the Arabian coast. Sir Henry confirmed the accuracy of Damberain's report on Bassidu, since he himself had heard similar complaints and proposals when he had visited the island with Lord Curzon.

Regarding Sirri, Greater Tumb, Abu Musa and Bassidu, Damberain reported that, when had he visited the islands, the Arabian flag was flying and was being watched by a sentry who said he was in the service of the Sheikh of Sharjah. Damberain removed the Arab flag and planted the Iranian flagpole nearby. On Sirri Island, there was no Arab flag and the Iranian flag was hoisted without any complication.

Sir Arthur Herding asked Naus to use his high office to remove the Iranian flags from the Tumbs and Abu Musa. He warned that, should Iran insist on having her flag on Greater Tumb, the British would re-open the case of Sirri -- Sirri had been occupied by Iran in 1888, and Britain protested but without further pursuing the matter or pulling down Iran's flag.

According to Herding, Naus said he could not make a decision on his own, but he would immediately report the matter to the Minister of Foreign Affairs and seek his advice. Naus added that probably the Iranian authorities were not aware that the Qawasim flag had already been flying on the island when Dambrain visited there. Perhaps in the light of this new discovery, he should request the Persian government for new instructions. Herding concluded by saying that His Excellency Naus thanked him for having acted prudently, giving Iran an opportunity to reconsider her decision.

A few days later, Naus informed Herding that he had taken up the matter with the Foreign Minister, who was unyielding. Hence, Naus asked him to raise the matter himself with the Prime Minister. Sir Herding's appointment with the Prime Minister was for 8 May, but when he ran into the Foreign Minister a few days before, the latter asked Herding to wait until he had discussed the matter with the Shah, implying that, at this stage, it was only the Shah who could have a ruling on the case.

The following week, when Herding went to see the Minister of Foreign Affairs, Naus was likewise present and showed him the text of a telegram to be cabled to Dambrain. This telegraph purported that the sovereignty of the islands was in dispute, hence the flags should be removed until the matter was resolved. Moshir al-Dowlah told the British Minister that Iran considered these islands her own property and was preserving her rights. Nevertheless he was ready to discuss it with the British. Herding admitted that he agreed with all that was said by Mushir al-Dowlah and promised to convey the Minister's message to London.[95]

---

[95] Precis of the Affairs of the Persian Coast and Islands (1854-1904) Political Secret Dept. Reg. No. c/248.

Following the said agreement, Iran removed her flag on 14 June, 1904 with the understanding that the *status quo* would be maintained by both sides, namely no flag would be flown on the islands, until the issue had been resolved. But much to Iranian's surprise and anger, a few weeks later, the flag of Sharjah was re-hoisted by the British. Moshir al-Dowlah summoned the British Minister in Tehran to his office and protested the breach of agreement. Herding said that there had not been any change in the status quo. By "status quo", the British meant the status quo before the Arab flag had been removed by Iranians. When Moshir al-Dowlah called the reasoning flawed, the British Minister brought up the issue of Sirri and suggested that, in that case, Iran should also withdraw from Sirri. He warned that, should Iran insist on the Arab flag being removed, Britain would renew its opposition to Iran's occupation of Sirri, since Britain had not formally accepted Iran's claim of sovereignty over that island.

In Iran's view, this was political blackmail and a betrayal of trust, yet she was unable to take a firm stand. The want of a naval force in the Gulf and the lack of a railway and good internal communications on shore had effectively tied her hands. The only recourse was protest, through political channels. Iran pursued this continuously between 1904 and 1970, namely until the time of withdrawal of the British forces from the Persian Gulf.

Since 1904, when the Anglo-Persian strife over the islands intensified, the India Office started compiling plausible accounts justifying Britain's efforts in keeping Iran out of the islands. Alwyn Parker's "Memorandum respecting the Persian Gulf islands of Abu Musa, Tumb, and Sirri" of 1907;[96] J.G.Laithwaite's "Memorandum on the

---

[96] F.O. 371/310 1907, Persia 34/41755

Status of the Islands of Tumb, Little Tumb, Abu Musa and Sirri" prepared in 1928[97] ; and D.W. Lascelles' "Memorandum on Persian Claim to Tumb and Abu Musa", written in 1934[98] represent such accounts. These memorandums contain many factual misstatements, and as a result, judgmental errors, due to their "subjective approach".

It is noteworthy that the writer of the memorandum of 1928, J.G. Laithwaite, states that "the islands were *apparently* part of the hereditary estates of the Qawasim Arab Sheikhs". The word "apparently" implies that even the writer of the memorandum was not certain of the truth of the claim. The writer opines that, while the sheikhs of the Lower Gulf and Lingeh had "equal interests" in the island, it was managed by the Sheikh of Lingeh. If correct, this can explain why the Sheikh of Ras al-Khaimah corresponded with the Sheikh of Lingeh on the pasturing rights on Greater Tumb; it may also clarify the nature of "equal interest", which must have been the right of usufruct.

The Qawasim's Historical Title

The documents produced by the Qawasim in support of their title to the islands by virtue of tribal patrimony are scanty. They consist of the letters exchanged between the Qawasim rulers of Ras al-Khaimah/Sharjah and the Qawasim Governors of Lingeh before 1904. The Sheikhs also stress their exercise of ownership rights after 1904 in their granting of concessions to foreign companies. Such transactions had been approved by their protector, Britain,

---

[97] F.O. 371/13010 1928, Arabia E 49266/421/91
[98] F.O. 371/17827 1934, Arabia E 5652/3283/91

under the "Exclusive Agreements" between the Trucial sheikhdoms and Britain. If anything, Iran argues, such transactions were an excercise of suzerainty by the British, conveniently using the agreements as a veil.

The first group of documents consisting of six letters has already been scrutinized in connection with Iran's claim and should not detain us here. It suffices to say that the contents of these letters were not taken seriously by the Sheikhs of Lingeh inasmuch as Al Bu Sumait continued his use of Greater Tumb's pastures effectively during that time, a sign of the exercise of sovereignty by Iran. They affirmed that the letters written by the Qawasim Sheikhs of Lingeh were written as a matter of tribal courtesy without legal significance, and at most, Iran argues, the letters were ultra vires the Sheikhs of Lingeh. The subsequent statement of one of those sheikhs to the Agent of the British Residency, that the Tumb Islands belong to Lingeh undermines the credence of the Sheikh of Lingeh's prior letter; particularly so, because the message was conveyed at the time to the Sheikh of Ras al-Khaimah.

The second group of evidence, according to Iran, directly or indirectly relates to Britain's conspiracy. The building of a lighthouse on Greater Tumb in 1912, the demand of the Anglo-Iranian Oil Company to prospect the island's natural resources in 1935, the grant of a concession to a British company to mine the red iron oxide in Abu Musa in 1935, the grant of a concession to Golden Valley Colors for the export of red iron oxide in 1952, and the grant of a concession to Unison Oil Exploration of California and Southern Natural Gas Company of Delaware (U.S.A.), were all protested by Iran as soon as they were discovered. Iran maintains that the confirmation of these concessions by the British, or the admission of the sovereignty of the Sheikh in the case of the building of the lighthouse, does not carry any legal weight, in view of the British conspiracy against Iran.

In the meantime, the persistence of Iran in asserting her rights to the island is weighty evidence alone. In 1923, when Moin al Tojar Bushehri applied to the Iranian government for a mining concession of red iron oxide in Abu Musa and Bahrain, Iran was about to file a complaint with the League of Nations against Britain, only to be warded off by the British gunboat policy. British threats notwithstanding, Foroughi, the Iranian Minister of Foreign Affairs, sent a letter to his British counterpart reminding him of the 1904 Agreement and reasserting Iran's rights.[99] In the fall of 1925, the Director-General of the customs offices of Fars, dispatched a mission to Abu Musa to investigate the quality and quantity of the red iron oxide. Faced with British protest and military threats, Iran withdrew, while reiterating her claim of sovereignty to the island.[100] In July 1928, Iran's coastal patrol boats seized a Dubai boat off Greater Tumb's waters, suspected of carrying contraband. The cargo was confiscated and the crew detained. After British intervention, the crew and boat were released and sent back to Dubai, but the cargo was confiscated. Iran maintained that it was from the Greater Tumb, hence it belonged to Iran.

The political tension between Iran and Britain intensified in 1928. This is evidenced by the letter of Lord Cushendon, the Foreign Minister of Britain to the British Minister in Tehran. In this letter, Cushendon expressed his concern

---

[99] F.O. 371/8941 Persia, from Sir P. Loraine to Foreign Office no.162/30, May, 1923.
[100] F.O. 371/8941 British Residency, Bushehr no. 11/85, 6 March, 1926 to Minister Loraine.

over the toughening of Iran's policy in the Gulf, threatening British interests. He cited many examples: The renewal of Iran's claim on Bahrain and the filing of a complaint thereon with the League of Nations, the seizure of an Arab boat near the Tumbs, the commissioning of Iranian medical personnel to replace English doctors in Iran's ports without prior notification, an attempt to occupy Bassidu, and the instruction to governors of the ports to treat the Arab residents from the shores of Oman, Muscat, and Kuwait as Iranian subjects. Lord Cushendon added that these acts indicated Iran's intention to expand her influence in the Gulf region and Arabian coast at the expense of Britain. The Minister went on to say that the information obtained by the British revealed that Iran was pressing for the consideration of Bahrain's status by the League of Nations, the failing of which could push Iran to occupy Bahrain and other islands. In his view, the eventuality of occupation of Bahrain and the islands would place Britain in a disadvantage. Also, Cushendon stated that Britain was researching and sponsoring investigations that would support Qawasim tribal patrimony over the islands.[101] British documents reveal that in November 1928, the British Cabinet approved military intervention should Iran seize the islands. In 1929, Teymoor Tash, Iran's Minister of Court requested the British to stay out of the dispute, leaving the matter of the three islands to Iran and Sharjah who would have it resolved through bilateral negotiations.[102]

With the building of a naval force in the Persian Gulf, Iran frequented her intermittent visits to the Tumbs and Abu Musa as proof of her suzerainty over the islands. Among

---

[101] F.O. 371/13070 Foreign Office Memorandum regarding defense of Abu Mussa and Tumb against agression, 23 October, 1928.

[102] F.O. 371/13721 Persia, from Sir Clive to Mr. A. Henderson, Tehran, 3 August, 1929. No 450.

the Iranian expeditions was the landing of several officers on Greater Tumb on 20 April, 1934, and again on 13 September, 1934 and the questioning the Sheikh's representative there. Following this was a visit to Greater Tumb by an Iranian delegation from the Ministries of Foreign Affairs and the Interior in November 1953, the surveyance of the island in September 1961 to determine the most convenient spot for fixing certain weather-monitoring station equipment, and the missioning a warship in 1968 to patrol her waters. Each time, upon learning of such incidents, the British would protest and direct the commander of the British naval forces in East India to watch Iran's movement and use force, should Iran encroach on the islands.[103]

The lack of vigilance on the part of the Sheikh of Ras al-Khaimah and Sharjah in the exercise of sovereignty over the islands was demonstrated by the number of times the British admonished them for not keeping their flags hoisted on the islands. In a telegram dated 15 August, 1928 the British Foreign Office recommended that the Arab flags be flown constantly in a highly visible place as a sign of ownership. In 1935, the Sheikh of Ras al-Khaimah pulled down and removed his flag on the islands, as the British had refused to pay rent for the lighthouse. At first the British suspected a conspiracy between the Sheikh and Iranian authorities. Consequently, a warship was dispatched to Greater Tumb. At the same time, a notice was sent to the Sheikh to rehoist his flag, otherwise the flag of another Qawasim sheikh would be installed.[104]   The British were obviously more

---

[103] Mohammad Ali Movahed , op. cit., p. 73.
[104] F.O. 371/18901 From Political Resident in the Persian Gulf to Foreign Secretary, 2 January, 1935.

concerned with the possession of the islands than the islands' purported "owners". The sheikhs' interest in the islands did not sharpen until the discovery of oil in the region.

Iran's Assertion of Her Rights Since Post W.W.II

After the termination of W.W. II, specifically after the liberation of India and Pakistan, Iran hoped to see a radical change in British policy in the Persian Gulf. This proved to be a mistake; if the sub-continent of India had been lost, Middle-eastern oil was still there. In a telegram dated 14 December, 1948 from the British Foreign Office to its political agent in the Gulf, it is stated that, despite the disinterestedness of Sheikh of Ras al-Khaimah in Greater Tumb and despite the fact that he had once offered to lease it to Iran, it seems unlikely that the Sheikh and Iran would be able to come to any agreement, all because of the oil and the natural resources of the continental shelves. Hence British policy should remain the same, namely, *unreserved support for the rulers of Sharjeh and Ras al-Khaimah* and, whenever Iran resubmitted her claim to the islands, the British would reiterate the response given in 1905, that is, any renewal for the claim by Iran would force Britain to raise the question of ownership over the island of Sirri. The British Foreign Office believed that the Iranians would realize that it was not to their advantage to seek a confrontation in the Gulf; in such eventuality, the only winner would be the Soviets. If Iran were to insist on her claims, she would be referred to the International Court in Hague. However, in the telegram it is mentioned that, should the case go before the International Court, the British might not have a strong case to argue. If the Court's ruling were to be for Iran, this would embolden the Iranian government to refer the case of Bahrain to the International Court as well. With these considerations, the British Foreign Office thought it was imperative to make a comprehensive study in advance.[105] In the same telegram, the British Political Resident in the Gulf spoke of the disinterestedness of the ruler of Ras al-Khaimah in Greater Tumb and emphasized the need for alerting him to the importance of the island. Writing to the Political Agent in Bahrain, the British Agency in Sharjah again complained of Sheikh Saqr ibn Mohammad's neglect of the island, remarking that he had not visited Greater Tumb for many years. "I have invited him to visit the island with me in the near future when a warship calls in Ras al-Khaimah; he has consented to it."[106] The Agency hoped that in doing so the Sheikh would begin to recognize the island's significance and act with more resolve.

Files in Iran's Ministry of Foreign Affairs disclose that, in 1949, Iran was considering various options to exercise her sovereignty over the islands, including the installation of a garrison on Greater Tumb; and referring the conflict to relevant international organizations. She also debated approaching the British and informing them of Iran's intention, should the British not recognize Iran's legitimate

---

[105] F.O. 371/68329 Persian Gulf Residency, Bahrain, 20 December, 1948 to C. J. Pely, Political Agency, Bahrain; Valid Hamdi Al-Azami, "Al Neza; Baine Dowlat al Imarat al-Arabi wa Iran Hawl-e Jazar Abu Mussa Wa Tumb al-Kobra wa al-Soghra Fil Wasaeq al-Britania, (London: 1993), p. 133.

[106] R/15/2/625; Valid Hamdi op. cit., p. 138, quoted by Movahed , op. cit., p. 78.

right. In August 1949, Iran's Foreign Minister, 'Ali Asqar Hekmat, instructed Iran's Ambassador to inform the British of Iran's determination to exercise her sovereign rights over the island as they were Iran's "indisputable and incontestable territories".[107]

During the period of 1950-1953, Iran, under Mossadeq, was engaged in the nationalization of Iranian oil and a bitter strife with Britain followed. In February 1951, Iranian naval officers arrived on Abu Musa and held dialogues with the residents of the island for two hours. At that time, there was no flag flying on the island. In March, the Commander of the British Navy in the Gulf visited the island with the Assistant to the Sheikh of Sharjah and hoisted the Sheikh's flag there. In May, the ruler of Ras al-Khaimah reported to the British that Iranians had planted Iran's flag on the island of Greater Tumb. From the correspondence between the British Agent and the British Foreign Office, it appears that in 1949, too, the Iranian flag had been hoisted there. The relevant passage reads: "Since the removal of the Persian flag in 1949, Iranians had not made any effort to install it. However the phrases, 'The Iranian territory', painted on the rocks still are visible. I have instructed my officers to wipe them out."[108]

In 1953, a special committee was set up by the Iranian government to survey various Iranian options. Iran feared that the occupation of the island would provoke a forceful reaction by Britain, and furthermore would be in contravention of the United Nations Charter that recommends the peaceful resolution of disputes. Iran also

---

[107] Guive Mirfendereski, The Tumb Islands Controversy: 1887-1971", Ph.D. thesis submitted to The Fletcher School of Law and Diplomacy, (Boston: 1985), p. 579.

[108] F.O. 371/9185. British Residency, Bahrain, 20 June, 1951 to the Foreign Office; quoted by Movahed, p. 79.

feared that the Security Council and General Assembly might not entertain Iran's complaint because, at this stage, it did not pose any risk to peace and security. The weight of opinion was in favor of referring the matter to the International Court. In the meantime, the British, detecting Iranian vigilance in the Gulf, ordered the British Royal Force to keep surveillance over the islands. On 19 May 1953, Iran protested the flight of the British Air Force over the Iranian islands, to which the British gave their usual reply denying Iran's suzerainty.

During Mossadeq, diplomatic relation between Iran and Britain were severed, and the Swiss Embassy in Tehran looked after British interests in Iran. An Iranian memorandum to the Swiss Embassy dated 10 August, 1953, evidences that on 22 May, Iran sent a note through the Swiss Embassy to the British Foreign Ministry, stating that, based on historical evidence, Iran's sovereignty over the islands is undeniable. Britain had violated the Bilateral agreement of 1904, and Iran requested an immediate withdrawal of the British Marines and the removal of its telegraph installation from the island.[109]

Throughout 1954 and 1955, Iran reorganized its administrative structure, proclaiming Greater Tumb a dependency of Qishm and Lesser Tumb and Abu Musa dependencies of the island of Kish. In November 1954, the British Political Agent in Bahrain reported that, during his discussion with the Iranian authorities, it had been suggested that should the British change their policy on the three islands, Iran would forgo her claim to Bahrain, helping

---

[109] F.O. 371/109852 for Iran Minister of Foreign Affairs to Swiss Legation Custodian of British interests in Iran, 10 August, 1953, no. 3455.

improve relations between the two countries. The British Agent promptly rejected this; if Iran relinquished her claim to Bahrain, the raison d'être of the British presence in the Gulf would disappear. Hence, the lingering of the dispute over Bahrain was actually in the British interest. Finally, the British Agent reported that British warships on a monthly or bimonthly basis visited Abu Musa and the Tumbs. His impression was that the Sheikh of Sharjah was actively involved in protection of Abu Musa, whereas the Sheikh of Ras al-Khaimah continued to be indifferent to the Tumbs' defense.

Iran continued to stress her sovereign rights. On 18 December, 1954, Roger Stevenson, the British Ambassador to Iran, met with Entezam, the Iranian Minister of Foreign Affairs. On this occasion, Entezam told him that Iran's claim to Abu Musa, the Tumbs, and Sirri is based on compelling evidence, and Britain could cooperate with Iran in the preservation of security in the Gulf. The British Ambassador said that these considerations could help the resolution of the dispute.

On 31 January, 1955 in a letter to the First Lord of Admiralty, Anthony Eden (the Foreign Minister of Britain) expressed his desire to resolve Britain's disputes with Iran, following the settlement of the oil issue. Anthony Eden thought one option would be for Iran to forgo her claims to Bahrain and Abu Musa. In return, the British would recognize Iran's sovereignty over Sirri and broker the sale of the Tumbs to Iran. The ruler of Ras al-Khaimah had asked for fifty million rupees as well the exemption of the fishers of Ras al-Khaimah and their boats from all taxes and duties. The Sheikh had also asked for a share in the revenue accruing from the lighthouse on Greater Tumb, and from oil and other minerals that may be extracted in the future. Obviously, such conditions were unacceptable to Iran.[110]

Abdollah Entezam, during his visit to London in August 1955, warned the British that the Irano-British conflict over the three islands might soon explode. The British proposed that the matter be referred to the International Court. Entezam agreed, on the condition that the Bahrain issue be referred as well; they should be considered as a package.[111] This was not palatable to the British.

In June 1960, the Shah ordered Iranian security officers to install certain equipment on the island, such as a "weather-monitoring station" in an "unobtrusive and gradual"[112] manner as an additional token of Iran's sovereignty. In May 1961, an Iranian helicopter landed on Greater Tumb and interrogated the British personnel in the lighthouse. In September 1961, another Iranian helicopter landed on the island, carrying a group of surveyors to determine the most convenient location for the system. All these incidents were followed by the usual British protest and the usual Persian claim of sovereignty.

In November 1965, Iran received information that the Sheikh of Ras al-Khaimah was planning to build an airport as well as a naval base on Greater Tumb. The Iranian government ordered its navy to stand alert and watch the events to ensure that no action by the Sheikh would weaken Iran's position. In the meantime, Iran had representation, both in Tehran and London, demand the immediate removal of the Arab flags and guards from the island, issuing the

---

[110] Movahed, op. cit. p.82, quoting Vahid Hamdi, op. cit., p. 162.

[111] F.O. 371/114641 Foreign Office to the British Embassy, 14 August, 1955.

[112] Guive Mirfendereski, op. cit. p.585.

warning that "should such actions continue, Iran will act in the manner that she sees fit in protecting her "interests"[113]

The last confrontation before the occupation of the islands, occurred on 11 January, 1968, when an Iranian warship patrolling in Tumb waters was harassed by a British plane flying at low altitude. In a note sent to the British Embassy, Iran warned that, should such maneuvers by the British Air Force be repeated over Persian waters, Iran would take necessary measures to defend her sovereignty. Again, Iran's protest was rebuked by the British in the usual manner.[114]

Subsequently, Iran dispatched a "civilian boat" to Greater Tumb to obtain factual information about developments on the island. The captain of the boat reported that on 14 January, 1968, a British helicopter carried the Sheikh's son, together with two British officials to the island with the intention of stationing twenty Arab policemen there.[115] Follow-up expeditions revealed that on 15 January, British planes in international waters harassed the Iranian warship, *Hurmoz*, and on 16 January it was reported that the British Navy was engaged in a "vigilant patrol" off Greater Tumb waters.[116] The British Foreign Ministry on 23 January, 1968 "made a strong protest against continued presence of Iranian warship in Tumb waters" and warned Iran "against any attempt to lower the Sheikh's flag".

Tax Evidence

---

[113] ibid., p.587.
[114] ibid., p.588.
[115] ibid., p.589.
[116] ibid., p.589.

In general, the payment and collection of taxes may be used as an evidence of sovereignty by conflicting parties.

In December 1887, in response to the British protest over Iran's occupation of Sirri, the Persian government stated that "for nine years Sirri and Tumbs had paid taxes to the Persian government" and that "the documents in support of the Persian claim were kept in Bushehr".[117]   Iran mentioned that the Governor of Lingeh intermittently visited the islands of Sirri, Greater Tumb and Abu Musa and collected taxes. On the same subject, in January 1888, the Persian government sent copies of letters submitted by Sheikh Yusif, Deputy-Governor of Lingeh, to the Governor of Bandar Abbas, about the purpose of his visits: collecting government dues. These letters demonstrate Iran's exercise of control over the islands.   However, when the British Resident sought the Sheikh of Sharjah's confirmation, the latter, Sheikh Saqr ibn Khalid, rebuked this claim by saying that Greater Tumb was uninhabited. The British Resident was referred by the Iranian government to Malek al-Tojar (the head of the merchant guild) in Bushehr for records of the tax, and the latter in turn referred the matter to Amin al-Sultan, who promised to send them soon to the British Agent in Bushehr.[118] The British say that the records were never received. The Sheikhs hold Iran's failure to produce the documents as evidence against her.

On the other hand, the sheikhs claim that, in the early nineteenth century, the Qawasim paid the religious tax, Zakat (alms tax), to the Wahhabi Sa'udis and not to Iran.[119]

---

[117] F.O. 371/13010, 1928, Arabia E4266/421/91

[118] I.O., L/P & S/18/B397, 1928.

[119] Kelly, op. cit. p.103.

Iran maintains that the Qawasim of Lingeh did not pay Zakat to the Sa'udi treasury because a majority of them had not yet embraced Wahhabism. Even if they had, this does not prove that they were not Iranian subjects; many Iranian Shi'a paid their khoms to their mentor, Mojtahed in Najaf, without becoming Iraqi subjects. The Sa'udis had also demanded that the Qawasim pirate tribes remit one fifth of the booty taken in war, to the Sa'udi Treasury as it was the practice of other Wahhabis.[120] However, a booty was not a tax.

It is noteworthy that when the Iranian authorities stated that they collected taxes from the residents of Greater Tumb during the previous nine years, the sheikhs answered that nobody lived on Greater Tumb to pay a tax. According to the sheikhs, Greater Tumb was open to all: When there was rain and grass, any tribesman could take his cattle to the island for pasturing. When the Sheikh of Lingeh had planted a number of date trees on the island, they were removed by other sheikhs, because they considered Greater Tumb nobody's, or everybody's, land, not only the Sheikh of Lingeh's.

Map Evidence

In order to substantiate her claim to the islands, Iran also advances maps, which were printed and published in the nineteenth century not only by Germans, French and Americans but also by the British themselves, as evidence. On these maps, the islands of the two Tumbs and Abu Musa bear the same color as Iran and not that of the Arab coast. Among them are three maps published by the Germans in

---

[120] ibid. p.106.

1804, 1811, and 1875,[121] one by the French in 1877,[122] two by the Americans in 1882 and 1885,[123] and at least six by the British in 1853, 1861, 1870, 1881, 1884 and 1886.[124]

The most important of these, for Iran's case are the "Persian Gulf Pilot, 1870" (a British Admiralty publication), and the Map of Persia of 1886 (prepared by the Intelligence Branch of the British War Office). Dr. Jalal Abdo, in his Memorandum of 28 April, 1953, on behalf of the Iranian Foreign Office, regarded the Persian Gulf Pilot as compelling evidence in favor of Iran's sovereignty. However, the British War Office Map of 1886 is the most crushing evidence against the British claim.

On 22 June, 1888, one copy of the map was presented by the British Ambassador to Nasser al-Din Shah, during a discussion on the border between Iran and Afghanistan. Two months later, in the Irano-British conflict over Sirri, Iran, relying on the same map, argued that Sirri belonged to Iran. At that time Sir Henry Drumond Wolff, the British Ambassador to Iran, warned the British that Iran would use the same map in establishing her claim over the two Tumbs and Abu Musa. That is exactly what happened.

The British came up with an incredibly naive explanation in self-defense. Their first argument was that the "Persian Gulf Pilot" was a nautical and not a political compilation;

---

[121] Harvard College Library Nos: 2276/8, 2276/10 and 2276/16

[122] Atlas universel de géographie (Paris, Hachette;1877)

[123] Edward Stak, Six Month in Persia (New York: 1882); Harvard College Library 2276/21.

[124] Harvard College Library No. 2275/1853; Harvard College Library No. 2276/17; the British Admiralty Publication IMFA, File No. 33/150A; Edward Weller, F.R.G.S. Persia, Afghanistan and Ballochestan (London:1881); The Royal Atlas of Modern Geography (Edinburgh: 1884); F.O. 371/18917, 1935.

and that appurtenance of the islands to Iran in the "British war map" was an "innocent mistake". The British Foreign Office said that "the error in question is extremely regrettable from the standpoint of his Majesty's government and that "it cannot be taken as a formal declaration by His Majesty's government of their view of the status of the islands".[125] In that connection the Marquis of Salisbury, the British Foreign Minister, uttered some "words of wisdom", saying that "...maps shall never be presented in future."[126] Meanwhile, C.W. Baxter, the head of Eastern Department at the Foreign Office, said that "the evidence of the map is in no way conclusive but it is inconvenient."[127] In 1934, D.W. Lascelles, Assistant Head of the Eastern Dept., again called the map of Persia "unfortunate."[128]

Regarding admissibility and conclusiveness of the maps, advocates of the U.A.E. title rely on the Island of Palmas Case in 1928[129] between the United States and the Netherlands. In this case, the maps submitted by the conflicting parties were not identical, some favored the United States and some favored the claim of the Netherlands. Yet, in the Irano-U.A.E. dispute, all the maps, which are drawn by foreign geographers, unanimously place the islands within Iran's territory. The U.A.E. has not been able to produce one map depicting otherwise. Hence, the advocates of Iran's title maintain that the Island of Palmas Case has no relevance to the Gulf situation.

---

[125] Mosely Abdullah op. cit. pp.238, 242; J.G. Laithwaite on the Status of the three islands and Sirri. supra , p 42

[126] F.O. 371/13009, 1928 Arabia E 4152/421/91

[127] F.O. 371/13009,

[128] Dan W. Lascelles, on the " Status of Islands of Tumb, Little Tumb, Abu Mussa and Sirri" supra p 43

[129] Permanent Court of Arbitration at Hague, Award of 4 April, 1928.

In the Palmas case, Max Huber stated: "A map affords only an indication -- and that, a very indirect one -- and, except when annexed to a legal instrument, has not the value of such an instrument, involving recognition or abandonment of rights". Nonetheless, the map of Iran had been annexed to a legal instrument in the case of the delimitation of the boundaries between Iran and Afghanistan. The map was submitted, according to Iran, by the British, the main conflicting party. How can Britain, or its wards, the Sheikhs of Ras al-Khaimah and Sharjeh, deny that?

In this case, the map is not an indirect, but a direct indication, falling within the "exception" in Max Huber's award. It represents the appurtenance of the two Tumbs and Abu Musa to Lingeh. It is reliable and based on data carefully collected by the British Intelligence and Marines, concurring with maps independently drawn up by the Germans, Americans and French. It was an official map. It has been reprinted, used in negotiations by the highest British authorities -- it was issued not by Iran for the assertion of its sovereignty over the islands but by the British government who denies Iran's claim.

Thus, the subsequent characterization of the map as an innocent error will not be admissible in court. Moreover, a case of acquiescence and estoppel may be made against the British, in as much as the British were aware of Iran's claim to the islands as early as 1887 (with her seizure of Sirri) yet they did not make any presentation to the contrary until 1904. Most significant is the fact that the British, in 1888, by presenting the map of persia to Iran, tacitly recognized, or acquiesced, to Iran's claims to the island. A case in point is the Costa Rica-Nicaragua Boundary Dispute of 1886, in which the Arbitrator stated that "...the government of

Nicaragua was silent when he ought to have spoken, and so waived the objection now made".[130] In the Temple of Preah Vihear Case (1962) the tribunal decided that "...it is clear that the circumstances were such as called for some reaction on the part of the Siamese authorities, if they wanted to disagree...They did not do so...and thereby must be held to have acquiesced."[131] Iran can argue that she intended to occupy the Tumbs and Abu Musa after occupying Sirri; but did not do so with the assumption that Britain, by not objecting to Iran's claim to the islands of the Tumbs and Abu Musa, had assented to Iran's claim of sovereignty.

In 1903, Iran sent a mission to Greater Tumb in connection with the reorganization of customs offices throughout the country. The Iranian Foreign Ministry in April 1953 charged the British with making contradictory statements, which are not admissible according to *Mascim allegans contraria non est audiendus*![132] The British government, relying on the British-produced Map of Persia (1886) demonstrated its belief that the islands of Tumbs and Abu Musa belonged to Iran. In 1904, Britain contended that sovereignty over the island was in dispute; in 1934 she changed her stand, saying that the islands belonged to the Qawasim Sheikhs. British political behavior was actually more than inaction, constituting acquiescence. In fact, it was overt action, constituting the confirmation of Iran's claim.

---

[130] Costa Rica-Nicaragua Boundary Dispute, 1886, J.B. Moore "International Arbitrations", Vol.II p.1945.
[131] The Temple of Preah Vihear (Cambodian V. Thailand) 1962, International Court of Justice Reports 1962, p.23.
[132] Guive Mirfendereski op. cit., pp.430-432, quoting the Abdo Memorandum on the Status of Tumb and Abu Mussa (File No.33/50A), Part I, p.23.

The Aquisition of Territory Under International Law

Both Iran and the U.A.E. must prove that their title to the Tumbs and Abu Musa before 1904 was historical or that they acquired the islands under the accepted rules of international law.

Iran contends that she has owned the three islands from time immemorial, that during the nineteenth century they were dependencies of Lingeh, and administered by the Governor of Lingeh as an appointee of the government of Iran. No other state, including Britain, exercised any sovereignty over the island. Britain, to further her colonial ambitions, forged a title for her wards, the Qawasim sheikhs, preventing Iran from exercising sovereignty over the islands.

The Qawasim assert tribal patrimony and claim that, since the middle of nineteenth century, the islands have belonged to the Qawasim and the Qawasim sheikhs of Lingeh, although appointees of the government of Iran administered those islands on behalf of the Qawasim Sheikhs of Sharjah and Ras al-Khaimah.

The Qawasim sheikhs can hardly deny Iran's suzerainty before the eighteenth century. The British, as protector of the sheikhs, cannot repudiate Iran's title before 1904. Hence the question of ownership of the islands becomes one of the legal acquisition of the islands. Were the islands *terra nullius* in 1904? And can the Sheikhs prove an intentional and effective acquisition of the islands, namely *animus occupendi* combined with *corpus occupendi*?

The British, on behalf of the Sheikhs, have argued that, at the turn of the century, the islands were "not yet formally occupied by any government" and that the Sheikhs, by "hoisting their flags" on the islands, were the first occupants. Thus, the British contend that the islands were *terra nullius*.[133] This is a claim that cannot be substantiated. In the "British Guinea-Brazil Boundary Case" (1904)[134] , the arbitrator defined terra nullius as a territory "not in the dominion of any state". Yet, at least fifteen years before the hoisting of the flag on the islands by the sheikhs at the behest of the British government, the British were cognizant of Iran's suzerainty claim As early as in 1870, the British government's published maps show beyond any reasonable doubt, that the British government knew that the islands were in Iran's dominion. Hence, the British assertion that the Sheikhs were the first occupants of the islands is baseless. For the determination of the historical sovereignty of the islands, one should look to the historical records and evidence that prove that these islands have belonged to Iran throughout the centuries. It is noteworthy to recall that in 1887 the Iranian government had declared Iran's ownership of the islands to the British and the latter did not protest.

In 1887, Sharjeh and Ras al-Khaimah were not states as defined under international law. In the British Guinea-Brazil Boundary Case and the Clipperton Island Case, the arbitrators clearly state that terra nullius is a territory not belonging to a state, but that it may be occupied by a state. The British assertion that, prior to the hoisting of Sharjah's flag, the island of Greater Tumb was not yet occupied by another government proves that, prior to 1904, the sheikhs

---

[133] F.O. 371/310 1907, Persia 39/41755 No.1.
[134] The Boundary between the Colony of British Guiana and the United State of Brazil, 1904:99 British and Foreign States papers (1905-1906), p. 93.

did not have dominion over the island, thus dashing the sheikh's claim that they have owned the island since the middle of the eighteenth century.

For Iran to have lost her proprietary right to the islands, there would have had to have been dereliction under international law.   Dereliction requires an intended, voluntary and actual abandonment.   Not only did Iran not intend to quit the island, she also made every effort to keep it.

Even an actual temporary dereliction does not amount to a legal dereliction.   In the Delagoa Bay Case (1875), between England and Portugal, the arbitrator stated that the interruption of occupation in itself does not constitute abandonment.   In the Clipperton Island Case (1931), the Arbitrator ruled that the non-exercise of sovereignty during 37 years "was no reason to suffice that France had lost her right by dereliction, because she had never the animus of abandoning the island".[135]   The fact that in 1904 Iran intended to establish customs services on Greater Tumb shows that Iran was maintaining her suzerainty over the islands.

Once it is proven that Iran had never abandoned her rights to the islands, the sheikhs' claim (Britain's claim) of the acquisition of the islands as *terra nullus* fails.

The occupation of the islands by the sheikhs in 1904 can scarcely be called intentional or effective.   During the period of 1904-1934, the British had to admonish the sheikhs several times for not keeping their flags hoisted on the islands.   And, in 1934, the Sheikh of Ras al-Khaimah, removed his flag because the British had not paid rent for

---

[135] American Journal of International Law, Vo. 26 (1932), pp. 391-393.

the lighthouse. Hence, animus to occupy, unless it can be ascribed to the British, is missing in this case. The hoisting of flag under Iran's protest can hardly be called an "effective" exercise of sovereignty by the Sheikh, after it had been removed by Iran. The effective exercise of the gunship policy by the British characterizes the nature and scope of occupation.

The British and the U.A.E. have failed to prove that the islands were terra nullus before 1903 and have not shown that the occupation since 1904 has been valid under the recognized principles of international law. It is obvious that the sheikhdoms did not possess independence and were not members of the family of nations; with the "Exclusive Agreements" of 1892, the British conducted their foreign relations. Hence, whatever took place in the Trucial States, from the signing of the Exclusive Agreement of 1892 to the British withdrawal from Gulf in 1970, was a British decision. It is remarkable that the British, on 15 and 22 June, 1903, maintained that the sheikhs' occupation was the basis of their title, whereas thereafter they ascribed this title back to the middle of the eighteenth century. Such contradictions further weaken any other arguments for lawful occupation.

Can the U.A.E. resort to "acquisitive prescription" to prove her case against Iran? Acquisitive prescription is realized through the continuous, uninterrupted and peaceful exercise of sovereignty, even if the initial occupation was unlawful. Such conditions were not present in the case of islands from 1904 to 1970.

Iran, as the legitimate owner of the islands, asserted her rights but, in the face of British political and military might in the area, could not exercise any control on the islands. The exercise of sovereignty by the British/Sharjeh and the British/Ras al-Khaimah, however meager, has been continuous, though not peaceful.   And as Oppenheim proports, the exercise of sovereignty in spite of "protest and claims" cannot be regarded as "undisturbed".[136]

This is particularly true when the title is based on acquisitive prescription. Starting in March 1904, the Iranian custom officers pulled down the Sharjeh flag, hoisted the Persian flag and put a sentry to guard it. Thereafter, the Persian government protested the construction of buildings in 1905, and the lighthouse in 1912 and 1913. In 1923, Iran intended to raise a complaint against Britain in the League of Nations over Bahrain, Abu Musa and the Tumbs, but stopped after British threats of naval operations against her. Iran renewed her claim on the three islands in 1923. She landed customs officers on Abu Musa for the inspection of the island's red oxide mines. This lasted several hours and they returned with a bag of the mineral as a sample. The British protested and warned that a gunboat would be sent to the waters of Abu Musa. In July 1928, Iran seized a Dubai boat off Greater Tumb. This caused intense tension between London and Tehran. On 15 August, 1928, the Governor of Lingeh ordered that boats flying Arab flags be barred from Lingeh. On the following day, India ordered all Iranian boats off Abu Musa and Greater Tumb. The gunboat policy risked an armed clash.

Around 10 November, 1928, a Persian customs officer visited Greater Tumb to inspect the island and reported that British flags had been hoisted on the islands. Seven months later, another inspection mission was performed and the British flags were still there. Iran protested.

---

[136] L.Oppenheim "International Law". ed. H. Lawlerpacht, 8th ed. (New York:1967) Vol. I pp.576-577.

On 17 May, 1933, the Governor of Bandar Abbas and two other men visited Greater Tumb and apparently inquired about the lighthouse's rent.   The British government protested a year later. In the summer of 1933, Iran planned to administer all the lights and buoys on the Persian Coast including those on Greater Tumb.   She employed French and Italian experts for this purpose.   In fact, French experts and their Persian counterparts visited all Iran's ports and islands, including Greater Tumb, on 23 July, 1933, on board a Persian ship.   Twice more, visits by Iranian naval officers took place in August and September of 1934. In 1935, Iran attempted to send letters demanding taxes and informing the population of Greater Tumb of the forthcoming Majlis election, inviting them to vote as part of the Bandar Abbas electorate.

An important exercise of dominion over Greater Tumb was the grant of a concession to Algemeine Exploratie, a Dutch Company, for the exploration of mineral resources in a large region comprising, inter alia, Qishm, the Tumbs and Abu Musa.[137] The British Minister in Tehran intervened and told the Dutch Minister that the Tumbs and Abu Musa did not belong to Iran. The Dutch responded that the company was interested primarily in Qishm and therefore operations on the three islands were most unlikely. The British Foreign Office viewed protest as unwise; however it ordered the British Navy in the Gulf to be on watch that the officers of the Dutch Company indeed did not land in the islands. Although the Dutch were not interested in the Tumbs or Abu Musa, Iran's willingness to negotiate a contract shows that she was neither disinterested in the islands nor inclined to allow the sheikhs reign without protest. With the above list, which may or may not be comprehensive, the Sheikhs'

---

[137] F.O 371/23264, 139.

titles through acquisitive prescription cannot be upheld; they was disturbed throughout the sixty-six years.

A report from the Subcommittee of Imperial Defense on issues related to the Middle East, the island of Greater Tumb, prepared on 8 March, 1935, confirms that the claim of the ruler of Sharjah on Greater Tumb, and its occupation by Britain, temporary or permanent, may raise protests and problems.[138] In a response to a query by the British Resident in the Persian Gulf, the British Agent in Bahrain, on 13 November, 1948, wrote that there is no evidence that Britain had ever recognized Ras al-Khaimah's sovereignty over Greater Tumb. However, Britain admitted that, since the dismissal of the Sheikh of Lingeh in 1887, there had been no relations between Greater Tumb and Ras al-Khaimah. Also, the British recognized the independence of Ras al-Khaimah in 1931, when it ceased to be ruled by the Sheikh of Sharjah.[139] These admissions on the part of British undermine other statements denying Iran's sovereignty over the Tumbs.

Unsuccessful British efforts to re-establish Sheikh Sultan Saqr in his seat in Ras al-Khaimah after he was deposed by Wahhabis indicate that the British hoped to forge a monolithic Qawasim tribe and use it as her political tool in the area. Britain's denial of Iran's sovereignty was a device for establishing her hegemony on the region.

In 1887, when the Tumb issue was raised, the British admitted that the island was part of the governorship of Lingeh, except that the Governor of Lingeh administered it on behalf of the Qawasim of Oman. but the British failed to

---

[138] F.O. 371/18901, paper No. ME. (0) 176.
[139] R/15/2/625, Political Agency Bahrain, NO. CR-231, 13 November, 1948 to the Residency.

show when and how the ownership of the island had passed to the Qawasim. The islands had never been terra nulla and Iran had never abandoned them.

After Nader Shah's assassination, the government of Iran leased certain cities which were exposed to the pirate tribes in the gulf, and farmed the customs offices to individuals.   To further this policy, Bandar Abbas was leased to the Imam of Muscat, and Lingeh to some Qawasim sheikhs who were Iranian subjects. One of the requirements of the lessee was his acceptance to become a subject of Iran in relation to that city and as a lessee.   Even the Imam of Muscat was not exempt from this requirement. The text of the lease of Bandar Abbas to the Imam of Muscat, recorded in 1855, confirms this. According to the first article of the lease, the Imam of Muscat, Sayid Sa'id, accepted the condition that the Governor of Bandar Abbas would be a subject of Iran, subordinate to the Governor of Fars. In this context, Sayid Sa'id pledged in writing to be a subject of Iran. According to the fourth article, the Imam of Muscat obligated himself and his successors not to transfer the lease to a third party, irrespective of nationality.[140] When the central government in Tehran was in a position to exercise control over the cities and the administration of the customs offices, the government changed its policy, terminating the lease of the towns and the farming of the customs offices.

Attached to the lease is a document, bearing the same date signed and sealed by Imam of Muscat, in which he makes the following statement:

---

[140] Mohamad Ja'afar Khor Mowji, "Haqayeq al-Akhbar Nasseri" p.163; Mirza Mohamad Khalil Mar'ashi "Majma al-Tavarikh", ed. by Abbas Eqbal p.38; Mohamad Ali Sadid al-Saltaneh Kababi, "Bandar Abbas and Khalij-e Fars: p. 199, quoted by Mohammad Ali Movahed op. cit. pp. 95-96.

I, hereby confess that I am one of the subjects and servants of the government of Iran; and hereby obligate myself to remit the taxes and dues of Bandar Abbas, Qishm, Hurmoz, etc. which have been leased to me, to the government of Iran in instalments as perscribed in the lease without delay or deferment...and do my utmost to keep the cities in good conditions and take good care of the residents of those cities. I further undertake to refrain from any act or adoption of any measure which will be against Iran's interest. Should there be a breach of these pledges by oversight or by design, the government of Iran has absolute authority to pass any ruling it consider fit and I shall obey such rulings.[141]

This was a prototype lease contract.[142] A similar lease was signed by Seiyid Salem Tharini in 1868, who succeeded his father, Sa'id, as Imam of Muscat.

Under the first lease agreement, the Imam agreed to pay annually sixteen thousand tooman as a tax to the Iranian government, twelve thousand to the Sadr-e A'zam, and two

---

[141] Haj Mirza Hassan Hosseini Fassai, op. cit., Vol I, p. 806. The agreement contained a preamble and sixteen provisions. The preamble reads: "Whereas by the order and permission of the sublime and mighty authorities of the Iranian government, the governorship of Bandar Abbas and its dependencies, which are an inalienable part of Iran's territory, is conferred upon Sayid Sa'id khan (Inman of Muscat and Oman) and his agents, therefore hereby it is agreed that: First, the governor of Bandar Abbas, like other governors of the Province of Fars, be subordinate to the Governor-General of Fars....Fifthly, the flag of the Iranian government should fly in Bandar Abbas all the time and be guarded by several Iranian soldiers...Twelvethly, should the government of Muscat be passed to a usurpor, this agreement will be annulled...and finally, the Inman does not have the right to lease or alienate any part of Bandar Abbas to a foreign state."
[142] ibid. p.98.

thousand to the Governor of Fars.[143] Due to the similarity of the situations, comparable agreemnts must have been signed with the Qawasim Sheikh of Lingeh, who was, in any case, an Iranian subject.   Thus the burden of proof is upon the British to establish that the Qawasim Sheikh of Lingeh held the Greater Tumb for the Qawasim of Oman.

---

[143] ibid. p.96.

V

The Last Episodes And Conclusion

On 3 November, 1971, Iranian troops occupied Abu Musa peacefully, following a bilateral agreement between Sharjah and Iran, brokered by the British. The seizure of the Tumbs by force caused the loss of seven lives on Greater Tumb.

Before withdrawing from the Gulf, the British offered certain alternatives to the conflicting parties, with a view to both prevent armed collision and induce Iran to recognize the existence of the United Arab Emirates.[1] The alternatives included the partitioning of Abu Musa between Iran and Sharjah and the return of the island to Iran, without entertaining the question of sovereignty.[2]

Also, the British in May 1971, as an act of goodwill towards Iran, directed the American Oil Company, Occidental Petroleum, to defer drilling operations off the shore of Abu Musa. In February 1971, the Shah announced that, if the restoration of Iran's sovereignty over the island could not be achieved peacefully, he would not hesitate to resort to force.[3]

---

[1] Daily Telegraph (London), 21 July, 1971; The Times (London), 2 November, 1971.
[2] The Financial Times, 23 May, 1970, p.224.
[3] The Times (London), 12 February, 1971.

Before the occupation of the islands, Iran had always maintained that the dispute was really between Iran and Britain and not Iran and the Arabs. She endeavored to avoid an Irano-Arab polarization in the Gulf. Thus, the Shah decided to occupy the islands before the departure of the British.

On the eve of the formation of the U.A.E., Iran and Sharjah signed an agreement whereby the Sheikh of Sharjah consented to the occupation of the island by Iranian troops, though, as the Britain's representative stated to the United Nations Security Council, "neither party (had) given up its claim to the island, nor recognized the other's claim".[4]   In return, Iran agreed to pay 3.75 million dollars annually to the sheikhdom, until the revenue realized from the sale of oil from the island or offshore reached 7.5 million dollars. After this time, the proceeds of the sale of the island's oil would be divided equally between Iran and Sharjah. Despite Britain's efforts to strike a similar deal with regard to the island of Greater Tumb, the Sheikh of Ras al-Khaimah did not accept it.   Consequently on 30 November,1971, one day before the British departure, Iran occupied the islands. At this same time, the deputy ruler of Sharjah was assassinated, seemingly, for his cooperation with Iran.

The attitude of the moderate Arab countries towards Iran was one of low-profile disapproval. Before Iran's intervention, Kuwait suggested to Iran that she might consider leasing the islands for 99 years, keeping a joint Irano-Arabian garrison in the islands, and recognizing the two Sheikhs' sovereignty over the islands. This proposal

---

[4] United Nations Security Council, Provisional Records, 9 December, 1971, New York Times, 1 December, 1971.

was unacceptable to Iran. After the occupation, naturally, the situation changed.

Except for Egypt and Saudi Arabia, who refused to sever diplomatic relations with Iran or protest in the United Nations, other Arab countries voiced disapproval in varying degrees, with different tones. Demonstrations against Iran were organized in Sharjah and Ras al-Khaimah, and the property of Iranian residents there was damaged. Iraq severed its relations with Iran and Britain, charging the latter with conspiracy against Arab nations. Libya severed its relations with Iran and nationalized the British Petroleum Company in Libya because of Britain's supposed collusion with Iran. Furthermore, the four radical Arab States (Iraq, Libya, Algeria, and the People's Democratic Republic of Yemen) on 9 December, 1971 requested the U.N. Security Council to consider "the dangerous situation arisen from the occupaton of the three islands by Iran's armed forces. Follwing a low-key debate, the U.N. Security Council opted to adopt a proposal tabled by the Somali delegate, deferring the consideration of the issue, in favor of the use of diplomacy and some third party efforts.[5]

The role played by the superpowers helped Iran. The Unites States was not disposed to changing the status quo; Iran had been chosen to act as gendarme of the Gulf, filling the vacuum created by the British withrawal from the region. The Soviet Union preferred to assume a low-key posture so as not to irritate either Iran or Iraq or other radical Arab states. The British, too, aligned herself with the two superpowers.

During the 1970's, the tension between Iran and the Arab states remained dormant. After the change in regime

---

[5] The Security Council, Provisional Records, 9 December, 1971.

in Iran and the establishment of the Revolutionary Islamic Republic, the situation changed. During the Irano-Iraqi war, the Arab countries in the Gulf sided with Iraq. In the last phase of the war, so did the United States. After the declaration of a cease fire in the Irano-Iraqi conflict and particularly after the war between Iraq and Kuwait with the mounting presence of the U.S. in the region, the 1971 Irano-U.A.E. dispute re-emerged.

Iran has always maintained that the question of the three islands -- Abu Musa and the Tumbs -- is purely an Iranian domestic matter and that the Arab League, the G.C.C. or the U.N. have no jurisdiction over it. The United Arab Emirates continues to insist that the matter be referred to the Internaitonal Court in Hague, or submitted to international arbitration.

The likelihood of Iran's submission to the jurisdiction of the Hague Court or the ruling of the Security Council is extremely remote. Even during the Shah, Iran's experience with the U.N. in the case of Bahrein was an unhappy one. In 1978, the Secretary-General of the U.N. organized a "fact-finding mission" to Bahrein, in order to discover the wishes of the people of Bahrein. The accuracy of that survey, which was in favor of Bahrein's independence, has always been dubious to the Iranian people. In 1946, the Security Council of the U.N., in response to Iran's plea for the evacuation of Iran by Soviet troops, only hoped that the Soviet Union would leave of her own initiative.

The experience of the Islamic Republic of Iran with the U.N. is more negative. In the wake of the Irano-Iraqi war, the U.N. Security Council rebuffed Iran's request for support against Iraqi invaders; the U.N. refused to support Iran, who had disregarded its recommendations on the American hostage crisis. In 1981, the Security Council, adopting Resolution 479, agreed to a cease-fire short of the

Iraqi invaders leaving Iranian occupied territory. In that year, Iran not only pushed back the Iraqi troops from Iran, but also conquered some Iraqi cities approaching Baghdad. On July 1982, the U.N. adoption of Resolution 514 called for a cease-fire and the evacuation of this Iraqi territory by Iranian troops. With these incidents very much alive in Iranians' memories, it would be far too optimistic to assume that Iran would submit to international arbitration or ruling in a matter that she considers a domestic concern.

Relations between Iran and the moderate Arab states of the Gulf is also influenced by the these states' relations with the U.S.A. Arab states have always regarded the non-Arab Muslim country of Iran as expansionist, a perception strengthened by the fear of Iran's proclaimed desire to export her revolution to other Muslim countries. The Islamic Republic of Iran considers moderate Arab states in the Gulf who are U.S. clients, as well as international forums (the U.N. and the Hague Court), secure bases for intrigue by the United States against her.

At the same time, Iran's foreign policy is not exclusively a product of religious fanaticism. As Iran marches into the twenty-first century, she wants to be a full international player in Gulf politics. Her recent offer of entering into non-agression treaties with the Gulf Arab states indicates the desire to allay Arab fears of Iran, and to resolve the existing conflict over the three islands. In the new world order, interstate conflict should be resolved by negotiation and through diplomatic channels and not by military confrontations. Conscious of this truism, in recent months the conflicting parties have shown greater constraints in their rhetoric, without advancing any feasible method, or agenda, for resolving the dispute.

Appendix I

Sheikh of Sharjah's Announcement of the Abu Musa Agreement
29 November, 1971

In the name of God, the merciful and compassionate: Brother compatriots, I warmly greet you with all the love and esteem I have in my heart for each of you. I salute you all for your awakening and complete sense of responsibility. You have always stood by me with your hears, arms and sentiments, and placed your hands in mine on the road of work and enterprise. Today I announce to you that our views and the views of the Iranian Government have coincided in the form of an agreement about the island of Abu Musa. Under this agreement we preserve for Sharjah and its people their legitimate right to a dear part of our good land.

The agreement read as follows:

> Putting our faith in almighty God, in order to preserve the interests of the people of Sharjah, to maintain the fraternal and friendly relations with Iran, to sere the purposes of preserving peace an security in the area, agreement has been reached

between us and the Iranian Imperial Government regarding the island of Abu Musa as follows:

1.   Arrangements under this agreement shall not affect Sharjah's view regarding its sovereignty over the island of Abu Musa. The Sharjah flag shall continue to be hoisted on the island. A police station and government offices shall remain on the island. Citizens on the island shall also remain under the authority and jurisdiction of the Government of Sharjah.

2.   Buttes Gas and Oil Company will prospect and drill for oil and natural minerals in the island of Abu Musa and in its 12-nautical mile territorial waters. Income from natural minerals produced in this area shall be equally shared between Sharjah and Iran.

3.   The Iranian forces will be deployed in an area on the island agreed upon by the two sides.

4.   An agreement for financial aid has been signed between Sharjah and Iran whereby Sharjah will receive 1.5 million pounds sterling annually for a period of 9 years. This sum will be paid directly to Sharjah for use on its public services. Payment of these installments will cease when Sharjah's oil revenue reaches 3 million pounds sterling annually.

These are the points in the agreement between us and the Iranian Imperial Government. Finally I can only say that this agreement coincides with our people's hopes and aspirations.

[Signed] Khalid ibn Muhammad al-Qasimi, ruler of Sharjah and dependencies.

Source: FBIS, *Daily Report, Middle East & Africa*, V, no. 230 (November 30, 1971).

Appendix II

Premier Hoveyda's Statement on Abu Musa and the Two Tumbs to the Majlis on 30 November, 1971

MR. SPEAKER: It gives me great pleasure to inform the honorable deputies and my dear countrymen that Imperial Iranian Armed Forces landed on greater and Lesser Tumb islands at 0615 today and also established themselves at strategic points on Abu Musa island. [applause] The Iranian flag was raised at the summit of Halva Mountain – the highest point on Abu Musa – at 0650 today. [applause]

Thus, after a period of nearly 80 years during which colonial policy prevented the establishment of Iranian sovereignty over these islands despite incontestable historical rights, these islands again came under Iranian control thanks to the wise policy of His Imperial Majesty the Shahanshah, Arya Mehr [applause] and prolonged and persistent negotiations with the British Government.

Following the resolution of the Bahrain issue, which was achieved as a result of Iran's correct policy, the solution of the problem of these islands through peaceful means has once again proved the validity of Iran's foreign policy. At the same time, with the elimination of the last vestiges of

218

colonialism in the Persian Gulf the road has been opened for close and all-round cooperation with our brothers on the other side of the Persian Gulf. This is a source of great pleasure. In line with the policy of good neighborliness, one of the clear principles of the Iranian independent national policy, and refraining from resorting to the use of force in solving the present issue, which in itself is proof of this attitude, we will now be able to have harmony and positive and constructive cooperation, now and in the future, with all the peoples bordering the Persian Gulf. We can do this with sincerity and without worrying about Iran's national interests or about the security of the region and international peace.

I deem it necessary to point out here, however, that his imperial majesty's government has in no conceivable way relinquished or will relinquish incontestable sovereignty and right of control over the whole of Abu Musa island. Thus, the presence of local agents in parts of Abu Musa should in no way be regarded as contradictory to this policy.

Another point is that the Imperial Iranian Government, in order to prove its absolute good will in solving this issue through peaceful means, brought an oil agreement which had been previously concluded between Sharjah and an oil company into line with the recent regulations of the Organization of Petroleum Exporting Countries so that it would be acceptable to Iran. Iran has further agreed that should oil be found, the income from it will be equally divided between Iran and Sharjah to help the progress of our brothers in Sharjah. In addition, Iran will provide financial and technical aid to further social and development progress in Sharjah. I would like to mention that in the past, several development projects have been implemented in a number of shaykhdoms. In the future, however, no efforts will be spared to help our brothers on the other side of the Persian Gulf. Now that confidence based on the elimination of the vestiges of colonialism in the Persian Gulf, the evacuation of foreign forces, the independence of the emirates, and more importantly on the social awareness of our Persian Gulf brothers with whom we share the same religion has provided all the necessary conditions for preserving peace and stability in this part of the world in the interests of all the littoral peoples, the Imperial Iranian Government, in line with the sacred wishes of the Iranian people's sagacious leader, will spare no efforts to achieve mutual confidence and all-round cooperation with all the peoples and governments in this region.

Appendix III

Mohammad Reza Shah's Press Interview, January 29, 1972

Question: Your Majesty, what in general do you think Iran's role should be in the future of the Persian Gulf? Will Iran contribute to the development of the Arab emirates as well as that of the islands belonging to Iran? Will Iran play an economic and developmental role in the region as well as a defense role?

Answer: Yes, I think that we have no doubt about that. Therefore, any of those countries, the emirates in the Persian Gulf, who would solicit and welcome our help will receive it without a doubt. We shall do even more than that. I believe that our country, within the next few years, will assume the role of a donor of aid without imperialistic designs. I can say that this will be done not only without any imperialistic designs but also without any individual and selfish motives. This is because I believe we can fulfill that role. Furthermore, we have duties towards entire mankind – especially towards that section of mankind that needs help. There was a time when we were ourselves recipients of such aid. Fortunately, that era ended a few years ago and now it is our turn to become a donor of aid. Obviously, the region of immediate interest to us is the Persian Gulf. In this region we can give technical aid to some countries while contributing to the area's stability and security.

Q.: We would like to know who is considered by His Majesty as an "enemy" in the Persian Gulf region. This is because while visiting military bases we were told that if the islands of Abu Musa and the two Tumbs fell into enemy hands a grave situation would ensue. Who is this enemy in the Persian Gulf?

A.: Well, you could consider all those who are against free navigation as enemies – all those who aim at instability in the region as their primary interest. I cannot name a special enemy in this connection. But one can classify the enemy in that genre.

Q.: What do you think about the American presence in Bahrain?

A.: Well, you know that we declared long ago that we should not like to see a foreign power in the Persian Gulf. Whether that power be Britain, the United States, the Soviet Union or China, our policy has not changed.

Q.: Does your Majesty consider the defense of the Persian Gulf – to which Iran wishes to contribute – as separable or inseparable from the defense of the Indian Ocean in general?

A.: It is obvious that in the final account all free seas are related to each other. Every ocean is the prolongation of another ocean. Naturally, if the Indian Ocean becomes troubled we shall feel the effects and counter-effects. There is no doubt about that.

Q.: Do you intend to establish bases further afield – for example in the Gulf of Oman?

A.: You mean on our own territory? Yes, it is normal, it is something utterly normal. It will depend on the future development of the entire Indian Ocean region. The reinforcement of our military position on our own territory – which borders on the Gulf of Oman – will depend on the situation prevailing in the Gulf of Oman, the Arabian Sea and the Indian Ocean.

Q.: Now a precise question. Have you had contacts with the United Arab Emirates?

A.: There has been an exchange of telegrams. Yes. And naturally there are often separate meetings with the heads of those states individually.

Q.: Have you recognized their union?

A.: Yes, certainly. We have exchanged greeting cables. They informed us of their formation and we congratulated them.

Q.: Hasn't the Arab League started or probed the possibility of conversations with you concerning the issue of the three islands?

A.: In our view the issue is a purely internal matter that does not concern anyone else. Well, we don't speak of three islands – I mean, we have concluded a separate agreement concerning Abu Musa.

Q.: Could one know, more or less, the elements of that agreement? Of what kind is it? Little has been publicized on this subject or, at least, there has been some misunderstanding.

A.: I think much has been said on that subject. We maintain our position that the whole of the island belongs to us. The Emir of Sharjah is apparently making the same claim. Of course, the agreement between the shaikh and the oil companies was changed so that it would be in line with our laws. We recognize that agreement which is now effective. On the other hand, our forces were sent to the island to take up positions on strategic heights there so that they could ensure the stability of the region. You have no doubt been told that it is nothing new for us to ensure the control of the Persian Gulf and the Strait of Hormoz. Having 2,000 kilometers of coast and dozens of air force and naval bases we can always close the strait. But it is exactly the opposite of this that is important. This is because a country like ours – a country that has a population of 30 million, a country that is responsible and serious and has a good future while it supports peace, calm and stability will never risk adventures. For such a country problems are not posed in that way. It is the opposite that we are discussing – that is to say a situation in which the islands could fall into irresponsible hands. A small ship, even a motor-boat armed with bazookas attacked a tanker – a big tanker and nearly sank it. Just imagine, we are constructing a jetty at Kharg Island which you have visited to receive 500,000-ton tankers. Well, if a 500,000-ton tanker is sunk in the Persian Gulf the whole of the Gulf will be lost, completely lost, because the pollution that would thus result will be on a scale unimaginable. Then clearing that pollution would be as harmful as the oil itself, bearing in mind the huge quantities of detergent one would have to use. All marine life as well as life along the coast could be destroyed. This is a very important matter – a very serious matter – because the Gulf is neither very wide nor very deep. It is almost like a closed sea. Further, historic facts and documents prove that these islands belong to us. We are not here to watch the annexation of a part of our territory to please no matter which country. Furthermore, it was in our interest as well as in the interest of other countries that the islands that could have had "nuisance value" would have it no longer.

Q.: Begging your pardon, could we know whether negotiations with the Emir of Sharjah have ended or are still going on?

A.: No, they have ended. They had ended before our troops landed on the island.

Q.: When did the attack on the tanker Your Majesty has referred to take place?

A.: Two or three months before we took up positions on the islands. It happened near the mouth of the Red Sea.

Q.: Has the Indo-Pakistani War, in Your Majesty's view, altered the strategic situation in the region? Could the outcome of that war have an effect on Iran's defense policies?

A.: It could.

Q.: In what sense, may I ask?

A.: If Pakistan remains a powerful country, strong and united, the danger will be less. But if what happened on the other side ever shook the unity of West Pakistan then very grave problems could be created for us. The same would be true from the international point of view as well. The entire international scene would be changed.

Q.: Do you think that, as a result of this situation, changes should take place in the CENTO alliance?

A.: Yes. CENTO has never been really serious, you know.

Q.: Could your Majesty explain to us the way you see the current problem with Iraq?

A.: Well. I don't know if we can call it a current problem since it is something to which we have almost become accustomed. We are serious. We are a country that thinks before taking any measure and we like our respectability. Facing us we have leaders that are, perhaps, not like that and who, finally, do not all follow the same ideas. To deport 60,000 people all of a sudden is a thing we would never do. Separating fathers from their children, men from their wives, is to us something extraordinary. You can see those people yourselves and ask them questions. The equilibrium is lost because we do not think in the same way. That sort of behaviour is beyond our conception because we shall never do a thing like that. One is put off a bit in the face of acts like that. Everyone believed that fascism was over in the world. We are exposed to acts that have the same consequences. But, once again, one should not lose one's *sang froid*. Our country is not going to change its mentality and methods because of such provocation. All the same, they should be careful because no one can go beyond a certain point in a policy of provocation. After a certain point those subjected to that policy will no longer tolerate it.

Q.: Could you give us any idea why the influx of deportees suddenly slowed down? Could one say this resulted from intervention by the Soviet Union?

A.: Everything is possible.

Q.: Did you demand Soviet intervention?

A.: No, never. We informed our friends about the whole event. But we did not seek any direct intervention. Of course, we kept the world informed of the whole event.

Q.: During our visit to one of the camps set up for the deportees we noticed that many of them were of Kurdish origin. To what extent would Your Majesty say the deportation of Iranians was connected with Iraq's domestic problems and its relations with Kurdish forces?

A.: I don't think the two are connected at all. This is an entirely separate issue. Of course, since the Kurds are Aryans, and very pure Aryans too, one could see a racist angle in the event too in the sense that they took action against those people who are called Aryan. Otherwise, I don't think there was any direct relationship between the two issues.

Q.: Your Majesty, do you think Iraq's aggressiveness indicates, prefigures, heralds a change of orientation in the policy of Arab states who might concentrate themselves on the Persian Gulf abandoning, perhaps, Israel's region, etc...? What is your opinion?

A.: Obviously, that would be easier since there would be less danger of war. The Iraqis – I mean the leaders since I do not wish to refer to the people of Iraq for whom we still have sentiments of friendship – do not, I believe, want their troops on the Israeli front so much, especially if they would have to fight. It is a bit early for replying to your question which, nevertheless, cannot be excluded. But let us wait for the formation of the new Egyptian government. So far the Egyptians have not behaved like that. Throughout what happened between us they have maintained friendly relations. But even though Iran today might not be considered a formidable military power I do not recommend anyone to try and meddle against us and that, especially, not in five years time....

Q.: There is a clear impression of Iran's reinforcement – of an Iran which is wighing more and more in a considerable way.

A.: Yes, obviously. It is one of the factors that form the context of power politics. If all the weight of the United States behind Israel makes one hesitate to attempt anything over there, one might believe it possible to find a mere "nothing" elsewhere -- perhaps to try and avenge oneself in another direction. But that would be something very dangerous to do. I believe that the consequences would be at least as dangerous, if not more so, since we, and the region that would be affected, are precisely the region that contains nearly 60 per cent of the world's oil resources.

A.: Your Majesty, do you have problems with the United States?

A.: No. I can say that our relations have never been as good as they are now. Our relations with your country might well further expand and a major and important conference dealing with economic and industrial questions is currently meeting in New York, so the people of the United States will become better acquainted with the possibilities that exist in our country. On the other hand, I believe that America has realized it can no longer play the role of an international gendarme and that the world's stability and security should, in any case, be guarded by countries that can assume that duty in each region. Vietnam has already developed into an impossible problem for you. How many more times can one repeat the experience of Vietnam?

Q.: Do you see a corresponding tendency in Soviet policy? Do you see any changes in that policy? Do you think the Soviet Union is playing a more peaceful role than in the past?

A.: The Soviets are quite flexible and , naturally, very intelligent while they also act in accordance with plans. They always construe their policy in their own country in a certain way which, in any case, I consider to be very intelligent and wise. Perhaps a new American policy could lead us to expect closer ties with others too. Here, we are talking about the "super-powers" and one can say that the role of these powers will gradually become smaller.

Q.: Would the presence of Soviet ships in the Persian Gulf, and especially in Iraqi bases, disturb the order and peace Your Majesty desires?

A.: If you are referring to creation of bases, then that would created new problems. But if we are talking about visits, then one cannot prevent military vessels of another country from paying visits anywhere in international waters. But if there should be a question of bases, it is obvious that that would create an entirely new situation.

Q.: What are Your Majesty's plans for the island of Abu Musa which we have visited? Does Your Majesty think that the island will become habitable?

A.: No, Certainly not. But the forces stationed on Abu Musa should be able to meet their logistic needs. Greater Tumb is inhabited by a few fishermen and we should, naturally, meet their needs. Lesser Tumb, however, has been inhabited by snakes up to now. What should we do next? We should certainly not issue new identity cards for those snakes – isn't that so?

Source: *Keyhan* (International Edition), January 29, 1972.

Appendix IV

A Sample of the Exclusive Agreement of the Shaikh of Bahrain with the British Governemnt Dated 13 March, 1892

I Esau bin Ali, Chief of Bahrein, in the presence of Lieutenant-Colonel A.C. Talbot, C.I.C=E., Political Resident, Persian Gulf, do hereby solemnly bind myself and agree, on behalf of myself, my heirs and successors, to the following conditions, viz.: --

1st. – That I will on no account enter into any agreement or correspondence with any Power other than the British Government.

2nd. – That without the assent of the British Government, I will not consent to the residence within my territory of the agent of any other Government.

3rd – That I will on no account cede, sell, mortgage or otherwise give for occupation any part of my territory save to the British Government.

Dated Bahrein, 13th March 1892, corresponding with 14th Shaaban 1309.

Esau Bin Ali,

Chief of Bahrein

A.C. Talbot, Lieut.-Col.,
Resident, Persian Gulf

LANSDOWNE,
Viceroy and Governor General of India

Ratified by His Excellency the Viceroy and Governor-General of India at Simla on the twelfth day of May 1892.
H.M. Durand,
Secretary to the Government of India, Foreign Dept.

Source: Aitchison, A Collection of Treaties etc. p. 238

Appendix V

A Sample of the Undertaking by the Shaikh of Shargah, Regarding Oil – 1922

Letter from Sheikh Khaled ben Ahmed, chief of Shargah, to the Hon'ble Lieutenant-Colonel A.P. Trevor, C.S.I., C.I.E., Political Resident, Persian Gulf, Bushire, dated 18th Jamadi-os-Sani, 1340 (= 17 February 1922).

After Compliments –

My object in writing this letter of friendship is to convey my compliments to you and to enquire after your health.

Secondly, let it not be hidden from you that I write this letter with my free will and give undertaking to Your Honour that if it is hoped that an oil mine will be found in my territory I will not give a concession for it to foreigners except to the person appointed by the High British Government.

This is what was necessary to be stated.

NOTE. – A similar undertaking was given by the Chief of Ras-al-Khaima, on the 22nd February 1922.
source: Aitchison p261

Bibliography

Abdullah, Muhhamad Morsy, *The United Arab Emirates*, (London: 1978).

Abrahamian, Edward, *Iran Betwen Two Revolutions*, (Princeton, N.J.: 1982).

Adamiyat, F., *Bahrein Islands: A Legal and Diplomatic Study of the British-Iranian Controversy*, (New York: 1917).

Aitchison, C.U.A, *A Collection of Treaties, Engagements, and Sanads relating to India and Neighbouring Countries*, 3rd edition, Volume 11, (Calcutta: 1933).

Al Bahaina, Husain M., *The Legal Status of the Arabian Gulf States: A Study of their Treaty Relations and their International Problems*, (Manchester, U.K.: 1968).

Al-Istakhri, *Al Masalik Wal-Mamalik*, (Leyden: 1939).

Anthony, John Duke, *Arab States of the Lower Gulf: People, Politics, Petroleum*, (Washington D.C.: 1975).

Belgrave, Sir Charles, *The Pirate Coast*, (London: 1966).

Brown, Edward, *Persian Revolution 1905-1909*, (Cambridge: 1910).

Chester, Edward W. *United States Oil Policy and Diplomacy*, (Connecticut: 1983).

Chubin, Shahram and Zabih, Sepehr, *The Foreign Relations of Iran: A Developing State in a Zone of Great Powers Conflict* (California: 1974).

Cottrel, Alvin J., General Editor, *The Persian Gulf States*, (Baltimore: 1980).

Curzon, George N., *Persia and the Persian Question*, (London: 1892).

Gregorian, Vartan, *The Emergence of Modern Afghanistan*, (Stanford, California: 1969).

Haj Mirza Hossein Husseini Fassai, *Farsnameh Nasseri*, edited by Mansur Rastigar Fassai, (Tehran: 1988).

Hamdullah, Mostowfi, *Nuzhat al-Qolub*, edited by Muhammad Dabir Siyaqi, (Tehran: 1336 A. H.).

Hamid al-'Azami, Valid, *Al Neza' Baine Dowlat al-Imarat al-Arabi Wa Iran Hawl-e Jazar Abu Mussa Wa Tumb al-Kobra Wa al-Soghra Fil Britania*, (London: 1993).

Hawley, Donald, *The Trucial States*, (London: 1971).

Hourani, George F., *Arab Seafaring in the Indian Ocean in Ancient and Medieval Times*, (Princeton: 1951).

Huart, C., *Kara Koyunlu*, (London: 1927).

Hurewitz, J.C., *Diplomacy in the Middle East*, (New York: 1951).

Ibn Balkhi, *Fars Nameh*, (London: 1921).

Ibn Battuta, *The Travells of Ibn Battuta*, translated into English by H.A.R. Gibb (London: 1959).

Ibn Hawkal, *Surat al-Ardh*, (Leyden: 1939).

Kazemzadeh, F., *Russia and Britain in Persia: 1864-1914*, (New Haven: 1968).

Kelly, J. B., *Britain and the Persian Gulf: 1795-1880*, *(Oxford: 1989)*.

Khalij-e Fars, *Proceedings of the Seminar on Khalij-e Fars*, 2 volumes (Tehran: 1962).

Lockhart, Laurence, *Nader Shah*, (London: 1938).

Lorimer, J. G., *Gazetteer of the Persian Gulf, Oman and Central Arabia*, Official publication of the government of India, 2 volumes, (Calcutta: 1908-15).

Mahmood, Mahmood, *Tarikh-e Ravabet-e Iran va Englis*, (Tehran: 1934).

Malcolm, John, *The History of Persia*, (London: 1829).

Merrir, Sir William, *The Caliphate: Its Rise, Decline and Fall*, (Edinburgh: 1924).

Miles, S. B., *The Countries and Tribes of the Persian Gulf*, (London: 1919).

Mirfendereski, Guive, "The Tumb Island Controversy: 1887-1971; A Case Study in Claims to Territory in International Law", Ph.D. Thesis, (Boston: 1985).

Movahed, J., *Bastak va Khalij-e Fars*, (Tehran: 1970).

Movahed, Mohammad 'Ali, *Mobalegh-e Mosta'ar: Asnad-e Britania va Ede'ay-e Shoyoukh bar Jazayer Tunb va Abu Mussa*, (Tehran: 1373 A. H.).

Oppenheim, L., "International Law", ed. by H Lauterpacht, Vol. 1, 8th edition, (London: 1955); Vol. 2, 7th edition, (London: 1952).

Qaem Maqami,Jahangir, *Bahrein va Massael-e Khalij-e Fars*, (Tehran: 1350 A. H.).

Ramazani, Rouhollah K., *The Foreign Policy of Iran 1500-1914*, (Virgina: 1966).

Rawlinson, Sir Henry, *England and Rusia in its East*, (London: 1875).

Salih ibn Razik, *History of the Imams and Seyyids of Oman from 61-1856*, translated into English by George Percy, (London: 1871).

Salmon, Thomas, *Modern History or the Present State of all Nations*, (London: 1744).

Schwartzenberger, G., *International Law through International Court*, Vol. 1, 3rd edition (London 1957).

Shuster, Morgan W., *The Strangling of Persia*, (New York: 1912).

Sykes, Sir Percy, *History of Persia*, 2 volumes, 1st edition (1915); 3rd edition (London: 1951)

Tadjbakhsh Gh.R., *La Question des Iles de Bahrein*, (Paris: 1960).

Ward, Sir A.W. and Gooch, G.P., *The Cambridge History of British Foreign Policy*, (New York: 1923).

Wilson, Sir Arnold T., *The Persian Gulf*, (London: 1928).

Zahlan, Rosemarie Said, *The Origins of the United Arab Emirates*, (New York: 1978).

Public Records

Bombay Secret Proceedings, Persia and Persian Gulf series, Vols. 21, 33, 34, 85.

British Foreign Office Papers (F. O.) relating to Persia (F.O.371) Eastern Affairs.

India Office Records (I.O.), Foreign and Commonwealth Office, London, (R/15/2: Bahrein Political Agency; R/15/4/1: Sharjah Affairs; R/15/4/4: Copies of Agreements and Concessions.

International Arbitration.

International Court of Justice Reports.

Iranian Foreign Office Papers relating to Britain.

Political and Secret Proceedings, (L/P & S/12; L/P & S/18).

Selection from the Records of the Bombay Government, Vol 24.

United Nations Security Council Records.

Mass Media

Agence France Press, June 1993.
Al-Ittihad (Abu Dhabi), September 1992.
APS Diplomat Recorder, December 1992, July 1993.
Ayandegan (Tehran), April 1970.
Blitz (India), June 1971.
Daily Telegraph (London), February 1971.
Dutch Press-Agent, September 1994.
The Financial Times, April 1970.
The Guardian (Manchester), November 1992.
Inter-Press Service, September 1993.
Iran Times, September 1994.
Keyhan International (Tehran), April 1970, October 1971.
Middle East Economic Digest, December 1992, January 1993, March 1993, August 1993.
Middle East Mirror, September1993, January 1993.
The Press Association, Ltd., September 1993.
Reuter from Nicosia, November 1992, December 1992, February 1993, April 1993, December 1993.
Tehran Times, December 1992.
The Times (London), April 1970, February, 1971.

Professional Journals

Journal of Near Eastern Studies, October 1942.
The American Journal of International Law.

Index